KT-215-507

F

Hampshire
COUNTY COUNCIL
County Library

FAREHAM REFERENCE LIBRARY

For use
in Library

339111

94

C003254256

CL.14(2/95).

3.96

Sources for
ENGLISH LOCAL HISTORY

Sources for
ENGLISH
LOCAL HISTORY

W.B. Stephens

FAREHAM REFERENCE LIBRARY

Phillimore

This edition first published in 1981 by
THE SYNDICS OF THE CAMBRIDGE UNIVERSITY PRESS
Reprinted 1983, 1986

1994
Reprinted by permission of Cambridge University Press by
PHILLIMORE & CO. LTD.
Shopwyke Manor Barn, Chichester, Sussex

© Cambridge University Press, 1986, 1994

ISBN   ɔ033 911 1

HAMPSHIRE COUNTY LIBRARY

942 0850339111
  .
         C003254256

FAREHAM REFERENCE LIBRARY

Printed and bound in Great Britain by
BUTLER & TANNER LTD.
Frome, Somerset

For my wife, and
for Susan and Mark

J U

Contents

Contents

General editor's introduction

By what right do historians claim that their reconstructions of the past are true, or at least on the road to truth? How much of the past can they hope to recover: are there areas that will remain for ever dark, questions that will never receive an answer? These are problems which should and do engage not only the scholar and student but every serious reader of history. In the debates on the nature of history, however, attention commonly concentrates on philosophic doubts about the nature of historical knowledge and explanation, or on the progress that might be made by adopting supposedly new methods of analysis. The disputants hardly ever turn to consider the materials with which historians work and which must always lie at the foundation of their structures. Yet, whatever theories or methods the scholar may embrace, unless he knows his sources and rests upon them he will not deserve the name of historian. The bulk of historical evidence is much larger and more complex than most laymen and some professionals seem to know, and a proper acquaintance with it tends to prove both exhilarating and sobering – exhilarating because it opens the road to unending enquiry, and sobering because it reduces the inspiring theory and the new method to their proper subordinate place in the scheme of things.

G. R. ELTON

Preface to the second edition

In the ten years or so since I wrote the first edition of this book a great deal of work has been undertaken in the area of local history and much also written on source materials and techniques. This new edition has provided me with the opportunity of drawing attention to some of this new work where it relates to the themes I discuss. It has made it possible, too, for me to correct minor errors, to augment certain parts which required strengthening (particularly on Anglo-Saxon charters, religious history, topography and early settlement, enclosure records, and insurance records), and to add new paragraphs and sections on such topics as family history and oral history, and a new chapter on houses, housing, and health. In addition I have been able to bring up to date information on the whereabouts of certain records where these have altered in recent years (particularly, for example, the records of the British Transport Commission, the nonconformist chapels, and wills and vital records) and to provide changed addresses of institutions, libraries and record depositories. The appendix of examples of some records, included in the first edition, received a mixed reception from reviewers and others, and is not included here.

In this task I have had assistance from many people including again my former colleagues, Dr R. W. Dunning and Mr M. W. Greenslade, as well as Mr A. G. Esslemont of the United Reformed Church History Society, the Revd N. S. Moon of Bristol Baptist College, Mr D. W. Riley of John Rylands University Library of Manchester, Mr Malcolm Thomas, Mr J. F. Wilkinson, Mr J. Anthony Williams, the Revd P. J. Wortley of the Baptist Historical Society, and my colleagues at the University of Leeds, Mr R. S. Mortimer and Dr G. L. Turnbull.

Preface to the second edition

My thanks are due to them and also to reviewers who drew attention to omissions and errors in the first edition. The presentation of this new edition has been greatly improved in many particulars as a result of the careful vetting given to the text and notes by the subeditor at Cambridge University Press, and I am most grateful to her for this. In addition I have continued to receive valuable information from colleagues and students at the University of Leeds and University College London. I wish to record, too, my debt to Dr V. Ben Bloxham and Dr David H. Pratt of the Department of Family and Local History Studies, Brigham Young University, Utah, for helpful criticism and advice in response to my lectures there in 1979, and for showing me that my strictures on genealogical research in the first edition were unfair, and that family history and genealogy at their best are not mere antiquarian pursuits, and have a relevance to local history.

There will still inevitably be errors and omissions. Moreover there are certainly topics which have been left untouched or only briefly treated, and I have expanded on these in the initial paragraphs of the Introduction.

Finally I wish to express my thanks to the general editor of this series, Professor Geoffrey Elton, for his advice, support, and useful suggestions.

W.B.S.

May 1980
The University
Leeds

Preface to the first edition

Interest in English local history has grown considerably in the last twenty years; this book attempts to meet the widespread need for a fairly detailed introduction to its sources. It is hoped that it will be of use to undergraduates reading history, to college of education students, to postgraduate students training for teaching or archive work, to those beginning research for higher degrees, to members of adult education classes, and to teachers at various levels, as well as to the many interested amateurs who wish to pursue seriously the study of their neighbourhood.

It is too much to hope that my work contains no errors, for the field I have sought to cover is wide, and in compiling the book I have continually been confronted by the fact of my own ignorance. Clearly I have had to be selective and there are, of course, large numbers of sources with which I have not been able to deal. It will be realized, too, that references can only be up-to-date at the time of going to press. Articles on sources and reference books continue to be published, and some of the older works referred to may well appear as photographic reprints in the near future.

Various friends have been kind enough to read and comment on individual chapters, and I have to express my thanks for this to Professor A. M. Everitt of the University of Leicester, Professor M. W. Flinn of the University of Edinburgh, Dr A. G. Watson of University College London, Mr D. Woodward of the University of Hull; to my former colleagues on the staff of the *Victoria History of the Counties of England*, Institute of Historical Research, University of London: Dr K. J. Allison, Dr Robert W. Dunning, and Mr M. W. Greenslade; and to my present colleagues at the University of Leeds: Mr G. C. F. Forster, Dr P. H. J. H. Gosden, and

Mr D. W. Sylvester. The work has been much improved by their criticisms. For the faults which inevitably remain I must bear sole responsibility.

For assistance in certain areas I am grateful, too, to my friends Dr E. A. G. Clark and Mr William Kellaway, and also to the Revd F. Edwards, Dr J. Kitching, Dr D. P. Leinster-Mackay, Miss Elisabeth Poyser, Professor L. S. Pressnell, Dr E. O. Whiteman, the Librarian and Deputy Librarian of Dr Williams's Library, and to others whose names are to be found in several footnotes. I am greatly indebted as well to a number of societies, publishers, historians, and others for permission to reproduce records published by them. Their names and publications will be found in footnotes to documents in the appendix.[1] My thanks are due, too, to Mrs E. Brass who has typed much of the text. To my wife I owe thanks not only for compiling the index, but in many particulars too numerous to mention.

Finally I should say that this book derives to a certain extent from lectures delivered in recent years to postgraduate students training to be archivists at University College London, and to history graduates training as history teachers or working for higher degrees at the University of Leeds, and owes a great deal to conversations with these students.

W.B.S.

March 1972
The University
Leeds

---

[1] The appendix has been omitted from the second edition.

Abbreviations

Parliamentary papers are normally referred to in the footnotes merely by short title, Commons session, and volume number. Often the information referred to is, in fact, contained in appendixes rather than in the text of the reports, etc., cited, but for the sake of brevity this has not been specified.

The following other abbreviations have been adopted:

Ag.H.R.	Agricultural History Review
B.I.H.R.	Bulletin of the Institute of Historical Research
B.L.	British Library, Bloomsbury
B.M.	British Museum Library (now part of the British Library)
E.H.R.	English Historical Review
Ec.H.R.	Economic History Review
Hist. Assoc.	Historical Association
i.p.m.	inquisition post mortem
Jnl	Journal
K.R.	King's Remembrancer
L.T.R.	Lord Treasurer's Remembrancer
N.R.A.	National Register of Archives
P.R.O.	Public Record Office
Rep.	Report
R. Commission	Royal Commission
ser.	series
T.R.H.S.	Transactions of the Royal Historical Society
V.C.H.	Victoria History of the Counties of England

CHAPTER I

Introduction

This book is intended to provide an introduction to the detailed study of the general history of a region, town, village, or other local area, or of particular aspects of local history. What is 'local' will often differ according to the topic being investigated or the period of time with which the research is concerned, but most sensible researchers will not be greatly worried whether their work is properly considered 'local' or 'regional'. Such a distinction in the context of modern scholarship is both artificial and unimportant.

It would be quite impossible to write a definitive or comprehensive guide to source materials local historians might find of value in their researches. Apart from the inevitable lack of omniscience in any author or group of authors, there is the fact that history is a living subject. Both the questions historians pose and seek to answer, and the topics in which they are interested, are always changing and being expanded. The chapters in this book are arranged to provide a general guide to the sources for certain aspects of local history in which there is currently an interest. Such subject divisions arc naturally artificial and many researchers will be interested in topics which cut across those divisions. Others will wish to investigate as wide a spectrum of topics as possible so as to provide a rounded picture of a local community in a particular period. Yet others may want to compare certain aspects of life in one place with the same aspects in others. It is hoped that a judicious use of this book, with particular attention being paid to cross references, the general information given in this introductory chapter, and the Index, will serve the needs of all these investigators.

It must be admitted, however, that there are topics which are treated here less fully than might be wished for by some, or hardly touched on at all. It is clear, too, that new areas of interest are likely to emerge. Moreover the inevitable discovery of sources not previously exploited and the use of well-known sources for new purposes mean that this work can provide only a basic introduction. It is certainly not arranged in the way it is with any intention of structuring or restricting future developments in local history research.

Lack of space accounts for certain aspects of local history receiving scant attention. This is particularly so with the ever expanding topics which may broadly be considered under the umbrella of 'social history'. If Harold Perkin is followed in his view that social history really embraces all aspects of life looked at from a 'social' point of view,[1] it is indeed difficult, even without restrictions of space, to provide all the information about sources such a definition implies, although many types of evidence noted in the pages which follow may well be of use. No attempt has been made, however, to suggest a corpus of types of sources for such open-ended topics as the life style of persons of different kinds and classes over the ages. And it must be admitted that the sources discussed in Chapter 2 for 'social structure' provide the means only for a rudimentary investigation of what some might regard more properly as occupational structure or the gradation of the inhabitants of local communities according to wealth.

Family structure and the intimacy of family relationships,[2] social class structure, the place of women in local communities, child rearing customs, child life, eating habits and diet, political attitudes – all these and more are proper fields for

[1] H. J. Perkin, 'Social History', in H. P. R. Finberg (ed.), *Approaches to History* (1962).

[2] For local studies, see, e.g., N. Smelser, *Social Change in the Industrial Revolution* (1959); M. Anderson, *Family Structure in Nineteenth Century Lancashire* (1971).

2

investigation for which it would at present be difficult to prescribe specific and commonly available types of source material for local study. Likewise local drama, music, art, folk-culture, religious attitudes, reading habits, voluntary societies[3] – indeed the whole spectrum of local cultural life (apart from institutionalized religion and education) – are subjects too disparate for more than passing advice to be given in a book of this kind, however desirable it is that they should not be ignored.

Examples of other topics of local significance which require more information than it has been possible to deal with here include crime, the police, and prisons[4] (though attention is given to the records of quarter sessions, the assizes and other royal courts and to those of the administration of the laws of settlement), social unrest, and military history. Other topics have had to be treated rather narrowly. Thus religion has been considered largely from an institutional point of view and even then some institutions, like local monasticism in medieval and early modern times, and parish organizations in more recent periods, are given little attention. The whole subject of sources for the local study of politics has proved difficult. Like social history, political history is almost boundless in its ramifications, particularly when topics like political influence and patronage, working-class movements, and the like are added to the history of local representation in parliament and the more formal aspects of the politics of local government. Moreover in the area of politics, local history comes nearest to being part and parcel of various national movements and events so that potential source material is endless.

Again while it has been possible to draw attention to a

[3] But see S. Yeo, *Religion and Voluntary Organisations in Crisis* (1976); W. B. Stephens, *Adult Education and Society in an Industrial Town: Warrington, 1800–1900* (1980).

[4] But see R. B. Pugh, *Imprisonment in Medieval England* (1968) (especially good for sources). There are many works on these topics in modern times.

considerable number of sources of biographical information for the landed classes, the clergy, politicians, and other local dignitaries, source materials for other local persons, both prestigious and humble, are so various that easy generalization is not possible and searchers are best advised to comb the catalogues of their local libraries intelligently. This is true, too, of specific events or movements associated with particular places or parts of the country without general applicability, as, for example, the Pilgrimage of Grace in the lake counties, or Peterloo in Manchester. Nor has it been possible here to deal with the work of pioneer local historians in regard to particular towns and counties.[5]

Some guidance to techniques in using the evidence obtainable from the sources discussed is given below. This cannot, however, be comprehensive or always as detailed as may be necessary for researchers to put the techniques into use. For many significant topics, however, reference has been made to articles and books which will assist the local historian by providing suggestions for procedures and outlining the strengths and drawbacks of specific types of source material. As new sources emerge from time to time, however, so, too, do new techniques, and local historians must be aware of new work being undertaken not only on their own locality but on the history of other parts of the country and in the area of more general history. The recent increase in the use of quantitative techniques in history, for example, cannot be ignored by local historians wishing seriously to work on certain aspects of the past. Yet these methods require special study.[6]

[5] See D. C. Douglas, *English Scholars* (1951); W. G. Hoskins, *Local History in England* (1959); A. Gransden, *Historical Writing in England* (1974); J. Simmons (ed.), *English County Historians* (1978); F. S. Fussner, *The Historical Revolution: English Historical Writing, 1580–1640* (1962).

[6] See R. Floud (ed.), *Essays in Quantitative Economic History* (1974); M. Drake, *The Quantitative Analysis of Historical Data* (1974); E. A. Wrigley (ed.), *Nineteenth-Century Society: Essays in the Use of Quantitative Methods for the Study of Social Data* (1972).

Professor G. R. Elton has rightly pointed out that 'far more history than is written remains unwritten', and that is true for local as well as other aspects of history. For most aspects of human activity in the nineteenth and twentieth centuries there is an almost embarrassing amount of evidence. As we go back in time evidence becomes sparser, and the task of the historian embraces less the skills of selection than those of discovery, detection, and interpretation. The sources for the period before the Conquest and the light they can throw on the life of local communities in that period, for example, are comparatively limited. For the Middle Ages there is a great deal more information, yet the legal and institutional nature of many of the sources may sometimes suggest a picture rather different from the actual situation. The local researcher needs a great deal of background information on the period being studied before he can get the most out of his investigations, and this of course cannot be provided in this book (though relevant bibliographies are cited below). Even then for some aspects of medieval and early modern local history, particularly with regard to economic activities and the life of humbler individuals, it is difficult to find out very much. Even for comparatively modern times there are large and surprising gaps in the sort of evidence needed to answer adequately certain questions, particularly, for example, those concerned with the activities of businessmen, especially the less successful, the politics of local government, and industrial processes and craft techniques, to cite at random only a few.

Finally, by way of initial introduction to this volume, it must be stressed that though there is much specific bibliographical material alluded to in footnotes and there are many references to particular types of records and their whereabouts, the volume does not set out to provide a general guide to record offices and libraries, or a detailed general bibliography of local history sources. Readily available good works of this kind already exist and may be consulted with advantage.[7]

The sources surveyed here are mostly arranged under topics and unnecessary duplication has been avoided by cross references. Nevertheless a brief introduction drawing attention to certain manuscript and printed collections and other types of records which have a general use for many aspects of local history seems appropriate. Also included in this introduction are some references to a few sources not dealt with in any detail elsewhere, and to some peripheral aspects of local history which it has not been possible to treat in the following chapters. The writer's prejudice against what he regards as antiquarian aspects of local studies has perhaps, however, been responsible for the absence of some subjects from this volume, and no mention will be found of heraldry,[8] brass-rubbing, campanology, and the like. Largely omitted, too, is any guidance in depth to the study of aspects of local history which appear to require a technical knowledge not normally at the disposal of even the trained historian, such as archaeology and geology.[9] Also not discussed here are the obvious difficulties which will confront

[7] See, e.g., F. G. Emmison, *Archives and Local History* (1966); R. Douch, *Local History and the Teacher* (1967); W. B. Stephens, *Teaching Local History* (1977); and the *British Humanities Index, Regional Lists* (Library Assoc., annually from 1962: until 1961 these were part of the *Subject Index to Periodicals*). See also H. Hall, *A Repertory of British Archives*, i, *England* (1920).

[8] Those interested should consult the works cited in Douch, *Local History*, 83, and also A. C. Fox-Davies, *Complete Guide to Heraldry* (1929 edn); A. C. Fox-Davies, *Book of Public Arms* (1915 edn); C. W. Scott-Giles, *Civic Heraldry of England and Wales* (1953).

[9] For archaeology, see, D. P. Dymond, *Archaeology for the Historian* (1967); *British Archaeology: A Booklist* (Council for British Archaeology, 1960); *Field Archaeology: Some Notes for Beginners issued by the Ordnance Survey* (H.M.S.O., 1963 edn); O. G. S. Crawford, *Archaeology in the Field* (1953); M. W. Beresford, *The Lost Villages of England* (1954); G. L. Gomme, *Index of Archaeological Papers, 1665–1801* (1907); and below, p. 179n. 65. For industrial archaeology, see below, pp. 138–9. Gazetteers include:

those unfamiliar with Latin or palaeography when they meet medieval and early modern original manuscripts. Sufficient is it to say that there are now good guides to help the learner, [10] and that success is largely a matter of practice and perseverance.

Many people have first been led to an interest in local history by pursuit of the history of their own family. There is often an overlap between genealogy, family history, and

J. Hawkes, *Prehistoric and Roman Monuments in England and Wales* (1951); N. Thomas, *A Guide to Prehistoric England* (1976 edn); E. S. Woods, *Collins's Field Guide to Archaeology in Britain* (1972 edn); *Ancient Monuments and Historic Buildings* (H.M.S.O., periodically revised).

For geology, see Douch, *Local History*, 34–5, 43 sqq.; H.M.S.O. pamphlets, *British Regional Geology*, prepared by the Geological Survey of Great Britain (now the Institute of Geological Sciences); and the Survey's 1-inch geological maps (1835–83), now being revised. See also p. 31 n. 90.

[10] For Latin, see R. E. Latham, 'Coping with Medieval Latin', *Amateur Historian* iii (1956–8); E. A. Gooder, *Latin for Local History: An Introduction* (1978 edn); R. F. Glover and R. W. Harris, *Latin for Historians* (1963 edn); R. E. Latham (ed.), *Revised Medieval Latin Word List* (1965); C. T. Martin, *The Record Interpreter* (1910 edn). For palaeography, see A. Wright, *Court Hand Restored* (1912 edn); C. Johnson and H. Jenkinson, *English Court Hand, 1066–1500* (1915); H. Jenkinson, *Court Hands in England, 15th to 17th Centuries* (1927); C. B. Judge, *Specimens of 16th Century English Handwriting* (1935); H. E. P. Grieve, *Examples of English Handwriting, 1150–1750* (1959 edn); G. E. Dawson and L. Kennedy-Skipton, *Elizabethan Handwriting, 1500–1650: A Guide to the Reading of Documents and Manuscripts* (1966); F. G. Emmison, *How to Read Local Archives, 1550–1700* (1967). A good recent work which might serve as an introduction is L. C. Hector, *The Handwriting of English Documents* (1966 edn). See also K. C. Newton, *Medieval Local Records: A Reading Aid* (1971); K. C. Newton, 'Reading Mediaeval Local Records', *Amateur Historian* iii (1956–8); W. le Hardy, 'How to Read 16th and 17th Century Handwriting', *ibid.* i (1952–4). A series published by the Borthwick Institute of Historical Research is also useful: A. Rycraft, *Sixteenth and Seventeenth Century Handwriting* (2 parts, 1969 edn); A. Rycraft, *English Mediaeval Handwriting* (1973 edn). For old and new style dating and keys to dating by regnal years, see C. R. Cheney (ed.), *Handbook of Dates for Students of English History* (1970); F. M. Powicke and E. B. Fryde, *Handbook of British Chronology* (1961 edn).

local history, though they remain distinct studies. Genealogists, family historians, and local historians make use of many of the same sources and sometimes the same research techniques. There exists a whole library of introductory and more advanced works in which advice on the main sources for family research can be found, and it would be foolish to attempt to duplicate them here.[11] Suffice it to say that the main sources (parish registers, nonconformist and Roman Catholic registers, recusant rolls, nineteenth-century census records,[12] wills and administrations, tax records, poll books, directories, rate books, manorial records, poor-law documents) are all dealt with in various places in this book, together with other records of value to the family historian and the genealogist.[13] The Registrar General's records of civil registration of births, deaths, and marriages from 1837, not noted elsewhere, may, however, be mentioned here. Indexes to the registers may be found at St Catherine's House, Kingsway, London, WC2B 6JP, whence copies of entries

[11] See, e.g., M. J. Kaminkow, *A New Bibliography of British Genealogy* (1965); L. G. Pine, *The Genealogists' Encyclopaedia* (1969); P. Spufford and A. J. Camp, *The Genealogists' Handbook* (1969 edn); J. Hall, *The Genealogical Handbook for England and Wales* (1976). Also useful are D. E. Gardner and F. Smith, *Genealogical Research in England and Wales* (3 vols., 1956, 1959, 1968); A. J. Camp, *Tracing your Ancestors* (1972 edn); E. Wagner, *English Genealogy* (1960); G. Hamilton-Edwards, *In Search of Ancestry* (1974 edn); G. Hamilton-Edwards, *In Search of Army Ancestry* (1977); A. Willis, *Genealogy for Beginners* (1980 edn). For specific families for which there is already something in print, see G. B. Barrow (comp.), *The Genealogists' Guide* (1977); J. B. Whitmore, *The Genealogical Guide* (1953); G. W. Marshall, *The Genealogist's Guide* (1903); T. R. Thomson, *Catalogue of British Family Histories* (1976 edn); Jane Cox and Timothy Padfield, *Tracing Your Ancestors in the Public Record Office* (1981).

[12] The Registrar General (St Catherine's House) will consider the release (for a fee) from some census returns less than 100 years old of the ages and places of birth of named persons if sought for genealogical purposes by relatives.

[13] See the Index and especially pp. 25–8, 50 sqq.

(births, deaths, marriage certificates) may be obtained. Registers of banns are found with parish records, marriage licences[14] and allied records in diocesan registries and county record offices, and the library of the Society of Genealogists[15] contains a general index of some three million names and information on thousands of families.

The Church of Jesus Christ of Latter-day Saints (the Mormons) has for many years been active in genealogical studies. The International Genealogical Index at Salt Lake City, Utah, contains reference to millions of individuals derived from, among other sources, British vital records of which copies are held in Utah.[16] The index, though not always accurate, can save a searcher much time. Many county record offices have a shortened version of the part of the index relevant to their locality, and a complete copy for the British Isles is located at the Society of Genealogists in London.

The records of the heralds' visitations between 1530 and 1686 (mentioned only briefly below) are of considerable value in tracing some family relationships. The original returns are the property of the College of Arms (Queen Victoria Street, London EC4) and are closed to researchers, though the heralds will conduct searches for a fee. Many copies of the visitations, however, have found their way into other record collections, especially the Harleian MSS. at the British Library. Of these many have been published in

---

[14] D. J. Steel, *National Index of Parish Registers* i (1976), 223–44; C. R. Humphery-Smith, *Marriage Licences, Bonds and Allegations* (1967).

[15] 37 Harrington Gardens, London, SW7 4JX. The Society has many useful publications and guides, and a publication list may be obtained free of charge.

[16] See *Parish and Vital Records Listings of the Genealogical Society of the Church of Jesus Christ of Latter Day Saints Inc.* (1975). Drawbacks are noted in H. Peskett, *Guide to the Parish and Non-Parochial Registers of Devon and Cornwall, 1538–1837*, Devon and Cornwall Record Soc., extra ser., ii (1979), p. xxiv.

county volumes by the Harleian Society.[17] Biographical information on families and persons of note is also treated below.[18]

PUBLISHED SOURCES, PRIMARY AND SECONDARY

Before embarking on any original research it is essential that the local historian ascertains what work has already been done on the subject or district he has chosen. For many places the most obvious first stage will be the appropriate volumes of the *Victoria History of the Counties of England*. The *V.C.H.*, founded in 1899, is still currently at work in its virtually endless task of providing a standard work of reference on English local history. Each county series is planned to comprise a number of 'general' volumes covering for the whole county certain aspects of its history, as, for example, prehistory, ecclesiastical history, political history, agriculture, economic and social history, and endowed schools, and to include a translation and commentary of the county section of Domesday. In addition to the 'general' volumes, 'topographical' volumes cover in detail the history of each parish, town, or city under various aspects, such as manors, churches, charities, Roman Catholicism, Protestant nonconformity, schools, local government, and economic history. Much attention is paid to topography. It must be noted that the topics covered in both the general and the topographical volumes have changed over the years, on the whole the number of themes being greater and their content fuller in the more recently published volumes; those published before the First World War are necessarily greatly out of date, though still useful. It should also be noted that not all

[17] See R. Sims, *Index to the Pedigrees and other MSS. and Arms contained in the Heralds' Visitations* (1849); G. D. Squibb, *Visitation Pedigrees and the Genealogist* (1964). List of visitation returns and their availability are to be found in Whitmore, *Genealogical Guide* (to 1953), and *Family History*, Oct. 1962. See also p. 27 n. 80.

[18] See pp. 27–8.

counties are as yet fully covered nor are volumes necessarily published in any particular order.[19] The topical arrangement of the volumes, while sometimes criticized as preventing a truly historical approach, is convenient for reference, and the practice of the compilers of carefully footnoting their sources of information makes the *V.C.H.* volumes a valuable guide to what work had been done to the time of publication and to the available records for the study of the subject and area concerned.[20]

The next step may well be to work through the older county and town histories, standard modern works, and books published on the history of the town or area.[21] For a

[19] For the contents of the volumes so far published, see *Victoria History of the Counties of England: General Introduction,* ed. R. B. Pugh (1970).

[20] See R. B. Pugh, 'The Structure and Aims of the *Victoria History of the Counties of England*', *B.I.H.R.* xl (1967).

[21] See C. Gross, *A Bibliography of British Municipal History including Gilds and Parliamentary Representation* (1966 edn, ed. G. Martin); G. H. Martin and S. McIntyre, *A Bibliography of British and Irish Municipal History,* i, *General Works* (1972); J. P. Anderson, *The Book of British Topography* (1881); A. L. Humphreys, *A Handbook of County Bibliography, being a Bibliography of Bibliographies* (1917). The volumes of the *Oxford Bibliography of British History* (Clarendon Press, for Royal Historical Soc. and American Historical Assoc.) (*to 1485,* ed. E. B. Graves (1975); *1485–1603,* ed. Conyers Read (1959 edn); *1603–1714,* ed. G. Davies, revised M. F. Keeler (1970); *1714–1789,* ed. S. Pargellis and D. J. Medley (1951); *1789–1851,* ed. L. M. Browne and I. R. Christie (1976); *1851–1914,* ed. H. J. Hanham (1976)) contain sections on local history, as do J. C. Lancaster (comp.), *Bibliography of Historical Works issued in the United Kingdom, 1946–56* (1957); W. Kellaway (comp.) *ibid. 1957–60* (1962); *1961–65* (1967); *1966–70* (1972); R. Taylor (comp.), *ibid. 1971–75* (1977). For publications starting in 1975, consult the volumes of the *Annual Bibliography of British and Irish History,* ed. G. R. Elton, (from 1976). Also useful are M. Altschul, *Anglo-Norman England 1066–1154* (1969); D. J. Guth, *Late Medieval England, 1377–1485* (1976); M. Levine, *Tudor England, 1485–1603* (1965); W. L. Sachse, *Restoration England, 1660–89* (1971); G. R. Elton, *Modern Historians on British History, 1485–1945: A Critical Bibliography, 1945–1969* (1970); J. L. Altholz, *Victorian England, 1837–1901* (1970). See also the works cited below, p. 13 n. 25.

number of counties recent bibliographies have been published,[22] and borough and county libraries usually have large
local collections. The published transactions and proceedings
of local historical and archaeological societies[23] will have to
be searched, and of course many articles on particular areas
are to be found in national periodical publications such as the
Economic History Review, the *Agricultural History Review,* the
English Historical Review, and so on.

In addition much unpublished work in recent times exists
in the form of dissertations written for higher degrees, and
the existence and availability of these should be checked.[24]

Having surveyed secondary works the local historian will

[22] E.g., A. G. Dickens and K. A. MacMahon, *A Guide to Regional Studies
on the East Riding of Yorkshire and the City of York* (1956); R. Douch, *A
Handbook of Local History: Dorset* (1952) (a work of more than purely local
value).

[23] For a list of such bodies, see S. E. Harcup, *Historical, Archaeological and
Kindred Societies in the British Isles* (1968 edn). See also *Directory of National
Organisations: Local History Societies in England and Wales . . . 1978* (National
Council of Social Service, 2 vols., 1978).

[24] See *Index to Theses Accepted for Higher Degrees in the Universities of Great
Britain and Ireland* (Aslib, annually from 1950–1 (1953)); *American Doctoral
Dissertations* (Association of Research Libraries (U.S.A.), annually); *His-
torical Research for University Degrees in the U.K.* (Part I, *Theses Completed;*
Part II, *Theses in Progress*) (Institute of Historical Research); but P. M.
Jacobs (comp.), *History Theses, 1901–70* (1976) covers all these to 1970. See
also S. P. Bell, *Dissertations on British History, 1815–1914: An Index to
British and American Theses* (1974); R. Bilboul and F. R. Kent (eds.),
Retrospective Index to Theses of Great Britain and Ireland, 1716–1950, i, *Social
Sciences and Humanities* (1975); Warren F. Kuehl, *Dissertations in History: An
Index to Dissertations Completed in History Departments of United States and
Canadian Universities, 1873–1960* (1965); *1961–70* (1972); Canadian Historical
Assoc., *Register of Postgraduate Dissertations in Progress in History and Related
Subjects compiled by the Public Archives of Canada* (Canadian Historical
Assoc., annually from 1966); *Comprehensive Dissertation Index, 1861–1972*
xxviii (History) (Xerox University Microfilms, 1973) covers many U.S.
theses and some from other countries. Also useful is S. T. Bindoff and J. T.
Boulton, *Research in Progress in English and Historical Studies in the Universi-
ties of the British Isles* (1976), to be revised periodically.

be able to turn to primary sources. Before embarking on the direct investigation of unpublished records, he must, however, make himself aware of the existence of the multitude of original records which have been published in full or abbreviated form.[25] The publications of local record societies are naturally of great importance, but the volumes of national record societies such as the Early English Text Society, the Pipe Roll Society, the Selden Society, and others must not be ignored.[26]

Often indispensable are the large number of government and government-sponsored publications, many of which are mentioned in subsequent chapters. They include the texts and calendars published by the Record Commissioners and the State Paper Commissioners in the first half of the nineteenth century, among which are the *Statutes of the Realm*,[27] the *Placita de Quo Warranto*, calendars of inquisitions

---

[25] Useful guides to the existence of particular records, to the publications of individual record societies, and also to modern secondary works, including articles, are: E. L. C. Mullins (ed.). *Texts and Calendars: An Analytical Guide to Serial Publications,* Royal Historical Soc., Guides and Handbooks, no. 7 (1958) (a supplement is in preparation); a microfiche edn of a series of English record societies' publications into the 1970s, produced by Chadwyck-Healey, Teament, N. J., U.S.A.; R. Somerville, *Handlist of Record Publications* (1951); E. L. C. Mullins (ed.), *A Guide to the Historical and Archaeological Publications of Societies in England and Wales, 1901–1933* (1968); *Writings on British History, 1901–1933* (5 vols., 1968–70), and continuations: *Writings on British History, 1934,* etc., ed. A. T. Milne (1937–60) (covering in several vols. the years 1934–45); *1946–48* and *1949–51,* ed. D. J. Munro (1973, 1975); *1952–1954,* ed. J. M. Sims (1975); *1955–1957,* ed. J. M. Sims and P. M. Jacobs (1977); *1958–1959,* ed. H. J. Creaton (1977); *1960–1961,* ed. C. H. E. Philpin and H. J. Creaton (1979); *1962–1964,* ed. H. J. Creaton (1979); A. T. Milne (ed.), *A Centenary Guide to the Publications of the Royal Historical Society, 1868–1968, and of the former Camden Society, 1838–1897* (1968). See also L. W. Hanson, *Contemporary Printed Sources for British and Irish Economic History, 1701–1750* (1963); and the annual volumes of the *British Humanities Index, Regional List.*

[26] See, e.g., the brief list in *English Local History Handlist.*

[27] See below.

post mortem, the hundred rolls, and Domesday.[28] Of more recent date the Public Record Office texts and calendars[29] include (largely for the period from the thirteenth to the sixteenth centuries) calendars of charter, patent,[30] close,[31] fine, liberate, and curia regis rolls, inquisitions post mortem, inquisitions miscellaneous, the Black Prince's register, the letters and papers of Henry VIII, the calendars of state papers, domestic (from 1547), of treasury books and papers (from 1666), the Privy Council registers (from 1542),[32] and others. The published topographical index to the so-called Ancient Correspondence (P.R.O., Class S.C.l) is worth searching for many aspects of local history.[33]

The reports and calendars of the Royal Commission on Historical Manuscripts form another significant official series.[34] The many Historical Manuscripts Commission

[28] P. Walne, 'The Record Commissions, 1800–1837', *Jnl Soc. Archivists* ii (1960). For lists of these publications see Mullins (ed.), *Texts,* 3 sqq.; *British National Archives*, Sectional List, no. 24 (H.M.S.O., periodically revised).

[29] Also listed in Sectional List, no. 24 (see previous note).

[30] For indexes and calendars for James I's reign, see List and Index Soc., xcvii, xcviii, cix, cxxi, cxxii, cxxxiii, cxxxiv (1974–7), and also, for Elizabeth I's reign, cxli (1977), Chancery Patent Rolls 23–29 Eliz. I; Index to Grantees.

[31] Full texts for 1227–72.

[32] Calendared as *Acts of the Privy Council.* N.b. also the *Privy Council Registers Preserved in the Public Record Office* (12 vols., 1967–8), a photographic reproduction of the registers and their indexes for 1637–45.

[33] *Ancient Correspondence of the Chancery and Exchequer; Index*, P.R.O., Lists and Indexes, suppl. ser. xv (1), (2) (1969). See also P.R.O., Lists and Indexes xv (1968).

[34] For lists, see Mullins (ed.), *Texts,* 61 sqq.; *Publications of the Royal Commission on Historical Manuscripts*, Sectional List no. 17 (H.M.S.O., periodically revised). For more details, and the history and activities of the H.M.C., see R. H. Ellis, 'The Historical Manuscripts Commission, 1869–1969', *Jnl Soc. Archivists* ii (1962); H. M. G. Baillie, 'The Use of the Resources of the Historical Manuscripts Commission', and R. H. Ellis, 'Origins and Transformations', in *ibid.* iii (1969); R. H. Ellis, 'The Royal

volumes are a mine of information for the local historian and he will need to examine them carefully. The collections reported on include those of the House of Lords,[35] of many great landowners and noble families, of some towns, and of institutions such as colleges of universities, borough corporations, hospitals, gilds, monasteries, and cathedrals. The arrangement of the volumes, however, may cause some initial confusion. It is necessary to distinguish between the Commissioners' reports to the Crown, and Inspectors' reports to the Commissioners. It is in the latter that the historian will find his material. The Inspectors' reports for the period 1870 to 1884 appear as appendixes to the Commissioners' reports to the Crown and are bound in with the reports; for the years 1885 to 1899 they are also appendixes to the Commissioners' reports but are published in separate volumes. From 1899[36] the Inspectors' reports appear as independent volumes. There are volume indexes, and also a topographical guide to reports issued between 1870 and 1911. A similar guide to later reports is in preparation. In addition an index of persons covers reports issued from 1870 to 1957.[37]

Less useful for the normal needs of the local historian are the Rolls series (which does, however, include the year books of Edward I and Edward II), certain monastic cartularies, and the red book of the Exchequer.

Commission on Historical Manuscripts', *Archivalische Zeitschrift* lxv (1969); F. Ranger, 'The Historical Manuscripts Commission and Northern History', *Northern History* v (1970). The Commission's offices at Quality Court, Chancery Lane, London WC2, house a register of manorial and tithe records. See also below, p. 41.

[35] See below.

[36] The Calendar of Salisbury Manuscripts was published separately from 1883.

[37] See also E. S. Upton, *Guide to the Sources of English History from 1603 to 1660 in Reports of the Royal Commission on Historical Manuscripts* (1952).

Other official publications include the Ordnance Survey maps, the inventories of the Royal Commission on Historical Monuments (which are dealt with below), and other records deriving from the activities of parliament.

Perhaps the most fruitful, and often the most ignored, set of sources for local history from the late eighteenth century are the official series of parliamentary papers or 'blue books'.[38] These comprise thousands of volumes, the most easily available comprehensive collection being that in the Official Publications Room of the British Library. University libraries and a few public libraries also often have large collections.[39] The reprinting of the volumes on a large scale by photographic means[40] and the availability in large libraries of microcard copies of the complete series should soon overcome the difficulties of access that have long hampered their full use by local historians.

Many of these parliamentary (sessional) papers are referred to in ensuing chapters, but it would be possible if space permitted to mention many more, and the local historian will need to find out for himself what others of the series may add to his store of knowledge. Practice is required in tracing the sessional papers because of the ways they are arranged and the difficulties which derive from various ways of citing them. Several guides are, however, available to help

---

[38] Strictly speaking, the *Journals* of the two Houses, Acts of Parliament (both described elsewhere in this chapter), the officially published debates (see pp. 94–5), some other official publications described elsewhere, and certain unpublished material are 'parliamentary papers'. What are dealt with here are those parliamentary papers called sessional papers.

[39] For a list of libraries holding Commons sessional papers, see W. R. Powell, *Local History from Blue Books: A Select List of the Sessional Papers of the House of Commons* (1962), 15 sqq.

[40] By the Irish Universities Press, and for the eighteenth century by Scholarly Resources Inc.

students,[41] and there are also select lists arranged by topics.[42] The serious local historian, however, will diligently search the official indexes.[43] In order fully to understand them,

[41] The ensuing account draws on M. F. Bond, *Guide to the Records of Parliament* (1971); Powell, *Blue Books;* M. F. Bond, *The Records of Parliament: A Guide for Genealogists and Local Historians* (1964), 20 sqq.; P. and G. Ford, *A Guide to Parliamentary Papers* (1959 edn); H. H. Bellot, 'Parliamentary Printing, 1660–1837', *B.I.H.R.* xi (1933); S. Lambert, 'Guides to Parliamentary Printing, 1696–1834', *ibid.* xxxviii (1965); See also J. G. Ollé, *An Introduction to British Government Publications* (1965); J. E. Pemberton, *British Official Publications* (periodically revised); F. Rodgers, *Serial Publications in the British Parliamentary Papers, 1900–1968: A Bibliography* (1971).

[42] Powell, *Blue Books*; and the following works edited and compiled by P. and G. Ford: *Hansard's Catalogue and Breviate of Parliamentary Papers, 1696–1834* (reissue, 1953) – for the limitations of this, see Lambert, 'Guides', 114–15; S. Lambert (ed.), *House of Commons Sessional Papers of the Eighteenth Century: Introduction and Lists:* i, *1715–1760* (1975); ii, *1761–1800* (1976), containing indexes; S. Lambert (ed.), *List of House of Commons Sessional Papers, 1701–1750*, List and Index Soc., special ser., i (1968); *Select List of British Parliamentary Papers, 1833–99* (1953); *Breviate of Parliamentary Papers, 1900–16* (1957); *Breviate of Parliamentary Papers, 1917–39* (1951); *Breviate of Parliamentary Papers, 1940–54* (1961); *Select List of British Parliamentary Papers, 1955–64* (1970). See also K. A. C. Parsons, *A Checklist of British Parliamentary Papers (Bound Set), 1801–1950* (1958); [B. L. Gabine], *A Finding List of British Royal Commission Reports: 1860 to 1935* (Harvard University Press, 1935) – unfortunately this does not distinguish between different sets of Command papers, referring to all as Cd.: see below p. 18 n. 45. N.b. J. Morgan, *A Breviate of Parliamentary Papers Relating to Wales, 1868–1964* (1975).

[43] For the series as a whole there is from 1801 an index volume for each session forming the last volume of the sessional set, from 1870 consolidated decennial indexes, and also general indexes. The general indexes include: *Catalogue of Papers Printed by Order of the House of Commons, 1731–1800* (1807); *General Index to the Bills, Printed by Order of the House of Commons: 1801–1852* (1853); *General Index to the Reports of Select Committees, printed by Order of the House of Commons: 1801–1852* (1853); *General Index to the Accounts and Papers, Reports of Commissioners, Estimates Etc. Etc., Printed by Order of the House of Commons or Presented by Command: 1801–1852* (1854, reprinted 1938); *General Alphabetical Index to the Bills, Reports, Estimates, Accounts and Papers, printed by Order of the House of Commons, and*

however, some guidance as to the nature of the parliamentary papers and the arrangement of these publications is
needed. Sessional papers, with which we are concerned here,
exist in separate Lords and Commons sets for each session.
The most important to the local historian are the Commons
sessional papers.[44] Each session's papers are arranged in
volumes into four main groups (alphabetically arranged by
subject within each group): Public Bills; reports from committees and royal commissions; annual reports of standing
councils, commissions, inspectors, boards, ministries, etc.;
and 'accounts and papers'. Each volume has a number within
its sessional set so that it may be referred to by session and
volume number (as, e.g., P.P. 1884, viii). Individual papers
within each volume may also be referred to by the sessional
or command numbers where they are given. Sessional numbers, which start afresh each session, are reserved for papers
originating from an address of the Commons and are indicated in round brackets. Command numbers run consecu-
tively for periods of years and are assigned to papers originating 'by command' from the Crown.[45] Most papers useful to
local historians belong to this group.

to Papers Presented by Command: 1852–1899 (1909) (unfortunately omits
session and command numbers); *General Index to the Bills, Reports and
Papers Printed by Order of the House of Commons and to the Reports and Papers
Presented by Command, 1900 to 1948–49* (1960). For other official indexes to
the House of Commons series, and for official indexes to the House of
Lords series, see 'British Parliamentary Papers: Catalogues and Indexes',
B.I.H.R. xi (1933–4). For earlier papers, see the important list and
introduction to Lambert (ed.), *House of Commons Sessional Papers*, i.

[44] The published Lords sessional papers contain little not in the Com-
mons papers. For differences between the printed sets of Lords and
Commons sessional papers, see Parsons, *Checklist*; Bond, *Guide to the
Records of Parliament*, 127 sqq., 232 sqq. See also K. A. Mallaber, 'The
House of Lords Sessional Papers', *Jnl of Librarianship* iv (1972).

[45] These are distinguished by letters and numbers in square brackets. The
1st series (covering the years 1833 to 1868–9) are numbered 1–4222; the
2nd (1870–99), C. 1–C. 9550; the 3rd (1900–18) Cd. 1–Cd. 9239; the 4th

It is usual to cite these papers by short title and either by session and volume,[46] session and session number, or by Command number. Confusion may arise over references to page numbers for in many volumes pages of all but the first paper in each will have two official numbers – a printed one and a manuscript one. The manuscript numbers run in sequence throughout the volume, but unfortunately they have not always been inserted in copies held in local libraries, which anyway may possess only individual unbound papers rather than whole volumes. It is, however, the manuscript page numbers to which the official indexes refer.

Some volumes of parliamentary papers, particularly reports of select committees and royal commissions and their appendixes, are rendered more useful by having their own indexes of contents, or are indexed in another volume. Many, however, are unindexed, and for these careful perusal of the contents pages may be rewarding if they are sufficiently detailed. For some papers, however, only lists of witnesses are provided and unless these can be recognized, or places of residence are given, the local historian's task is made the more difficult. Some reports and other papers, are, however, arranged topographically. A very useful index (by subjects and places) has been compiled for those parliamentary papers containing reports on the employment of women and children in industry between 1816 and 1867.[47]

(1919–55/6) Cmd. 1–Cmd. 9889; the 5th (from 1956/7) Cmnd. 1– (in progress). The numbers are printed on the papers except for those in the first series (here they are to be found in the indexes). Useful is E. Di Roma and J. A. Rosenthal, *A Numerical Finding List of British Command Papers Published 1833–1961/62* (1967). For earlier papers, see Powell, *Blue Books*, 4–5.

[46] This is the practice followed in this work, where reference to a report or return may be taken to refer not only to the text but to the appendixes, without specific reference to these. Unless otherwise stated it is the Commons series which is cited.

[47] *Index to British Parliamentary Papers on Children's Employment* (Irish Universities Press, 1973).

As with many other sources the investigator needs to be aware that reports of select committees and royal commissions and evidence attached to them are political documents which may have been tailored to suit particular interests, and should not necessarily be taken at their face value. Local historians would be wise to seek general information on the historical context of the investigations and modern comments on them by general historians, with such caveats in mind.

Apart from the sessional papers just described, other records of the Houses of Parliament provide much material for the local historian. The proceedings of medieval parliaments are to be found in the parliamentary petitions and the rolls of parliament, published by order of the House of Lords – an important source for local history from 1278 to 1503 not commented on in subsequent chapters.[48] For modern times the journals of the two Houses are also published,[49] the *Journals of the House of Commons* from 1547[50] and the *Journals of the House of Lords* from 1510 (new style).[51] Through them may be traced the presentation of petitions[52]

[48] *Rotuli Parliamentorum: the Rolls of Parliament* (6 vols. and index, 1783–1832): see Mullins (ed.), *Texts*, 12. See also H. G. Richardson and G. Sayles, 'The Early Records of the English Parliaments, III', *B.I.H.R.* vi (1928–9); G. R. Elton, *England, 1200–1640* (1969), 84–5.

[49] The following is based partly on Bond, *Records of Parliament;* M. Bond, 'Acts of Parliament: Some Notes on the Original Acts Preserved at the House of Lords, their Use and Interpretation', *Archives* iii (1958).

[50] A most informative guide is D. Menhennet, *The Journal of the House of Commons: A Bibliographical and Historical Guide,* House of Commons Library, Document no. 7 (1971). This lists libraries which have copies of the *Journal* and its indexes. A microprint version for 1547–1900 has been produced by the Readex Microprint Corporation (U.K.).

[51] T. Erskine May, *Treatise on the Law, Privileges, Proceedings and Usage of Parliament* (1964 edn), 262–3; H. S. Cobb, *The Journals, Minutes and Committee Books of the House of Lords,* House of Lords Record Office Memorandum no. 13 (1957 edn).

[52] The texts of some public petitions are included. Others are printed in House of Commons, *Votes and Proceedings*: see Menhennet, *Journal*, 48–50; May, *Treatise*, 264–5.

and the formal passage of Bills, the moving of amendments, and the results of motions. Except for the period 1580 to 1628 they do not record actual debates, which are dealt with below.[53] Legislation and its effects are, of course, important locally as well as nationally. Acts of Parliament may be either Public Acts (also known as Statutes) or Private Acts.[54] Public Acts may be traced through the annual *Chronological Table of the Statutes* (H.M.S.O.), which lists all Acts and Statutes since 1235,[55] showing which are still in force and the effect of later legislation on them.[56] The texts of Public Acts will be found in the *Statutes of the Realm* (for the medieval period to Anne)[57] and the *Sessional* (later *Annual*) *Volumes of Public Acts* (from 1714).[58] The original texts are in the House of Lords (from 1497) and the Public Record Office.[59]

[53] See pp. 94–5.

[54] *Acts of Parliament: Some Distinctions in their Nature and Numbering*, House of Commons Library, Document no. 1 (1955). See also S. Lambert, *Bills and Acts: Legislative Procedure in Eighteenth Century England* (1971).

[55] See also *Index to the Statutes, 1235–1969* (H.M.S.O., 1971), periodically revised (formerly called *Index to the Statutes in Force*).

[56] See also *Halsbury's Laws of England* (1952 edn), with supplements; arranged alphabetically by subjects.

[57] *Statutes of the Realm, 1278–1714*, ed. A. Luders *et al.* (Record Commission, 11 vols., 1810–28). For limitations, see Bond, 'Acts of Parliament', 215–16, where other collections of the Statutes are noted. See also *Rotuli Parliamentorum*; R. Steele, *Tudor and Stuart Proclamations* i (1910); P. L. Hughes and J. F. Larkin, *Tudor Royal Proclamations*: i, *1485–1553* (1964); ii, *1553–1587* (1969); iii, *1585–1603* (1969); and *Stuart Royal Proclamations*, i, *1603–25* (1973); C. H. Firth and R. J. Rait, *Acts and Ordinances of the Interregnum, 1642–1660* (1911).

[58] Various editions of the *Statutes at Large* give the texts of many Acts from 1702 (sometimes in a shortened form): see Bond, 'Acts of Parliaments', 216, for details.

[59] For enrolments at the P.R.O., see Bond, 'Acts of Parliament', 201, 217–18; R. B. Pugh, *How to Write a Parish History* (1954), 27; *Guide to the Contents of the Public Record Office* (3 vols., P.R.O., 1963–8), i, 21–2; *List of the Chancery Rolls*, P.R.O., Lists and Indexes xxvii (1908) (Statute and Parliament rolls). For a detailed account of Acts and their texts, see Bond,

Often more important to the local historian are the Private Acts, also known as Local and Personal Acts. They include among other things Acts concerning enclosure, estates, and public works (such as, bridges, ferries, roads, railways, tramways, canals, rivers, harbours and docks, water supply, drainage, and gas and electricity undertakings). Private Acts are each published separately and are not accumulated into volumes. There are, however, annual and cumulative indexes, in particular an index to Acts passed between 1801 and 1947.[60] The *Statutes at Large* (published in various editions, 1758–1811) prints the long titles of all Acts from 1509. The texts of Private Acts before 1798 are not universally available in print. Often individual prints exist, but they tend to be inaccurate, being really the texts of Bills without the comprehensive addition of subsequent amendments. Some Private Acts which were 'declared Public' are to be found in the *Sessional Volumes of the Public Acts.* From 1798 most Private Acts are published in two series of volumes, *Local Acts* (from 1798) and *Private Acts* (from 1815). The original Acts are in the House of Lords Record Office.

It may be convenient here to refer to other records preserved at the House of Lords. These include original texts of Bills, some of which with amendments became Acts and others which never reached that stage. For the local historian it is Private Bills (especially those concerning estate, enclosure, highways and turnpikes, canal and railway, and other public works Bills) and their ancillary records which are often very fruitful.[61] Particularly informative may be the

Guide to the Records of Parliament, 93 sqq. (on pp. 96–7 are references to Lists and Calendars of Acts).

[60] *Index to Local and Personal Acts (1801–1947)* (H.M.S.O., 1949) with supplements. See also G. Bramwell, *Analytical Table of the Private Statutes passed between 1727 and 1812* (1813).

[61] For Public Bills, see Bond, *Records of Parliament,* 9; Bond, *Guide to the Records of Parliament,* 65 sqq.; H. S. Cobb, 'Sources for Economic History

petitions to introduce Bills and those opposing them, evidence given, and judges' reports.[62]

Also at the House of Lords Record Office are other petitions[63] and papers which may provide information of considerable interest to local historians,[64] and some of these are mentioned in more detail in later chapters. Records deriving from the judicial powers of the Lords may also be worth looking at.[65]

Some legislative action affecting localities has, of course, been taken by means of Orders in Council and Statutory Rules and Orders, the more important of which are reported in the *London Gazette*.[66]

More primary printed material for the local historian exists in the form of newspapers and other periodicals, guide books and directories, other topographical and biographical works and the like, and these will often prove a mine of information. Before the nineteenth century local newspapers are

amongst the Parliamentary Records in the House of Lords Record Office', *Ec. H. R.,* 2nd ser., xix (1966).

[62] Bond, *Records of Parliament,* 10 sqq.; Bond, *Guide to the Records of Parliament,* 70 sqq.; Cobb, 'Sources', 159 sqq. See also E. R. Poyser, *The Private Bill Records of the House of Lords,* House of Lords Record Office Memorandum no. 16 (1957).

[63] Bond, *Records of Parliament,* 20 sqq.; H. S. Cobb, *A Guide to the House of Lords Papers and Petitions,* House of Lords Record Office Memorandum no. 20 (1959).

[64] They are calendared for the period 1497 to 1718 in the *Reports of the Historical Manuscripts Commission,* i–xiv, and the *Manuscripts of the House of Lords,* NS. For a full list of these volumes, see Bond, *Records of Parliament,* 43–5; Bond, *Guide to the Records of Parliament,* 8–10. From 1801 many of these papers are printed in the Lords and Commons sessional papers discussed above. See also *A List of the Main Classes of Records,* House of Lords Record Office Memorandum no. 1 (G) (1969 edn); Bond, *Guide to the Records of Parliament,* part 1.

[65] For details, see Bond, *Records of Parliament,* 34–8, 48; Bond, *Guide to the Records of Parliament,* 106 sqq.

[66] For details, see Pugh, *Parish History,* 28. Also useful is *Table of Government Orders* [1671–1965] (H.M.S.O., 1966).

often disappointing for local news, though they may contain advertisements and notices which can provide useful evidence.[67] For the nineteenth century, however, newspapers must be regarded as an essential source for the local historian. The wealth of detail they contain cannot be summarized briefly, but for almost any local topic they may well provide a mass of material. Annual reports of local associations, local government officers and local institutions, reports of elections, church and chapel affairs, information on schools, local businesses, communications, the state of agriculture, trade and industry, indications of local prices and wages and social conditions – all these and much else besides may well be there.[68] Unless, however, there happen to be

---

[67] Guides for the searcher include: D. C. Collins, *A Handlist of News Pamphlets, 1590–1610* (1943); B. M., *Catalogue of the Pamphlets, Books (etc.) relating to the Civil War (etc.) collected by George Thomason, 1640–1661* (1908); R. S. Crane, F. B. Kaye, and M. E. Prior, *A Census of British Newspapers and Periodicals, 1620–1800* (1927); G. R. Cranfield, *A Hand-List of English Provincial Newspapers and Periodicals, 1700–1760* (1952) (for additions to this, see *Transactions of the Cambridge Bibliographical Soc.* ii (1956), and G. R. Cranfield, *The Development of the Provincial Newspaper, 1700–1760* (1962), which also refers to many histories of newspapers); G. Pollard in *Cambridge Bibliography of English Literature* (1940) ii, 720–30, iii, 801–6; *The Times Tercentenary Handlist of English and Welsh Newspapers, Magazines and Reviews, 1620–1919* (1920); P. Hollis, *The Pauper Press* (1970), 318 sqq.; and J. Weiner, *A Descriptive Finding List of Unstamped British Periodicals, 1830–1836* (1970) (for lists of early nineteenth-century radical and other publications); D. J. and A. E. F. Steel, *National Index of Parish Registers* i (1968), 288 (for a list of the 'longer-lived' London newspapers before 1837); Mitchell's *Newspaper Press Directory* (annually from 1846); *Willing's Press Guide and Advertisers' Directory* (annually from 1890; gives foundation date of each extant paper); J. Grant, *The Metropolitan Weekly and Provincial Press* iii (1872); D. Read, 'North of England Newspapers c. 1700 – c. 1900 and their Value to Historians', *Leeds Phil. Soc.* viii, part III (1957). The Library Association is compiling a bibliography of newspapers on a county basis.

[68] G. M. Mellor, 'History from Newspapers', *Amateur Historian* ii (1954–6); K. A. MacMahon, 'Local History and the Newspaper', *ibid.* v (1961–3).

indexes, or the searcher knows about what dates to look at, the use of newspapers is likely to be a time-consuming affair. It will nevertheless usually prove worthwhile.

Many newspapers will be found in local libraries in the original or on microfilm. The offices of the local press may also contain files of back issues, including those of other papers that have been absorbed; sometimes these are indexed. The British Library Newspaper Library at Colindale (Hendon) contains copies of English, Irish, Scottish, and Welsh provincial newspapers since 1690, and London and national newspapers from 1801, many of which are no longer available locally. Its catalogue should therefore be searched.[69] The Bodleian Library, Oxford, has a large collection of earlier newspapers.[70] National newspapers, too, may yield provincial news and in this connection attention is drawn to the published indexes to *The Times.*

As well as newspapers other contemporary periodicals are often extremely useful, and many are mentioned in later chapters. Of general value are such publications as the *Annual Register* (from 1758), *Notes and Queries* (from 1849), and the *Gentleman's Magazine* (1731–1868).[71]

Guidebooks, handbooks, and directories (local, national, trade, and specialist) also find frequent mention in subsequent chapters, and no local historian dealing with the modern period can avoid searching them,[72] though they

[69] B.L., *Catalogue of the Newspaper Library* (8 vols., 1975). Earlier London and national newspapers before 1801 are kept in the B.L. at Bloomsbury.

[70] See R. T. Milford and D. M. Sutherland, *Catalogue of English Newspapers and Periodicals in the Bodleian Library, 1622–1800* (1936).

[71] These may be traced through the *British Museum Catalogue of Printed Books to 1955*; the *British Union–Catalogue of Periodicals* (1955–8, with supplement 1960), and *British-Union Catalogue of Periodicals: New Titles* (1960–); Library Assoc., *Subject Index to Periodicals, 1915,* etc. (annually to 1922, 1926–53; quarterly 1954–61). See also the references given in A. T. Milne *et al.* 'Indexes to Periodicals', *B.I.H.R.* xi (1933–4).

[72] Particularly useful for tracing the whereabouts of directories is J. E. Norton, *Guide to National and Provincial Directories of England and Wales,*

must be used with caution, for they are by no means always reliable. The *Post Office Directories* (from 1800)[73] and the local directories of White, Kelly, Pigot, and Slater deserve particular mention. Also worth consulting are national gazetteers such as Nicholas Carlisle's *Topographical Dictionary of England* (1808), S. Lewis's *Topographical Dictionary of England, Wales, Scotland and Ireland* (1840–7), and D. and S. Lysons's *Magna Britannia* (1806–22) (vols. i–vi only completed, covering counties alphabetically to Devon).

The descriptions of contemporary travellers, and diaries, biographies, and letters of individuals[74] may often provide the sort of detail on many local subjects not found in official records. Large numbers of these have appeared in print. Well known are the works of travellers like John Leland, William Camden, William Smith, Richard Blome, Celia Fiennes, and Daniel Defoe,[75] but there are many others whose works are

excluding London, published before 1856 (1950). See also C. W. F. Goss, *The London Directories, 1677–1855* (1932); S. Horrocks (ed.), G. H. Tupling (comp.), *Lancashire Directories, 1684–1957* (1968); J. E. Vaughan, 'Early Guide Books as Sources of Social History', *Amateur Historian* v (1961–3); J. L. Oliver, 'Directories and their use in Geographical Inquiry', *Geography* xlix (1964). One of the largest collections of directories is at London Guildhall Library; the Society of Genealogists also has an important collection.

[73] Oliver, 'Directories'.

[74] See W. Matthews, *British Diaries: An Annotated Bibliography of British Diaries written between 1442 and 1942* (1950) (covers both published and unpublished diaries); A. Ponsonby, *English Diaries from the 16th to the 20th Century* (1923); R. A. Fothergill, *Private Chronicles: A Study of English Diaries* (1975).

[75] *Itinerary of J. Leland* (various edns, but see especially that ed. by L. Toulmin Smith); W. Camden, *Britannia* (many edns from 1586); W. Smith, *Particular Description of England, 1588* (not published till 1879); R. Blome, *Britannia* (1672); C. Morris (ed.), *The Journeys of Celia Fiennes* (1949 edn); D. Defoe, *A Tour through the Whole Island of Great Britain* (various edns from 1724–7, onwards, but see especially G. D. H. Cole's edn of 1927).

worth examining.[76] Biographies[77] of and references to other evidence concerning eminent local people and families may be traced through the older county histories, the *Dictionary of National Biography* and its supplements,[78] and *Musgrave's Obituary*.[79] Compilations such as those dealing with the pedigrees of the landed and ennobled classes and the careers of those who attended Oxford and Cambridge universities and the Inns of Court may also be useful.[80] For church

[76] See p. 129. Good bibliographies are J. P. Anderson, *The Book of British Topography* (1881); E. G. Cox, *Reference Guide to the Literature of Travel* i (1935); G. E. Fussell, *Exploration of England: A Select Bibliography of Travel and Topography, 1570–1815* (1955). L. B. Mayne, 'Tourists of the Past', *Amateur Historian* iii (1956–8), contains a select bibliography.

[77] N.b. W. Matthews, *British Autobiographies: An Annotated Bibliography of British Autobiographies Published or Written before 1951* (1955); F. Boase, *Modern English Biography* (6 vols., 1892–1921, reissued 1965) (contains notices of many persons not in the *Dictionary of National Biography* who died between 1851 and 1900).

[78] To 1900 published 1885–1900; supplements cover 1900–60 (1912–60). There is also a *Concise Dictionary of National Biography* (in two parts: I to 1900; II 1901–50). Corrections to the *D.N.B.* are periodically published in the *B.I.H.R.* (see also *Dictionary of National Biography Corrections and Additions, Cumulated from the Bulletin of the Institute of Historical Research, 1923–63* (1965)). At the Institute of Historical Research there is a manuscript catalogue of recent corrections. See also H. J. Hanham, 'Some Neglected Sources of Biographical Information: County Biographical Dictionaries, 1890–1937', *B.I.H.R.* xxxiv (1961); *Biographia Britannica* (1743–66).

[79] Ed. G. J. Armytage, Harleian Soc. Publications, xliv–xlix (1889–1901). See also Boase, *Modern English Biography*.

[80] See, e.g., A. B. Emden, *Biographical Register of the University of Oxford to A.D. 1500* (1957–9); ibid. *1501–40* (1974); A. B. Emden, *Biographical Register of the University of Cambridge to 1500* (1963); J. Foster, *Alumni Oxonienses* (1887–92) (covers 1509–1886); J. and J. A. Venn, *Alumni Cantabrigienses* (1922–7) (covers years to 1751); ibid. ii (1940–54) (covers 1752–1900); C. H. and T. Cooper, *Athenae Cantabrigienses, 1500–1611* (3 vols., 1858, 1861, 1913); Middle Temple, *Register of Admissions* (1949); Inner Temple, *Students Admitted to the Inner Temple, 1547–1660* (1877); Lincoln's Inn, *Records of the Honorable Society of Lincoln's Inn (Admissions, 1420–1893)* (1896); Gray's Inn, *Register of Admissions to Gray's Inn,*

dignitaries, John le Neve's *Fasti Ecclesiae Anglicanae* is useful.[81]

For older and more obscure books and periodicals the resources of local libraries are sometimes insufficient, and many local historians may have to have recourse at some time or other to the collections of printed works in the large public libraries, particularly the British Library,[82] or to such specialist libraries as the Goldsmiths' Library of Economic Literature at London University.[83]

1521–1889 (1889); G. E. Cockayne (ed.), *The Complete Peerage* (1910–59); Sir (John) B. Burke (ed.), *Genealogical and Heraldic History of the Peerage* (from 1826); G. E. Cokayne (ed.), *The Complete Baronage* (1900–9); Sir (John) B. Burke (ed.), *Genealogical and Heraldic History of the Landed Gentry* (1952 edn, supplement 1954; and earlier edns); Burke's Peerage, *Burke's Family Index* (1976) (a list of all families in Burke's publications, 1826–1976); *Kelly's Handbook to the Titled, Landed and Official Classes* (annually from 1880); J. J. Howard and F. A. Crisp, *Visitation of England and Wales* (35 vols., 1893–1921); the publications of the Harleian Society (visitation section) (for a list, see Mullins (ed.), *Texts*), and the many editions of visitations listed in the *British Museum General Catalogue of Printed Books to 1955* lxiv, England III, College of Arms; G. D. Squibb, *Visitation Pedigrees and the Genealogist* (1964); G. W. Marshall, *The Genealogist's Guide* (1903); T. R. Thomson, *Catalogue of British Family History* (1976 edn); J. B. Whitmore, *The Genealogical Guide* (1953). The early compilations of the peerage, baronetage, and landed gentry contain many errors and should be used with caution. For the clergy, see references in the sections on religious history (Chapter 8).

[81] A revised and expanded edition in progress at the Institute of Historical Research (vols. publ. from 1962) will supersede the edn by T. D. Hardy (1854).

[82] A. J. K. Esdaile, *National Libraries of the World* (1957 edn, rev. by F. J. Hill), chapter on B.M. *The British Museum General Catalogue of Printed Books to 1955* and its supplements to 1975 are available in large libraries and can be consulted before a visit to London is contemplated.

[83] M. Canney and D. Knott (eds.), *Catalogue of the Goldsmiths' Library of Economic Literature*, i (1970) (covers works published before 1801), ii (1975) (covers works, 1801–50).

SOURCES FOR TOPOGRAPHY AND EARLY SETTLEMENT

It is rare today for a researcher into the history of local topography, particularly urban topography, to be the first to carry out an investigation. For that reason secondary works should be searched at the start, in particular the volumes of the *Victoria History of the Counties of England*, where topography is made a special feature. Apart from that it is often best to proceed from the present backwards.

Unlike some other aspects of local history the study of topography will necessarily involve field work and the physical examination of the existing landscape and townscape for clues to the past. The value of physical remains in the shape of buildings, walls, streets, roads, and so on is obvious. The existence and nature of, for example, burial sites, and the positioning of churches, may give clues to the whereabouts and chronology of early settlement. The building of new churches and chapels may help to indicate the stages of urban expansion. The survival of earthworks and of ridge and furrow, the lines taken by streets, paths and waterways, and the botanical composition of hedges,[84] for example, may all assist in the reconstruction of the historical topography of a locality. Several good books exist to demonstrate how the skilled observer, combining such physical evidence of the past with information derived from the sorts of documentary sources described below, may reveal the

---

[84] For the dating of hedges from the study of their vegetation, see *Hedges and Local History* (National Council of Social Service, 1976 impr.), and works cited there; M. D. Hooper, 'Historical Ecology', in A. Rogers and T. Rowley (eds.), *Landscape and Documents* (1974); W. G. Hoskins, *Fieldwork in Local History* (1967), 117–30 (and for dating stone walls, 130–4); M. D. Hooper, 'Dating Hedges', *Area* iv (1971); R. Tillyard, 'Hedge Dating in Norfolk: The Hooper Method Examined', *Norfolk Archaeology* xxxvi (1977); W. Johnson, 'Hedges – A Review of Some Early Literature', *Local Historian* xiii (1978). Cf. G. Hewlett, 'Reconstructing a Historical Landscape from Field and Documentary Evidence', *Ag. H.R.* xxi (1973).

characteristics of urban and rural local topography and its changes over time.[85]

In recent years much effort has gone into making collections of photographs, and these, together with drawings, pictures, and prints, can often provide evidence on topography as well as on social and economic life.[86] Air photographs, though recent, may reveal evidence for earlier periods,[87] and these can be obtained from various places.[88]

Maps and plans, however, must be regarded as the chief single type of source for the study of local topography,[89] and they are, of course, of value to the local historian for the

[85] W. G. Hoskins, *The Making of the English Landscape* (1955); Hoskins, *Fieldwork*; M. W. Beresford, *History on the Ground* (1957). See also p. 181.

[86] See J. Wall (comp.), *Directory of British Photographic Collections* (1977) (with a topographical index); W. A. Nunn, *British Sources of Photography and Pictures* (1951); C. E. Wright, 'Topographical Drawings in the Department of Manuscripts, British Museum', *Archives* iii (1957–8); and works cited below, p. 299.

[87] See, e.g., D. Knowles and J. K. St. Joseph, *Monastic Sites from the Air* (1952); M. W. Beresford and J. K. St. Joseph, *Medieval England: An Aerial Survey* (1979 edn).

[88] For aerial films taken after 1966: Air Photo Cover Group, Ordnance Survey, Ramsey Road, Maybush, Southampton, SO9 4DH. For previous years: Air Photography Officer, Department of the Environment, Prince Consort House, Albert Embankment, London, SE1 7TF, or, for Scotland, the Registrar, Central Register of Air Photography of Scotland, Scottish Development Department, York Buildings, Queen Street, Edinburgh, EH2 1HY. Other collections include: University Collection of Air Photographs, Cambridge. The largest commercial collection is that of Aerofilms Ltd, 4 Albermarle Street, London W.1. Local newspapers, local planning departments, and local photographic firms are also sometimes willing to lend or sell photographs. See also Aerofilms Ltd, *The Aerofilm Book of Aerial Photography* (1965 edn). The Department of the Environment maintains a Central Registry of Air Photography and can supply names of commercial companies which can provide photographs.

[89] Historicus, 'Topography and Maps', *Amateur Historian* iii (1956–8); B. Roberts, 'The Study of Village Plans', *Local Historian* ix (1970–1). See also A. R. H. Baker and R. A. Butlin (eds.), *Studies of Field Systems in the British Isles* (1973); M. D. Lobel, 'The Value of Early Maps as Evidence for the Topography of English Towns', *Imago Mundi* xxii (1968).

pursuance of many other topics, too.[90] They are of particular interest for the student of agriculture, land use, communications, urban development, and industry and trade. They may also shed light on less obvious matters, such as, for example, the existence of schools or chapels. Some types of maps and plans, in particular those relating to landed estates,[91] enclosures, tithes, railways, canals, and roads, are described in some detail in the chapters dealing with agriculture and communications, but it should be noted here that these maps may have more general uses, too. They may show not only physical features and communications but provide field names, names of landowners, tenants, and farms, and show the existence of quarries, mines, manor houses, mills and factories, and buildings generally.[92]

Older printed maps are of less value but must not be ignored. Before the sixteenth century there are virtually no regional maps and we must rely on national ones.[93] Early county maps, such as those of Saxton, Norden, and Speed and their copiers, are sparse in useful detail though they may be of some value for some towns where marginal plans are

[90] J. B. Harley, *Maps for the Local Historian: A Guide to British Sources* (1972), is a *sine qua non* for this topic. See also, e.g., A. M. Lambert, 'Early Maps and Local Studies', *Geography* xli (1956); E. H. Yates, 'History in a Map', *Geographical Jnl* cxxvi (1960); Hoskins, *Fieldwork, passim.* For geological maps, see K. W. Earle, *The Geological Map* (1936); the maps in the Land Utilization Survey (see p. 200); and the maps and other publications of the Geological Survey of Great Britain (now the Institute of Geological Sciences).

[91] J. West, *Village Records* (1962), 67–8; L. J. Redstone and F. W. Steer, *Local Records* (1953), 144, 211–12. For the use of estate maps, see three articles by A. R. H. Baker: 'Local History in Early Estate Maps', *Amateur Historian* v (1961–3); 'Some Early Kentish Estate Maps and a Note on their Portrayal of Field Boundaries', *Archaeologia Cantiana* lxxxvii (1962); 'Field Patterns in Seventeenth-Century Kent', *Geography* lix (1965); see also p. 201.

[92] Sources for buildings are dealt with below.

[93] For these, see G. R. Crone, *Early Maps of the British Isles, A.D. 1000–A.D. 1579* (1961).

provided.[94] From the late seventeenth century, however, roads are shown on county and other maps, and John Ogilby's *Britannia* (1675) and some of his later publications indicate among other things industrial sites. County maps for the eighteenth century are of greater interest, for in that period a revolution in map making occurred.[95] For the eighteenth and nineteenth centuries enclosure and tithe maps may furnish the first really detailed topographical information for a locality in cartographic form, and these are dealt with in detail below.[96]

For the nineteenth and twentieth centuries, many plans and maps prepared for the use of local government officials, such as those concerned with water supplies and sewerage, are often available for consultation in local government offices or record depositories.[97] For this period, however, the most authoritative maps are those prepared by the Ordnance Survey. A detailed guide to the various editions is available and should be studied by all those seeking to use

[94] L. B. Mayne, 'Maps from Saxton to Royal Ordnance, *Amateur Historian* i (1952–4); Harley, chapter 6. For the existence of local maps, see T. Chubb, *The Printed Maps in the Atlases of Great Britain and Ireland: A Bibliography, 1579–1870* (1927); E. M. Rodger, *The Large Scale County Maps of the British Isles, 1596–1850: A Union List* (1972 edn); A. V. Tooley, *Maps and Map-Makers* (1952 edn); R. A. Skelton (ed.), *County Atlases of the British Isles, 1579–1850: A Bibliography* (4 parts, 1964–8; section covering 1579–1703 published as separate volume, 1970). For a short list of county maps arranged topographically, see West, *Village Records*, 70–2. Several county bibliographies have been published: e.g. G. C. Cowling, *A Descriptive list of the Printed Maps of Shropshire, A.D. 1577–1900* (1959) (see Harley, *Maps*, 168–70); P. M. G. Dickinson, *Maps in the County Record Office, Huntingdon* (1968); F. W. Steer, *Catalogue of Sussex Maps*, Sussex Record Soc. Publications lxvi (1968).

[95] For details, see J. B. Harley, 'The Re-Mapping of England, 1750–1800', *Imago Mundi* xix (1965); Harley, *Maps*, chapter 6.

[96] See pp. 180–1, 193. See also C. Taylor, *Fields in the English Landscape* (1975).

[97] Cf. Redstone and Steer, *Local Records*, 212–13; Emmison, *Archives and Local History*, 32–3.

these maps.[98] The original series (called the first edition) of the 1-inch (to the mile) O.S. maps was published between 1805 and 1873, though those for most of the country had appeared by 1840.[99] Subsequent revised printings of the first edition, however, continued to carry the date of the first printing, and investigators must be aware of this. The dating on further series of 1-inch maps (called second, third, fourth editions, and so on) and their revisions is more reliable.[100] Larger O.S. maps (the 6-inch and 25-inch being most useful to historians) vary in their coverage and content according to their dates of publication. The 6-inch maps (dating from 1840) cover the whole country, and the 25-inch maps (dating from 1853) all but waste and mountainous districts.[101] The larger maps are specially welcome because of their great accuracy and detail, showing fields, waterways, administrative boundaries, and buildings, and marking all geographical

[98] *The Historian's Guide to Ordnance Survey Maps* (publ. for the Standing Conference for Local History by the National Council for Social Service, 1964) (much of it is based on articles by J. B. Harley and C. W. Phillips in *Amateur Historian* iv (1961–3)). The following account derives much from this excellent publication. See also the *Catalogue of Maps and Other Publications of the Ordnance Survey* (various dates, 1862–1924); C. Close, *The Maps of England: About England with an Ordnance Map* (1932). For current O.S. maps, see *Ordnance Survey Maps: A Descriptive Manual* (Ordnance Survey, 1975).

[99] A reprint of the first edition edited by J. B. Harley (with introductory notes, for each sheet, on dating and interpretation) was published by David and Charles in 1969. Another is being produced by Harry Margary in a number of volumes.

[100] The second edition begins in 1840, the third in 1901, the fourth in 1913. The seventh was completed in 1961.

[101] There were also later revisions. See the Ordnance Survey publications: *A Description of the Ordnance Survey Large Scale Maps* (1954) (for the 25-inch maps); *A Description of the Ordnance Survey Medium Scale Maps* (1955) (for the 6-inch maps); H. St. J. L. Winterbotham, *The National Plans*, Ordnance Survey Professional Papers, NS, xvi (1934). For the 2½-inch O.S. maps, see the O.S. publications already cited, and F. J. Monkhouse, 'The New Ordnance Survey Maps Series, Scale 1 : 25,000', *Town Planning Review* xxi (1950).

and man-made features. They are helpful, too, for minor place names and the identification of antiquities.[102]

For many towns with populations of over 4,000 there are large-scale O.S. plans for the later nineteenth century. These are in three series: those of 5 feet to the mile, those of 10 feet to the mile, and those of 10·56 feet to the mile.[103] Clearly these, used with earlier maps and plans, are invaluable in the tracing of urban development and change.[104]

The local availability of O.S. maps is patchy, and though many, especially of the immediate district, are to be found in local libraries and record offices, complete sets are rare except in university libraries and the British Library. Indeed for all local historians seeking to use maps a visit to the British Library Map Room and a search through its catalogues may prove fruitful.[105] A great collection of maps and plans also exists in the Public Record Office,[106] and the urban historian should be aware of a new project, the Historic Towns series

[102] The local historian should be aware of the O.S. period maps which include: Roman Britain; Seventeenth-Century England; Neolithic Wessex; Britain in the Dark Ages; Neolithic South Wales; Neolithic Map of the Trent Basin; Celtic Earthworks of Salisbury Plain; Ancient Britain; Monastic Britain; South Britain in the Iron Age; Hadrian's Wall. For the local study of Roman roads, see I. D. Margary, *Roman Ways in the Weald* (1965 edn); I. D. Margary, *Roman Roads in Britain* (1965), especially the introduction; W. Bonser, *Romano-British Bibliography (55 B.C. – A.D. 449)* (1964), topographically arranged, is useful for the Roman period. See also *Field Archaeology* (H.M.S.O., 1963).

[103] 1 : 1056; 1 : 528; 1 : 500. For the towns for which these exist, with dates and scales, see *Historian's Guide to Ordnance Survey Maps*, 29, 30.

[104] For these and other town plans, see M. R. G. Conzen, 'The Use of Town Plans in the Study of Urban History', in H. J. Dyos (ed.), *The Study of Urban History* (1968); M. R. G. Conzen, *Alnwick, Northumberland: A Study in Town Plan Analysis* (1960).

[105] N.b. the *British Museum Catalogue of Printed Maps, Charts and Plans to 1964* (15 vols., 1967), and supplements; *1965–70* (1971–2), *1971–5* (1978–); *British Museum Catalogue of Manuscript Maps* (3 vols., 1844–61, reprinted 1962).

[106] *Maps and Plans in the Public Record Office*, i: *British Isles c. 1410–1860* (H.M.S.O., 1967) (topographically arranged).

of maps and plans of British towns and cities, which is to cover the period up to *c.* 1800 with commentaries,[107] and there are a great number of contemporary town maps and plans.[108] The many volumes of plans of parts of British towns published by Charles E. Good Ltd from the 1880s are in the British Library and elsewhere.[109]

For modern times, as well as cartographic and pictorial evidence, there are many written and printed sources available for the study of local topography. Guide books, directories, older local histories, and contemporary travellers' descriptions have already been described. Many of the sources examined elsewhere in this book for other purposes may provide topographical information; such sources include, particularly, borough records, estate records, deeds, fire insurance records, and a great number of other sources described in the chapters on agriculture, local government, housing and public health, and communications.[110] The numerous parliamentary papers concerned with towns, public services, boundaries, communications and transport, industry, and the employment of women and children, all touched on below in various chapters, should be particularly noted.

For earlier times, quarter-sessions rolls and books provided details of such matters as road and bridge maintenance while borough council minutes and financial accounts con-

[107] This is part of an international series set up by the International Congress of Historians, under the aegis of the International Commission for the History of Towns. The first British volume (1969) covers Banbury, Caernarvon, Glasgow, Gloucester, Hereford, Nottingham, Reading, Salisbury; the second (1975) covers Bristol, Cambridge, Coventry and Norwich. Other towns will be covered in subsequent volumes.

[108] See Harley, *Maps*, chapter 1. There are maps, too, in *Reps. on the Parliamentary Boundaries of Counties and Boroughs* (1831–2) xxxviii–xli, and in the reports, cited p. 84 n. 65.

[109] P. J. Aspinall, 'The Use of Nineteenth Century Fire Insurance Plans for the Urban Historian', *Local Historian* xi (1974–6).

[110] See Index.

tain much miscellaneous information on urban topography, as do deeds of various kinds. More specifically topographical in nature are glebe terriers and the extents and surveys of manors and estates, cartularies, and for some areas the thirteenth-century hundred rolls.[111] The *Calendar of Miscellaneous Inquisitions* (from 1219)[112] includes many extents and has been found a fruitful source for the medieval topographer.[113] Monastic suppression papers in the Public Record Office (Class S.P. 5) may provide information on lands, farms, and granges, as well as some details of the buildings.[114]

For the characteristics of the landscape in early times and for evidence of early settlement and migration, the main source, apart from physical remains, Domesday, and land charters,[115] and what in skilled hands can be revealed by modern O.S. and geological maps, we have the names of farms, fields,[116] streets, villages, towns, and of other physical features. The study of early place names, derived particularly from maps, Domesday,[117] land charters, and manorial

[111] All treated in detail elsewhere in this volume: see Index. Very useful is the bibliographical essay: D. M. Palliser, 'Sources for Urban Topography', in M. W. Barley (ed.), *The Plans and Topography of Medieval Towns in England and Wales* (1976.) For town plantation in the Middle Ages, see L. Baker, 'The Evolution of Towns: Planted Towns after 1066' in *ibid.*; M. W. Beresford, *New Towns in the Middle Ages* (1967).

[112] *Calendar of Inquisitions Miscellaneous (Chancery) Preserved in the Public Record Office* (7 vols., covering the years 1219–1422).

[113] Hoskins, *Fieldwork*, 48.

[114] See J. W. Clay (ed.), *Yorkshire Monasteries Suppression Papers*, Yorks. Archaeological Soc. Record Ser. xlviii (1913).

[115] For Anglo-Saxon charters, see p. 166.

[116] See p. 166.

[117] See W. G. Hoskins, *Provincial England* (1963), 15–52, for some interesting theories on the topographical interpretation of Domesday. N.b., too, the more recent comments by S. Harvey, 'Evidence for Settlement Study: Domesday Book', in P. H. Sawyer (ed.) *Medieval Settlement* (1976), and Sawyer in *ibid.*, on the values and drawbacks of Domesday for this purpose.

records, is, however, a subject in its own right and not one to be tackled lightly by the ill- or half-informed.

A start, apart from the study of recent general works,[118] must be, for many areas, the county volumes of the English place-name survey, published by the English Place-Name Society,[119] and other references of long standing.[120] It must be pointed out, however, that contemporary place names experts have radically revised some of the theories and the views expressed in previous works, including the earlier volumes of the place-name survey, and the beginner should beware of accepting outdated theories (still unfortunately kept alive in print by non-experts).[121] Much work remains to be done and generally speaking place name specialists in England seem to have underrated the survival of Celtic elements. Both for early place names and for the reconstruction of pre-Conquest topography, Anglo-Saxon land charters form a very significant, and still underused source. Many of them are in print, and references are noted elsewhere.[122]

Allied to place names as a historical source are those surnames which derive from the names of places. Much research on medieval migration has been undertaken recently

[118] E.g., K. Cameron, *English Place Names* (1977 edn); P. H. Reaney, *The Origin of English Place Names* (1960); M. Gelling, *Signposts to the Past* (1978). N.b. also the *Journal of the English Place-Name Society*.

[119] Published from 1924; in progress. A. H. Smith, *The Preparation of County Place-Name Surveys* (1954), explains the basis of the compilation. See also F. M. Stenton, *Introduction to the Survey of English Place Names* (1925).

[120] E. Ekwall, *Concise Oxford Dictionary of English Place Names* (4th edn, 1960); A. H. Smith, *English Place Name Elements* (1956); E. Ekwall, *English River Names* (1928); O. S. Anderson, *The English Hundred Names* (1934–9); R. J. Roberts, *Bibliography of Writings on English Place- and Personal Names* (*Onoma* viii, (1958–9)) (1961).

[121] Cf. M. Gelling, 'The Evidence of Place Names', in Sawyer (ed.), *Medieval Settlement*; N. Lund 'Thorp-Names' in *ibid.*; M. Gelling, 'Recent Work on English Place Names', *Local Historian* xi (1974).

[122] See p. 166 for details.

based on the distribution of such names[123] as found in tax records, especially poll-tax returns and lay subsidy rolls, as well as in manorial court rolls, extents, surveys and rentals, and the hundred rolls.[124]

Other clues to the chronology and relative density of early settlement, it has been suggested, may be found in the study of the distribution of parochial places of worship, since the English parish system was established by late Anglo-Saxon times.[125] Thus the siting of manorial (later parish) churches may indicate the whereabouts of the oldest and densest settlements, while other chapels are likely to have been built to serve more recent and less dense settlements. The plotting of such buildings on a map may, therefore, reveal settlement patterns of this kind. Lists of churches and chapels may be derived from Domesday, the *Valor Ecclesiasticus*, episcopal visitation returns, bishops registers, and monastic and other cartularies, among other records.[126]

The techniques of archaeology, palaeobotany, and the study of the distribution of blood groups, which may also be used to throw light on early settlement and migration, are too specialized to discuss here.[127]

[123] Hoskins, *Local History* (1972 edn), 179 sqq., and works cited there; Roberts, *Bibliography*; E. J. Buckatzsch, 'The Constancy of Local Populations and Migration in England before 1800', *Population Studies* v (1951–2); J. A. Raftis, 'Geographical Mobility in the Subsidy Rolls', *Medieval Studies* xxxviii (1976); G. Redmonds, 'Surnames and Place Names', *Local Historian* x (1972–3); P. A. McClure, 'Surnames from English Place Names as Evidence for Mobility in the Middle Ages', *ibid.* xiii (1978), and works cited there; R. A. McKinley, *Norfolk Surnames in the Sixteenth Century* (1968); R. A. McKinley, 'The Survey of English Surnames', *Local Historian* viii (1968–9); R. A. McKinley, *Norfolk and Suffolk Surnames in the Middle Ages* (1975); P. McClure, 'Patterns of migration in the late Middle Ages', *Ec. H.R.*, 2nd rev., xxxii (1979).

[124] For these records, see Index.

[125] D. Owen, 'Chapelries and Rural Settlement', in Sawyer (ed.), *Medieval Settlement*.   [126] See Index for these records.

[127] But see D. D. Bartley 'Palaeobotanical Evidence'; W. T. W. Potts, 'History and Blood Groups in the British Isles'; and comment on Potts by

THE WHEREABOUTS OF UNPUBLISHED SOURCES

The local historian will, of course, usually need to use unpublished sources. Some have already been mentioned and the following chapters draw attention to many more. They are to be found primarily in record offices and other depositories, including town and county record offices, libraries, museums, diocesan registries, and the offices of institutions and societies.[128] Many such depositories will possess printed guides and ancillary lists and catalogues of their collections, though these will vary in their exactness and detail.

Few adequate local studies of any depth will be able to rely entirely on locally available material. National collections of sources will inevitably have to be combed,[129] in particular the official archives at the Public Record Office, and the great collections at the British Library. The student is well catered for in aids to the use of the P.R.O. Apart from the published calendars[130] there are general guides[131] and more detailed lists and indexes[132] to be found in many large libraries, where

E. Sunderland; all in Sawyer (ed.), *Medieval Settlement.*

[128] For a topographical guide, see Historical Manuscripts Commission, *Record Repositories in Great Britain* (1979 edn). See also Emmison, *Archives and Local History*, 10 sqq.; J. Gibson and P. Peskett, *Record Offices: How to Find Them* (1981).

[129] P. Hepworth, *Archives and Manuscripts in Libraries* (1964 edn), which gives (pp. 16–18) a list of catalogues and guides, and also advice on locating collections; *Encyclopaedia Britannica* (1911 edn), under 'Libraries'.

[130] See above, p. 14.

[131] The most recent is the *Guide to the Contents of the Public Record Office* (H.M.S.O.), (3 vols., 1963–8), now (1980) being supplemented by the volumes of the *P.R.O. Current Guide* which includes record classes acquired by the P.R.O. since 1966. Older guides are still sometimes useful, especially M. S. Giuseppi, *Guide to the Manuscripts Preserved in the Public Record Office* (2 vols., 1923–4). See also *Public Record Office; Records of Interest to Social Scientists, 1919 to 1939: Introduction*, ed. B. Swann and M. Turnbull (H.M.S.O., 1971).

[132] P.R.O., Lists and Indexes (many vols.). There are also the large number of volumes of the List and Index Society which consist of photographic reproductions of unpublished P.R.O. search room lists and

they can be consulted prior to any visit to London. Since most of these were compiled, however, the P.R.O. has been separated physically into two parts, one at Chancery Lane and the other at Kew. It is worth making prior enquiry before a visit as to the whereabouts of particular classes. It seems likely (1980) that within a few years all records will be available only at the Kew branch. These libraries will often also possess the printed catalogues of manuscripts held in other great depositories like the Bodleian Library and the British Library.[133] British Library manuscript collections are indexed (not always satisfactorily),[134] and at the British Library Manuscripts Room there is a topographical index which, though by no means comprehensive, seeks to bring the collections together and is of some value to the local historian. The Bodleian collections are considerable, and the Dodsworth, Dugdale, Gough, Rawlinson, and Tanner manuscripts in particular are likely to contain material of value to local historians.[135] Other university libraries also have valuable manuscript collections.[136] Students interested in the post–1940 period may find material in government departmental libraries.[137]

indexes. A Special Series covers archives not in the P.R.O. The more important libraries receive these volumes, which are at present appearing at the rate of several a year.

[133] For the published calendars of the House of Lords manuscripts, see above, pp. 14–15.

[134] J. P. Gilson, *A Student's Guide to the Manuscripts of the British Museum* (1920); T. C. Skeat, *The Catalogues of the Manuscript Collections in the British Museum* (1962 edn); Esdaile, *National Libraries*; M. A. E. Nickson, *The British Library: Guide to the Catalogues and Indexes of the Department of Manuscripts* (1978).

[135] See *A Summary Catalogue of the Western Manuscripts in the Bodleian Library at Oxford* (7 vols., including index, 1922–53).

[136] See G. K. Clark and G. R. Elton, *Guide to Research Facilities in History in the Universities of Great Britain* (1964 edn).

[137] A. F. Comfort and C. Loveless (comps.), *Guide to Government Data: A Survey of Unpublished Social Science Material in the Libraries of Government Departments in London* (1974).

A boon to the student for tracking down collections of records is the National Register of Archives, part of the Royal Commission on Historical Manuscripts. This seeks to record the location, content, and availability of collections of documents (apart from those of the central government) in England and Wales. Its *Bulletin* (now discontinued) includes short accounts of some important collections, and its annual *List of Accessions to Repositories* is also worth searching.[138] Most important are its detailed reports of collections held in various depositories which are duplicated and distributed to certain important libraries.[139] Local libraries and record offices often have copies of those reports which concern their own areas. A complete set is at the N.R.A.'s offices[140] where there are also indexes to places, persons, and subjects.[141]

ORAL EVIDENCE

The recent popularization of the term 'oral history' is unfortunate since it suggests a branch of history on a par with others, as, for example, ecclesiastical history, or economic history. It would be more appropriate to speak of oral evidence and methods of using it. Even so, there is often some confusion between actual oral evidence gathered by the historian and already existing manuscript or printed evidence enshrining originally spoken words – as autobiographies, memoirs, statements of evidence to committees or officials as in parliamentary papers, poor-law examinations, and the like. Many of the latter category are numbered among the

[138] From 1973: *Accessions to Repositories and Reports added to the National Register of Archives.*

[139] Including that of the Institute of Historical Research, University of London.

[140] Quality Court, Chancery Lane, London wc2.

[141] F. Ranger, 'The National Register of Archives, 1945–1969', *Jnl Soc. Archivists* iii (1969); Baillie, 'Use of Resources', 464–6; R. A. Storey, 'Indexing Archives', *Indexer* v (1967).

records treated elsewhere in this volume, and are not strictly speaking oral evidence.

The use of actual oral evidence collected by historians is of long standing,[142] and in local history the many 'ex inf.' references in the footnotes of the *Victoria History of the Counties of England* testify to its academic acceptance. Commonly the evidence here referred to by the *V.C.H.* is information on a specific factual point from an informed individual where no documentary evidence exists. The types of oral evidence available to the local historian are, however, more extensive than this.

We may distinguish a number of different kinds. First there is the direct evidence of sound recordings of actual events, such as a speech given at a political meeting. Except for very recent times such evidence is unlikely to be common for local history. In the future, however, local record offices may well have extensive sound archives of this kind available to the researcher. Then there is the information verbally supplied by a former leading local figure (like a local education officer) concerning important local events in which he was involved and giving an insight not discernible from written evidence. Similar to this is evidence provided by humbler persons who may nevertheless have special knowledge, such as, for example, a factory hand who can explain the workings of a particular obsolete machine or process in a local industrial plant or a clerk who witnessed otherwise unreported conversations between important local figures.

In a somewhat different category is oral tradition relying on the memory of more than one generation. Thus in Upton Hellions parish (Devon) the field in front of Haske farm is known as 'barton', a likely indication that the farm itself was once known as Haske Barton (that is, a medieval demesne

[142] See P. Thompson, *The Voice of the Past: Oral History* (1978), 228–9. This book contains extensive bibliographical references to various aspects of oral evidence. For new work, see the journal *Oral History*.

farm),[143] though as far as I know there is no documentary record of this. Again Professor John MacCormack of Nova Scotia knows the Christian names of the main line of his Hebridean ancestors back to the seventeenth century, handed down by word of mouth.[144] Somewhat similar are the recollections of a previous generation.

Finally there is the kind of evidence that the historian may collect and process in the same way as contemporary sociologists analyse the answers to questionnaires they have distributed. This involves the use of interviews to collect information from a comparatively large number of local people with a similar background about aspects of life at a particular time in the past: by seeking answers to the same questions a form of check on accuracy is introduced. In this work skilled interview technique is essential and proper attention must be given to the nature and size of the group to be interviewed if the many dangers are to be avoided.[145]

Except in the case of the sound recording of actual events, oral evidence of the kinds outlined above has obvious drawbacks. Chief among these is the reliance on human memory, now recognized as the product of unconscious analysis and processing, rather than direct recall, and often lacking in accuracy. Then there are the results of conscious or unconscious bias on the part of the recollector and sometimes of an interviewer, deliberate fabrication of evidence for a variety of reasons, and the introduction in the guise of recollection of what is really logical reflection. These or similar drawbacks, however, attach also to many documentary sources, and oral evidence cannot be ignored on such accounts. So long as the local historian views oral sources with the same circumspection and treats them with the same

[143] This would seem to fit the Domesday evidence for this part of Devon: cf. Hoskins, *Provincial England*, 33–4, 64–8.

[144] Ex inf. J. R. MacCormack.

[145] Good advice is given in Thompson, *Voice of the Past*, with bibliographical references.

care as other source materials, oral evidence can be of considerable use.

Oral evidence is of particular value for those aspects of local (and general) history for which documentary evidence is slight or recorded only through the eyes of contemporary observers of a different social class: home life and family relationships; specific family history; working-class life, particularly that of women; behind-the-scenes politics and business activity; and social relationships generally. There is considerable scope in the future for work based on interview surveys. But it should be noted that in 1980 the number of persons able to recollect with accuracy the period before 1900 is small indeed. For the period from 1900 onwards the value of oral archive material available seems likely to grow greatly.[146] Oral evidence, however, will generally speaking be of value only for twentieth-century history.

[146] Useful is: Oral History Society, *Directory of British Oral History Collections* (1981). For the difficulties of organization etc., see R. L. Filippelli, 'Oral History and Archives', *American Archivist* (1976).

CHAPTER 2

Population and social structure

Before the official censuses which begin in 1801 there is no body of records (apart from bills of mortality) compiled primarily to obtain demographic or sociological information. Moreover the historian, unlike the social scientist, cannot create his own raw material, but must use what time and chance have allowed to survive. Nevertheless there is a great variety of sources available, and only the chief ones are dealt with here. Up to 1538 the sources available for the study of population and social structure in England are largely feudal or fiscal in nature; after that, until 1801, they are mainly ecclesiastical. Since such records were compiled for other purposes than the study of demography and social structure, the investigator is faced with a double problem of how reliable the records are even for what they purport to be or to do, and to what extent and in what way they can be utilized to give answers to the questions which interest modern historians.

The first problem requires awareness that administration in the past was often weak, corrupt, and inefficient. Taxes, for example, were evaded, laxly enforced, or became stereotyped. The second problem involves taking into account such considerations as the fact that most tax returns did not cover total population (sometimes omitting those under a certain age, those below a certain income level, those who were not heads of households, and so on). This involves the historian in estimating the proportion of children to adults and of paupers to the rest of the population, the average size of families, and, for this purpose, in employing multipliers. Similarly, religious returns sometimes provide the number of communicants rather than total populations. It is clear that so many factors are involved that conclusions based on such material must be tentative. Yet with skill and intelligence the local historian can make these records contribute to his historical knowledge.[1]

There are many sources which would throw light on the topics being surveyed. Here we confine ourselves to the more common types, most of which shed light on both population and social structure and may conveniently be treated together. Many of these can also be used for the study of migration.[2]

For most places the Domesday survey of *c.* 1086–7 is the earliest source of information. The original text consists of two volumes both housed in the Public Record Office. One covers Essex, Norfolk, and Suffolk, and is in greater detail than the other which embraces the rest of the country except Cumberland, Durham, Northumberland, and parts of Westmorland. London, Bristol, and some other towns known to

---

[1] For some of the techniques involved, see J. C. Russell, *British Medieval Population* (1948); D. V. Glass and D. E. C. Eversley (eds.), *Population in History* (1965) (and reviews of this in *Ec.H.R.*, 2nd ser., xx (1967), 131 sqq.); E. A. Wrigley (ed.), *Introduction to English Historical Demography* (1966); W. G. Hoskins, 'The Population of an English Village, 1086–1801', in his *Provincial England* (1963); *V.C.H.: Leicestershire* iii, ed. W. G. Hoskins and R. A. McKinley (1955), 129 sqq.; J. Z. Titow, *English Rural Society, 1200–1350* (1969); W. B. Stephens (ed.), *Sources for the History of Population and their Uses* (Leeds University Institute of Education, 1971); and T. H. Hollingsworth, *Historical Demography* (1969), which is useful, too, for bibliographical references and for warnings on the tentative nature of conclusions drawn from some of the sources cited below. For a good bibliography, including local monographs, together with a survey for recent times, see M. W. Flinn, *British Population Growth, 1700–1850* (1970), q.v. also for the Rickman estimates, not dealt with here. *Daedalus* xcvii (2) (1968), has a number of interesting articles on aspects of historical demography.

[2] For sources on migration before the official censuses, see E. J. Buckatzch, 'Constancy of Local Populations and Migration in England before 1800', *Population Studies* v (1951–2), and also pp. 37–8, 54.

have existed at the time are also not included. A remarkably accurate text of Domesday was published in record type in 1783, and it was also reproduced by the Ordnance Survey in facsimile in 1861–4 (in county sections). The *Victoria History of the Counties of England* provides translations of the Domesday entries for the majority of counties[3] and these are usually sufficient for most purposes. Some record society publications also exist, as for Devon and for Lincolnshire. It should be realized when working with Domesday that entries are not topographically arranged (except under counties) but appear under landholders' names. Domesday poses many problems of interpretation which cannot be gone into here,[4] nor can all the information normally found in each entry be discussed. Significant for our purpose are those entries which indicate the number of tenants, arranged into classes. The population figures there recorded are probably households (i.e. one villein is really one villein and his household), except in the case of slaves (*servi*)[5] and clergy, who are probably individuals. It is usual to employ a multiplier to obtain some

[3] They exist for Beds., Berks., Bucks., Cambs., Corn.,* a very small part of Cumb.,* Derby., Devon, Dorset, Essex, Hants., Herefordshire,* Herts., Hunts., Kent, Lancs., Leics., Middx., Norfolk,* Northants., Notts.,* Oxon., Rutland, Shropshire,* Somerset, Staffs., Suffolk,* Surrey, Sussex, War., Wilts., Worcs., Yorks. All except those marked * have indexes. For other indexes to Domesday, see F. M. Stenton, *Anglo-Saxon England* (1947 edn.), 693–4. A new translation of Domesday is being published by Messrs Phillimore.

[4] But see W. G. Hoskins, *Local History in England* (1959), 37–40; R. E. Welldon Finn, *The Domesday Inquest and the Making of Domesday Book* (1961); F. W. Maitland, *Domesday Book and Beyond* (1897); A. Ballard, *The Domesday Inquest* (1906); E. King, 'Domesday Studies', *History* lviii (1973); and books edited by H. C. Darby and his collaborators: see p. 167 n. 11.

[5] But see also J. C. Russell, 'The Pre-plague Population of England', *Jnl of British Studies* vi (2) (1966), 2; J. C. Russell, 'The Short Dark Folk of England', *Social Forces* xxiv (1946), 340–7; M. Postan, 'The Famulus: the Estate Labourer in the Twelfth and Thirteenth Centuries', *Ec.H.R.* supplement no. 2 (1954).

indication of total population of a Domesday manor; perhaps 4 or 5 for each head of household.[6]

In addition to Domesday proper there are also certain roughly contemporaneous surveys, some of which may well represent the preliminary work for the compilation of Domesday itself. The chief of these 'satellite surveys'[7] are the Exon Domesday (for Wiltshire, Dorset, Somerset, Devon, and Cornwall), housed at the Dean and Chapter's Library, Exeter, the Ely Inquest and the Cambridge Inquest, both in the British Library. There are also the Winton (Winchester) Domesday, a similar survey of 1107–28 held by the Society of Antiquaries,[8] and the Boldon Book, a survey of 1183 of the Palatinate of Durham.[9] The texts of some of these surveys have been published.[10]

The next source, of particular use for several counties, is the hundred rolls of the late thirteenth century, which contain the results of enquiries undertaken by hundreds

[6] The size of a medieval household is a matter of dispute. Russell, *British Medieval Population*, 22–3, 57–70, suggests 3·5, but this is questioned by H. E. Hallam, 'Some 13th-century censuses', *Ec.H.R.*, 2nd ser., x (1958), 340 sqq. (q.v. for serf lists, an uncommon population source), and J. Krause, 'The Medieval Household: Large or Small?', *ibid.* ix (1957), 420–32, who suggest a higher multiplier. See also J. C. Russell, 'Demographic Limitations of the Spalding Serf Lists', *Ec.H.R.*, 2nd ser., xv (1962); H. E. Hallam, 'Further Observations on the Spalding Serf Lists', *Ec.H.R.*, 2nd ser., xvi (1963), and, for further reference to this dispute, Titow, *English Rural Society*, 67, 89.

[7] D. C. Douglas, 'The Domesday Survey', *History* xxi (1936–7), 251. See also J. J. Bagley, *Historical Interpretation: Sources of English Medieval History, 1066–1540* (1965), 22.

[8] A translation is in M. Biddle (ed.), *Winchester in the Early Middle Ages* (1976).

[9] Original not extant. Copies in B.L., Bodleian Library, and at Durham.

[10] E.g., N. E. S. A. Hamilton, *Inquisitio Comitatus Cantabrigiensis and Inquisitio Eliensis* (1876). The Exeter Domesday is published in the third volume of the Record Commission's edition of the Survey. See also R. W. Finn, *Domesday Studies: The Eastern Counties* (1967); R. W. Finn, *Domesday Studies: The Liber Exoniensis* (1964).

(divisions of counties) into royal rights and prerogatives in Edward I's reign. The most useful, and the best known, are those for 1279–80, described in more detail elsewhere.[11] From the point of view of population and social structure, the enumeration of the villeins, freemen, and cottage tenants, with their obligations and holdings, are the significant items, and are found in detail for certain counties in the 1279–80 returns. It is argued that estimates of population can be made from this evidence and a picture of social structure built up.[12] Serious drawbacks, however, are that those who do not hold land – the famuli, the hired labourers, and servants, perhaps numerous – are not included, that individuals appear more than once (sometimes in other villages), and that the same person may appear in one social category in one place and in a different one in another.

For many counties the hundred rolls are not sufficiently detailed to be of value so that the next class of records available for general examination is the lay subsidy rolls of the period 1290 to 1334. This subsidy was sometimes known as the tenths and fifteenths, because the contribution of townsmen was based on one-tenth of the current valuation of certain personal property, and that of country dwellers on one-fifteenth.[13] Returns note the tax to be paid by named individuals arranged by vills and boroughs. These rolls are more useful for giving a comparative picture of the wealth of different places than for any other purpose. They do not cover all property owners (let alone all inhabitants), since certain types of goods were exempt, and there was, moreover, considerable evasion. For total population they are, therefore, useless, each return being 'rather like an

[11] See p. 168.

[12] See J. B. Harley, 'The Hundred Rolls of 1279', *Amateur Historian* v (1961–3), and other works cited in notes on p. 168.

[13] For these taxes, see M. W. Beresford, *Lay Subsidies and Poll Taxes* (1963); J. F. Willard, *Parliamentary Taxes on Personal Property, 1290–1334* (1934); A. M. Erskine, *The Devonshire Lay Subsidy of 1332*, Devon and Cornwall Record Soc., NS, xiv (1969), pp. vii–x.

iceberg the size of whose submerged depths is unknown'.[14]
What one can surmise, however, is a rough indication of
who the richer lay inhabitants of each village were (and here
significant families may be identified) and a vague idea may
be obtained of their relative wealth and of the wealth of one
place relative to that of another. The assessments for 1334
have been published with a useful index and grid references,
and references to other published assessments.[15] The lay
subsidies from 1334 onwards no longer give the names of
individuals, since (like the seventeenth-century monthly assessments levied by Parliament) they fell not on individuals
any longer but on communities. Moreover, reassessment
became rare so that, although the 1334 returns may indicate
the relative wealth of different places in that year, these
differentiations tended to become fossilized in subsequent
levies right through to their abolition in the seventeenth
century. Reductions for tax, however, might follow disasters
such as plague.[16] The lay subsidies are to be found in the
Public Record Office, Class E.179.[17]

Of greater use are the fourteenth-century poll taxes, of
which there were three – 1377, 1379, 1381. Of these the most
valuable for the purpose of estimating total population was
the first, since the tax levied was 4*d.* per head for all lay
inhabitants over 14 years of age, except regular beggars.
Clergy paid 1*s.* Even when only the total sum collected in a
parish is available the number of groats involved will indicate
roughly the number of persons subject to poll. Professor
Russell suggests adding half this number again to account

---

[14] M. W. Beresford, 'Fifteenths and Tenths: Quotas of 1334', *V.C.H.:
Wiltshire* iv, ed. E. Crittall (1959), 294.

[15] R. E. Glasscock (ed.), *The Lay Subsidy of 1334* (1975).

[16] Cf. Hollingsworth, *Historical Demography*, 124.

[17] See *Exchequer (K.R.) Lay Subsidy Rolls*, List and Index Society: xliv
(Beds.–Essex) (1969); liv (Gloucs.–Lincs.) (1970); lxiii (London–Somerset)
(1971); lxxv (Staffs.–Yorks.; Wales) (1972); lxxxvii (Wales; Cinque Ports,
etc.) (1973).

also for those under 14. He also considers 5 per cent a reasonable figure to cover the exempt and evaders,[18] but Professor Postan argues for 40–50 per cent and up to 25 per cent for undernumeration.[19] The two other polls, those collected in 1379 and 1381, are less valuable for this purpose, because it is known that there were large-scale evasions. The 1379 poll differed from the 1377 one, however, in being graded according to rank. For example, its incidence varied from £4 for earls to 6s. 8d. for esquires and substantial merchants, to 2s., 1s., or 6d. for artificers, and to 4d. for poor couples and individuals (not being beggars) over 16. Clergy were exempt. From the returns to this tax, therefore, a rough picture of social stratification can be worked out. The 1381 tax was levied on all over 15 (not beggars), the richer to help the poorer.[20] The fourteenth-century poll tax returns are also found in the Public Record Office, Class E.179.

Manorial extents, which are to be found for centuries from the thirteenth to the seventeenth, sometimes enumerate the heads of families rather like Domesday, and can thus in the same way provide an estimate of total population. Many extents are attached to inquisitions post mortem in the Public Record Office, but they are also to be found elsewhere.[21] In

[18] Russell, *British Medieval Population*, 119–46. To this would have to be added a few clergy (*c.* 1·5 per cent of the population, according to Russell, 145).

[19] M. Postan (ed.), *Cambridge Economic History of Europe* (1966 edn), 561–2.

[20] For details of these taxes, see S. Dowell, *History of Taxation* (1881 edn) i, 91 sqq; Beresford, *Lay Subsidies and Poll Taxes*, Professor Beresford is (1980) preparing all the 1377 returns for publication.

[21] For how to go about searching for relevant i.p.m.s, lists, indexes, and calendars, etc., see M. McGuiness, 'Inquisitions Post Mortem', *Amateur Historian* vi (1963–6); D. J. Steel (ed.), *National Index of Parish Registers* i (1968), 367–77; *P.R.O. Guide* i, 27–8. See also R. E. Latham, 'Inquisitions Post Mortem', *Amateur Historian* i (1952–4). Calendars published by the Record Commission in the nineteenth century indicate which inquisitions have extents; each has an index of places. See also pp. 73 n. 12, 169–70, 174 n. 48.

Russell's *British Medieval Population* there is an interesting chapter on the uses of inquisitions post mortem, where the opinion is expressed that from a demographic point of view the inquisitions themselves (i.e. apart from the extents) are useful for working out an average expectation of life of the upper classes; they state the age of the heir on inheritance, and can often be followed through several generations. Manorial court rolls may also yield information on population and social structure.[22]

There are no sources peculiar to the fifteenth century useful for our purpose, but from the sixteenth century there are the parish registers which are certainly the most important of all demographic sources before the nineteenth century provides the official censuses and the Registrar General's reports (see below). Advice on the best methods for the use of parish registers by the local historian cannot, however, be briefly given and are anyway already available in some detail in *An Introduction to English Historical Demography*.[23] Because of the availability and authority of this work the amount of space devoted to the parish registers here is not proportionate to their significance.

The keeping of registers of baptisms, marriages, and burials was made compulsory in 1538, and some date from then. Many more, however, record registrations from 1558, for in 1598 the keeping of such records was again ordered and the copying into books of entries as far back as the year of Elizabeth I's accession was encouraged.[24] The registers are of greater use for the sixteenth and seventeenth centuries than

[22] Cf. J. A. Raftis, 'Social Structure in Five East Midland Villages', *Ec.H.R.*, 2nd ser., xviii (1965); K. C. Newton, 'A Source for Medieval Population Statistics', *Jnl Soc. Archivists* iii (1969). For court rolls, see also pp. 74–5.

[23] Ed. E. A. Wrigley (1966).

[24] For the history of parish registers, see J. C. Cox, *Parish Registers of England* (1910); J. S. Burn, *History of Parish Registers in England* (1862 edn); G. H. Tupling, 'Parish Registers', *Amateur Historian* i (1952–4); Hollingsworth, *Historical Demography*, 139 sqq.

later, when the spread of legal nonconformity destroyed their comprehensiveness.[25] The spread of dissent in the eighteenth century thus detracts, especially in some areas, from the value of parish registers for demographic purposes, since, although for long all but Jews and Quakers were obliged to marry in church, they were permitted baptism and burial elsewhere. Other sources, such, for example, as visitation returns, may help if they indicate the proportion of nonconformists in the population. If nonconformist registers exist[26] this also may ease the problem.

Two methods are currently used to obtain demographic information from parish registers – aggregative analysis and family reconstitution. For both, acceptable results normally require data drawn from a larger area than a single parish.[27] The aggregative method has a long history and is likely still to be the most commonly used by the individual historian. Even simple compilations of totals of baptisms, marriages, and burials can yield useful results. Rather rudimentary ways of estimating totals of populations have been suggested,[28] and though these may be of some value, especially if other evidence is available, they must contain 'a large element of

[25] In the Civil War and Interregnum, however, the system broke down, and registers for these years are unreliable. During the years 1694–1706 (and 1783–94) taxes were payable on registration and a large number of births and deaths are thought to have gone unregistered. In 1837 civil registration of births, deaths, and marriages began; records at Office of Population Censuses and Surveys, St Catherine's House, 10 Kingsway, London, WC2B 6JP.

[26] Now housed at the Public Record Office (Classes R.G.4, R.G.5). See pp. 273–4, 293 for a detailed discussion. They are chiefly for the later eighteenth and early nineteenth centuries. For a printed example, see *Bradford Historical and Antiquarian Soc., Local Records Series* iv (1953).

[27] Cf. M. Drake, 'An Elementary Exercise in Parish Register Demography', *Ec.H.R.*, 2nd ser., xiv (1962), 430.

[28] See, e.g., methods of estimating total population in W. E. Tate, *The Parish Chest* (1960), 80–2; Hoskins, *Provincial England*, 189; N. L. Tranter, *Population since the Industrial Evolution* (1973), 21–2. For a more sophisticated method: Wrigley (ed.), *Introduction to Historical Demography*, 264–5.

uncertainty' and cannot be used in calculating birth, death, and marriage rates.[29] Elementary totalling can, however, provide information on such matters as migration and occupational structure. Yearly totals of baptisms, burials, and marriages, 'plotted on a graph give a very fair guide to general population trends',[30] and burial totals, for example, can pin-point periods of high mortality and perhaps suggest the relationship between climatic conditions, the price of food, and mortality.[31]

The family reconstitution or nominal method has been pioneered in this country by the Cambridge Group for the History of Population and Social Structure (University of Cambridge). Since this method consists of reconstituting a random sample of all the families in a parish it involves a great deal more work, expense, and expertise than the aggregative method, and indeed would normally require a team of workers. It can, however, provide more sophisticated information and more accurate results than are possible by the aggregative method, as, for example, on 'such key variables as age at marriage, infant mortality, pre-nuptial conception rates, average intervals between births, age-

[29] E. A. Wrigley, 'Parish Registers in Population History' (two articles), *Amateur Historian* vi (1963–5), 148. Cf. M. W. Flinn, 'Population in History, II', *Ec.H.R.*, 2nd ser., xx (1967), 141–2.

[30] Wrigley, 'Parish Registers', 149.

[31] For detailed advice on sophisticated aggregative analysis, see D. E. C. Eversley, 'Exploitation of Anglican Parish Registers by Aggregative Analysis', in Wrigley (ed.), *Introduction to Historical Demography*; D. Turner, *Historical Demography in Schools* (Hist. Assoc. pamphlet, 1971), 20–6. Good examples of the use of this method are Drake, 'Parish Register Demography'; J. D. Chambers, *The Vale of Trent, 1670–1800, Ec.H.R.* supplement no. 3 (1957); D. E. C. Eversley, 'A Survey of Population in an area of Worcestershire from 1600–1850 on the Basis of Parish Records', *Population Studies* x (1957); A. H. French, 'The Population of Stepney in the Early Seventeenth Century', *Local Population Studies Magazine* iii (1969). See also R. S. Schofield, 'Some Notes on Aggregative Analysis, *Local Population Studies* v (1970). For criticism of the claims made for aggregative analysis, see Flinn, 'Population in History, II', 141–2.

specific fertility, average duration of marriage',[32] and so on. It can also perhaps provide the reasons for the direction of population trends which aggregative analysis can reveal but not explain.[33]

Family reconstitution is, however, likely to remain a less commonly used technique than aggregative analysis not only because it is so time-consuming but because there are only a limited number of registers complete over sufficiently long a period and in adequate enough detail for this method.[34] The method is, however, not without other difficulties and drawbacks.[35]

Parish registers have traditionally been found in the parish chest. The Parochial Registers and Records Measure of 1978, however, requires all registers and records more than a century old and not still open for entries normally to be deposited with the diocesan records within a given period. The existence of such registers should thus be simpler to

[32] Wrigley, 'Parish Registers', 149.

[33] E. A. Wrigley, 'Family Reconstitution', in Wrigley (ed.), *Introduction to Historical Demography*, 97 sqq. This article provides detailed advice on procedure for undertaking this method. See also J. A. Johnson, 'Family Reconstitution and the Local Historian', *Local Historian* ix (1970–1); Turner, *Historical Demography in Schools*, 26–34. Cf. E. A. Wrigley, 'Family Limitation in Pre-Industrial England', *Ec.H.R.*, 2nd ser., xix (1966); E. A. Wrigley, 'Mortality in Pre-Industrial England: The Example of Colyton, Devon, over Three Centuries', *Daedalus* xcvii (2) (1968). For further sophisticated work (not family reconstitution), see R. D. Lee, 'Methods and Models for Analyzing Historical Series of Births, Deaths, and Marriages', in R. D. Lee (ed.), *Population Patterns in the Past* (1977).

[34] Wrigley, 'Parish Registers', 150.

[35] See, e.g., Hollingsworth, *Historical Demography*, 181 sqq.; Eversley, in Wrigley (ed.), *Introduction to Historical Demography*, 44–5. See also D. J. Loschky, 'The Usefulness of England's Parish Registers', *Review of Economics and Statistics* xlix (1967); Flinn, *British Population Growth*, 18–19; and, for advice on avoidance of error, L. Henry, 'The Verification of Data in Historical Demography', *Population Studies* xxii (1968); E. A. Wrigley, 'Some Problems of Family Reconstitution using English Parish Register Material', *Third International Conference of Economic History, Munich 1965*, iv (1972).

ascertain in the future. The Society of Genealogists has published several guides of use in tracing parish registers and copies.[36] Copies of entries known as bishops' transcripts (mainly dating from 1598) may be with the diocesan records, and can sometimes be used to fill a gap where the originals are missing. They are, however, not exact copies and can be inaccurate, so that caution is advised.[37] Bills of mortality, derived from registers, are dealt with elsewhere.[38]

Other ecclesiastical sources can give information for specific periods. The chantry certificates of 1547,[39] for example, often give an estimate of the number of 'housling people' (i.e. communicants) in the parish. This possibly meant all those over the age of 14 or 15 so that the certificate may

[36] E.g., *Parish Register Copies*: i, *Society of Genealogists' Collection*; ii, *Other than the Society of Genealogists' Collection* (1977). D. J. Steel *et al.* (eds.), *National Index of Parish Registers* i (1968), v (1966), xi (1) (1979): vol. i (*Sources of Births, Marriages and Deaths before 1837*) is a general introd.; vol. v covers the registers of Gloucs., Herefordshire, Oxon., Shropshire, War., Worcs.; vol. xi (1) covers Durham and Northumberland. They list the years of the registers, treating baptisms, burials, marriage registers separately, noting missing years and all known register copies. Roman Catholic and other dissenting registers are also listed but for these see esp. vols. ii, iii (1973–4): see pp. 274–6, 293. These are the first of a 12 vol. series. See also the publications of the Parish Register Soc., founded 1896, dissolved 1934 (those published between 1901 and 1922 are listed in E. L. C. Mullins (ed.), *A Guide to the Historical and Archaeological Publications of Societies in England and Wales, 1901–1933* (1968)), and *Original Parish Registers in Record Offices and Libraries*, Local Population Studies (1974) with supplements (1976 and 1978). A. M. Burke, *Key to the Ancient Parish Registers of England and Wales* (1908), lists all parishes with dates of earliest known registers. *Parish Maps of the Counties of England* (Institute of Heraldic and Genealogical Studies, 1977), gives dates of surviving parish registers and maps of ancient parochial boundaries.

[37] Steel (ed.), *National Index of Parish Registers*, i, 167; Eversley, in Wrigley (ed.), *Introduction to Historical Demography*, 46.

[38] See p. 320.

[39] For the nature of these records, see L. S. Snell, 'Chantry Certificates', *History* xlviii (1963). See also J. Thirsk, 'Sources of Information on Population, 1500–1760 – I', *Amateur Historian* iv (1958–60), 131–2.

indicate 60 per cent of the population.[40] The larger the place the more likelihood there was of exaggeration.[41]

For the sixteenth and seventeenth centuries certain specific collections may be of value. The Harleian Manuscripts contain returns of 1563 by the bishops to the Privy Council of the number of households in each parish, and similar returns for 1603 giving numbers of communicants, Protestant dissenters, and Roman Catholics.[42]

The ecclesiastical census of 1676 (often called the Compton Census)[43] provides by parishes the number of Anglican communicants, Protestant dissenters, and Roman Catholic dissenters, presumably over the age of 16 (though there is some reason to believe that in some places the returns incorrectly give those under 16 as well, and that in others only males are included). The returns probably vary in their reliability. Some, by reason of the roundness of the figures,

[40] Roughly following Gregory King, *Natural and Political Observations and Conclusions upon the State and Condition of England* (1696). For doubts on assuming 14 as the age of confession in the sixteenth century and before, however, see J. Cornwall, 'English Population in the Early Sixteenth Century', *Ec.H.R.*, 2nd ser., xxiii (1970), 32; E. L. Cutts, *Parish Priests and their People in the Middle Ages in England* (1914), 496; *Catholic Encyclopaedia* (1913–14), under 'Communion of children'.

[41] Cf. *V.C.H.: Warwickshire* viii, ed. W. B. Stephens (1969), 5 (for Coventry).

[42] B.L., Harleian MSS. 280, 594, 595. *The Catalogue of the Harleian Manuscripts* i (1808), 359–61, gives the names of the dioceses concerned. Some of these returns are in other depositories. For details, see Thirsk, 'Sources of Information', 132–3, who also suggests means of comparing the two returns. Hollingsworth, *Historical Demography*, 79 sqq., discusses ecclesiastical and other censuses of the sixteenth to eighteenth centuries, including one of 1688 for the province of Canterbury.

[43] See A. Browning (ed.), *English Historical Documents, 1660–1714* (1953), 411. For some bibliographical references and some strictures on its reliability, see Hollingsworth, *Historical Demography*, 80; W. B. Stephens, 'A Seventeenth Century Census', *Devon and Cornwall Notes and Queries* xxix (1958). See also C. W. Chalklin (ed.), *The Compton Census for the Dioceses of Canterbury and Rochester*, Kent Archaeological Soc. Records Branch xvii (1960).

are clearly estimates, others give the appearance of careful counting. Many of the returns are at Lambeth Palace, at the William Salt Library, Stafford, and at the Bodleian Library, Oxford.[44]

Episcopal visitation records are a most important source for they very often give an estimate of the population or of the number of families or communicants in parishes. Again the accuracy tends to vary from place to place.[45]

Before turning to some fiscal sources for the sixteenth and seventeenth centuries, mention may be made of the military records, known as the muster rolls and books,[46] which are extant for periods of national crisis from the early sixteenth to the mid-seventeenth century.[47] Their nature varies very considerably. They are basically lists of men between the ages of 15 or 16 and 60 and also often of their weapons. From 1558 many returns list or enumerate men in three categories – those unfit for military service, those able, and those actually chosen; but some returns give only the able, or only the chosen. It is thought that those from 1569 were more carefully compiled.[48] Where the number of able men is

[44] The Stafford returns are to be published by the Stafford Record Soc. together with those for the southern province which are at Lambeth. It is incorrect (Hollingsworth, *Historical Demography*, 80) that only the province of Canterbury was covered. Some returns for the province of York are at Oxford in Bodleian MSS: Tanner 144, 150. The Lambeth returns were printed by G. Lyon Turner, *Original Records of Early Nonconformity* (1911), and include extracts for the York province. See also D. M. Owen, *The Records of the Established Church in England* (1970), 28n.

[45] For other ecclesiastical sources, see Thirsk, 'Sources of Information'.

[46] E. E. Rich, 'The Population of Elizabethan England', *Ec.H.R.*, 2nd ser., ii (1950), 264n.

[47] Originals are in P.R.O., Classes S.P.12/50, 52, 55–7, 61–5, 70, 72, 94; E.101; E.36/16–55a; E.315 (Bucks. and Norfolk), and in local repositories. Quite a number have been published by local record societies (see E. L. C. Mullins (ed.), *Texts and Calendars, An Analytical Guide to Serial Publications*, Royal Historical Soc., Guides and Handbooks, no. 7 (1958)), and the introductions to these should be consulted.

[48] Rich (in 'Population of Elizabethan England') indicates those years for

known a multiplier may be applied to give an indication of total population. E. E. Rich suggests a multiplier of 4,[49] Professor Hoskins one of 6 or 7.[50] Generally these records are not of much use for social structure, though it is possible that an occasional return giving occupations may come to light.[51] For some places the muster return for 1522 is of particular value since it was the basis of the subsidy of 1523–7 (see below).[52]

The taxes known as the Tudor and Stuart subsidies, first introduced in 1523, are generally regarded as most useful for providing an indication of the better-off inhabitants of each parish or township. The first subsidy, however, collected over four years between 1524 and 1527, fell in its first two years (1524, 1525) on the working as well as other classes and for that reason can provide a good idea of the general social structure of localities,[53] since the tax was graded.[54] Later subsidies fell only on the wealthier classes, and are useful mainly as an indication of the number, apparent relative wealth, and names of such persons. As time went on, however, the collection of the tax became more and more stereotyped and evasion became common. The returns are, therefore, less and less reliable for our purpose.[55] The rates of

which he considers the records most reliable, and discusses some of the problems of interpretation.

[49] *Ibid.*

[50] Hoskins, *Local History*, 146–7.

[51] For such a return for Gloucestershire in 1608, see R. H. and A. J. Tawney, 'An Occupational Census of the Seventeenth Century', *Ec.H.R.* v (1934).

[52] J. C. K. Cornwall, 'A Tudor Domesday', *Jnl Soc. Archivists* iii (1965).

[53] W. G. Hoskins makes good use of this in 'English Provincial Towns in the Early Sixteenth Century', *T.R.H.S.*, 5th ser., vi (1956), also printed in Hoskins, *Provincial England*. See also J. C. K. Cornwall, 'English Country Towns in the Fifteen Twenties', *Ec.H.R.*, 2nd ser., xv (1962).

[54] For the incidence of the assessment on different classes, see Dowell, *History of Taxation* i, 131–2.

[55] Hoskins, *Local History*, 104, finds that the 1546 subsidy is the last one to give any very exact indication of social structure. See also S. A. Payton,

tax varied considerably from time to time.[56] They are to be found in the Public Record Office, Class E.179[57] and local depositories.

More useful sources for the seventeenth century are the poll-tax and hearth-tax records. The hearth taxes were levied in the later seventeenth century at different times from 1662 to 1689.[58] Most exist in the Public Record Office (Class E.179)[59] but contemporary copies are to be found locally. Some rolls or books are 'assessments' (what was due for collection), others are 'returns' (what was actually collected). The most valuable are those assessments which indicate the persons exempt as well as those who paid or ought to pay. Those for 1664 are generally the best from this point of view. Sometimes separate lists of exempt households exist.

The hearth-tax records provide lists of householders together with the number of hearths in their dwellings. On the assumption that the richer the person the more hearths and

'The Village Population in the Tudor Lay Subsidy Rolls', *E.H.R.* xxx (1915).

[56] They are set out well in J. Tait, *Taxation in Salford Hundred*, Chetham Soc., NS, lxxxiii (1924).

[57] See List and Index Soc. vols. cited above, p. 50 n. 17.

[58] C. A. F. Meekings, *Surrey Hearth Tax*, Surrey Record Soc. xvii (1940), and *The Hearth Tax, 1662–1689: Exhibition of Records, 1962–3* (P.R.O., n.d.), provide a good introduction to the significance of the returns. C. A. F. Meekings, *Dorset Hearth Tax Assessments, 1662–4* (1951) gives summaries of the 1662 assessment for the chief towns, and all counties. F. G. Emmison and J. Gray, *County Records* (Hist. Assoc. pamphlet, 1948), list extant returns in local record offices. J. West, *Village Records* (1962), gives a list of hearth-tax assessments which have been printed. For a general survey and bibliography, see R. Howell, 'Hearth Tax Returns', *History* xlix (1964); Thirsk, 'Sources of Information', 183, and Hollingsworth, *Historical Demography*, 124–5.

[59] See List and Index Soc. vols. cited above, p. 50 n. 17. *Exchequer (K.R.) Lay Subsidy Rolls: Analysis of the Hearth Tax, 1662–1665 and 1666–1669*, List and Index Soc., cliii, clxiii (1979 and 1980), comprise C. A. F. Meekings's analysis by counties of the charge, payment, and discharge of the tax.

stoves he possessed, a rough idea of the spread of wealth may be obtained. Generally speaking houses with only one hearth may be regarded as an indication of humbler inhabitants, and this may apply to those with two hearths in some areas. Those with seven or more hearths lived in some affluence.[60] In addition relative or actual sizes of populations may be estimated by the use of a multiplier of perhaps 4 to 5 per household (or more in towns), remembering, of course, that maybe a third of the householders were exempt from tax.[61]

The seventeenth-century poll taxes of 1641, 1660, 1666, and 1677 (also in P.R.O., Class E.179, and local depositories) can likewise be used to give some idea of the distribution of wealth, since they were graduated taxes.[62] The incidence of the 1641 poll, for example, ranged from £100 for a duke to £10 for an esquire, while other persons generally paid on an assessment of their annual expenditure (from £5 for a gentleman spending £100 a year, to 1s. for a man spending £5). For all others over 16 a poll tax of 6d. was levied. Usually women were included with husbands, but indicated (*et uxor*). The

[60] A degree of caution is required, however, since some houses with a large number of hearths were inns, poorhouses, etc. (though usually not indicated as such). Smiths' forges (but not industrial hearths) paid the tax. See also below, p. 306.

[61] Thirsk, 'Sources of information', 183. For examples of the use of a hearth tax for population and social structure, see W. G. Hoskins, *Industry, Trade and People in Exeter, 1688–1800* (1935), 111 sqq.; G. C. F. Forster, 'York in the Seventeenth Century', in *V.C.H.: City of York*, ed. P. M. Tillott (1961), 162–5. P. Laslett, in 'Size and Structure of the Household in England over Three Centuries', *Population Studies* xxiii (1969), suggests that the household size stayed fairly constant at *c.* 4·75 between 1574 and 1821. See also R. S. Schofield, 'Estimates of Population: Hearth Tax', *Local Population Studies Magazine* i (1968); J. Patten, 'The Hearth Taxes, 1662–1689', *Local Population Studies* vii (1971); R. Fieldhouse, 'The Hearth Tax and other Records', in A. Rogers (ed.), *Group Projects in Local History* (1977); and Chambers, *Vale of Trent*, 20, and works cited there.

[62] See W. B. Stephens, 'Sources for the History of Agriculture in the English Village and their Treatment', *Agricultural History* xliii (1969), 230. There were other poll taxes, particularly after the Revolution.

adolescent children of well-to-do parents, however, paid the poll tax of 6*d*. and the number of sixpenny-poll-tax payers, though largely an indication of the size of the working-class sector of the community, does include these. Also to be taken into account are paupers, who were not listed since they were exempt. For total population an estimate of the number of those under 16 (perhaps 40 per cent) and of paupers must be made. The post-Restoration poll taxes were similarly graded.[63]

Parish rate books,[64] such as those for church and poor rates, usually list householders with the value of their property and the rate levied. They are most common from the mid-eighteenth century but some exist for the seventeenth. If they list both the families who paid and those who did not[65] they can be useful for estimating population as well as the spread of wealth.

One way of building up a more detailed picture of social structure in a place for which tax returns, such as those for the hearth and poll taxes, exist, is to use as ancillaries records which identify the occupation and social standing (e.g. official positions such as mayor) of some of the persons known to fall in each tax category. Such records are very miscellaneous and too numerous to mention individually but include quarter-sessions records, freemen's books, and other town records. Most important for this purpose, however, are wills, and, more especially, probate inventories which list the possessions of the deceased (e.g., houses, furniture, clothes, livestock, crops, tools, stock, ready money, money due and owing, etc.), except real estate. Using these the relative wealth of different social groups and their size (from the tax returns) can be estimated.[66] If one can find the names

[63] *Statutes of the Realm* v (18 Chas. II c.1; 29 and 30 Chas. II c.1).

[64] See I. Darlington, 'Rate Books', *History* xlvii (1962).

[65] E.g., Hoskins, *Provincial England*, 200.

[66] For examples of the analytical use of such records, see W. B. Stephens, *Seventeenth Century Exeter: A Study of Industry and Trade* (1958), 40–3,

of some people who died soon after being listed in a tax return, their wills and inventories, if they can be found,[67] will indicate, for example, how different were the economic circumstances of those who paid £5 for the poll tax and those who paid 2s. The inventories often list belongings room by room so that a picture of what, for example, the five-hearth house for the person concerned (identified in a hearth-tax return) was like, and so the probable degree of prosperity of other householders in that category whose inventories are not extant, may be deduced.[68] The number of householders listed also gives clues to the density of settlement in an area.[69]

Wills before 1858 came under the jurisdiction of the church courts where they were proved and administration was granted. Generally speaking the wealthier the testator the more important the court where his will was proved. Usually if a man held property in more than one province, his executors had to prove his will at Canterbury; if in two dioceses within the same province, then the will was to be proved at the archbishop's court – at Canterbury or York. If he held property in, say, two archdeaconries in the diocese, then the episcopal court was the place. If his property lay

155–6; W. B. Stephens (ed.), *History of Congleton* (1970), 50–4; R. Grassby, 'The Personal Wealth of the Business Community in Seventeenth-Century England', *Ec.H.R.*, 2nd ser., xxiii (1970).

[67] For an explanation of the legal procedure involved in testamentary matters, the documents deriving from it, lists of local depositories, and the wills they held at date of publication, see A. J. Camp, *Wills and their Whereabouts* (1974 edn); J. S. W. Gibson, *Wills and Where to Find Them* (1974). Books and articles published before 1974 are out of date as regards whereabouts, but otherwise useful are: P. Walne, *English Wills* (1964); O. Ashmore, 'Inventories as a Source of Local History', *Amateur Historian* iv (1958–60), 157–61, 186–95; H. Thacker, 'Wills and Other Probate Records', *ibid.* 1 (1952–4). See also pp 135, 172, 306.

[68] For inventories, see M. Cash (ed.), *Devon Inventories of the Sixteenth and Seventeenth Centuries*, Devon and Cornwall Record Soc., NS, xi (1966); and see p. 305.

[69] Cf. D. Foster, 'The Hearth Tax and Settlement Studies', *Local Historian* xi (1974–6).

solely within the area of an archdeacon's or other minor court, then the will could be proved there.[70] Nevertheless for reasons of prestige the wills of the better-off were at times proved in higher courts than strictly necessary, while humbler persons sought to prove their wills as cheaply as possible. In practice wills were usually proved at Canterbury if property was held in more than one county. Moreover till 1750 it was not obligatory to prove a will unless it was disputed, so that the less well-off often omitted to do so. It should be noted, too, that some secular courts, such as those of manors or mayors, had powers of probate, as did some minor ecclesiastical officials.[71]

From 1858 the powers of the church courts in these matters were assumed by the Probate Division of the High Court, and the testatory records of the church courts also passed to the lay administrators. For a long time wills both before and from 1858 were to be found at the Principal Probate Registry at Somerset House, Strand, as well as at the various district probate registries. In recent years many of the pre-1858 probate records have been distributed to local depositories. The Prerogative Court of Canterbury (P.C.C.) wills and administrations, dating from the fourteenth century to 1857, were removed from Somerset House to the Public Record Office in 1970. There are published indexes of these wills from 1383 to 1700,[72] and then year books called

[70] The areas of probate jurisdiction are shown in map form in Institute of Heraldic and Genealogical Studies (England), *Parish Maps of the Counties of England* (Utah, 1977), and in a series of county handbooks (*Pre-1858 English Probate Jurisdiction*), prepared by the Genealogical Society of Utah, from the 1960s.

[71] For some such wills, etc., see *A List of Wills, Administrations, etc., in the Public Record Office, London, England: 12th–19th Century* (Magna Carta Book Co., 1968).

[72] Published in a number of volumes (still in progress) by the British Record Society, Index Library. Also in this series are calendars of indexes to wills and administrations for various counties and ecclesiastical jurisdictions: for a list, see Mullins (ed.), *Texts*, 104 sqq. See also A. J. Camp, *An*

calendars. The registered copies of the wills may be con-sulted at the Public Record Office.[73] From 1858 originals or copies of all wills are available at Somerset House, and an annual index is printed which may be consulted at all district registries.[74]

The inventories deposited with the wills are very fruitful sources of information and many of these are to be found in various depositories including local record offices and dioce-san registries. The P.C.C. inventories are now available in the Public Record Office.[75]

Returns made under the 'Marriage Duties Act' of 1694 may occasionally be found. The Act imposed taxes on marriages, births, burials, childless widowers, and bachelors over 25, and lasted for ten years. It was a graded tax,[76] and although there are only a few examples extant, and none in the Public Record Office, others may well come to light. The form of the returns varies but they may provide names of householders and other residents (distinguishing relations, lodgers, and servants), indicating their liabilities under the Act, house by house (though these are not always clearly distinguished), in each parish.[77]

Index to the Wills Proved in the Prerogative Court of Canterbury, 1750–1800 (2 vols., 1976); and Camp, *Wills*, 72–6.

[73] P.R.O., Class PROB. 11. The 'original' wills (PROB. 10), as far as they exist, may also be seen. PROB. 12 contains alphabetical indexes to PROB. 11.

[74] For the direct use of the valuations of property mentioned in the various calendars for purposes of comparative studies of wealth, see W. D. Rubinstein and D. H. Duman, 'Probate Valuations', *Local Historian* xi (1974–6).

[75] Classes PROB. 2–5 and 31. See List and Index Soc., lxxxv–lxxxvi, cxlix (1973, 1973, 1978).

[76] For tables, see Dowell, *History of Taxation* ii, 543–4; D. V. Glass in *London's Inhabitants Within the Walls, 1695*, London Record Soc. ii (1966), pp. xi–xii.

[77] See *London's Inhabitants*, introduction by D. V. Glass (notes provide refs. to some extant returns); P. E. Jones and A. V. Judges, 'London

Political sources useful for our purpose include the protestation returns of 1641–2 and poll books. The protestation returns are a record of those males of 18 years and over who, at the behest of Parliament, signed an undertaking to support the rights of Parliament, and of those who refused to do so or for some other reason did not sign. Very occasionally (as in one Yorkshire and two Cornish parishes) the returns included women. Originals are in the House of Lords Record Office.[78] Many of the returns have been printed, and copies often exist in parish registers. Where returns have not survived in the House of Lords (as for Derbyshire, Leicestershire, and Norfolk) such other copies are important. They are of no value for social structure, except when they give occupations (this is not often), but a crude estimate of total population may be obtained by doubling (to include women) and adding an estimated 40 per cent to account for those under 18.

Poll books, a printed source, indicating the way parliamentary electors cast their votes, date from 1696 and go on until 1868, the last election before the Ballot Act. Some give additional information, such as occupations and places of residence. Many are in existence, the largest collection being

---

Population in the Late Seventeenth Century', *Ec.H.R.* vi (1935); D. V. Glass, 'Two Papers on Gregory King', in Glass and Eversley (eds.), *Population in History*; D. V. Glass, 'Notes on the Demography of London at the End of the Seventeenth Century', *Daedalus* xcvii (2) (1968); P. Styles, 'A Census of a Warwickshire Village in 1698', *Birmingham Historical Jnl* iii (1951); G. C. F. Forster, 'Hull in the 16th and 17th Centuries', *V.C.H.: York, E. Riding* i, ed. K. J. Allison (1969), 158; P. E. Jones, 'Local Assessments for Parliamentary Taxes', *Jnl Soc. Archivists* iv (1970); E. Ralph and M. E. Williams (eds.), *The Inhabitants of Bristol in 1696*, Bristol Record Soc. xxv (1968).

[78] For a list of places for which House of Lords returns survive, see *Fifth Rep. of the Historical Manuscripts Commission* (1876). For those in print, see L. W. Lawson Edwards, 'The Protestation Returns of 1641–2; A Checklist of Printed and other Sources', *Genealogists' Magazine* xix (1977).

at the Institute of Historical Research, University of London.[79]

Other printed records, important for towns, particularly from the later eighteenth century, are local directories, though they must be used with caution for they vary in reliability.[80] Their content is also varied. Most useful are those which give occupations, which the investigator may categorize, or which may already be listed under trade or professional headings. These directories can provide a rough and ready socio-economic picture of a town at a particular time, though, of course, not all inhabitants (especially not the working classes) are listed.

From 1801 there has been an official census every decade apart from 1941. The summarized findings are published as parliamentary papers and these are a mine of information. It must be remembered, however, that the form of the returns and the boundaries of the census districts have changed over the years and that thus difficulties of comparison of one census with another exist. In particular, occupational categories have altered a great deal. A detailed guide to what sort of social and other information may be obtained from the printed censuses up to 1951 exists, embracing also the partial census of 1966.[81] The printed censuses can be made to yield an enormous amount of sophisticated material.[82] They can provide, particularly if used together with the annual reports

[79] See J. Cannon, 'Poll Books', *History* xlvii (1962). See also p. 96.

[80] For reliability, see Jane E. Norton, *Guide to the National and Provincial Directories of England and Wales, excluding London, published before 1856* (1950). This work lists the whereabouts of directories. See also p. 25 n. 72.

[81] Office of Population Censuses and Surveys, *Guide to Census Reports: Great Britain, 1801–1966* (1977). See also D. V. Glass and P. A. M. Taylor, *Government and Society in Nineteenth-Century Britain: Commentaries on British Parliamentary Papers: Population and Emigration* (1976).

[82] See H. J. Dyos and A. B. M. Baker, 'The Possibility of Computerising Census Data', in H. J. Dyos (ed.), *The Study of Urban History* (1968); R. Smith, 'Demography in the Nineteenth Century', *Local Historian* ix (1970–1).

of the Registrar General of Births, Deaths, and Marriages, very detailed information on birth rates, mortality rates, fertility ratios, migration, and so on. The Registrar General's reports begin in 1837 but are of use to the local historian only from about 1840 when the statistics (varying in detail over the years) were given by registration districts and sub-districts, so enabling calculations in conjunction with the census data to be made. The censuses and the Registrar General's reports must be regarded as the major sources for local demographic history for the nineteenth and twentieth centuries. Their importance to the historian compared with other sources dealt with is out of all proportion to the space it has been possible to devote to them here.[83]

For the censuses of 1841, 1851, 1861, and 1871, many of the original manuscript enumerators' books, from which the printed census reports were compiled, are available for consultation at the Land Registry Office in Lincoln's Inn Fields.[84] Of these the most useful to the local historian are those for 1851 and 1871, since they give somewhat fuller information than those for 1841 and are generally better preserved than those for 1861. From 1851 books give, house by house, each individual resident's name, whether married, single, or widowed, his or her age, sex, and occupation. They also give the parish (or for those born outside England and Wales, the country) of birth,[85] and can be used for the

[83] But see Chapter 9, below.

[84] They form part of the Public Record Office records (Classes H.O.107 for 1841 and 1851, R.G.9 for 1861, and R.G.10 for 1871). By the time this book appears the schedules for the 1881 census should be available for consultation.

[85] See Beresford in R. L. Storey and M. Beresford, *A Short Introduction to Wills* [and] *The Unprinted Census Returns of 1841, 1851, 1861, for England and Wales* (1966). For the use of these records, see P. M. Tillott, 'The Analysis of the Census Returns', *Local Historian* viii (1968–9); W. A. Armstrong, 'Social Structure from the Early Census Returns' in Wrigley (ed.), *Introduction to Historical Demography* (and comments on this in *Ec.H.R.*, 2nd ser., xxi (1968)); and W. A. Armstrong, 'The Interpretation

provision of very interesting demographical information.[86]
Some statistics for 1961 for certain enumeration districts not
published in the census are available at the Office of Population Censuses and Surveys, as, too, are some for the partial
census of 1966, especially for those districts in which population fell below the limit of 15,000.[87]

Occupational structure is not the same as wealth structure,
though the two are related. Individual tax assessments do
not, however, exist for the nineteenth century, though for
the wealthier inhabitants probate valuations may be used.[88]
Totals of tax revenue do exist in the Public Record Office,
however, for counties, parishes, and other areas for certain
years, so that some idea of the relative spread of middle-class
wealth may be obtained from them.[89]

of the Census Enumerators' Books for Victorian Towns', in Dyos (ed.),
Study of Urban History; W. A. Armstrong, 'The Census Enumerators'
Books', in R. Lawton (ed.), *The Census and Social Structure* (1978).

[86] See, e.g., R. Smith, 'Early Victorian Household Structure: A Case
Study of Nottinghamshire', *International Review of Social History* xv (1970);
M. Anderson, 'Family, Household and the Industrial Revolution', in M.
Anderson (ed.), *Sociology of the Family* (1971) (adapted from the author's
'Household Structure and the Industrial Revolution: Mid-Nineteenth-
Century Preston in Comparative Perspective', in T. P. R. Laslett (ed.),
The Comparative History of Family and Household (1971)); M. Anderson,
Family Structure in 19th-Century Lancashire (1971); various essays in E. A.
Wrigley (ed.), *Nineteenth Century Society* (1972); D. R. Mills, 'The Techni-
que of House Repopulation', *Local Historian* xiii (1978), and works cited
there.

[87] See A. F. Comfort and C. Loveless (comps.), *Guide to Government
Data: A Survey of Unpublished Social Science Material in the Libraries of
Government Departments in London* (1974).

[88] See D. Rubinstein and D. H. Duman, 'The Probate Records as a Tool
of the Local Historian', *Local Historian* xi (1974); C. D. Harbury, 'Inheritance and the Distribution of Personal Wealth in Britain', *Economic Journal*
lxxii (1962); W. D. Rubinstein, 'The Victorian Middle Classes: Wealth,
Occupation and Geography', *Ec.H.R.*, 2nd ser., xxx (1977), 602–3n.

[89] For details, see Rubinstein, 'Victorian Middle Classes', 615 sqq.;
P.R.O. Guide ii, 197 (for Class I.R.2), iii (for Class I.R.16); and below, p.
199.

In conclusion one must note the possibility of the existence for a particular place of a list of inhabitants of one sort or another other than those already discussed. The Cambridge Group for the History of Population and Social Structure has made it one of its aims to register and collect such listings and it has evolved methods for studying social structure based upon them. They can be used not only for population counts but may also provide details of the size and structure of the family and household and the distribution of the population by religion or by sex and marital status.[90]

[90] For details, see P. Laslett, 'The Study of Social Structure from Listings of Inhabitants', in Wrigley (ed.), *Introduction to Historical Demography*; V. Smith, 'The Analysis of Census-type Documents', *Local Population Studies* ii (1969). P. Laslett, 'Size and Structure of the Household in England over Three Centuries', *Population Studies* xxiii (1969), makes use of a hundred such lists falling within the period 1574–1821. Agricultural publications often contained demographic information.

CHAPTER 3

Local government and politics

The variety of sources available for the study of local government in England is considerable. Some of the chief sources, however, have been described in detail for other purposes in other chapters so that some cross references may be made to avoid unnecessary repetition. The control of local administration in its fiscal, military, and judicial aspects in medieval and early modern times was to a great extent in the hands of royal officials, particularly sheriffs, coroners, itinerant justices, constables, and castellans. Information on their activities must be sought in the records of the central government.[1] The pipe rolls (P.R.O. Class E.372), some of which are published,[2] are perhaps the most valuable of these records for the local historian. They contain the financial accounts of sheriffs and other royal officials in the counties and provide much evidence not only on the local sources of royal revenue but of Crown expenditure in different places. They may be supplemented by the Exchequer K.R. and L.T.R. memoranda rolls,[3] and Exchequer accounts various.[4] The accounts of escheators (local officials concerned with certain types of royal revenue), originally included in the pipe rolls, were enrolled separately from 1323, and may throw light on, among other matters, the landholdings of local families.[5] Chancery records provide another corpus of

[1] See, e.g., J. F. Willard (ed.), *The English Government at Work* iii (1950).
[2] See p. 82 n. 50; G. R. Elton, *England, 1200–1640* (1969), 47–8; H. M. Jewell, *English Local Administration in the Middle Ages* (1972).
[3] P.R.O., Classes E.159, E.368, E.370.   [4] See p. 116 n. 93.
[5] P.R.O., Classes E.136, E.357 (see *P.R.O. Guide* i, 58, 72). See also inquisitions post mortem (p. 169, below).

materials for the history of local administration and justice. The charter, close, fine, and patent rolls[6] record grants of land and privileges to individuals and corporate bodies and orders to local royal officials. The records of coroners, and justices in eyre[7] and, from the fourteenth century, the justices of assize[8] are valuable for judicial matters.[9] All these records represent the direct extension of central government into the localities. The sources treated in this chapter reflect more the chief units of local self-government – the manor, the parish, the borough, and the county – together with some information on less important units and institutions,[10] and, briefly, on sources for political aspects of local history.

[6] See p. 82.

[7] For the P.R.O. Classes involved, see *P.R.O. Guide* i, 123–6. See also R. F. Hunnisett, *The Medieval Coroner* (1961); C. A. F. Meekings, *Crown Pleas of the Wiltshire Eyre, 1249*, Wilts. Archaeological and Natural History Soc. xvi (1960); H. M. Cam, 'On the Material Available in the Eyre Rolls', *B.I.H.R.* iii (1925–6).

[8] For the P.R.O. Classes, see *P.R.O. Guide* i, 127–31. See also J. S. Cockburn, *A History of English Assizes from 1558 to 1714* (1972); J. S. Cockburn, 'Early-Modern Assize Records as Historical Evidence', *Jnl Soc. Archivists* v (1975), and, for examples in print (except where otherwise indicated, ed. J. S. Cockburn): *Western Circuit Assize Orders, 1629–1648: A Calendar*, Camden Soc., 4th ser., xvii (1976); T. G. Barnes (ed.), *Somerset Assize Orders, 1629–1640*, Somerset Record Soc. xv (1959); T. G. Barnes (ed.), *Somerset Assize Orders, 1640–1659*, ibid. xxi (1971); and also *Calendar of Assize Records: Sussex Indictments, Elizabeth I* (1975); *Sussex Indictments, James I* (1975); *Hertfordshire Indictments, Elizabeth I* (1975); *Hertfordshire Indictments, James I* (1975); *Essex Indictments, Elizabeth I* (1978); *Kent Indictments, Elizabeth I* (1979); *Surrey Indictments, Elizabeth I* (1980) (H.M.S.O.).

[9] For justices of the peace, see below, pp. 90–2.

[10] Providing a useful background to many aspects of local government, but not generally cited further in this chapter, are the volumes of S. and B. Webb, *English Local Government* (1906–29, reprinted 1963): i, *The Parish and County*; ii, iii, *The Manor and the Borough*, pt I and pt II; iv, *Statutory Authorities for Special Purposes*; v, *The Story of the King's Highway*; vi, *English Prisons under Local Government*; vii, viii, and ix, *English Poor Law History*, pts I and II (part II in 2 vols.); x, *English Poor Law Policy*.

THE MANOR

Outside the boroughs the manor was 'the most pervasive unit . . . of local administration'[11] in the Middle Ages.[12] Manorial records embrace not only administrative and judicial aspects of country life but also economic and social affairs, and, indeed, it is difficult to treat them merely from the administrative point of view. Some are described in some detail in the chapter on agricultural sources below.

The chief types of document which throw light on manorial administration are ministers' accounts (*compoti*), that is, the accounts of various manorial officials. These take the form of sections or paragraphs often with marginal heads. Money sums are in the body of the text and not, as in modern accounts, in columns; but at the end of each section the total of the moneys involved appears. Pitfalls, however, await the investigator who attempts to draw conclusions from these sources without mastering the principles of such medieval accountancy, which are unlike those of their mod-

[11] Elton, *England, 1200–1640*, 128. The larger feudal unit, the honour, may also, where it existed, have left records similar to those of the individual manor.

[12] For a good introduction to the manor, see H. S. Bennett, *Life on the English Manor* (1937), 151–221, and R. B. Pugh, *How to Write a Parish History* (1954), 48 sqq. For manorial records, see especially N. J. Hone, *The Manor and Manorial Records* (1906; 2nd edn 1912; 3rd edn 1925), which reproduces facsimiles and translations of typical records, lists of articles on individual manors, and a glossary of terms found in court rolls; F. W. Maitland, *Select Pleas in Manorial and other Seigneurial Courts*, Selden Soc. ii (1889), which provides useful information on technical problems, and transcripts and translations of pleas in several thirteenth-century courts; J. West, *Village Records* (1962), which has a bibliography and useful glossary; A. E. Bland, P. A. Brown, and R. H. Tawney, *English Economic History: Select Documents* (1914), which prints some manorial records in translation. P. D. A. Harvey (ed.), *Manorial Records of Cuxham, Oxfordshire, 1200–1359* (1976), prints an excellent selection in the original Latin.

ern counterparts.[13] The content of these records is usually concerned largely with agricultural matters.[14]

The duties and rights of individual tenants or classes of tenants, and other manorial information, may be ascertained from manorial extents, custumals, inquisitions post mortem, and the hundred rolls, all described elsewhere.[15]

The most fruitful of manorial records for the reconstruction of current administration are court rolls, which began to be kept systematically during the thirteenth century and of which many long series are still extant. They provide enrolled accounts of the proceedings of the manorial courts. Manorial lords held by right periodical courts (usually at fortnightly or three-weekly, but sometimes at longer, intervals), attendance at which was one of the chief obligations of their tenants. Technically, jurisdiction over freemen was through the court baron, and over the servile through the court customary, but in practice the two types of manorial court were not usually distinguished. In addition to these basic manorial jurisdictions some lords obtained, or assumed prescriptively, cognizance of criminal cases otherwise heard in higher courts.[16] Thus certain court days might be distinguished from the normal manorial court meetings by being particularized as great courts or courts leet, though the distinction between courts leet, courts customary, and courts baron often tended to be blurred.[17] The most frequently held

[13] See p. 176 and note; A. E. Levett, *Studies in Manorial History*, ed. H. M. Cam, M. Coate, and L. S. Sutherland (1938), 41 sqq.; also printed in *Ec.H.R.* i (1927).

[14] See p. 176.   [15] See pp. 48–52, 168–70, 174.

[16] See J. J. Bagley, *Historical Interpretation: Sources of English Medieval History, 1066–1540* (1965), 82 sqq.; J. F. C. Hearnshaw (ed.), *Leet Jurisdiction in England*, Southampton Record Soc. v (1908); L. C. Latham, *The Manor*, Hist. Assoc. Leaflet 83 (1931), 14–16.

[17] Bagley, *Historical Interpretation*, 92; Hone, *Manor*, 21–6. For the distinctions between these different types of court, see Elton, *England, 1200–1640*, 131; Pugh, *Parish History*, 62–3. The election of manorial officers took place in courts leet.

additional franchise was the right to administer the local 'view of frankpledge', that is, to hear cases involving petty infringements of law and order, infringements of the assizes of bread and ale, and occasionally pleas of debt.

The judicial functions of the courts reflect some of the types of information to be found in the court rolls. Many of the offences recorded touched on the organization of the manor itself, such as those to do with landholding, dues, services, disputes over customs, rights, trespasses, theft of manorial property, and the like.

Much of the business of the courts was, however, administrative and economic, though in practice the distinction between economic, judicial, and administrative is often artificial. The courts dealt with the administration of tenurial matters, such as alienations of land, admittances or entries of tenants to holdings, the surrender of holdings, and the money payments (fines) relating to such events. The court rolls also record the outcome of matters concerning the lord's rights and dues, such as application for a villein's son to enter the Church, or for his daughter to marry. And, of course, they record the regulation of the agricultural activity of the manor. Later court rolls also give much topographical information and details of such institutions as markets and fairs.[18]

Many manorial records have appeared in print[19] and many more exist in manuscript. A large number of manors were in the hands of the Crown, and their records may be found among the public archives, particularly in the P.R.O., Class S.C.2.[20] Local record offices house many more manorial

[18] For some guidance, see W. B. Johnson, 'Notes before reading Court Rolls', *Amateur Historian* iv (1958–60); N. F. Mumford, 'Studying Medieval Court Rolls', *Local Historian* x (1972).

[19] See E. L. C. Mullins (ed.), *Texts and Calendars: An Analytical Guide to Serial Publications*, Royal Historical Soc., Guides and Handbooks, no. 7 (1958); West, *Village Records*, 37–42.

[20] These include manors belonging, before the Dissolution, to the monastic foundations. For manorial records in the P.R.O., see P.R.O., Lists and Indexes vi (1896); *P.R.O. Guide* i; Hone, *Manor*, 243 sqq. Hone

documents; others are still in private hands.[21] An attempt to make a register of the whereabouts of manorial records has been undertaken by the National Register of Archives,[22] and an investigator ignorant of the existence of the records of manors in his area should consult this register, which is not, however, comprehensive. The topographical volumes of the *Victoria History of the Counties of England*, where they exist, will provide accounts of the descent of each manor within the parish,[23] and the footnotes may also draw attention to the whereabouts of privately held manorial records. It should also be remembered that ecclesiastical depositories may house the records of manors belonging to the Church,[24] while others may be in the hands of Oxford or Cambridge colleges.

The economic changes of the fourteenth century and later, and the growth in the powers of the justices of the peace and in the activities of parish vestries, as well as the spread of towns, have rendered the manor less important in modern times, but the local historian may well find useful information in manorial records for the sixteenth and seventeenth centuries or even later.[25]

also lists (pp. 266 sqq.) manorial records in the B.L., Lambeth Palace, and the Bodleian Library.

[21] See Manorial Society's Monographs: *List of Manor Court Rolls in Private Hands* (1907–10), cited Elton, *England, 1200–1640*, 130n.

[22] Now part of the Historical Manuscripts Commission, Quality Court Chancery Lane, London WC2.

[23] For a detailed account of the highly technical process of tracing manorial descents, see A. Hamilton Thompson, *Parish History and Records*, Hist. Assoc., Pamphlet 66 (revised edn, 1961), 21 sqq.; Pugh, *Parish History*, 48 sqq.; for examples, see the manorial sections of the topographical volumes of the *V.C.H.* Some advice to the local historian on the usefulness of such activity is given in W. G. Hoskins, *Local History in England* (1959), 46.

[24] See Chapter 8.

[25] Cf. Pugh, *Parish History*, 98–9; F. G. Emmison, *Archives and Local History* (1966), 55.

THE PARISH

The parish has in the past been a unit of both ecclesiastical and civil government, and, although this chapter is concerned particularly with the parish's functions in secular administration, the records described often also pertain to the religious history of the locality. The parish and its archives have been the subject of a large and exhaustive monograph, W. E. Tate's *The Parish Chest*,[26] which should be referred to for detailed information.

It is not possible here to examine the origins of the parish. It was developed as a unit of local secular government by the Crown in the sixteenth century, as the manor declined, and it was in Tudor times that it was organized on a statutory basis, though to a certain extent this merely legitimized existing practice.

Apart from some churchwardens' accounts and some 'books of record', containing, for example, memoranda, leases, and wills, most parish records date from the sixteenth century, becoming more prolific as the parish became more important in the structure of government. It was not until the nineteenth century that the parish government set up by the Tudors passed away: responsibility for the relief of poverty fell to the boards of guardians established after 1834, compulsory church rates were abolished in 1868, the office of parish constable disappeared in 1872, and the remaining secular functions of the parish vestries were transferred to the secular parish councils from 1894. Parish records are thus important in the study of local government from the sixteenth to the nineteenth centuries. They are most frequently found in the parish itself, but also elsewhere, particularly in local and diocesan record offices.[27]

[26] 1946; reprinted 1951, 1961. The following account inevitably owes much to this work, which is not, therefore, except in a few instances, cited further in the footnotes.

[27] On this, see L. J. Redstone and F. W. Steer, *Local Records* (1953), 179–81; Emmison, *Archives and Local History*, 51.

Purely ecclesiastical records and records normally deposited in the parish chest which are useful for various aspects of local history, such as parish registers, tithe and enclosure records, glebe terriers, licences, certificates, and apprentice indentures, are touched on in other chapters.[28] So, too, are the records relating to the poor law, especially the records of the overseers of the poor,[29] and though the information is not repeated here it must be emphasized how important in the history of local government was the administration of poor relief. Indeed in most places this activity was the most important civil function of the parish.

At the centre of parochial administration was the vestry, the parish 'parliament', an institution taking three main forms: open, select, and close.[30] An Act of 1818 required the vestry to keep its minutes but this merely made obligatory what was often long established practice. Such minutes (sometimes called parish or town books) record both the ecclesiastical and the secular activities of the vestry.[31] These included the selection by the vestry of churchwardens,[32] who were *ex officio* overseers of the poor, and of overseers of the highway, and the drawing up of short lists from which the J.P.s selected constables. The vestries audited the accounts of the parish officials, including the churchwardens and the overseers of the highway, sanctioned rates of various kinds, granted charity to those they thought deserving, sometimes regulated agricultural matters, and even in some instances arranged enclosure. The details of these activities are to be found in the minutes.[33]

[28] See especially pp. 55–6, 127–8, 177–83, 192–4, 271–2, 287–8.

[29] See pp. 99 sqq.

[30] For details, see Tate, *Parish Chest*, 131 sqq.

[31] See G. H. Tupling, 'Vestry Minutes and Church Wardens' Accounts', *Amateur Historian* i (1952–4).

[32] Sometimes, however, these were appointed by the incumbent, the patron, or the retiring churchwardens.

[33] For an example in print, see S. A. Peyton (ed.), *Kettering Vestry Minutes, 1797–1853*, Northamptonshire Record Soc. vi (1933).

As well as the overseers of the poor, other parish officers also had their own records. The accounts of the church-wardens (sometimes called stewards, guardians, wardens, reeves)[34] detail not only their ecclesiastical work, with regard, for example, to the church rates and the church fabric, but the execution of their civil responsibilities. These included, particularly, the relief of vagrants, as opposed to the settled poor, the destruction of troublesome birds and animals, and sometimes the administration of local charities.[35]

The parish constables[36] were responsible for matters of law and order, administrative matters concerning the militia, the collection of national taxes, the relief of itinerant vagrants holding passes and the physical removal of others, the execution of J.P.s' warrants, and many other duties. Their activities can be traced in their accounts.[37]

Since all these officials had duties relating to the treatment of the poor, it sometimes happens, particularly with the constables and overseers, that their records appear to deal with much the same sort of activity.

Surveyors (sometimes called overseers or supervisors) of the highway, for the upkeep of which the parish was responsible from 1555 usually to 1835, also kept accounts and books from which their activities, supervised by the J.P.s, may be deduced.[38]

The civil successors of the parish vestries were the parish councils originating in an Act of 1894, obligatory for every parish of 300 or more inhabitants, and permissive for smaller parishes. Their records include minutes, letter and order

[34] See J. C. Cox, *Churchwardens' Accounts* (1913).

[35] See, e.g., W. G. Hoskins, *The Midland Peasant* (1965), 206–7; J. E. Farmiloe and R. Nixseaman (eds.), *Elizabethan Churchwardens' Accounts*, Beds. Historical Record Soc. xxiii (1953).

[36] For the manorial origins of the post, see Tate, *Parish Chest*, 175–6.

[37] G. H. Tupling, 'Constables' Accounts', *Amateur Historian* i (1952–4); Cox, *Churchwardens' Accounts*, 323 sqq.

[38] G. H. Tupling, 'Highway Surveyors' Accounts', *Amateur Historian* i (1952–4).

books, and original correspondence, but their powers have been so restricted that the records are of comparatively little importance.[39]

For the nineteenth century there are parliamentary papers which give information on parish government, particularly on boundaries, and for these the official indexes should be searched.[40]

THE TOWN

It is possible that some information on towns – particularly on those which grew up on crown estates – and on royal grants of land, privileges and immunities, may be found in collections of Anglo-Saxon charters.[41] Generally, however, the first information on many towns is likely to be found in Domesday, though not all boroughs then in existence are recorded in that survey.[42]

The early history of boroughs is largely that of their emancipation from feudal control and their assumption of varying degrees of self-government. The grants of privileges, often collectively called 'charters', provide the basic information for tracing the evolution of a borough as a unit of local government.[43] The three volumes of *British Borough Charters*, noting borough by borough the dates and content

[39] Pugh, *Parish History*, 101.

[40] E.g., *Parishes of England and Wales* (1867–8), liii. For boundary changes, see especially the *Census* reports. See also W. R. Powell, *Local History from Blue Books: Select List of the Sessional Papers of the House of Commons* (1962), 32.

[41] For references to these, see p. 166 n. 8 and D. A. McKay, 'Medieval Boroughs', *Amateur Historian* ii (1954–6), 321.

[42] See pp. 46–7 and F. W. Maitland, *Domesday Book and Beyond* (1897), chapter on boroughs in existence at the time of the Survey. M. W. Beresford and H. P. R. Finberg, *English Medieval Boroughs, A Handlist* (1973), makes greater use of manuscript material than do the *British Borough Charters* (see below) and tracks down many minor places which at one time had borough privileges.

[43] See Bagley, *Historical Interpretation*, 70 sqq.; Elton, *England, 1200–1640*, 120 sqq.; *Borough Charters: Catalogue of an Exhibition* (British

of known charters and their whereabouts, with comments,[44] may well be a starting point for the investigator. They include both royal and seigneurial charters.

Seigneurial charters, which were chiefly of early date, may be found among town, estate, and family records, and in form are similar to deeds relating to land. Royal grants include charters proper and letters patent, forms of documents both often loosely called 'charters'. Inspeximuses are records of inspections and confirmations of previous grants, whether royal or private.[45]

An older large collection of charters is *Rymer's Foedera*,[46] and many others have been published by boroughs themselves, by local record societies, or are contained in local histories. Some historians will, however, wish or need to look at the originals, or at original transcripts or calendars. The original charters will usually be held locally, but the best collection of royal grants of privileges are the transcripts enrolled on official records housed in the Public Record Office. These and other contemporary records relating to these grants are to be found in the following sets of records, many of which have been calendared in official publications.

The charter rolls (P.R.O., Class C.53) consist of enrol-

Record Assoc., 1959), 5–25; G. H. Martin, 'The Origins of Borough Records', *Jnl Soc. Archivists* ii (1961).

[44] *British Borough Charters: 1042–1216*, ed. A. Ballard (1913); *1216–1307*, ed. A. Ballard and J. Tait (1923); *1307–1660*, ed. M. Weinbaum (1943). The last is the least satisfactory since it does not attempt the analysis undertaken in the other two volumes, and has errors and omissions. For some illustrations, see Hilary Jenkinson, 'Borough Charters of Britain', *Municipal Review* xxxi (1960). See also H. A. Merewether and A. J. Stephens, *The History of the Boroughs and Municipal Corporations* (1835, reprinted 1972).

[45] *Borough Charters Exhibition*, 14–15.

[46] *Rymer's Foedera: Syllabus in English with Index*, ed. T. D. Hardy (P.R.O., 1869, 1873, 1885); *Rymer's Foedera, 1066–1383*, ed. A. Clarke, J. Caley, F. Holbrooke, and J. W. Clarke (Record Commission, 1816–30, 1869).

ments of charters issued from chancery for the period 1199 to 1517 and are of great importance for many boroughs of medieval origin.[47] They are published in full for John's reign,[48] and for the remainder (from 1226)[49] an outline may be obtained from the P.R.O., *Calendar of Charter Rolls*. From 1517 the same sort of record is to be found in the patent rolls (Class C.66), for which the P.R.O., *Letters and Papers, Foreign and Domestic, Henry VIII* (for the years 1517 to 1547) and the P.R.O., *Calendar of Patent Rolls* (for the years 1547 to 1569), provide abstracts.

In the early Middle Ages transcripts of charters sometimes appear on the pipe rolls (Class E.372);[50] the close rolls (Class C.54) may also contain information touching upon borough privileges;[51] Class D.L.10 includes royal charters for towns in the Duchy of Lancaster, for which there is a calendar.[52] On the fine rolls (Class C.60) are entered payments for the grant of renewal of privileges, and there are transcripts and calendars of these rolls.[53]

[47] J. F. C. Hearnshaw, *Municipal Records*, S.P.C.K., Helps for Students of History, no. 2 (1918), 16.

[48] T. Hardy (ed.), *Rotuli Chartarum in Turri Londinensi Asservati, 1199–1216* (Record Commission, 1837).

[49] There are no rolls for the period of Henry III's minority.

[50] *P.R.O. Guide* i, 77–8. There are transcripts: *The Great Roll of the Pipe*, ed. J. Hunter: *1155–1158* (Record Commission, 1844; reprinted 1931); and *1188–1189* (Record Commission, 1844); and the many volumes of the Pipe Roll Soc. (from 1884), in current progress.

[51] For transcripts, calendars, and indexes, see *P.R.O. Guide* i, 18. Cf. A. A. Dibben, *Coventry City Charters*, Coventry Papers ii (1969), *passim*. This work has a good brief introduction to the subject of borough charters.

[52] P.R.O., *Deputy Keeper's Report* xxxi (1869), 3–4.

[53] For John's reign there is a full transcript: *Rotuli de Oblatis et Finibus in Turri Londinensi Asservati temp. Regis Johannis*, ed. T. Hardy (Record Commission, 1835); for Henry III's reign there are extracts: *Excerpta e Rotulis Finium in Turri Londinensi Asservatis, Henry III, 1216–1272*, ed. C. Roberts (Record Commission, 1835–6); for the years 1272–1509 there are the vols. of the P.R.O., *Calendar of Fine Rolls*; those for 1547–53 are calendared in the P.R.O., *Calendar of Patent Rolls*.

Confirmation of charters before 1483 may be found in the *Cartae Antiquae* rolls (Class C.52) of which rolls 1–10 have been printed.[54] From 1483 to 1625 confirmations are enrolled in the confirmation rolls (Class C.57), not calendared except for Henry VIII's reign for which they appear in the *Letters and Papers, Foreign and Domestic, Henry VIII*. From 1625, and sometimes before, lesser privileges and town charter confirmations are recorded in the patent rolls.

The political upheavals of the mid- and later seventeenth century led to the alteration of many borough constitutions with the object of securing control over future parliamentary elections as well as of gaining direct influence in the local governments of the towns themselves.[55] The local historian should be aware of the reasons for the series of changes in town charters[56] which he may come across in investigating borough government in this period. A list of charters granted between 1680 and 1688, for the purpose of restoring original privileges, can be found in the *Historical Manuscripts Commission, Twelfth Report*.[57] From this[58] may be extracted boroughs which obtained new charters in these years, and it may be ascertained whether a charter of restitution was granted.

Much information on towns and their governments in many periods may, of course, be culled from general series of

[54] *Cartae Antiquae*, Pipe Roll Soc., NS, xvii (1939): *P.R.O. Guide* i, 15.

[55] The following is largely based on a provisional (typescript) article by R. B. Pugh: 'Note on Borough Charters in the Later Seventeenth Century', prepared for contributors to the *V.C.H.* I am grateful to Professor Pugh for permission to refer to it here. Cf. R. H. Sacret, 'The Restoration Government and Municipal Corporations', *E.H.R.* xlv (1930); D. Ogg, *England in the Reign of Charles II* (1934) ii, 634–9; R. H. George, 'The Charters granted to English Parliamentary Corporations in 1688', *E.H.R.* lv (1940).

[56] Apart from the originals, usually in local depositories, the texts may be found in the patent rolls, and in the P.R.O., Signet Office, King's Bills (Class S.O.7).

[57] Appendix, pt VI (1889), 298–300.

[58] And from R. H. George's article cited above.

records and calendars, such as the hundred rolls,[59] parliament rolls,[60] the *Journals of the House of Commons*, the *Journals of the House of Lords*, the *Calendar of State Papers, Domestic*, the *Acts of the Privy Council*, and public, personal, and local Acts of Parliament.[61]

It should be recalled that present boroughs include not only ancient chartered boroughs but those incorporated by Act of Parliament in modern times, and that some ancient boroughs have lost their corporate status by legislation.[62]

The Royal Commission on Municipal Corporations, which reported in 1835, investigated the constitutions and history of 284 incorporated boroughs. Much contemporary and retrospective information may be obtained from its reports.[63] For 178 of these towns the subsequent Act of 1835 provided a common constitution. A later official investigation gives information on other boroughs.[64] The Boundary Commission's reports published in 1835 and 1837 provide details not only on boundaries of many towns but on public utilities, rates, and so on, and provide useful town maps.[65] For towns, local directories and newspapers will prove mines of material, but they vary in accuracy and should be used cautiously.[66]

There are many other parliamentary papers concerned with towns, particularly, for example, with finance and

[59] See p. 20, and Hearnshaw, *Municipal Records*, 18–19.

[60] P.R.O., Class C.65. Printed in *Rotuli Parliamentorum* (6 vols., 1783–1832).

[61] See pp. 14, 20–2.

[62] Redstone and Steer, *Local Records*, 157.

[63] *Rep. R. Commissioners to Inquire into Municipal Corporations* (1835) xxiii–xxvi, xl; (1837) xxv; (1837–8) xxxv; index vol. (1839) xviii.

[64] *Rep. R. Commissioners to Inquire into Municipal Corporations* (1880) xxxi. See Pugh, *Parish History*, 94–5; F. Lavendar, 'Municipal Corporations Acts and Local History', *Amateur Historian* ii (1954–6).

[65] *Rep. R. Commission on Municipal Corporations' Boundaries* (1835) xxxvii; (1837) xxvi–xxviii.

[66] See pp. 23–6.

public health. The official indexes should be searched,[67] especially under the name of the town concerned and under 'Boroughs', 'Municipal Boroughs', 'Local Government', and the 'Local Government Board', whose annual reports from 1872 provide much information for towns, not only on poor relief but also on public health and other matters.[68] For recent times much statistical material is available in official publications.[69]

Most towns will, of course, in varying degrees possess collections of their own records[70] and the nature of these may perhaps be most easily sought from local archivists and librarians. There are also printed works which can give a lead. In particular the reports of the Historical Manuscripts Commission which calendar or list the records of many towns, the typescript lists of the National Register of Archives obtainable in most large libraries, and Gross's bibliography,[71] may be valuable. Some older county and town histories may print extracts from local records which have since disappeared.[72]

The variety of records held by towns themselves is too great for an exhaustive description to be given here, but the most commonly useful may be mentioned.

Usually incorporated towns will possess minutes of the meetings of their governing bodies,[73] and these may go

[67] See also Powell, *Blue Books*, 31–3.

[68] See p. 17.

[69] See Interdepartmental Committee on Social and Economic Research, *Guides to Official Sources, no. 3: Local Government Statistics* (H.M.S.O., 1953).

[70] See *Third Rep. Royal Commission on Public Records* (1919) xxviii.

[71] C. Gross, *A Bibliography of British Municipal History including Gilds and Parliamentary Representation* (1897), and ed. G. Martin (1966). See also G. H. Martin and S. McIntyre, *A Bibliography of British and Irish Municipal History*, i, *General Works* (1972).

[72] E.g., R. Head, *Congleton Past and Present* (1887).

[73] See G. H. Tupling, 'Borough Records: Common Council Minutes', *Amateur Historian* ii (1954–6).

under various names. At Exeter, for example, they are known as the city act books, at Southampton the assembly books, at Coventry the leet book, at Liverpool the town books, and so on. Few dating before the fifteenth century exist. Often two sets of minutes were kept: journals, which were narrative accounts of the proceedings of council meetings; and order books, which recorded the executive orders and acts passed by the council. More frequently only one set of minutes was kept. The record of each meeting is usually prefaced by a list of those members who were present and the most useful may give details of the debates and touch on the reasons behind the decisions taken. Once a year, usually, the election and appointment of officers and officials will be entered in the minutes.

These records are an important source of information not only on the working of local government but on every aspect of town life, political, social, religious, and economic. Evidence is to be found on the relationship between membership of the corporation and the different social, economic, or religious groups in the town, the attitude of the corporation to business, trade, and industry, its relationship with other towns, with local aristocracy, and with Parliament and the central government. Details of public health, town planning, public services, charities, poor relief, education, law and order, markets and fairs, and many other subjects may be discovered in the minutes, together with much information on local topography.

Publication of council minutes and their availability for public inspection was required by the Municipal Corporations Act of 1835, though many towns did not in fact have their minutes printed. Many earlier records remain in manuscript, but some of these have been published by local authorities or record societies.[74]

---

[74] E.g., M. D. Harris (ed.), *The Coventry Leet Book, 1420–1555*, Early English Text Soc., cxxxiv, cxxxv, cxxxviii, cxlvi (1907–13); J. Dennett

All boroughs kept annual financial accounts,[75] though not all these will survive for earlier periods. They may be called treasurers', receivers', stewards', or chamberlains' accounts, according to the local name given to the responsible official. With the important exception of rates, which before 1835 were levied for particular purposes and recorded in separate accounts, they will provide information on the revenues of the town such as its income from lands and buildings,[76] profits from market tolls, freemen's entry fees, investments, borrowed money, and so on. Details of expenditure made include among other things moneys spent on town properties, salaries and wages, gifts and bribes, public festivities, charities (apart from normal poor relief), and the annual fee-farm paid to the Crown. In some places, as, for example, at Exeter, the original bills or vouchers involved in the payments still survive and can fill out the pictures supplied by the annual accounts.

Where no council minutes exist, careful examination of the treasurer's accounts may provide a considerable body of evidence of the activities of the town authorities. Where both types of records survive a very detailed account of town government may be built up.

Modern council records are voluminous and many are published. They include, in particular, the minutes of committees and sub-committees, and reports, correspondence, and so on of council officials, and records of departments. They are too varied to describe here, and the student should

(ed.), *Beverley Borough Records, 1575–1821*, Yorks. Archaeological Soc. Record Ser. lxxxiv (1933).

[75] G. H. Tupling, 'Borough Records: Chamberlain's or Treasurer's Accounts', *Amateur Historian* ii (1954–6). For examples in print, see F. D. Wardle (ed.), *The Accounts of the Chamberlains of the City of Bath*, Somerset Record Soc. xxxviii (1923); G. A. Chinnery (ed.), *Records of the Borough of Leicester*, vi, *The Chamberlains' Accounts, 1688–1835* (1967).

[76] Deeds and leases will also be of great value for town property and its uses, and for housing generally. See also below, Chapter 9.

consult the local archivist. He may wish also to give attention to public services, some of which, like gas and electricity supplies, and tramways, may have originated as private enterprises.[77]

All boroughs possessed legal courts of one kind or another. Borough civil courts, often called mayor's courts, leet courts, and the like, met every three or four weeks, and charters usually gave the right to hold a criminal court with all the jurisdiction formerly held by the county sheriff's court. Other types of courts could include manorial courts, piepowder courts, and orphans' courts.[78] Incorporated boroughs would also have their own quarter sessions.[79] All such courts kept records, often well preserved, and these provide evidence on many aspects of town life.

Some towns kept special books where local customs, important town or gild acts, copies of town charters, privileges, and exemptions, the results of significant legal cases, important wills, and such like information, were recorded as precedents and evidence for future reference.[80] For many towns, too, there exist town chronicles noting important events in their history.[81]

Freemen's books and rolls are also important, especially where freedom of the town carried with it the right to

[77] Useful leads for early public services are local Acts of Parliament, newspapers, and parliamentary papers (see Powell, *Blue Books*, 38–9). See also pp. 162–3.

[78] For the considerable variety of these, see Emmison, *Archives and Local History*, 35; Redstone and Steer, *Local Records*, 158; Martin, 'Origins', 149–50; L. C. Lloyd, 'The Records of a Borough Court in the Seventeenth Century', *Archives* vii (1965–6).

[79] For quarter-session records, see below, pp. 90–2.

[80] E.g., the Black Book at Warwick, the Red Book at Bristol, the Oak and Black Books at Southampton.

[81] Hearnshaw, *Municipal Records*, 22–4. These are found not only locally but in, e.g., B.L. collections (as Harleian, Lansdowne, Egerton MSS.). Some have been published: see Gross, *Bibliography* (1897), xviii sqq., for the whereabouts of both MSS. and printed copies. See also A. Dyer, 'English Town Chronicles', *Local Historian* xii (1976–7).

participate in elections, local or parliamentary, and to serve as council members or officials. Apart from their value for occupational structure, freemen's records can also yield information on urban immigration,[82] the social background of freemen, and the significance of gilds in local politics.[83] They tend to become less useful from the eighteenth century when the old pattern of industry and the economic significance of freedom tended to decline.[84] Gild records (some of which predate other records),[85] poor-law records, the records of boards of health, school boards, and charities are also valuable sources of information for town history generally, including local government, and these are dealt with elsewhere.[86]

Not all towns which had an effective local administration were governed under charters by town councils. Some, like Manchester, long remained under the control of manorial courts. In the eighteenth and early nineteenth centuries local 'street' and 'improvement' commissioners were sometimes given by Act of Parliament general powers of local administration, and so were able to act as town governments.[87] Birmingham, where the street commissioners performed many of the functions of a local government before the town was incorporated, is an important example.[88] Other towns,

---

[82] See also, for other sources, J. H. C. Patten, 'Some Notes on Sources for the Study of Urban Immigration before 1841', *Urban History Newsletter* xi (1968).

[83] See W. G. Hoskins's foreword to M. M. Rowe and A. M. Jackson, *Exeter Freemen, 1266–1967*, Devon and Cornwall Record Soc., extra ser., i (1973).

[84] D. M. Woodward, 'Freemen's Rolls', *Local Historian* ix. (1970–1).

[85] Martin, 'Origins', 149–52.

[86] See pp. 93, 99 sqq., 111–13, 127–8, 223–4.

[87] See chapters in F. H. Spencer, *Municipal Origins, 1740–1835* (1911); S. and B. Webb, *English Local Government*, iv.

[88] Cf. C. R. Elrington, 'Local Government and Public Services', *V.C.H.: Warwickshire* vii, ed. W. B. Stephens (1964), 324–7; A. Redford, *History of Local Government in Manchester* ii (1940), 3.

for example, Peterborough and Ely, were governed by bodies of trustees or the feoffees of local charities.[89] Where this was so the records of these bodies are, of course, important.

The records of the central government may also be useful to the investigator of town administration. In the Public Record Office the records of the Ministry of Health embrace those of the Poor Law Commissioners, the Poor Law Board, the General Board of Health, the Local Government Act Office, and the Local Government Board. The most fruitful of these may well be the poor law union papers (1834–1900: Class M.H.12) which cover not only poor-law matters but many aspects of local government, and are also an excellent source for general social history. There are subject indexes, and the papers are arranged topographically.[90] Class T.96 contains the minutes of the Boundary Commissioners of 1867–8 together with assistant commissioners' reports on borough and county boundaries.[91] The Home Office Class H.O.90 consists of a volume (1841) giving the names, occupations, and dates of appointments of borough J.P.s, arranged topographically.

Year books also provide much information (see the publications cited at the end of the next section).

THE COUNTY AND OTHER BODIES

Before the establishment of county councils by the Act of 1888, county government was in effect carried out by the royal officials noted in the introductory paragraphs of this chapter, the lieutenants, and increasingly, by the J.P.s, whom the Tudors made one of their main instruments of government with not only judicial but also considerable

[89] Pugh, *Parish History*, 98–9.
[90] For details of all these, see *P.R.O. Guide* ii, 171.
[91] The records of the 1837 Boundary Commission (see above) (Class T.72) contain only draft maps.

administrative functions.[92] To be found in local record offices or private hands, the records of quarter sessions and of the clerks of the peace are of enormous importance to the local historian.[93] They have, however, been exhaustively described elsewhere in accessible publications,[94] and are consequently not dealt with in any great detail here.

Sufficient is it to say that apart from their purely judicial activities the J.P.s' administrative functions included the oversight of the poor law and vagrancy, gaols, asylums, houses of correction, fairs and markets, the regulation of wages and prices and weights and measures, the upkeep of roads and bridges, the licensing of nonconformist meeting houses, alehouses, playhouses, and pedlars, and the levying of rates.[95] Their records are thus of great significance from Tudor times until 1888, although the establishment of ad hoc bodies, such as the poor-law guardians, highway boards, and local boards of health, in the nineteenth century considerably

[92] For good introductions to the history of the office of J.P., see D. L. Powell, *Quarter Sessions Records with Other Records of the Justices of the Peace in the County of Surrey*, Surrey Record Soc. xxxiii (1931), introduction; E. A. L. Moir, *The Justices of the Peace* (1969); G. C. F. Forster, *The East Riding Justices of the Peace in the Seventeenth Century* (1973). For the identity of J.P.s, see T. G. Barnes and A. H. Smith, 'Justices of the Peace, 1558–1688: A Revised List of Sources', *B.I.H.R.* xxxii (1959).

[93] For the clerk of the peace, see S. C. Ratcliff and H. C. Johnson (eds.), *Warwick County Records* (1935), pp. xxiii–xxiv.

[94] See, e.g., F. G. Emmison and I. Gray, *County Records* (revised edn, 1961), which includes a list of printed catalogues and transcripts; Redstone and Steer, *Local Records*, chapter 14; F. G. Emmison, *Guide to the Essex Record Office*, pt I (1946). These are drawn on extensively in what follows here. See also *Third Rep. R. Commission on Public Records*, pt II (1919), xxviii, appendix: 'Specimen List of Classes of Records which may be found with Clerks of the Peace'.

[95] See E. H. Bates (ed.), *Quarter Sessions Records for the County of Somerset*, Somerset Record Soc. xxiii (1907), introduction, for types of business. Another good introduction is in J. Wake (ed.), *Quarter Sessions Records for the County of Northampton, 1630, 1653, 1657–8*, Northamptonshire Record Soc. i (1924).

reduced their powers. The main types of records are the sessions order books (containing the formal orders of the court on very many matters, reports from officers and committees, and wage assessments),[96] sessions rolls and bundles (including, among a multitude of other matters, presentments of offenders, indictments, informants' reports, bonds, lists of offences, petitions, religious certificates of one sort or another, licences, and pauper removal orders), sessions minute books (recording, as well as other things, the verdicts and orders of the court, and lists of registered meeting houses), records of committees (such as those dealing with licensing, finance, asylums, police), accounts (especially for the different rates levied by the justices for specific purposes, and later for a general rate) including books or rolls, cash books, ledgers, and bills and vouchers.

Quarter sessions were also used for the enrolment, registration, and deposit of documents. These include, for example, the registration of oaths (as under the Test Act), of licences granted, of electors after 1832, of dissenters' places of worship, and the enrolment and deposit of deeds of bargain and sale, of enclosure and tithe commutation documents, of taxation records, poll books, and plans of projected canals, turnpikes, railways and other utilities. Sometimes records of petty or special sessions will also exist.[97]

In the early modern period the Privy Council registers and the state papers, domestic (in the Public Record Office), and, of course, the *Acts of the Privy Council* and the *Calendar of State Papers, Domestic*, will contain much information on local J.P.s and their relationships with the central government.

In recent times the records of the county councils esta-

---

[96] For a full description, see R. Hunt, 'Quarter Sessions Order Books', *History* lv (1970).

[97] See Emmison, *Archives and Local History*, 31. See this work also for sheriffs' records and lieutenancy records.

blished in 1888 are important.[98] Briefly these comprise the minutes and other records of the council itself and of its committees, the letter books and files of the clerk, and the treasurer's accounts. In addition there are the records of the poor-law guardians, school boards, turnpike trusts, and improvement commissioners, described elsewhere.[99] Highway boards (established in 1862 and later superseded by the county councils and rural district councils), the urban and rural district councils and their forerunners, the local boards of health established from 1848 – all had their own minutes, accounts, letter books, and so on.[100] There are also a number of parliamentary papers which will give helpful information.[101] After the establishment of the county councils many parliamentary papers concerning county government (particularly for financial affairs) may be found,[102] and for very recent times there is much statistical information.[103] Naturally local newspapers will be invaluable, as also will local government directories, such as the *Municipal Corporations Companion, Diary, Directory and Year Book* (1877–89) (later the *County Councils and Municipal Corporations Companion*), and the *Municipal Year Book of the United Kingdom* (from 1897), which provides details of all sorts of local government bodies and their personnel. By the end of the nineteenth century the Ordnance Survey was publishing county admini-

[98] See p. 90.

[99] For greater detail on the records of these bodies and of county councils, see Index, and Redstone and Steer, *Local Records*, 130 sqq.

[100] N.b. *Records of District Councils* (British Record Assoc., 1974).

[101] E.g., *Return of Urban and Rural Sanitary Authorities* (1875) lxiv; *Returns of Counties, County Boroughs, Urban Sanitary Districts, Rural Sanitary Districts and Unions* (1888) lxxxvi; (1893–4) lxxvii. The following note also applies.

[102] See official indexes to the parliamentary papers, and also Powell, *Blue Books*, 31–3. See also the previous section of this chapter, where some of the P.R.O. records apply also to areas outside towns.

[103] See *Guides to Official Sources No. 3: Local Government Statistics*.

strative maps and diagrams showing the boundaries of local government areas.[104]

POLITICS

For the local historian interested particularly in political events, it is difficult to give very detailed advice. Local newspapers, pamphlets, broadsheets, archives of local families, together with the sources already described for local government will provide much information on local politics, but many of the primary and secondary sources for national political history will contain much on individual places, and clearly these works cannot be listed here. Attention may, however, be drawn to a few sources where information on legislation, elections, and local M.P.s may be sought.

Local Acts of Parliament are, of course, important and are dealt with above.[105] Records of debates in the two Houses of Parliament[106] are to be found in various sets covering parts of the seventeenth, eighteenth, and early nineteenth centuries, and are often referred to by the names of their compilers.[107]

[104] For details, see *The Historian's Guide to Ordnance Survey Maps* (National Council for Social Service, 1964), 33–4.

[105] See p. 21.

[106] See *A Bibliography of Parliamentary Debates in Great Britain*, House of Commons Library, Document no. 2 (1967 edn).

[107] As, e.g., *Grey's Debates*; *Chandler's Debates*; *Almon's Debates*; *Woodfall's Debates*; *Debrett's Parliamentary Register*; *Almon's Parliamentary Register*; W. Cobbett, *Parliamentary History of England from the Norman Conquest in 1066 to the year 1803* (36 vols., 1806–20). This last was taken over by T. C. Hansard who was responsible for the volumes from 1743 to 1803, and so is sometimes referred to as the first series of *Hansard's Debates* (vols. i–iii of this work compress the information for the period to 1660 contained in [W. Sandby], *The Parliamentary or Constitutional History of England* (24 vols., 1751–6)). See also H. H. Bellot *et al.*, 'General Collections of Reports of Parliamentary Debates for the Period since 1660', *B.I.H.R.* x (1932–3), for full details, other similar sources, and bibliographical references. For an earlier period, see R. C. Johnson, M. F. Keeler, *et al.* (eds.), *Commons Debates, 1628* (3 vols., 1977–8).

From 1803 five series of publications cover the debates of the Lords and Commons verbatim and are usually known as *Hansard* or *Parliamentary Debates*.[108] The *Journals of the House of Commons*, the *Journals of the House of Lords*,[109] and, for earlier periods, the *Rotuli Parliamentorum*[110] may also be useful. Reports of debates were also published in newspapers and journals.[111]

Such sources provide numbers and sometimes names of those voting in divisions. Although there were no official division lists until 1836, unofficial lists exist and are among the most important sources for determining the politics of individual M.P.s. They must, however, be used with caution for they often contain inaccuracies. Many are to be found in the British Library and elsewhere.[112] Draft lists for the period 1553 to 1695 are in the P.R.O., Class C.193. Some unofficial

[108] First series: 1803–20; second series: 1820–30; third series: 1830–91; fourth series: 1892–1908; fifth series from 1909. The first three series were published by the firm of Hansard, the fourth by various contractors, the fifth by H.M.S.O. In 1943 the name of Hansard was restored to the title pages. The fifth series is published separately for Lords and Commons. See also P. D. G. Thomas, *Sources for Debates of the House of Commons, 1768–1774*, B.I.H.R., special supplement no. 4 (1959).

[109] See p. 20.

[110] The *Rotuli Parliamentorum: the Rolls of Parliament* cover the years 1278–1504 in 6 vols. (1783); index by J. Strachey, J. Pridden, and E. Upham (1823). (See index, especially under 'Parliament'.)

[111] E.g., in the *Historical Register* (for the period 1716–38); the *Gentleman's Magazine* (from 1732): see M. Ransome, 'The Reliability of Contemporary Reporting of the Debates of the House of Commons, 1727–1741', B.I.H.R. xix (1942–3).

[112] For lists for certain periods, see A. F. Pollard, 'Thomas Cromwell's Parliamentary Lists', B.I.H.R. ix (1931–2); R. R. Walcott, 'Division Lists of the House of Commons, 1689–1715', *ibid.* xiv (1936–7); M. Ransome, 'Division Lists in the House of Commons, 1715–60', *ibid.* xix (1942–3); E. S. de Beer, 'Division Lists of 1688–1715: Some Addenda', *ibid.* xx (1942–3); I. F. Burton, P. W. J. Riley, and E. Rowlands, *Political Parties in the Reigns of William III and Anne: The evidence of Division Lists, ibid.* special supplement no. 7 (1968) (and a supplementary note in B.I.H.R. xliii (1970)). See also M. F. Bond, *Guide to the Records of Parliament* (1971), 215.

lists are broadsheets, and political broadsheets of a more general nature are also often found in local record offices. These, of course, are of great interest to the historian of local elections and politics generally.[113]

For the period 1696 to 1868 poll books, to be found in many large libraries,[114] will indicate who cast their votes for what candidates at elections.[115]

A nineteenth-century parliamentary paper is useful for M.P.s,[116] and another provides a list of pre-1832 parliamentary boroughs indicating the nature of the suffrage qualifications existing in them.[117] Not an official publication, *The*

[113] There is much election literature in local depositories, especially in family papers, including those associated with the management of borough constituencies: cf. M. Ransome, 'Parliamentary History', *V.C.H. Wiltshire* v, ed. R. B. Pugh and E. Crittall (1957).

[114] Especially at the Institute of Historical Research, University of London. See also J. R. Sims, *A Catalogue of Directories and Poll Books in the Possession of the Society of Genealogists* (1964); *A Handlist of Poll Books and Registers of Electors in Guildhall Library* (Corporation of London, 1970); and see above, p. 67 n. 79.

[115] See p. 66, J. R. Vincent, *Pollbooks: How Victorians Voted* (1967); and W. A. Speck and W. A. Gray, 'Computer Analysis of Poll Books: An Initial Report', *B.I.H.R.* xliii (1970).

[116] *Returns of Names of Members Returned to Serve in the Lower House of the Parliament of England, Scotland, and Ireland, 1213–1874* (1878) lxii (I–III). It is, however, incomplete. Part III contains an index, corrections, and additions. A further volume ((1887) lxvi) contains later returns (1880–5) and more corrections (see also (1890–1) lxii). A MS. list of later corrections and additions is in the P.R.O. For original writs and returns of M.P.s (Class C.219), see *P.R.O. Guide* i, 40. See also W. W. Bean, *The Parliamentary Returns of the Members of the House of Commons* (1883). Browne Willis, *Notitia Parliamentaria* (1715–50), is an older reference work.

[117] (1867) lvi. For other useful parliamentary papers, see the official indexes, especially under 'Elections'; 'Representation of the People'; and the names of constituencies (for election petitions). For a convenient brief list, see P. and G. Ford, *Select List of British Parliamentary Papers, 1833–1899* (1953), 135 sqq. T. H. B. Oldfield, *The Representative History of Great Britain and Ireland* (6 vols., 1816), contains information on individual unreformed parliamentary boroughs, including abstracts from election petitions, the number of voters, and the political character of these

Parliamentary Papers of John Robinson, 1774/1784,[118] illustrates the Crown's interest in influencing borough constituencies in the eighteenth century, and has much on M.P.s and constituencies for the elections of 1774, 1780, and 1784.

Other works in print which may well yield useful information are the volumes currently being produced by the History of Parliament Trust,[119] and for some periods certain secondary works may be very fruitful.[120] Sometimes the

constituencies: see Pugh, *Parish History*, 96–7. C. R. Dod, *Electoral Facts from 1832 to 1853* (1972 edn), includes accounts of constituency politics.

[118] Ed. W. T. Laprade, Camden Soc., 3rd ser., xxxiii (1922); Pugh, *Parish History*, 97.

[119] Already published are: J. C. Wedgwood and A. D. Holt, *History of Parliament: Biographies of the Members of the Commons House, 1439–1509* (1936); *History of Parliament: The House of Commons, 1715–1754*, ed. R. Sedgwick (1970); *History of Parliament: The House of Commons, 1754–1790*, ed. L. Namier and J. Brooke (1964). See also J. Cannon, 'Polls Supplementary to the History of Parliament Volumes, 1715–90', *B.I.H.R.* xlvii (1974); and the *Dictionary of National Bibliography*.

[120] E.g., J. S. Roskell, *The Commons in the Parliament of 1422* (1954); M. McKisack, *The Parliamentary Representation of the English Boroughs during the Middle Ages* (1932) (n.b. the useful bibliography); J. E. Neale, *The Elizabethan House of Commons* (1949); D. Brunton and D. H. Pennington, *Members of the Long Parliament* (1954); M. F. Keeler, *The Long Parliament, 1640–1641; A Biographical Study of its Members*, Memoirs of the American Philosophical Soc. xxxvi (1954); G. P. Judd, *Members of Parliament 1734–1832* (1955); M. Stenton, *Who's Who of British Members of Parliament*: i, *1832–1885* (1976); ii, *1886–1918* (1977); iii, *1919–1945* (1979); L. B. Namier, *The Structure of Politics at the Accession of George III* (1957 edn); E. Porritt, *The Unreformed House of Commons*, i, *England and Wales* (1909); J. E. Hanham, *The Reformed Electoral System of Great Britain* (1968); N. Gash, *Politics in the Age of Peel: A Study in the Technique of Parliamentary Representation, 1830–1850* (1953). For recent times, the following are useful: *British Parliamentary Election Results: 1832–1885* (1977); *1885–1918* (1974); *1918–1949* (1969); *1950–1970* (1971), and *British Parliamentary Election Statistics* (1971), all compiled by F. W. S. Craig; and *F. H. McCalmont's Parliamentary Poll Book of all Elections, 1832–1918* (1971 edn), ed. J. R. Vincent and M. Stenton. For selected organizations and societies, and the private papers of M.P.s and others, it is worth searching C. Cook (comp.), *Sources in British Political History, 1900–1951* (5 vols., 1975–8).

records of local political parties, trade unions, other organizations, and pressure groups exist.[121] Occasionally there were periodicals connected with them.[122] There is, for example, a useful *Bibliography of the Chartist Movement, 1837–1976*.[123] For modern times, the biographies and reminiscences of politicians should not be overlooked.[124]

[121] *Guide to the Modern Records Centre* (University of Warwick Library, 1977), lists some such deposits. For trade union sources, see p. 121.

[122] See J. Weiner, *A Descriptive Finding List of Unstamped British Periodicals, 1830–1836* (1970); R. Harrison, G. B. Woolven, and R. Duncan, *The Warwick Guide to British Labour Periodicals, 1790–1970* (1977).

[123] Ed. J. F. C. Harrison and D. Thompson (1978).

[124] N.b. J. O. Baylen and N. J. Gossman (eds.), *The Biographical Dictionary of British Radicals since 1770*, i, *1770–1832* (1978) (other vols. projected); J. Bellamy and J. Saville, *Dictionary of Labour Biography* (5 vols., 1972–8); *The Labour Who's Who* (1924, 1927).

CHAPTER 4

Poor relief, charities, prices and wages

POOR RELIEF

The concern of the state, local authorities, and individuals with the relief of the poor is reflected in England in a mass of records. For long periods the chief community action on a local basis lay in the administration of the poor law and other charitable acts. Thus local historians seeking to deal with this aspect of the history of their town or area will need to be well acquainted with the general history of the poor law, while at the same time the many local variations make the subject particularly worthy of study.[1]

The history of the poor law in England falls conveniently into two periods broken by the Poor Law Amendment Act of 1834, and the types of records also fall into these two chronological categories and are dealt with below in this way.

Generally speaking the administrative unit for the relief of

[1] See, e.g., E. M. Leonard, *The Early History of English Poor Relief* (1900); S. and B. Webb, *English Local Government*, vii–x (see p. 72 n. 10 for details); E. Lipson, *Economic History of England* iii (1947 edn), chapter 6; D. Marshall, *English Poor in the Eighteenth Century* (1926); J. D. Marshall, *The Old Poor Law, 1795–1834* (1968); M. E. Rose, *The English Poor Law, 1780–1930* (1971); and bibliography in W. E. Tate, *The Parish Chest* (1960 edn), 331–2. The last named work prints extracts from many of the types of records described below and also has a good summary (pp. 1–35) of parish administration. For a good local study, see E. M. Hampson, *The Treatment of Poverty in Cambridgeshire* (1934). J. D. Marshall, *The Old Poor Law*, 47–8, lists other local monographs. For a good list of the types of records which might be found locally, see *Poor Law in Hampshire Through the Centuries: A Guide to the Records* (Hampshire Archivists Group, 1970).

poverty for the period before 1834 was the parish, and it is in parochial records that much of the history of early poor relief must be sought. The researcher will find that these records incidentally provide a great deal of information on other aspects of local social history.

The basic sources for the parochial poor-law administration are the accounts of the overseers of the poor, officials established under an Act of 1597 and including the church-wardens.[2] These records provide details of the amounts of poor rate collected from the better-off parishioners, as well as how it was expended. From such evidence may be deduced the policy of the parochial officers towards the poor, both ordinary paupers and vagrants,[3] and the effectiveness of government legislation. In the eighteenth century, for example, details of outdoor relief as well, possibly, as of parish or 'Gilbert Union' workhouses may be found in the accounts.[4]

The overseers' accounts may also indicate sources of revenue other than the rates. Many parishes, for example, had a 'poor-stock' of money from gifts, the interest from which was used for poor relief; sometimes fines for certain offences were also applied to poor relief. The way the money was spent may reveal the methods of relief favoured.[5] Details of who paid the poor rate and how much individuals paid are to be found in separate rate books.

The overseers were directly responsible to the J.P.s. Those of them who were churchwardens were elected in the parish vestry which also nominated the others for the approval of

[2] Normally overseers were parish officers, but by an Act of 1662 they were permitted for townships within large northern parishes. See G. H. Tupling, 'Overseers' Accounts', *Amateur Historian* i (1952–4).

[3] C. P. Ketchley, 'Vagrancy', *Amateur Historian* ii (1954–6).

[4] For an example of how a detailed picture of poor relief in a parish may be written from overseers' accounts, see F. G. Emmison, 'Relief of the Poor at Eaton Socon, Beds., 1706–1834', *Beds. Historical Record Soc.* xv (1933); F. G. Emmison, 'Poor Relief Accounts of Two Rural Parishes in Bedfordshire, 1563–1598', *Ec.H.R.* iii (1931).

[5] Tupling, 'Overseers' Accounts', 270.

the justices. The vestry decided the poor rate, audited the overseers' accounts, heard petitions and complaints from the poor, and took important decisions, such as to farm out the workhouse, establish a 'roundsman' system, and so on.[6] All these matters are of interest to the local historian and may be discovered in the vestry minute books.

Before the end of the seventeenth century the workhouse system became common. Such institutions might serve a single parish, or (from Gilbert's Act in 1782) a union of parishes.[7] Details about the workhouses can often be extracted from the overseers' accounts, but sometimes separate accounts were kept, especially where the house was administered by a separate committee. Where these exist they may include evidence on the conditions of life in the house, including the accommodation and diet, the rules imposed on inmates, and sometimes details of the work they were required to undertake. Where the workhouse was farmed out to a contractor for a fixed fee, as permitted under the 1722-3 Act, it is much less likely that records will exist.

The overseers were empowered with consent of the justices to apprentice pauper children and the masters chosen were bound to accept the youngsters on penalty of a fine. The indentures of such apprentices may still be extant, and sometimes copies are to be found in parish registers, vestry minute books, or overseers' accounts.[8]

The Settlement Acts of 1662 sought to restrict paupers or potential paupers to their own parish.[9] After 1795 their

[6] Cf. Tate, *Parish Chest*, 231–4.

[7] Some union workhouses were established before this under an Act of 1722–3 and private Acts.

[8] C. P. Ketchley, 'Apprentices – Trade and Poor', *Amateur Historian* ii (1954–6). See also A. J. Willis and A. L. Merson (eds.), *A Calendar of Southampton Apprenticeship Registers, 1699–1740*, Southampton Record Series (1968).

[9] C. P. Ketchley, 'Settlement and its Legal Definition', *Amateur Historian* ii (1954–6). See also A. J. Willis, *Winchester Settlement Papers, 1667–1842* (1967).

removal to their parish of origin was to take place only after they actually became a charge on the rates. The Acts never worked properly, were open to many abuses, and broke down in the industrial areas in the later eighteenth century. Nevertheless the attempt to enforce settlement was a bone of contention between parishes for many years, absorbed much of the energies of the parish officers, and has left behind a great body of records. The overseers' accounts and records ancillary to them give details of cost of removal (often also found in the constables' accounts) and the like. And there frequently exists in the parish archives correspondence with the officers of other parishes and, from 1697, settlement certificates. These certificates permitted men to move about by providing a guarantee that their own parish would receive them back if they fell into need.[10] There may also be, for the period 1744 to 1824, copies of examinations of vagrants by J.P.s seeking to discover what parish was legally responsible for them.[11] W. E. Tate has pointed out the value of these to the local social historian, for they are in fact brief autobiographies of a class of person for whom such personal details are rarely found: 'they give the place of birth . . . and often his whole history over a long period of years, especially with reference to apprenticeship, the length of time for which he has been hired, the rental value of any property he has occupied, and, in short anything bearing upon the question whether or not he has acquired a settlement'.[12] Providing interest of a similar nature are inventories of paupers' goods. Such records may exist where overseers were mean enough to take advantage of their right to sell dead paupers' property.

The parish records may also include removal orders made by the justices, particularly following the Settlement Acts of

[10] S. Farrant, 'Some Records of the Old Poor Law as Sources of Local History', *Local Historian* xii (1976–7).

[11] After 1824 they are only concerned with Scottish and Irish vagrants.

[12] Tate, *Parish Chest*, 201.

1662, passes provided for unmolested progress back to a parish of origin, counsels' opinions, warrants to whip and maybe documents recording such punishments, commitments to houses of correction, copies of appeals to quarter sessions, petitions, and the like.[13]

Extra-parochial records also throw light on local poor relief up to 1834. In towns the poor law may have been administered by parish officials in the same way as in rural parishes, and there were often parochial workhouses. In many towns, however, borough councils also had a say in the matter, and it was in large towns that most experiments occurred. Sometimes parishes were united for poor-law purposes and there was often a borough house of correction. Thus the records of the borough itself, as well as those of the parishes within it, are likely to contain much information on the poor. Council minute books[14] and treasurers' accounts may prove the most fruitful.[15] Some towns under local Acts conducted a poor-law administration somewhat different from that of the rest of the country. At Bristol, for example, there was a Corporation of the Poor, established in 1696,[16] and at Coventry poor relief was administered under an Act of 1801 (not set aside by the general Act of 1834) by Directors of the Poor, who have left behind detailed minute books.[17]

Since the oversight and enforcement of the poor law was entrusted by the government to the J.P.s, the records of quarter sessions[18] contain details of the relations of the

[13] *Ibid.* 201.

[14] See, e.g., M. D. Harris, *The Coventry Leet Book, 1420–1555*, Early English Text Soc. (1907–13); A. E. Bland, P. A. Brown, and R. H. Tawney, *English Economic History: Select Documents* (1914), 366–7 (for Chester).

[15] See pp. 85–7.

[16] Printed in E. E. Butcher (ed.), *Bristol Corporation of the Poor*, Bristol Record Soc. iii (1932).

[17] Preserved in Coventry City Record Office. See W. B. Stephens, 'Poor Relief', *V.C.H.: Warwickshire* viii (1969), 176–7.

[18] See pp. 91–2.

justices with the vestries and overseers as well as of other actions taken by the justices themselves.[19] Much of the business of quarter sessions concerned matters of poor relief, such as, for example, disputes between parishes, appeals on orders of removal, and conditions of workhouses.[20] Sometimes J.P.s inaugurated particular systems of outdoor relief. The example of Speenhamland is well known, though neither outdoor relief nor the concept of subsidizing wages according to the price of food was new in the 1790s.

In the sixteenth and seventeenth centuries, particularly before the Civil War, the impetus to enforcement of the national system of poor relief came from the Privy Council, and the *Calendar of State Papers, Domestic,* and the *Acts of the Privy Council*[21] are full of instructions to local J.P.s and other information on matters of poor relief. Likewise assize records may contain useful information on poor relief, bridewells, settlement, bastardy, and so on. Tax records of this period, such as those of the poll and hearth taxes, may also give some indication of the extent of poverty.[22]

For the late eighteenth and early nineteenth centuries there are many parliamentary papers which throw light on the subject at a local level, and for these reference should be made to the indexes.[23] Mention may, however, be made of a few

---

[19] E.L.C. Mullins (ed)., *Texts and Calendars: An Analytical Guide to Serial Publications,* Royal Historical Soc., Guides and Handbooks, no. 7 (1958), lists many sessions records now in print.

[20] See above for removal orders, examinations, and settlement disputes.

[21] And, of course, the manuscript records to which they pertain: see p. 14. For examples see Bland, Brown, and Tawney, *English Economic History,* 382–3, 387. [22] See pp. 60–2.

[23] See, for a select list, W. R. Powell, *Local History from Blue Books: Select List of the Sessional Papers of the House of Commons* (1962), 36–7. This includes references to some papers, not mentioned here, which give totals of relief by county. Many of the papers dealing with agriculture (see pp. 197–9) are also useful for poor relief. See also Interdepartmental Committee on Social and Economic Research, *Guides to Official Sources, no. 3: Local Government Statistics* (H.M.S.O., 1953), 1 sqq.

which are particularly useful. A return for 1777 gives information by hundreds and parishes on the poor, poor rates, houses of industry, and workhouses, for the years 1772 to 1774. For 1777 and 1787 there are very detailed abstracts of returns by overseers of the poor relating to 1776 and to 1783, 1784, and 1785.[24] A similar very detailed abstract by parishes for 1803–4 gives an enormous amount of information for 1803 and for years in the 1780s.[25] Reports of 1817 and 1818 on the poor laws are also useful, providing assessments of poor relief by counties only, in 1748, 1749, and 1750, 1776, 1783, 1784, 1785, 1803, and 1815.[26]

Very useful, too, is an 1817 report of a House of Lords Committee on the Poor Laws,[27] which contains in its appendixes extremely detailed information on many places in several counties, and more details may be culled from the evidence. Perhaps even more valuable is an abstract of this report giving details county by county and place by place, of rates, numbers of poor, workhouses, charities, friendly societies, and so on for the years 1813, 1814, and 1815.[28] A return of 1824 gives evidence, by hundreds, about poverty and about systems of relief,[29] and the *Digest of Parochial Returns to the Select Committee on the Education of the Lower Orders*[30] includes a statement of the number of poor in each parish in 1815. Information on expenditure on poor relief in

[24] These form part of the *First Series of Sessional Papers*, ix (1774–1802).

[25] *Abstract of the Answers and Returns Relative to the Poor* (1803–4) xiii (this volume is not housed with other parliamentary papers in B. L. Official Publications Room, but at call mark 433 i 12 (2). See P. Grey, 'Parish Workhouses and Poorhouses', *Local Historian* x (1972–3), 71–2, for details.

[26] *Rep. Select Committee on the Poor Laws* (1817) vi; *First and Second Reps. Select Committee on the Poor Laws* (1818) v.

[27] *Rep. Lords Committee on the Poor Laws* (1818) v.

[28] *Abridgement of the Abstract of Returns Relative to the Poor* (1818) xix. For workhouses, see also Grey, 'Parish Workhouses', 72.

[29] *Abstract of Returns on Wages of Labourers* (1825) xix.

[30] (1819) ix (3 vols.).

individual parishes for each year from 1815 to 1835 is to be found in a series of reports of this period.[31]

For some towns the reports of the Municipal Corporations Commission of 1835[32] is useful. More significant is the report of 1834 of the Royal Commission on the Poor Law[33] which contains detailed reports on many places.[34]

Evidence can be gathered, too, in many unofficial publications. The anonymous *Account of Several Workhouses, as also of Several Charity Schools* (1725; 2nd edn 1732) contains references to over a hundred workhouses.[35] Eden's *State of the Poor*[36] has very detailed reports on a number of parishes in the English, and some Welsh, counties, for the end of the eighteenth century. These include, for example, tables of baptisms, burials, and marriages from the late seventeenth century, poor rates collected for many years in the eighteenth century as well as rates in the pound, and expenditure. They may also contain, for the years immediately prior to the survey, details of wages, prices of food, land tax, friendly societies, workhouses, types of relief, actual details of recent recipients of relief, and general information about the parish concerned.

The incidence of the poor rate was considered to be so heavy in the eighteenth and early nineteenth centuries that many contemporary publications contain evidence about poor-law matters. These are too numerous and miscella-

---

[31] *Rep. Select Committee on Poor Rate Returns* (1822) v; *Money Expended for Relief of Poor in Every Place in England and Wales* (1825) iv; (1830–1) xi; (1835) xlvii.

[32] See p. 84.

[33] (1834) xxvii–xxxviii.

[34] For criticism of this enquiry, see J. D. Marshall, *The Old Poor Law*, 16 sqq.; M. Blaug, 'The Poor Law Report Re-examined', *Jnl of Economic History* xxiv (1964).

[35] Lipson, *Economic History of England* iii, 478 q.v.

[36] F. M. Eden, *State of the Poor together with Parochial Reports* (1797), 3 vols. The parochial reports appear in vols. ii and iii. There is an abridged edn (1928) (ed. A. G. L. Rogers), but the original is to be preferred.

neous to list here, but mention may be made of the *Annals of Agriculture*[37] which often contains local information on poor relief in this period. The volume for 1795,[38] for example, publishes many answers to a questionnaire asking, among other things, about methods of poor relief employed locally. Again a work of 1816[39] contains details about poor relief for some parishes in each county. Sometimes these are very detailed, and information on the wages of labourers and on prices of certain crops is also provided. The *General Views* of the Board of Agriculture[40] also give details about the state of the poor.

Houses of correction, or bridewells, for the idle unemployed were really penal institutions and detailed information about individual establishments may be found in John Howard's, *State of the Prisons in England and Wales*[41] and his *Account of the Principal Lazarettos in Europe*,[42] which give such information as the accommodation for each sex, sanitary and heating arrangements, diet, whether employment was provided, the salary of the keeper, and the number of inmates. James Neild's *State of the Prisons in England, Scotland and Wales* (1812) contains similar information with numbers of prisoners for various years in the early nineteenth century.

With the Poor Law Amendment Act of 1834 the parish basis of poor relief ceased and poor-law unions and elected boards of guardians[43] replaced the parish officers and the

[37] See p. 185–6.

[38] Vol. xxiv.

[39] Cited fully on p. 185. The information on the poor is given in answer to: 'What is the state of the Labouring Poor; and what is the proportion of Poor-Rates compared with the years 1811 and 1812?'.

[40] See pp. 183–5.

[41] 1777–80; 2nd edn 1780; 3rd edn 1784; 4th edn 1792; all should be searched since in this way changes in the accommodation and administration may be traced.

[42] 1789; 2nd edn 1791.

[43] Except in a few places where former local Acts continued in force, as at Coventry.

J.P.s as the directors of local poor relief. For the century
following the 1834 Act the chief sources are the records of the
local guardians, those of the central body set up to administer
the Act,[44] and published parliamentary papers.

Local records for the period[45] include workhouse records,
such as day books, accounts, and admission registers,[46]
copies of the guardians' correspondence, and files of 'in'
letters, especially those from the central authority. Most
important, however, are the guardians' minute books and
general ledgers.[47] The minute books must form the basis of
any local study of poor relief after 1834. They contain much
detail on the administration of the union workhouse, including workhouse schools,[48] the erection and alteration of
workhouse buildings, reports from the workhouse officials,
and much on the general social conditions of the area.
Sometimes they include reports of subcommittees on aspects
of the guardians' work. The general ledgers or account books
of the boards of guardians also exist in large numbers and are
of vital importance to the local historian in investigation of
the financial history of poor-law administration and for a
multitude of general matters, including settlement.[49]

At the Public Record Office records relating to the poor

[44] To 1847 this was the Poor Law Commission; from 1847 to 71 it was
the Poor Law Board; from 1871 to 1919 it was the Local Government
Board (also responsible for health); and from 1919 to 1929, the Ministry of
Health. Thereafter county councils and county borough councils became
responsible.

[45] Sometimes held now in local hospitals, once poor-law institutions.
Sussex Poor Law Records (West Sussex Record Office, 1960), introduction,
is worth consulting for these records.

[46] See R. M. Gutchen, 'Paupers in Union Workhouses', *Local Historian* xi
(1974-5).

[47] See Jane M. Coleman, 'Guardians' Minute Books', *History* xlviii
(1963).

[48] For poor-law schools, and the education of paupers generally, see pp.
218-20.

[49] K. H. Baker, 'General Ledgers of Boards of Guardians', *Jnl Soc.
Archivists* ii (1963).

law are now filed under the Department of Health. The
P.R.O. Guide should be consulted, but the most useful class
may well be the poor law union papers (M.H.12, covering
1834 to 1900), consisting of the correspondence (arranged by
counties and unions) of the central government department
with poor-law unions and other local authorities.[50] After
1871 these contain also information on health and general
local government matters. In the Second World War the
Germans destroyed most of the papers after 1900.[51] The
correspondence of assistant poor-law commissioners and
inspectors (M.H.32) are less conveniently arranged under the
officers' names. The census enumerators' books[52] list the
inmates of workhouses.

Printed parliamentary papers relating to poor relief are
very numerous for the period after 1834. Generally useful are
the annual reports of the Poor Law Commission (1835–47),
and subsequently of the Poor Law Board (1848–71) and the
Local Government Board (from 1872); the usually annual
papers – Poor Rate Returns (1840), Poor Relief Returns
(1842–57), and Statements of Paupers, etc. (1857–1948);[53] the
reports of a select committee of 1861;[54] the returns of unions
and parishes of 1862, which provide populations of unions
and the dates of their formation;[55] the report of a Lords
Committee of 1888;[56] and the reports of the Royal Commission on the Aged Poor of 1895[57] and of the Royal Commis-

---

[50] There are also subject indexes (M.H.15). See also *Ministry of Health,
Poor Law Union Papers* pts I–III, List and Index Soc., lvi, lxiv-lxx (1970,
1971, 1972).

[51] Where any survive they are to be found also in Class M.H.48.

[52] See pp. 68–9.

[53] After 1928–9 information is for counties. See parliamentary paper
indexes. See also Grey, 'Parish Workhouses', 72–3.

[54] (1861) ix (indexed).

[55] (1862) xlix (2).

[56] *Rep. Select Committee of the House of Lords on Poor Relief* (1888) xv.

[57] (1895) xiv, xv.

sion on the Relief of Distress of 1909–10.[58] A specially useful
return of 1847 consists of a nationwide collection of parochial
details on poor rates and expenditure from 1834. The same
parliamentary paper volume also contains details of numbers
relieved in each union in 1846 and 1847, and much other
information.[59] Parliamentary papers concerned with agriculture also often contain information on the poor law.[60]

Also useful are the reports of 1837 of the Boundary
Commission, the reports of the Select Committee on the
Health of Towns of 1840,[61] of the Poor Law Commissioners
on the Sanitary Conditions of the Labouring Population of
1842,[62] and of the Royal Commission on the State of Large
Towns of 1844–5.[63] The views and evidence contained in
official reports and their appendixes cannot, of course,
always be taken at face value.

From 1875 to 1930 the volumes of *Poor Law Conferences*[64]
contain articles and appendixes which at times include very
detailed local information. The volume for 1901–2, for
example, contains abstracts of replies from boards of guardians about the treatment of the poor in various unions in
different parts of the country. *Shaw's Union Officers' and Local
Board of Health Manual*[65] gives lists of poor-law unions,
officers, and workhouses. The *Municipal Year Book* (from
1897), the *Poor Law and Local Government Journal* (later

[58] (1909) xxxvii–xlv; (1910) xlvi–lv.

[59] (1847–8) liii.

[60] See pp. 197–8.

[61] *Rep. R. Commission on Municipal Corporations' Boundaries* (1837)
xxvi–xxviii; *Rep. Select Committee on Health of Towns* (1840) xi.

[62] H.L. (1842) xxvi–xxviii.

[63] (1844) xvii; (1845) xviii (information not easy to find: poor relief not
indexed).

[64] Central Committee of Poor Law Conferences, *Poor Law District
Conferences* (1875 to 1896); *Poor Law Conferences* (1897/8 to 1930).

[65] Published under this title 1854–75. Otherwise: *Shaw's Union Officers'
Manual of Duties* (1846–53); *Shaw's Local Government Manual and Directory*
(1876–1921); *Local Government Manual and Directory* (from 1923).

Magazine) (1891–1930), and the *Poor Law Unions Gazette* may also be useful. The sources for the history of the education of pauper children are dealt with in the chapter on education.[66]

CHARITIES

Investigations into the relief of poverty cannot, of course, confine themselves to the official poor law without giving a distorted picture. They will have to take into account, too, the part played by private charity which certainly down to the mid-seventeenth century amounted to a great deal more than official poor relief. Some charities were and still are concerned with education, the upkeep of bridges, bells, churches, and so on, but here we are interested in the many designed to assist the needy.

The first place to seek information on these may well be the account of the history of a town or parish in the volumes of the *Victoria History of the Counties of England*. This, if it exists, should include a section on charities for the poor, providing an abbreviated account of each local charity with footnote references to sources. Some of these may be in unusual places otherwise difficult to track down. Moreover recourse may have been made by the *V.C.H.* contributors to recent records of the Charity Commission not open to general inspection.

The *V.C.H.* accounts draw widely on the reports of the Charity Commissioners published as parliamentary papers in the first half of the nineteenth century,[67] but these papers, which contain both contemporary and retrospective material, will need to be consulted by anyone delving deeper. Towards the end of the century other parliamentary papers

---

[66] Chapter 7; see pp. 218–21.

[67] See p. 207. There are indexes, and a digest arranged under parishes: *Analytical Digest* (1843) xvi, xviii. Local directories also often summarize the Charity Commission reports.

record fresh surveys of charities in certain towns and counties.[68]

The records of the Charity Commission are held at the Commission's offices in London and Liverpool.[69] Registered charities[70] may be traced through a register, arranged topographically, which is available at both offices. The register itself provides a brief description of a charity and its nature. Fuller evidence is to be found in the Commission's files, not all of which, however, are open to public inspection. Unpublished reports, available at both offices, bound in volumes, effectively continue the printed reports of the earlier Charity Commissioners,[71] giving details of the beginnings of charities (except the most recent) which have originated since the earlier investigation.

Earlier records in the hands of the central government are to be found in the Public Record Office itself, in the proceedings of the Commissioners for Charitable Uses,[72] established towards the end of Elizabeth I's reign. The

[68] *Digest of Endowed Charities* (various titles), published at irregular intervals 1867/8 – 1912/13. See official index under Endowed Charities', 'General Digest'.

[69] Central Register of Charities, St Alban's House, 57 Haymarket, London S.W.1; Charity Commission (Northern Office), Derby Square, Liverpool. The Liverpool office deals with the records of charities in Ches., Cumb., Derby., Dur., Herefordshire, Lancs., Leics., Lincs., Mon., Northumber., Notts., Rutland, Shropshire, Staffs., War., Westmorland, Worcs., Yorks., Wales.

[70] Unregistered charities are those of little importance financially, and places of public worship. Records of educational charities form part of the archives of the Department of Education and Science, where there is a register of them.

[71] The records on which the Brougham Commission based its published reports once formed P.R.O., Class Charity 2 (covering largely the period 1817–50), but these were removed to the Charity Commission in the early 1960s.

[72] For details, see *P.R.O. Guide* i, 13; P.R.O., Lists and Indexes x (1899), which provides a key topographically arranged.

chantry certificates of the mid-sixteenth century[73] in effect list charities then existing.[74]

The actual records of trustees of charities may well exist locally, in town or parish records, in county record offices, solicitors' offices, or with the existing trustees. In boroughs the town council often acted as trustee to many charities, and information may be found not only in the council minute books and treasurers' accounts, but in separately kept records. In all these places the records of greatest interest are the account books, deeds, leases, and correspondence. Among some parish records are registers of charities, and the records of clerks of the peace may include copies of returns of charities sent to Parliament, lists of registered charities, and copies of annual accounts.[75]

Self-help in the eighteenth and nineteenth centuries was often expressed in friendly societies, and the records of these may help to build up a general picture of working-class life and resources.[76]

PRICES AND WAGES

Associated with any attempt to evaluate the standard of living within the local community is the study of local wage rates and price levels.[77] The records from which information on such matters may be culled are, however, so miscellaneous that only a few can be touched on here. It must be

---

[73] See pp. 56–7.

[74] R. B. Pugh, *How to Write a Parish History* (1954).

[75] Tate, *Parish Chest*, 118; F. G. Emmison, *Archives and Local History* (1966), 50, 61; F. G. Emmison and I. Gray, *County Records* (1948), 12.

[76] See E. Hobsbawm, 'Friendly Societies', *Amateur Historian* iii (1956–8); P. H. J. H. Gosden, *The Friendly Societies in England, 1815–1875* (1961), 245 sqq.

[77] For the controversy over the standard of living in the eighteenth and nineteenth centuries, see A. J. Taylor (ed.), *The Standard of Living in Britain in the Industrial Revolution* (1975); and bibliography in M. W. Flinn, 'Trends in Real Wages', *Ec.H.R.*, 2nd ser., xxvii (1974), 412–13.

realized, too, that work on the topics of wages and prices requires special knowledge and expertise.[78]

Certain printed sources may be consulted first. For medieval prices Thorold Rogers's *History of Agriculture and Prices in England*[79] is a mine of information since the author used among other sources the accounts of several Oxford colleges with property in many parts of the country. His volumes provide in tabular form, topographically arranged, prices of grain, livestock, other foodstuffs, fuel, lighting and building materials, cloth, wool, and wages.[80] Most of his prices are, however, taken from scattered references rather than from continuous series, and this detracts substantially from their value.[81]

Rogers's prices go down to 1797, but for the period from the sixteenth century the first (and only) volume of Lord Beveridge's *Prices and Wages in England* is more reliable.[82] Using his account of twelve institutions (schools, hospitals, and government departments), he is able to provide prices for such goods as food, cloth, fuel and lighting, building materials, and grain.[83] For the eighteenth century Miss

[78] For introductory works, see E. V. Morgan, *The Study of Prices and the Value of Money*, Hist. Assoc., Helps for Students of History, no. 53 (1950); W. T. Layton and G. Crowther, *An Introduction to the Study of Prices* (1938 edn); W. Tooke and W. Newmarch, *A History of Prices and of the State of Circulation from 1793 to 1856* (1838–57). E. H. Phelps Brown and M. H. Browne, *A Century of Pay* (1968), examines real wages, 1860–1960.

[79] 7 vols. (1866–1902).

[80] Average prices (not topographically broken down) for some of these commodities, based on Rogers, are printed in 'Medieval Prices', *Amateur Historian* ii (1954–6). See also W. Beveridge, 'The Yield and Price of Corn in the Middle Ages', *Economic History* i (1926–9).

[81] For a criticism, see Morgan, *Study of Prices*, 17 sqq.

[82] W. H. Beveridge *et al.*, *Prices and Wages in England from the Twelfth to the Nineteenth Century* i (1939).

[83] Averages are worked out and printed in 'Post Reformation Prices', *Amateur Historian* ii (1954–6). Two articles have used Beveridge's tables to compile cost of living indexes: E. W. Gilboy, 'The Cost of Living and Real

Gilboy provides tables of wages for different parts of the country.[84]

Original evidence of prices and wages may, of course, be found in all sorts of accounts.[85] For the Middle Ages and later, manorial or ministers' accounts[86] are an important source, as, too, are the accounts kept by borough treasurers.[87] Sometimes as well as the formal borough accounts rough accounts were compiled as money was spent or received, and if these have survived they will often provide more detailed information. Even more important are actual vouchers and bills which show minutely what was paid or received, including prices of commodities and of wages to workmen of various kinds.[88] The same sort of information is obtainable from churchwardens' accounts, the accounts and other records of gilds,[89] estate accounts,[90] quarter-sessions

Wages in Eighteenth Century England', *Review of Economic Statistics* xviii (1936), provides an index of consumer goods for London, 1685–1816; E. B. Schumpeter, 'English Prices and Public Finance, 1660–1822', *ibid.* xx (1938), gives a general index for 1660–96 and others for 1695–1823. Provincial prices are not broken down into regions but it may be useful for local historians to be able to compare these general trends with those in the area being studied.

[84] E. W. Gilboy, *Wages in the Eighteenth Century* (1934). For the nineteenth century, see A. L. Bowley, *Wages in the United Kingdom since 1860* (1900). For references to agricultural wages for different counties for the eighteenth and nineteenth centuries collected by A. L. Bowley, see M. Blaug, 'The Myth of the Old Poor Law', *Jnl of Economic History* xxiii (1963). See also pp. 197–8.

[85] See, e.g., E. H. Phelps Brown and S. V. Hopkins, 'Seven Centuries of the Prices of Consumables, compared with Builders' Wage-Rates', *Economica,* NS, xxiii (1956), 306–10.

[86] See p. 176.

[87] See p. 87.

[88] W. G. Hoskins, *Local History in England* (1959), 96–7. For an example of the use of such records, see W. B. Stephens, *Seventeenth Century Exeter* (1958), 148–52.

[89] See pp. 77, 127–8.

[90] See pp. 200–1.

accounts,[91] diaries, and private account books,[92] all of which may with luck be backed up by the original vouchers. The Exchequer accounts various in the Public Record Office,[93] embracing the 'Ancient Miscellanea' used by Thorold Rogers, contain other accounts, too, which may be of use for different parts of the country.[94] The pipe rolls can provide detailed information about early livestock prices for places in many counties, and some of these have been tabulated.[95]

The practice of wage and price regulation has left many records. Wages were regulated by gilds, town authorities, and by the justices of the peace, and evidence of this activity is thus to be found in their records. Examples of price and wage fixing by gilds are usually recorded in their minute books, many of which are now to be found in local depositories.[96] The gilds were very much under the control of borough authorities, which often regulated not only wages but the prices charged by the gildsmen. Evidence of this activity is usually provided by town councils' minute books.[97] The central government had attempted to fix national maximum wages in the mid-fourteenth century and in 1389 placed the responsibility for local assessments on the J.P.s. Most wage assessments extant, however, derive from the Statute of Artificers of 1563 when the justices were

[91] See Emmison and Gray, *County Records*, 8–9.

[92] See F. G. Emmison, *Tudor Food and Pastimes* (1964).

[93] See P.R.O., Lists and Indexes xxxv (1912); *P.R.O. Guide* i, 50 sqq.

[94] E.g., accounts and receipts and expenses of the royal mines in Devon and Cornwall (Edward I to Charles I), including wages.

[95] See, e.g., three articles by D. L. Farmer: 'Some Price Fluctuations in Angevin England', *Ec.H.R.*, 2nd ser., ix (1956); 'Some Grain Price Movements in Thirteenth Century England', *ibid.* x (1957); 'Some Livestock Price Movements in Thirteenth Century England', *ibid.* xxii (1969); A. L. Poole, 'Live Stock Prices in the Twelfth Century', *E.H.R.* lv (1940); and publications of the Pipe Roll Soc.

[96] For examples of wage fixing, see E. Lipson, *Economic History of England* i (1945 edn), 335 sqq.

[97] See pp. 85–6.

instructed to assess the maximum wages of labourers and craftsmen 'by the yere or by the Daye, Weke, Moneth or otherwyse, with Meate and Drincke or Without'. In 1604 a minimum assessment for the textile industry was instituted though this probably lapsed after a decade or so. Assessments are to be found particularly in quarter-sessions order books. They must, however, be used with caution. Although the 1563 clauses remained in force until 1813, by the later seventeenth century the system was cracking, and by the period of the Industrial Revolution it had in most areas broken down. How far the assessments are to be trusted as realistic indications of local wage levels can only be determined by comparison with other data. The quarter-sessions records may also indicate whether the justices really sought to enforce their assessments by levying fines. Assessments which were repeated year after year without indication of changes to accommodate changing price levels are not likely to represent the real state of affairs as far as local wages are concerned.[98]

The central government rarely regulated prices, but the Books of Rates[99] provided for the Customs officials give a rough guide of values of goods normally imported and

[98] D. M. Woodward, 'The Assessment of Wages by the Justices of the Peace, 1563–1813: Some Observations', *Local Historian* viii (1968–9), q.v. for a detailed comment on the interpretation of assessments. For lists of examples in print, see Lipson, *Economic History of England* iii, 256–8 nn. See also R. K. Kelsall, *Wage Regulation under the Statute of Artificers* (1938) (appendix lists wage assessments and their sources); R. H. Tawney, 'The Assessment of Wages in England by the Justices of the Peace', *Vierteljahrschrift für Sozial- und Wirtschaftsgeschichte* xi (1913), 307–37, 533–64. Kelsall's and Tawney's studies are republished in W. E. Minchinton (ed.), *Wage Regulation in Pre-Industrial England* (1971).

[99] E.g., *The Rates of Marchandizes as they are set downe in the Book of Rates* (1610) and others (see Stephens, *Seventeenth Century Exeter*, p. x). T. S. Willan (ed.), *A Tudor Book of Rates* (1962), prints the Book of 1582 and has an informative introduction. See also R. C. Jarvis, 'Books of Rates', *Jnl Soc. Archivists* v (1977).

exported, especially at the time of their compilation – thereafter they tended to remain unchanged for years at a time.

Town authorities from the Middle Ages often laid down market prices especially in time of dearth, and by the assizes of bread and ale regulated the price of bread according to the price of wheat and the price of ale according to the price of wheat, barley, and oats. Records of these regulations are to be found in borough council minute books or mayor's court rolls. For the late eighteenth and the early nineteenth centuries the *London Gazette* printed weekly average prices for different types of crops for counties and regions. From the 1830s the prices in a number of individual towns are given.

Probate inventories[100] may also provide a rough indication of prices, particularly of farm stock and crops, though there was perhaps a tendency to undervalue. From the eighteenth century fire insurance inventories give valuations of stock and buildings, but again these are likely to be undervalued since it was quite usual not to insure for the full value.[101] For agricultural wages and prices many of the sources dealt with in Chapter 6 are likely to be fruitful. Of published sources the *Annals of Agriculture*, the *Journal of the Royal Agricultural Society*, and the parliamentary papers cited, are very important. John Houghton's *Collections for the Improvement of Husbandry*,[102] a periodical publication, contains, in its original form, price quotations for many agricultural products.[103] Eden's *State of the Poor*, too, contains much on rural prices.

[100] See p. 35. See also J. West, *Village Records* (1962), 128–31, for a list of inventories in print.

[101] For fire insurance records, see pp. 136–7.

[102] The collection later edited by R. Bradley does not contain this material but the original flysheets do. The B. L. has issues for the period 1692–1703. I am indebted to Dr Joan Thirsk for this information.

[103] Some eighteenth-century local returns of corn prices are at the House of Lords: H. S. Cobb, 'Sources for Economic History Amongst the Parliamentary Records in the House of Lords Record Office', *Ec.H.R.*,

For the nineteenth century the parliamentary papers are full of evidence on wages, and to a less extent on prices. The indexes should, therefore, be searched under these headings, but it should be noted that many details of this sort, especially on wages, may occur in parliamentary papers mainly devoted to other subjects – such as factory inspectors' reports, investigations into industries (particularly those important in the region being studied), papers dealing with poor relief, agriculture, reports on the employment of women and children, on the state of large towns, on hand-loom weavers, and on the truck system.[104]

Certain collections of statistical material are specially useful for areas where particular industries predominated.[105] The parliamentary papers include a Board of Trade *Return relating to Wage Rates, etc., between 1830 and 1886* (1887),[106] and a paper of 1890 has tables of the standard hours of work in the many centres of various important industries at ten-year internals between 1850 and 1890.[107] A *Report on Standard Time Rates of Wages in the U.K. in 1900*[108] contains information on wage rates in certain industries in the last

2nd ser., xix (1966), 169. For later periods, see P.R.O., Class M.A.F.10, which consists of returns from markets of average prices and quantities of corn sold, weekly and monthly, 1799–1959; and Class M.A.F.15, which provides returns of market prices of stock and crops, 1896–1936.

[104] E. H. Hunt, *Regional Wage Variations in Britain, 1850–1914* (1973), uses many such sources and should be consulted.

[105] The following is largely based on Interdepartmental Committee on Social and Economic Research, *Guides to Official Sources, no. 1: Labour Statistics* (H.M.S.O., 1958 cdn), 33 sqq., q.v. for greater detail. See also Bowley, *Wages and Incomes since 1860*, 100 sqq.; A. L. Bowley, *Elements of Statistics* (6th edn, 1937), 30–6.

[106] (1887) lxxxix. See also *Abstract of Returns, 1824, Relative to Labourers' Wages* (1825) xix.

[107] (1890) lxviii. Trades dealt with are: agricultural and dock labourers, bakers, building trades, chemicals, tobacco, clothing, coach-making, engineering, glass, manufactured iron, mining, pottery, printing, railways, shipbuilding, textiles.

[108] (1900) lxxxii.

quarter of the century; similarly, in 1908, the Board of Trade's Labour Department printed (but did not publish) 'Rates of Wages and Hours of Labour in Various Industries in the United Kingdom for a Series of Years', which has details about rates of wages from the mid-century to 1906.[109]

For the years from 1893 there is a series, first called *Standard Time Rates*, and then *Time Rates of Wages and Hours of Labour*, periodically published (eleven times between 1894 and 1946, and then annually). Similarly another periodic official publication, *Abstract of Labour Statistics*, published between 1894 and 1937, and the monthly *Labour Gazette* (later *Ministry of Labour Gazette*), published from 1893,[110] also contain much on wage rates and hours of labour in certain industries. For the present century the *Censuses of Production*[111] may also be of use.

Recent official publications on prices include a Board of Trade *Report on Wholesale and Retail Prices in the U.K.* (1903),[112] which has details of food prices, mainly for London, from the mid-eighteenth century. Also from the Board of Trade came a series of three *Memoranda, etc., on British and Foreign Trade and Industrial Conditions*, published in 1903, 1905, and 1909.[113] These provide data on working-class living costs. The 1903 issue, for example, tabulates, among other things, the retail prices of the main types of goods bought by working-class Londoners annually between 1893 and 1902. It contains also details of typical British working-class expenditure in 1890–1 with working-class budgets for certain individual families. The 1904 issue charts

[109] But see *Report of an Enquiry by the Board of Trade into Working Class Rents, Housing and Retail Prices, together with the Standard Rates of Wages in the Principal Industrial Towns* (1908) cvii.

[110] Annual parliamentary papers giving the same information were published as *Changes in Rates of Wages and Hours of Labour etc.*, from 1893 to 1913.

[111] See p. 130.

[112] (1903) lxviii.

[113] (1903) lxvii; (1905) lxxxiv; (1909) cii.

the cost of living for the working classes in large towns between 1880 and 1903. Another Board of Trade report, of 1908, gives information on rents and prices in 94 British towns in 1905, and a similar report covers 88 towns in 1912.[114]

In conclusion it may be noted that a large collection of materials for the study of price and wage history for the period *c.* 1200 to *c.* 1830 is at the British Library of Political and Economic Science.[115]

For the nineteenth century the records of trade unions may be of interest to the local historian not only with regard to wages but also to economic and social conditions generally. The scope of the present work does not, however, permit any detailed discussion of such records.[116]

[114] *Labour Statistics,* 52–3.

[115] London School of Economics and Political Science, Houghton Street, London, WC2A 2AE. This is the collection formerly held at the Institute of Historical Research. See Beveridge *et al., Prices and Wages.*

[116] Those interested should look at E. and E. Frow and M. Katanka, *The History of British Trade Unionism: A Select Bibliography* (1969) (includes references to primary sources and a guide to collections of documents and books); A. W. Gottschalk, T. G. Whittingham, and N. Williams, *British Industrial Relations: An Annotated Bibliography* (1969); V. L. Allen, *International Bibliography on Trade Unionism* (1968); A. Aspinall, *Early English Trade Unions: Documents from the Home Office Papers in the Public Record Office* (1949); E. J. Hobsbawm, 'Records of the Trade Union Movement', *Archives* iv (1959–60); A. E. Musson, 'Writing Trade-Union History', *Amateur Historian* i (1952–4); S. Pollard, 'Sources for Trade Union History', *ibid.* iv (1958–60); B. Grant, 'Trades Councils, 1860–1914', *ibid.* iii (1956–8). N. Scotland, 'Primary Sources for 19th-century Agricultural Trade Unionism', *Local Historian* xiii (1979). *Guide to the Modern Records Centre* (University of Warwick Library, 1977) lists deposits of some trade unions and employers' organizations. See P. S. Bagwell, *Government and Society in Nineteenth Century Britain; Commentaries on British Parliamentary Papers: Industrial Relations* (1974), for parliamentary papers concerning unions. For friendly societies, see p. 113.

CHAPTER 5

Industry, trade and communications

INDUSTRY AND INTERNAL TRADE

Before the eighteenth century the records of individual craftsmen or firms are very rare, and local historians must rely on information culled from a variety of sources too wide for all to find mention here. For medieval and modern times evidence for local extractive industries and for manufactures generally is likely to be found in deeds or charters, especially leases,[1] in manorial court rolls, and in manorial and other financial accounts. Many of these records will be found in local record offices, but since the Crown was so often involved in the control and taxation of industry generally, and more directly with mining and metal working, the collections of such records in the Public Record Office must be tackled by the serious investigator. These include the Classes S.C.6 and D.L.29 (ministers' accounts), S.C.2 and D.L.30 (manorial rolls), and, especially for the aulnage tax on cloth in various counties and the royal mines of Devon and Cornwall, E.101 (Exchequer accounts various).[2] Customs records can also throw light on local industry,[3] as can the Exchequer special commissions and depositions mentioned below, the memoranda rolls,[4] and the ancient

---

[1] For deeds, etc., see pp. 301–4.

[2] P.R.O., Lists and Indexes, v, xxxiv (1894, 1910) (for ministers' accounts); vi (1896) (court rolls); xxxv (1912) (various accounts).

[3] See below, pp. 140–1, 142–8.

[4] For the K.R. and L.T.R. memoranda rolls, see *P.R.O. Guide* i, 60–2, 75; P.R.O. calendar for the rolls for 1326–7 (1968); *Exchequer K.R. and L.T.R. Memoranda Rolls*, List and Index Soc. iv (1965).

correspondence of the Chancery and Exchequer.[5] Not all the other collections at the Public Record Office which may contain information on local industry and trade in the medieval and early modern period can be noted here. For some, however, there are published calendars with indexes, and this will facilitate research. Such collections include the close, charter, liberate, fine, patent and pipe rolls, inquisitions post mortem, inquisitions miscellaneous, the letters and papers of Henry VIII, the state papers, domestic, and the Privy Council registers.[6] In addition to these collections the catalogues of the manuscripts of the British Library, especially those of the additional manuscripts and of charters and rolls, should be searched.[7]

Particularly in towns the chief institutions of trade and industry in the Middle Ages and the early modern period were gilds, markets, and fairs. Though some early fairs and markets grew up without formal permission it was soon recognized that the right to possess a merchant gild or to hold a market or fair came from a royal or seigneurial grant of privileges.[8] From the early thirteenth century, for example, the *Calendar of Charter Rolls* records the original grants and renewal of grants of market charters. Apart from Domesday, where markets find mention, charters and other documents recording them are, therefore, the first place to look for the medieval existence or origins of such institutions. Such records are described fully in another chapter.[9]

---

[5] Class S.C.I. See *P.R.O. Guide* i, 190.

[6] See pp. 13–14. For the pipe rolls, see the publications of the Pipe Roll Soc.

[7] See p. 7. N.b. *Index to the Charters and Rolls in the British Museum* (B.M., 1900, 1912).

[8] For the origins of fairs, see C. Walford, *Fairs Past and Present* (1883); A. Everitt, 'The Marketing of Agricultural Produce', in J. Thirsk (ed.), *The Agrarian History of England and Wales*, iv, *1500–1640* (1967), 532 sqq. An instructive local investigation is B. E. Coates, 'The Origin and Distribution of Markets and Fairs in Medieval Derbyshire', *Derby. Archaeological Jnl* lxxxv (1965): those seeking to investigate other areas would profit from reading this.   [9] See pp. 80–3.

Also useful are the Chancery inquisitions *ad quod damnum* at the Public Record Office (Class C.143). These were instructions to escheators (local officials concerned with certain types of royal revenue) to enquire whether a proposed grant to hold a market or fair would affect the profitability of existing markets. There is a calendar of these records.[10] The *Placita de Quo Warranto* also contain references to markets and fairs.[11]

A nineteenth-century parliamentary paper, the first report of the Royal Commission on Market Rights and Tolls of 1888, has sought to extract from the records described above the details of all royal grants for markets and fairs made between 1199 and 1483,[12] and although this may not be entirely reliable it may serve as a starting point. Manorial and estate records, particularly inquisitions post mortem and extents, and the more detailed hundred rolls[13] will also record the existence of markets in medieval and early modern times.

Details of local regulation of markets and fairs, their changing nature, their profitability, and so on, are usually to be found in local records, including estate and family records, and records of boroughs, such as council minutes,

[10] *Inquisitions ad quod Damnum*, P.R.O., Lists and Indexes, xvii (1904), xxii (1906). Some of these inquisitions for the reigns of Henry VII to Charles I are preserved among the inquisitions post mortem (Class C.142); for James I's reign they are in the brevia regia of the petty bag office (Class C.202).

[11] Ed. W. Illingworth and J. Caley (Record Commission, 1818).

[12] See below. The grants are listed chronologically but there is a manuscript index at the P.R.O. William Owen, *An Authentic account of all the Fairs in England and Wales* (1756, and later editions as *Owen's Book of Fairs*) lists fairs. For markets in existence in the sixteenth and seventeenth centuries, see the lists and maps in A. Everitt, 'Marketing of Agricultural Produce', 468–75; A. Everitt, 'Urban Growth and Inland Trade, 1560–1770: Sources', *Local Historian* viii (1968–9) (q.v. also for other sources).

[13] See pp. 48–52, 168–70.

treasurers' accounts, and quarter-sessions records. There may be specific toll-books for fairs or markets, court rolls, or extents of town properties.[14]

The Public Record Office collections noted above may well have references to fairs and markets. The state papers, domestic, the letters and papers of Henry VIII and the Privy Council registers, for example, contain references for Tudor and Stuart times on the disruption of markets and fairs by plague, dearth, or civil war, or contain special orders to the justices and town officials concerning the regulation of these institutions and maybe petitions concerning them. The indexes to the calendars of these collections should therefore be searched.

Markets and fairs, of course, retained their importance to very recent times, and a handful are still significant. Older local histories and topographies, guide books, directories,[15] newspapers, and handbooks issued by town councils may yield much information, though often unreliable in detail. The *General Views* (of the Board of Agriculture) contain sections on fairs and markets. The reports of the Royal Commission on Market Rights and Tolls[16] are especially valuable for contemporary as well as historical details, the evidence of witnesses being especially significant. The first report (1888) gives lists of markets and fairs in existence in 1792 and in 1888. A parliamentary paper of 1836 lists amounts of wheat sold in 149 markets for each year between 1825 and 1834,[17] and another, a return of markets published in 1886, provides a useful tabulated list topographically arranged.[18]

[14] See, e.g., W. Hudson and J. Tingey, *Records of the City of Norwich* (1906) ii, 237 sqq.; A. E. Bland, P. A. Brown, and R. H. Tawney (eds.), *English Economic History: Select Documents* (1914), 159, 386.

[15] See especially *Lewis's Topographical Dictionary* (1833) and the *Imperial Gazetteer* (1870), which often note the existence of former markets.

[16] (1888) liii, liv, lv; (1890–1) xxxvii–xli.

[17] *First Rep. Select Committee on the State of Agriculture and the Causes of Distress* (1836) viii (1).   [18] (1886) lvi.

Legal disputes over fairs and markets or business conducted in them may be found in the local records of piepowder courts and quarter sessions, and in the Public Record Office in the records of the Court of Common Pleas, the Court of Exchequer, and Star Chamber. Thus, for example, the Exchequer special commissions and depositions (Classes E.134 and E.178) contain details of disputes about markets and fairs.[19] The Home Office records may also shed light on modern markets and fairs. Home Office correspondence and papers, registered papers (Class H.O.45), contains files on fairs and markets (1876–1939), and are largely concerned with orders for abolition or change of date. Correspondence on fairs for the years 1899 to 1923 is to be found in entry books (Class H.O.152), while for the period 1852–76 indexed warrant books (Class H.O.141) include licences to hold markets and fairs. A Ministry of Agriculture and Fisheries *Report on Markets and Fairs* (1927–30), in seven topographically arranged volumes, is useful for the inter-war period.[20] Orders to discontinue markets and fairs are reported in the *London Gazette* and local newspapers.

The national collections mentioned above[21] may well contain references to gilds. In addition the miscellanea of the Chancery (P.R.O., Class C.47, bundles 38–46)[22] contain returns for the late fourteenth century providing information, topographically arranged, of the ordinances, usages, and property of gilds and fraternities. About a tenth of these are in English and are printed in full in J. Toulmin Smith's *English Gilds* (1870).[23] Another printed source is C. Gross's *The Gild Merchant* (2 vols., 1890) which reproduces records

[19] Everitt, 'Urban Growth', 198. For calendars and lists, see *P.R.O. Guide* ii, 57, 66.

[20] List and Index Soc., xxii, xxiii, xxxix, l, lxxxiv (1967–72), provide a topographical index.

[21] See p. 125.

[22] *P.R.O. Guide* i, 38.

[23] Early English Text Soc. xl (1870).

of the sixteenth century and earlier concerning merchant gilds. Since these are arranged under the names of towns they are very useful, and the local historian may save himself a great deal of time by consulting this book at an early stage in his researches.

The craft gilds grew up later than the merchant gilds and their affairs were regulated closely by the town authorities. Borough council minute books[24] are, therefore, full of information on them, and treasurers' accounts may record the receipt of taxes paid by these gilds to the town. In many places freedom of the borough was open only to freemen of the various gilds, so that the town freemen's rolls or books will be useful for gild history.[25] The waxing or waning of their importance, for example, may be deduced from the numbers of a particular gild becoming borough freemen. The value of the official town records for gild history cannot, therefore, be overemphasized.

The most intimate detail, however, may only be obtainable from the records of the gilds themselves, where they exist.[26] From their ordinances and minute books and from their account books may be discovered details of their structure, policy, properties, and social and philanthropic activities. The entries of payments for freedom will indicate how the gild was prospering. If entry numbers vary greatly in certain years this may indicate periods of recession or expansion, or it may merely reflect the tightening up of regulations to force non-gild members already at work in a town to join the gild. Special freemen's books or rolls and

---

[24] See, e.g., R. H. Tawney and E. Power, *Tudor Economic Documents* (1935 edn) i, 91–7, 121–4; and also above pp. 85–6.

[25] See pp. 88–9.

[26] C. Phythian-Adams, 'Records of the Craft Gilds', *Local Historian* ix (1970–1). S. Kramer, *The English Craft Gilds* (1927), gives leads to the sources for the history of many gilds and also has a good bibliography. For the archives of the London city companies, see L. J. Redstone and F. W. Steer, *Local Records* (1953), 147 sqq.

apprenticeship registers will also give information on the numbers coming into the gild, the methods of entry, and the social and geographical background of entrants. Apprentice indentures will give similar details and in addition will tell something of the conditions of training. At the Public Record Office are apprenticeship books (Class I.R. 1) for the period 1710 to 1811 which record names, addresses, and trades of masters, and names of apprentices (and to 1752 of their parents).[27]

From the sixteenth century much more detailed evidence for general aspects of local trade and industry than for earlier periods is available. The records already described – borough and gild records, quarter-sessions material, the state papers, domestic, the Privy Council registers – are particularly important at a time when the central government attempted more vigorously than before to regulate economic affairs. National legislation is, of course, for the same reason significant. As well as public, local, and private Acts, the journals of both Houses of Parliament should also be searched.[28] Chancery enrolled decrees (Class C.78) contain many details of trading activities.[29]

For the Stuart period, in particular, the patent rolls, at the Public Record Office, for which there are published calendars, contain the incorporations of monopoly companies and the text of all important grants to individuals, some of which may have local significance. Another convenient source of information for patent grants is the signet office docket books (P.R.O., Class S.O.3) for the period 1584 to 1874

---

[27] For some in print, see C. Dale (ed.), *Wiltshire Apprentices and their Masters, 1710–1760*, Wilts. Archaeological Soc. Records Branch xvii (1961). There are indexes to names: P.R.O., Class I.R.17 (1710–74).

[28] See pp. 20–3.

[29] See M. W. Beresford, 'The Decree Rolls of Chancery as a Source for Economic History, 1547–c.1700', *Ec.H.R.*, 2nd ser., xxxii (1979), 8–9 and the list referred to on p. 179 n. 66.

which record the essence of the grants. The index volumes (Class S.O.4) are not trustworthy.[30]

From the early modern period, too, the writings of topographers and travellers, and older histories, will contain much on the general economic history of localities.[31] Well-known general works are John Leland's *Itinerary* (a sixteenth-century work first published in 1710–12), William Smith's *Particular Description of England, 1588* (not published until 1879), Celia Fiennes's *Travels through England on a Side Saddle*,[32] Daniel Defoe's *A Tour Thro' the Whole Island of Great Britain* (1724–7, and many later editions), Pococke's *Travels* of the mid-eighteenth century,[33] and D. and S. Lysons's *Magna Britannia* (1808–22) which covers counties alphabetically from Bedfordshire to Devon. Older town histories, too, will have to be searched.

For general aspects of local economic history in more recent times there are many published records which the researcher should refer to before embarking on the investigation of unpublished records. The decennial censuses of population, which began in 1801, will give much information on local occupations, and so indirectly on local industries. So, too, will unpublished parish registers and census enumerators' books.[34]

[30] W. H. Price, *The English Patents of Monopoly* (1913), 146. See also J. W. Gordon, *Monopolies by Patents* (1897). For patents, see also below, pp. 131–2.

[31] See pp. 26–7.

[32] Late seventeenth century, but not published until 1888. A useful edition is that of C. Morris, *The Journeys of Celia Fiennes* (1947; 2nd edn 1949).

[33] Published as *The Travels through England of Dr Richard Pococke*, Camden Soc., NS., xlii, xliv (1888–9): particularly useful for smaller towns.

[34] See pp. 68–9. The sort of material they contain for the period up to 1951 is summarized in Office of Population Censuses and Surveys, *Guide to Census Reports: Great Britain, 1801–1966* (1977). See also R. Hall, 'Early Nineteenth Century Occupational Structures', *Local Historian* xi (1974–6); J. M. Bellamy, 'Occupational Statistics in the Nineteenth Century', in R.

The present century has the *Censuses of Production*, statistics prepared by the Board of Trade, for 1907, 1912, 1924, 1930, 1933, 1934, 1935, 1937, 1938, 1946, 1948, and annually from 1949. These provide such information as numbers of firms of different sizes, output of industries, numbers of employees, costs (including wages, materials and fuel, transport, etc.), investments, and building. These details do not, however, pertain to individual towns or counties, but to larger regions.[35]

Perhaps the most fruitful sources for local economic history in recent times are parliamentary papers. In this area of study, however, these publications are so numerous and multifarious in nature, that it is not easy to pick out any for particular attention. The local historian should search the official indexes to the parliamentary papers[36] looking particularly for references under the names of the towns or counties in which he is interested, under the industry or industries he knows to have been important there,[37] and under factory, poor-law, charity, trade unions, handloom weavers' commissions and reports, and under commissions investigating the health of towns, the employment of women and children, apprenticeship laws, and so on.

For individual business firms[38] a start may be made by

Lawton (ed.), *The Census and Social Structure* (1978); N. K. Buxton and D. I. Mackay, *British Employment Statistics* (1977).

[35] For full details, see Interdepartmental Committee on Social and Economic Research, *Guides to Official Sources, no. 6: Census of Production Reports* (H.M.S.O., 1961). See also W. A. Armstrong, 'The Classification of Occupation', in E. A. Wrigley (ed.), *Introduction to English Historical Demography* (1966), 272–3; Buxton and Mackay, *British Employment Statistics*.

[36] See p. 17 n. 43.

[37] E.g., for the silk industry: *Rep. Select Committee on the Petitions of Ribbon Weavers and Silk Manufacturers* (1818) ix; *Rep. Select Committee on the Present State of the Silk Trade* (1831–2) xix.

[38] Many histories of firms have been published. Articles, lists of titles, and reviews are to be found particularly in the journals *Business History* and

consulting certain rather obvious sources. The stock exchange year books have lists of quoted commercial and industrial firms, indicating who controls them, with some historical data.[39] The publication *Who Owns Whom* (English edn; annually from 1958) gives details for large firms of the group to which they belong, indicating which firms control others. The *Register of Defunct Companies*, published periodically from 1934 under the auspices of the Stock Exchange Council, contains lists of companies removed from the stock exchange year books since 1825. The majority of these are defunct companies removed as a result of liquidation or dissolution. In some cases, it must be noted, liquidation is followed by the registration of another company of the same or similar name, marking the reorganization of a firm which is defunct only in the legal sense.

Printed records on bankruptcy include W. Bailey, *List of Bankrupts, 1772–1793* (1794), and William Smith and Co., *List of Bankrupts, 1786–1806* (1806). Commissions of bankruptcy and details of the dissolution of partnerships are to be found in the *London Gazette*.[40] Lists of bankrupts derived from the *London Gazette* are to be found from 1832 in the *Law Journal* and from 1833 in the *Bankrupts' Register*.

Also useful in certain circumstances are references to patentees of inventions,[41] and here the records and publica-

---

Business Archives. See also bibliography in T. C. Barker, R. H. Campbell, P. Mathias, and B. S. Yamey, *Business History* (1960); J. M. Bellamy (ed.), *Yorkshire Business Histories: A Bibliography* (1970). References to some early firms are in W. R. Scott, *Joint Stock Companies to 1720* (1910–12).

[39] These have appeared under various titles: *Burdett's Official Intelligence* (1882–98); *Stock Exchange Official Intelligence* (1899–1933); *Stock Exchange Year Book* (1875–1933); *Stock Exchange Official Year Book* (from 1934). For records of provincial stock exchanges, see J. R. Killick and W. A. Thomas, 'The Provincial Stock Exchanges, 1830–1870', *Ec.H.R.*, 2nd ser., xxiii (1970). For the London Stock Exchange, see E. Victor Morgan and W. A. Thomas, *The Stock Exchange: Its History and Functions* (1969 edn), 285 sqq.

[40] Barker *et al.*, *Business History*, 13.

[41] See T. Daff, 'Patents as History', *Local Historian* ix (1970–1); F.

tions of the Patent Office (created following an Act of 1852) may be consulted. *The Alphabetical Index of Patentees of Inventions, 1617–1852* (1854);[42] the *Alphabetical Index of Patentees of Inventions* (annually for 1853–88); and the *Index to the Illustrated Official Journal (Patents)* (from 1890) are those to which reference should first be made.[43]

Other published sources include trade journals for the industries predominant in the locality. These may yield not only the names of firms and individuals, but details of their products, the size of factories, numbers of employees, annual balance sheets, and reports to shareholders. Some may contain historical articles and reminiscences. National and local trade directories, as well as general directories and local newspapers, will often provide a great deal of information on firms, shops, and on local economic activity generally.[44] The published transactions of professional bodies, such as, for example, the *Proceedings of the Institute of Mechanical Engineers*, may print descriptions of individual firms or factories.

Occasional publications by such local bodies as chambers of trade and commerce sometimes contain, besides advertisements, short histories of firms with perhaps numbers of

Newby, *How to Find Out about Patents* (1963); A. A. Gomme, *Patents of Invention: Origin and Growth of the Patent System in Britain* (1946); H. G. Fox, *Monopolies and Patents* (1947).

[42] Reprinted 1969, with corrections.

[43] Available at the Science Reference Library, British Library Reference Division (at Chancery Lane and also at Bayswater), and elsewhere. The B.L. catalogue lists other indexes. For the weekly and bi-weekly publications from which the above are compiled, see B. M. D. Smith, 'Patents for Invention: The National and Local Picture', *Business History* iv (1961–2). This article should be studied carefully by anyone wishing to investigate this aspect of economic history. For the records of the Patent Office, see *P.R.O. Guide* ii, 272 sqq.

[44] For examples of trade journals in an account of the Coventry cycle and motor industries, see W. B. Stephens, 'Cycle Manufacture', 'Motor-Cycle Manufacture', 'Motor Vehicle Manufacture', in V.C.H., *Warwickshire* viii (1969).

employees, size of output, and names of owners and directors. Local newspapers also include advertisements which are invaluable for many aspects of trade in the eighteenth and nineteenth centuries.

When published sources have been reviewed the local historian will have to seek the unpublished records of local firms. Some of these may be found in the national archives. Files of papers relating to all joint-stock companies registered under Acts of 1844 and 1856 exist in the Public Record Office. For the years 1844 to 1860, for companies defunct or still existing, these are in Class B.T.41. For such companies continuing in existence after 1860 but since dissolved the papers are in Class B.T.31 (files of dissolved companies).[45] The Registrar of Companies[46] has files of more recently defunct and of existing limited liability companies, and these are available for inspection. All these files contain information required by law, such as the articles of association, the names of directors, subscribers, and shareholders, financial data, reports and balance sheets, copies of contracts, and, in the case of dissolved companies, dissolution documents.

The Court of Bankruptcy records do not survive before 1710, though some conveyances of bankrupts' property were enrolled in the close rolls from 1571 onwards. The Public Record Office houses the Court of Bankruptcy's records from 1710 to the later nineteenth century,[47] the remainder

[45] For indexes and details, see *Public Record Office Records of Interest to Social Scientists, 1919 to 1939: Introduction*, ed. B. Swann and M. Turnbull (1971), 71. See also P.R.O., Class B.T.34 (dissolved companies, liquidation accounts, 1890–1932). After 1932 these are found in Class B.T.31.

[46] Companies House, Cardiff.

[47] For details, see *P.R.O. Guide* i, 166–7. For other bankruptcy records, see *ibid.* 173; ii, 271. Class B.1 (order books in bankruptcy) (1710–1868) is indexed and sometimes gives the nature of the business before bankruptcy in some detail. Class B.3 contains the extant files of the Commissioners of Bankruptcy (c. 1780–1842) and is also indexed. For more detail on the P.R.O. bankruptcy classes, see S. Marriner, 'Accounting Records in English Bankruptcy Proceedings to 1850', *Accounting History* iii (1978); S.

being still with the court itself.[48] P.R.O., Class
C.217/58–188 (Chancery petty bag office, miscellaneous
papers, etc.) also contains bankruptcy records which include
the records of some business firms for the period
1774–1830.[49] Some Chancery and Exchequer records contain
details of law cases in which firms and individuals were
involved. The Exchequer records include bills and answers
(Class E.112), 'depositions taken by commission' from witnesses (Class E.134, arranged under counties),[50] and 'exhibits' (i.e. documents produced in a suit) (Class E.140). The
Chancery records include the series 'Masters' exhibits'
(Classes C.103–114) and proceedings (bills, answers, and
depositions) (Classes C.5–13).[51] Exchequer extents and inquisitions relating to Crown debtors (Class E.144) contains
for the period 1685–1842 a series of portfolios which include
valuations of debtors' houses and contents. These are a very
fruitful source but unfortunately there is no topographical
index. They are, however, chronologically arranged.[52] Class
E.145, Exchequer extents and inquisitions into excise for
1800–c.1830 contain similar material. Class E.167 contains
the records of the eighteenth and early nineteenth centuries of
proceedings by the attorney general against Crown
debtors.[53]

Marriner, 'English Bankruptcy Records and Statistics before 1850',
Ec.H.R., 2nd ser., xxxiii (1980).   [48] Barker *et al.*, *Business History*, 13.

[49] There is an index: *List of Records of Chancery: Petty Bag Office to 1842*,
List and Index Soc. xxv (1967), 113 sqq., q.v. also (pp. 123 sqq.) for a
'Catalogue of Business Records in Chancery Miscellaneous Papers, Exhi-
bits, etc.'.   [50] For calendars and lists, see *P.R.O. Guide* i, 57, 66.

[51] For a full description of these records, see *P.R.O. Guide* i, 32 sqq.,
which lists calendars. See also the appropriate records of the County
Palatinates of Durham and Chester and the Duchy of Lancaster; and
Barker *et al.*, *Business History*.

[52] I am indebted to Professor L. S. Pressnell for drawing my attention to
these records.

[53] T. Rath, 'Business Records in the Public Record Office in the Age of
the Industrial Revolution', *Business History* xvii (1975).

For earlier periods wills, and more particularly, probate inventories of business men, may provide a great deal of information. These have been dealt with elsewhere.[54]

The domestic records of individual firms are to be found with solicitors, and in local depositories, as well as, of course, with existing firms themselves.[55] Where they exist and are available no local historian dealing with commerce and industry can ignore them. Such records are miscellaneous in nature, but often include[56] minute books recording meetings of directors and shareholders. Many of these, particularly for later periods, may be rather formal, and they tend to be most useful for the period before 1870. Usually there will also be correspondence. Copies of 'out' letters were kept in books, while 'in' letters are in files or bundles. If not heavily weeded correspondence may prove a most fruitful source. Account books, too, can be mines of information. Of these, books of original entry (called rough books, waste books, day books, journals, etc.) record daily transactions. There may be separate books dealing with sales, purchases, consignments, and so on. In cash books were

[54] See pp. 62–5.

[55] The whereabouts of particular business records may sometimes be traced through the *Sources of Business History in the National Register of Archives* (annually, 1964–72) and the Business Archives Council (Dominion House, 37–45 Tooley St, London Bridge, London SE1), which keeps a register. The Council's journal, *Business Archives*, contains, from time to time, references to regional surveys of business records. Some deposits of records of business and trade associations are listed in *Guide to the Modern Records Centre* (University of Warwick Library, 1977).

[56] The following is based largely on Barker *et al.*, *Business History*; 'The Publication of Business Records', *Archives* i (1949–52); W. H. Chaloner, 'Business Records as a Source of Economic History', *Jnl of Documentation* iv (1948–9). See also: *History from Business Records* (Council for the Preservation of Business Records, 1937); P. L. Payne, 'Business Archives and Economic History: The Case for Regional Studies', *Archives* vi (1963–9); A. W. Coats, 'The Value of Business Archives to the Economic Historian', *Aslib Proceedings* xiii (1961). For banks, see *Survey of the Records of British Banking* (Historical Manuscripts Comm. 1980).

entered receipts and expenditures, and they may summarize more detailed books such as wages and freight books. The information in the books of original entry is generally summarized in ledgers.[57]

Among other financial records may well be bank statements, investment and insurance records, audited accounts, invoices, and receipts. There may also be books containing inventories of stock, prospectuses, trade circulars, apprenticeship indentures, and legal records of various kinds, such as partnership deeds, lists of shareholders, and contracts. Most important are the annual reports which were usually also published in local newspapers and trade journals. Professional diaries, if available, may also be useful.

Apart from insurance policies to be found among business papers and bundles of deeds, the fire insurance registers compiled by the insurance companies and their local agents mainly from the early eighteenth century provide a remarkably rich, and so far relatively unexplored, source for the local historian.[58] The register details usually include the number and date of the policy, the name of the policy holder and his occupation, and an inventory of the property insured, with its insurance valuation. Alone, or, better, in conjunction with other evidence, they can throw a great deal of light on many aspects of local economic history (for many are concerned with industrial and commercial property), as well as on local topography and building history.[59]

---

[57] For financial accounts, see Barker *et al.*, *Business History*, 30 sqq.

[58] See J. H. Thomas, 'Fire Insurance Policy Registers', *History* liii (1968); L. M. Wilcko, 'Fire Insurance Policies as a Source of Local History', *Local Historian* ix (1970); S. D. Chapman, 'Business History from Insurance Policy Registers', *Business Archives* xxxii (1970); S. D. Chapman (ed.), *The Devon Cloth Industry in the Eighteenth Century: Sun Fire Office Inventories of Merchants' and Manufacturers' Property, 1726–1770*, Devon and Cornwall Record Soc., NS, xxiii (1978), introduction.

[59] For work based on the registers, see Thomas, 'Fire Insurance Policy Registers', bibliography; and, e.g., S. D. Chapman, 'Fixed Capital Formation in the British Cotton Industry, 1770–1815', *Ec.H.R.*, 2nd ser., xxiii

The register entries can be used to investigate the owners, lessees, and sub-tenants of individual buildings, and, collectively, the distribution of ownership and tenantship in, say, particular local industries at certain times. They indicate the site of the insured buildings, very often with reference to adjoining property, and are thus of interest to the topographer. They provide for the historian interested in local building history an indication of the size of buildings, the dates of erection, and the materials of which they were constructed. Sometimes industrialists built tenements for their workmen and this is also discoverable.

Where substantial numbers of policies exist for an area for a particular period they will provide evidence of the topographical distribution of different industries, the extent to which individuals diversified their occupations, the extent and nature of partnerships, the occupational structure of specific industries, and so on. The registers are particularly valuable for the study of the scale of the business unit, measured in terms of fixed capital, in the form of building and plant. They can show the ownership of such fixed capital and its value,[60] the types of machines and other plant used or newly introduced, and the different sorts of buildings and their industrial function. The adding of extra policies to cover additional buildings or plant may give an indication of the growth of an enterprise, and times of prosperity and expansion in a local industry. Where merchants owned property in different places a clue may be given to such matters as their channels of distribution of goods. Some information will be provided, too, on the type of stock kept, but it should be noted that this kind of capital was generally undervalued, and some not insured at all. The calculation of total assets is,

(1970); N. B. Harte and K. G. Ponting (eds.), *Textile History and Economic History* (1973), 113–37, 247–80; D. T. Jenkins, *The West Riding Wool Textile Industry, 1770–1838: A Study of Fixed Capital Formation* (1975).

[60] But for the basis of valuation, see Chapman (ed.), *Devon Cloth Industry*, pp. x sqq.

however, not possible since trade credits, an important component of working capital, were not at risk by fire and so not insured.

The largest collection of registers, including those of the Sun Fire Company, the Royal Exchange, and London Assurance, are at Guildhall Library, London. The Phoenix Assurance Company retains its registers, which may nevertheless be consulted by students.[61] The available registers are both numerous and bulky, and a great drawback to their use lies in the fact that entries, although usually chronological, are in most cases unindexed.[62] For those at Guildhall there is, however, a catalogue giving the dates covered by each volume.

It is possible that for certain industries the study of physical remains may be significant.[63] The size of buildings, for example, may in some cases indicate crudely the scale of the enterprise, and the nature of buildings and machinery may

[61] There is a very useful guide to the existence and whereabouts of insurance (including fire insurance) records: H. A. L. Cockerell and E. Green, *Survey of the Records of British Insurance* (Historical Manuscripts Commission, 1976), reprinted in somewhat less detail in H. A. L. Cockerell and E. Green, *The British Insurance Business, 1547–1970: An Introduction and Guide to Historial Records in the United Kingdom* (1976).

[62] For advice on searching for policies for particular localities, however, see M. W. Beresford, 'Building History from Fire Insurance Records', *Urban History Yearbook* (1976). An index (by name, place, and occupation) of the main eighteenth-century registers is being (1980) prepared under the auspices of the Social Science Research Council.

[63] See J. Tann, 'Sources for Industrial History: 1: Archaeology and the Factory', *Local Historian* ix (1970–1); R. Chaplin, 'Discovering Lost Ironworks and other Industrial Remains of the Early Modern Period', *ibid.*; J. Tann, 'Industrial Archaeology and the Business Historian', *Business Archives* xxxi (1969); J. R. Harris, 'Industrial Archaeology and its Future', *Business History* xii (1970); N. Cossons and K. Hudson, *Industrial Archaeologists' Guide, 1971–3* (1971). Also useful are J. P. M. Pannell (ed.), *The Techniques of Industrial Archaeology* (1974); J. K. Major, *Fieldwork in Industrial Archaeology* (1975). M. Rix, *Industrial Archaeology* (1967), has a select bibliography. N.b. the journal *Industrial Archaeology*.

throw light on industrial processes. At its best industrial archaeology can contribute much information (especially on trades and crafts, technical processes, fixed capital, and the life of those engaged in such activities) that is not obtainable from documentary sources. At its worst it threatens to become the new antiquarianism.

Many towns have at one time or another possessed co-operative societies, and although many of their business records are similar to those of other firms, the political and social interests of the co-operative movement have given rise to special collections. At the library of the Co-operative Union Ltd, Holyoake House, Manchester, are the Robert Owen correspondence (1821–58), and the G. J. Holyoake collection (from 1835); at the Goldsmiths' Library of Economic Literature, University of London, are many journals and broadsheets including the William Pare collection of press cuttings for the 1820s and 1830s; at the Bishopsgate Institute, London, are another Holyoake collection and the George Howell papers; and there are other collections at the Co-operative College near Loughborough, the Manchester Central Reference Library, and the Plunkett Foundation for Co-operative Studies (31 St Giles, Oxford).[64]

SEA-GOING TRADE AND SHIPPING

The records of sea-going trade and shipping concern mainly the historian of port towns and of areas whose industries were particularly concerned with exports and imports. They are so vast that only the more important can be touched on here.[65]

[64] R. G. Garnett, 'Records of Early Co-operation with Particular Reference to Pre-Rochdale Consumer Co-operation', *Local Historian* ix (1970–1), q.v. (pp. 169–71) for a list of contemporary journals containing material on early co-operation, of contemporary pamphlets and broadsheets, and of contemporary books and records.

[65] For further information, see especially: G. N. Clark and B. M. Franks, *Guide to English Commercial Statistics, 1696–1782* (1938) (which does touch

For earlier periods local sources such as local government records, the archives of individuals and firms, and the records of gilds, are useful. In port towns the local borough council minutes[66] usually contain much about the state of trade and matters affecting the business of the port, together with details concerning dock facilities and the like. Because many boroughs had the right to levy local taxes and dues on shipping and on the movement of goods there may be fiscal records of considerable value to the local historian of trade. The most important of these imposts were petty or local customs duties.[67] These varied in nature from port to port, sometimes falling on imports only, sometimes on exports as well. Certain of them, as at Southampton, were levied on land as well as sea traffic.

The financial records of the collectors of these dues may be very helpful in illustrating and quantifying the nature and volume of the trade of a port, especially where there are gaps in the national customs records (see below). The best local accounts record the names of ships, of exporters and importers, and the details of the cargo and of the duty paid. Since

---

on records before 1696); S. H. Palmer, *Economic Arithmetic: A. Guide to the Statistical Sources of English Commerce, Industry and Finance, 1700–1850* (1977); R. C. Jarvis, 'Sources for the History of Ports', *Jnl of Transport History* iii (1957–8); R. C. Jarvis, 'Sources for the History of Ships and Shipping', *ibid.*; R. Davis, 'Shipping Records', *Archives* vii (1965–6); J. B. Harley, 'Marine Charts', *Local Historian* viii (1968–9); P. Mathias and A. W. H. Pearsall (eds.), *Shipping: A Survey of Historical Records* (1971). Useful for commodities are R. E. Zupko, *Dictionary of English Weights and Measures* (1968); R. E. Zupko, *British Weights and Measures* (1977); P. Grierson, *English Linear Measures* (1972).

[66] See pp. 85–6.

[67] N. S. B. Gras, *The Early English Customs System* (1918), 21–6 and (for examples) 153–99; H. S. Cobb, 'Local Port Customs Accounts prior to 1550', in F. Ranger (ed.), *Prisca Munimenta* (1973), q.v. for a survey of these records for individual ports. For a printed example, see H. S. Cobb, *The Local Port Book of Southampton for 1439–40*, Southampton Record Ser. v (1961). Others have been published.

freemen of the port town were usually exempt from the duties, some accounts omit to record their shipments thus detracting from the value of the accounts. In some ports, however, as at Exeter, the details of exempt shipments were nevertheless entered in the accounts. Yet in most cases it must be admitted that records of local customs duties do not provide the historian with such great detail as the Exchequer port books, described below. They do not, for example, indicate the direction of trade, and it is difficult to distinguish coastal from overseas trade. On the other hand the fact that coastal traffic was included may be significant since this traffic was not recorded in the national customs accounts until the mid-sixteenth century.

Similar local accounts sometimes exist recording the collection of harbour and port dues of various kinds. These may show the number of ships and their tonnage entering or leaving a port. Receipts over a period may show upward or downward trends and reflect the state of prosperity of a port. Sometimes duties such as these were collected with the local or petty customs duties and may be recorded in the same account rolls or books.

Other local materials which may yield information on this topic are quarter-sessions records,[68] and the records of harbour officials, which may include plans of docks. In more recent times the records of dock committees of borough councils and their successors may be fruitful.[69]

Local vice-admiralty court records sometimes exist, as they do at Exeter. The minute books of these courts are full of vital information in cases of shipping disputes, insurance, matters of salvage, prizes, and so on. The ownership of vessels, types of goods, methods of marketing cargoes, size of ships, information on crews, including wages, salvagers, and piracy, are all matters on which very detailed

[68] See pp. 91–2.
[69] Jarvis, 'Sources for the History of Ports', 89–91.

information may be culled from these records if they survive.[70]

In local depositories are most likely to be found merchants' letters and account books and diaries, and the records of companies involved in sea-going trade. Probate inventories of individual merchants will also be valuable.[71] In larger ports in the early modern period there were local regulated companies such as the York Merchant Venturers, the Exeter French Company,[72] and the Bristol Merchant Venturers,[73] some of which have left records similar to those of other gilds.[74] Records of national joint-stock and regulated companies, such as the Merchant Adventurers, may also contain local information.[75]

The local historian of trade must, however, inevitably regard the fiscal records of the central government as his basic source. In using them he should distinguish between details referring to a whole port (that is, the head port of each group of ports supervised by a particular customs establishment, together with its member ports and creeks) and those referring to an individual port in the group. For example, the port of Plymouth included all the Cornish ports, so that

[70] Cf. W. B. Stephens, *Seventeenth Century Exeter* (1958), 186. Some ports had exemption and the right to hold their own admiralty courts, the records of which provide similar information; see, e.g., E. Welch (ed.), *The Admiralty Court Book of Southampton, 1566–1588*, Southampton Record Ser. xiii (1968).   [71] See pp. 62–5.

[72] W. B. Stephens, 'Merchant Companies and Commercial Policy in Exeter, 1625–88', *Transactions of the Devonshire Assoc.* lxxxvi (1954); W. B. Stephens, 'The Officials of the French Company of Exeter in the Early Seventeenth Century', *Devon and Cornwall Notes and Queries* xxviii (1957).

[73] P. McGrath (ed.), *Records Relating to the Society of Merchant Venturers of the City of Bristol in the Seventeenth Century*, Bristol Record Soc. xvii (1952).

[74] See pp. 127–8.

[75] See, e.g., W. E. Lingelbach, *The Merchant Adventurers of England* (1902); F. W. Dendy and J. R. Boyle, *Extracts from the Records of the Merchant Adventurers of Newcastle-upon-Tyne*, Surtees Soc., xciii, ci (1895, 1899).

figures for 'Plymouth' may be for the whole group, or merely for Plymouth itself.[76]

For the period to the mid-sixteenth century the most important of these fiscal sources are the particulars of customs accounts, and the enrolled customs accounts, at the Public Record Office.[77]

The particulars of accounts (Class E.122), covering the period from Edward I to 1565,[78] are forerunners of the Exchequer port books dealt with below, and usually (except in the case of some early years) record for each port, in rolls or occasionally books, the arrival and departure of ships by

[76] See H. Crouch, *A Complete View of the British Customs* (1724), 247–50; Gras, *Early English Customs System*; E. E. Hoon, *The Organization of the English Customs System, 1696–1786* (1938); P.R.O., *Descriptive List of Exchequer, Queen's Remembrancer, Port Books, Part I, 1565–1700*, ed. N. J. Williams (1960); J. H. Andrews, 'Two Problems in the Interpretation of the Port Books', *Ec.H.R.*, 2nd ser., ix (1956). For a list of ports, creeks, and landing places in 1575, see P.R.O., S.P.12/135/1.

[77] Until the mid-sixteenth century for the ports of the counties of Chester, Lancaster, Cumberland, and Cornwall, and of Wales, the royal customs collected are not usually recorded in these series but are to be found in the records of the exchequers of the Palatinate of Chester, the Duchy of Cornwall, and the Principality of Wales: E. M. Carus-Wilson and O. Coleman, *England's Export Trade, 1275–1547* (1963), 8. For the Welsh ports, see E. A. Lewis in *Y Cymmrodor* xxiv (1913); for Chester, K. P. Wilson (ed.), *Chester Customs Accounts, 1301–1556*, Record Soc. of Lancs. and Ches. cxi (1969). The returns for the Cornish ports are in P.R.O., ministers' accounts, Duchy of Cornwall (Class S.C.6). See also H. S. Cobb, 'The Medieval Royal Customs and their Records', *Jnl Soc. Archivists* vi (1979).

[78] After 1565 they contain only miscellaneous material, of which tunnage (wine) rolls may be the most valuable. For an index, see *Exchequer K.R. Customs Accounts (E.122)*, List and Index Soc., xliii (1969), lx (1970). Examples are printed in Gras, *Early English Customs System*; H. J. Smit, *Bronnen tot de Geschiedenis van den Handel met Engeland, Schotland, en Ierland, 1485–1585*, Rijksgeschiedkundige Publicatien, lxxxvi, xci (1942, 1950) (which reproduces also many other records concerning British trade); E. M. Carus-Wilson, *The Overseas Trade of Bristol in the Later Middle Ages*, Bristol Record Soc. vii (1937), q.v. (pp. 7–9) for a description of the accounts.

name, the names of their masters, their home ports, the names of exporters and importers, and details of the goods concerned (with their official values), and the duty paid.

The enrolled accounts (Class E.356) cover the period from Edward I to the early years of James I,[79] and are short summaries of the particulars of accounts (above) and of the port books (below), and record the total customs dues collected on goods paying specific duties (e.g., wool and cloth) and on goods paying *pro rata* (usually 5 per cent of their customs' valuation). The substance of some of the enrolled accounts are readily available in print.[80]

In Elizabeth I's reign the basis of the customs duties was changed by a new Book of Rates. From then the most useful sources are the declared accounts and the Exchequer port books.

The declared customs accounts (Classes E.351 and A.O.1)[81] are accounts of farmers, commissioners, and collectors of the customs from 1534 to modern times, giving the yield and other details of different types of duties at various ports.[82] In using them it is necessary to be aware that they are

[79] *P.R.O. Guide* i incorrectly states that they end in Elizabeth I's time.

[80] G. Schanz, *Englische Handels-politik gegen ende des Mittelalters* ii (1881), gives money totals collected from various types of duties in individual ports, and also some totals of quantities of goods exported and imported (e.g., cloth). All are for Henry VIII's reign, except for wool exports for Henry VII's reign. Figures for individual headports for 1399–1482 are published in E. Power and M. Postan (eds.), *Studies in English Trade in the Fifteenth Century* (1933), 330–60. For specimens, see Carus-Wilson, *Overseas Trade of Bristol* (q.v., pp. 9–12, for a description of the records). Carus-Wilson and Coleman, *England's Export Trade*, prints totals for all the ports for wool and cloth exports. References to other accounts in print are in *ibid.* 5–6.

[81] E. 351/607–1268. See *List and Index of the Declared Accounts*, P.R.O., Lists and Indexes ii (1893).

[82] For the years 1689–1714 they are printed, port by port, in the introductions to the *Calendars of Treasury Books*. For an example of the use of these records, see W. B. Stephens, 'The Cloth Exports of the Provincial Ports, 1600–40', *Ec.H.R.*, 2nd ser., xxii (1969).

of two types: cash accounts and general accounts. The cash account is a statement of amounts actually paid into the exchequer after deductions of expenses, salaries, etc. The general account is a statement of sums actually received in the port concerned and is therefore the one the investigator of the volume of trade should seek.[83]

The Exchequer port books (Class E. 190)[84] are for the early modern period the most important source for the history of local overseas trade.[85] They exist in large numbers for many ports for the period from 1565 to 1799 although some ports ceased to return them to the exchequer in the mid-eighteenth century. For many ports, too, there are considerable gaps for the years of the Civil War and Interregnum. For the eighteenth century the existence of the Inspector General's ledgers, described below, make the port books less important.

The books fall mainly into two categories, with about equal numbers extant in each. First, there are those which record details of goods sent to or imported from overseas countries (including the colonies, Scotland, Ireland, and the Channel Isles). Second, there are books which deal with

[83] R. C. Jarvis, 'The Archival History of the Customs Records', *Jnl Soc. Archivists* i (1955–9), 242–3.

[84] The books for individual ports may be traced through P.R.O., *Descriptive List of Exchequer, Queen's Remembrancer, Port Books, Part I, 1565–1700,* ed. N. J. Williams (1960); *Exchequer Port Books, 1701–1798: Part I, East Coast: Berwick to Yarmouth; Part II, South-East, South and South-West Coasts: Ipswich to Barnstaple; Part III, South-West and West Coasts: Plymouth to Carlisle,* List and Index Soc., lviii, lxvi, lxxx (1970, 1971, 1972). A few port books are incorrectly filed in Class E.122.

[85] D. M. Woodward, 'Port Books', *History* lv (1970); W. B. Stephens, 'The Exchequer Port Books as a Source for the History of the English Cloth Trade', *Textile History* i (1969), q.v. (p. 213) for a bibliography of works concerned with and based on the port books; Clark and Franks, *English Commercial Statistics,* 52–6; Jarvis, 'Sources for the History of Ports'. W. E. Minchinton (ed.), *The Growth of English Overseas Trade in the Seventeenth and Eighteenth Centuries* (1969), 184, lists other works on the port books as a source.

coastal trade. For every port several overseas books were issued each year for completion by different officials. In most ports there were usually three books per year, one to be completed by the customer or collector, another by the controller, and a third by the searcher. For the larger ports each official sometimes had two books, one for exports and one for imports, and this became increasingly common after the Restoration. The information entered in the first two books was usually identical, and the searchers' books also contain much of the same information. Since it is unusual for all three books to have survived intact for any one year, the existence of one may be sufficient for the historian's purposes, or he may be able to obtain the information lacking in one book, because of illegible or missing pages, from another of the same year. For London there were in addition separate surveyors' and waiters' books, and sometimes surveyors' books exist for provincial ports.[86]

The coastal books were often jointly those of the controller and customer, though for London and sometimes provincial ports there were increasingly, as time went on, separate books for each of these officials and also searchers' books. Very occasionally, for the less important ports, books exist which combine details of coastal and overseas trade, though these details are entered in different parts of the books.

Most overseas books give a date against the ship. This is sometimes the date of arrival or departure, or sometimes the date the duties were paid. They also give the name of the importing or exporting ship; the tonnage of the ship (not to be taken as the tonnage of the cargo); the name of the master of the vessel; especially from 1600, the name of the foreign port for which the ship was initially destined or from which it had recently arrived (often for extra-European destinations

---

[86] For the duties of the various officers, see Hoon, *English Customs System*. For the special case of the London port books, see N. J. Williams, 'The London Port Books', *Transactions of the London and Middx. Archaeological Soc.* xviii (1955).

specific ports are not mentioned, but 'New England', 'the Azores', 'the Atlantic Isles', and so on, are given); the names of the merchants paying the duties for the imports or exports; and occasionally the home town of the merchant where this differed from the port town. Sometimes the words 'and partners' or 'and company' occur after the merchant's name, and it was usually stated whether they were natives or aliens (who paid higher duties). Then follow details of the goods, and the duties paid.

No duties were payable on coastal trade which was open only to indigenous merchants. Apart from lacking the money columns, however, many coastal books contain much the same sort of information as the overseas books. The purpose of the coastal books was really to record the taking of bonds and the issue of certificates or cockets to ensure that the goods went to the English or Welsh port declared and not overseas.

The chief criticism of the use of the port books has been that work based on them failed to take into account smuggling[87] or customs inefficiency and corruption,[88] but historians now generally regard these records with less suspicion than they previously did.[89]

The Exchequer records also contain many series concerning the collection of specific duties[90] and the Chancery

[87] See, e.g., Clark and Franks, *English Commercial Statistics*, 52–6; N. J. Williams, 'Francis Shaxton and the Elizabethan Port Books', *E.H.R.* lxvi (1951). Cases of detected smuggling may, however, be traced in the Exchequer (K.R.) memoranda rolls (P.R.O., Class E.159): see Stephens, *Seventeenth Century Exeter*, pp. xxi–xxv; Carus-Wilson, *Overseas Trade of Bristol*, 12. There are manuscript indexes to these rolls in the P.R.O.

[88] This may not have been serious for heavily taxed imports in the eighteenth century: P. Deane and W. A. Cole, *British Economic Growth, 1688–1959* (1967 edn), 45.

[89] See, e.g., T. S. Willan, *A Tudor Book of Rates* (1962), pp. xvii–xviii, xlviii.

[90] E.g. the pretermitted duties on cloth: see Stephens, 'Cloth Exports, 1600–40'; W. B. Stephens, 'The Overseas Trade of Chester in the early

records may also yield much information on the trade and shipping of a port.[91] The P.R.O. guides and indexes should be searched for these.

The Public Record Office also houses the records of the High Court of Admiralty and these may reveal information of a similar nature to that noted above for the vice-admiralty courts,[92] especially for the period from 1525. Most useful are the Classes H.C.A.24 (libels and answers), H.C.A.13 (examinations), H.C.A.15–20 (instance papers), H.C.A.23 (interrogatories), and H.C.A.30 (miscellanea).[93] Libels and answers contain accusations and refutations of those involved in the law cases; examinations and interrogatories record evidence given on both sides; instance papers contain documents presented as evidence in the cases, often business letters and accounts; and the miscellanea have within them ships' accounts and logs.

The records of the Board of Customs and Excise are also important.[94] The Inspector General's ledgers of imports and

17th Century', *Transactions of the Historic Soc. of Lancs. and Ches.* cxx (1968).

[91] See, e.g., Carus-Wilson, *Overseas Trade of Bristol*, 13–15; D. A. Gardiner (ed.), *A Calendar of Early Chancery Proceedings relating to West Country Shipping, 1388–1493*, Devon and Cornwall Record Soc., NS, xxi (1976). Cf. *List of Early Chancery Proceedings*, i, ii, P.R.O., Lists and Indexes, xii, xvi (1901, 1903).

[92] See pp. 141–2.

[93] For accounts of the court and its records, see *P.R.O. Guide* i, 156–62; C. M. Andrews, *Guide to the Materials for American History to 1783 in the Public Record Office of Great Britain*, Carnegie Institution of Washington, Publication no. 90A (1912–14) ii, 304 sqq. For an index, see *Records of the High Court of Admiralty*, List and Index Soc. xxvii (1967). See also D. O. Shilton and R. Holworth (eds.), *High Court of Admiralty Examinations (MS. Volume 53) 1637–8* (Anglo-American Records Foundation, 1932); R. G. Marsden (ed.), *Select Pleas in the Court of Admiralty*, Selden Soc., vi, xi (1892, 1897).

[94] For those in the P.R.O. there is an index: *List of the Records of the Board of Customs and Excise since 1697*, List and Index Soc. xx (1967).

exports (1696–1780) show the types and amounts of goods classified under London and the outports (P.R.O., Class Customs 3).[95] There are, however, problems in interpreting these records, which, because of the way they were compiled, reveal changes in quantities rather than in values.[96] The Class Customs 17 consists of annual statistical tables which give the number of vessels (with tonnages) registered in individual British ports and the accounts of ships entering or leaving the ports. For the later nineteenth century Classes Customs 23–6 give port abstracts of imports and exports. Records of the Board of Trade at the Public Record Office (especially in Class B.T.1) include letters and petitions from merchants and others for the period 1791 to 1863.[97]

The catalogues of the British Library manuscripts are also worth searching for material on trade and shipping and on general information about the fortunes of individual ports. The complementary Additional MSS. 11255 and 11256, for example, provide statistics (for each outport in England and Wales, and in some cases for London) of tonnages of ships employed in various aspects of trade (coastal and foreign) and in fishing in years between 1709 and 1782.

At the Custom House Library, London,[98] are other customs records. Runs of minute and letter books belonging to the central customs organization throw light on the trade of

---

[95] See Clark and Franks, *English Commercial Statistics*, 1 sqq., for the value and use of these records. This work also has (pp. 153 sqq.) a list of published abstracts from them (e.g. from the *Lords Journals*, *Commons Journals*, *Manuscripts of the House of Lords*, parliamentary papers, etc.) and of unpublished abstracts in the B.L., P.R.O., Custom House, Bodleian Library, etc. For format of the originals and comment, see T. S. Ashton's introduction to E. B. Schumpeter, *English Overseas Trade Statistics, 1697–1808* (1960).

[96] Minchinton (ed.), *Growth of Overseas Trade*, 54; Ashton, in Schumpeter, *English Overseas Trade*, 1–9.

[97] Some are indexed: Rath, 'Business Records'.

[98] King's Beam House, Mark Lane, London EC3.

individual ports.[99] In addition there are local customs establishments' records transferred to London in 1958.[100] These pertain mainly to the period from the early or mid-eighteenth century. The most valuable to the local historian are letter books recording the correspondence of local officials to the Board of Commissioners in London. These provide details of the nature of the trade of a port, some idea of its value, as well as evidence of the prosperity of local industries, and, of course, of the administration of the port. Parallel with and supplementary to these are letters and orders received from the Board of Commissioners. For some ports (King's Lynn, Harwich, Penzance, Southampton, Portsmouth, Cowes) a continuous series of 'in' and 'out' letters exist for a period of 150–200 years, mainly from the late seventeenth century onwards. Other correspondence was kept in separate letter books and was of a miscellaneous nature largely concerning non-fiscal matters such as wrecks, manning of ships, and so on. These and another class of local customs records, the establishment records, will be of less value to the historian of trade than the others described. The establishment records, concerning the customs personnel employed in the port, may, however, have a bearing on the efficiency and honesty of the customs service and, therefore, on the validity of their fiscal records.

Another category of customs records is still kept at the

[99] For a list, see Jarvis, 'Archival History of the Customs Records', 246–7. For a survey of the records preserved at the Custom House and elsewhere (not entirely accurate), see *Second Rep. R. Commission on Public Records* (1914) ii, 239–48. For examples, see G. G. Dixon, 'Notes on the Records of the Custom House, London', *E.H.R.* xxxiv (1919).

[100] The following is largely based on Jarvis, 'Archival History of the Customs Records'; R. C. Jarvis, 'Local Archives of H.M. Customs', *Bulletin of the Soc. of Local Archivists* ix (1952); R. C. Jarvis, 'H.M. Customs and Excise', in R. Staveley (ed.), *Government Information and the Research Worker* (1952); H. Hall, *Repertory of British Archives, Part I: England* (1920), 169, 179–252; E. A. Carson, 'The Customs Records of the Kent Ports – A Survey', *Jnl Soc. Archivists* iv (1970).

individual ports.[101] This consists of registers of property rights in ships, from which may be traced construction details, masters' names, and the ownership of the ships throughout their existence.[102] From 1698 ships engaged in the colonial trade had to be registered; from 1786 the requirement was applied to all ships except the smallest. The ships were registered at their home ports and the system is still in force.[103] Crew lists and agreements which give not only information on crews but on vessels and their voyages (but not of cargo) exist, though culled and dispersed.[104]

Apart from the statutory registration of vessels there is also a voluntary register known as Lloyd's Registry of Shipping. The extant records of Lloyd's Registry, arranged by ports, are deposited at the National Maritime Museum, Greenwich, and mainly provide details of insured ships.[105] Some of the

---

[101] But permission to view should be made through King's Beam House. For the names of the ports at which these records are kept and their availability see, Jarvis, 'Sources for the History of Ships', 221–3.

[102] Clark and Franks, *English Commercial Statistics*, 41–51; G. E. Farr, *Records of Bristol Ships, 1800–1838*, Bristol Record Soc. xv (1950), 13–16. For examples, see Farr, *Records*; R. Craig and R. Jarvis, *Liverpool Registry of Merchant Ships* (1967); G. E. Farr, 'Custom House Ship Registers of the West Country', in H. E. S. Fisher (ed.), *The South-West and the Sea*, Exeter Papers in Economic History (1968); R. C. Jarvis, 'British Ship Registry: The Quantification of Source Material', in H. E. S. Fisher (ed.), *Ports and Shipping in the South-West*, Exeter Papers in Economic History (1971) (provides references to shipping statistics for the various ports in records at the B.L. and elsewhere for the period *c.* 1707); see also R. Davis, *The Rise of the English Shipping Industry in the Seventeenth and Eighteenth Centuries* (1962), 401–6.

[103] Now maintained by the Dept of Trade and Industry. Copies of local entries are at the P.R.O. (since 1971). See Jarvis, 'Sources for the History of Ships', for other lists of shipping in various ports. Recently work has begun at the National Maritime Museum, Greenwich, on a central index of the information in the registers.

[104] For their whereabouts, see K. Matthews, 'Crew Lists, Agreements and Official Logs', *Business History* xvi (1972).

[105] Jarvis, 'Sources for the History of Ships', 224–5.

details were, however, published. The annual *Lloyd's Register of Ships* (the so-called Green Book) issued by a Society of Underwriters from 1704–6 to 1833, and the annual *New Register Book of Shipping* (the so-called Red Book), published by a Committee of Shipowners from 1799 to 1833, amalgamated as *Lloyd's Register of British and Foreign Shipping* (later *Lloyd's Register of Shipping*) which was issued from 1834 and is still in progress. This gives names of vessels, construction details, their owners, masters, home ports, tonnages, and normal places traded with. *Lloyd's List* (1726–1884, and from 1914; and as *Shipping Gazette and Lloyd's List*, 1884–1914), originally weekly, can be searched for details of shipping arriving at the main ports.

From 1820 to 1853 the Board of Trade's *Tables of the Revenue, Population, Commerce, etc. of the United Kingdom*, and after that the *Annual Statement of Trade and Navigation*, also give details of shipping.[106] For the nineteenth century printed daily shipping lists or weekly or bi-weekly intelligencers (often called bills of entry) exist recording the details of vessels doing business in a port.[107]

For the period from 1855 the Customs and Excise have published in one form or another monthly and annual statistics of British trade including statistics of the trade of individual ports. The annual reports of the Commissioners are parliamentary papers.[108] Other parliamentary papers throwing light on local sea-going trade and shipping are too numerous to list individually here, and recourse should be made to the official indexes. Particular mention may, however, be made to a paper of 1803 showing the individual trade of 74 ports for the years 1790 to 1792 and 1799 to 1802.[109]

[106] *Ibid.* 229.

[107] Clark and Franks, *English Commercial Statistics*, 43–4.

[108] Jarvis, 'Sources for the History of Ports', 89; Jarvis in Staveley (ed.), *Government Information*, 178–82, q.v. for full details.

[109] *Articles imported into England and Exported Therefrom* (1802–3) viii, cited in Jarvis, 'Sources for the History of Ports', n. 112. See also under

Other printed sources likely to prove useful include local newspapers which for the eighteenth century in port towns often contain details of trade, shipping movements, advertisements, and so on.[110] Two important collections of great value are the volumes of Adam Anderson's *Origin of Commerce* (1788–9) and D. Macpherson's *Annals of Commerce, Manufactures, Fisheries and Navigation* (1805), both of which present chronologically arranged materials on trade from early times, including reproductions of records which have since disappeared.[111] For a limited period the Danish Sound tables, now published, are an important source for the trade with the Baltic.[112]

The official *Calendar of State Papers, Domestic*, the *Calendar of State Papers, Colonial*, the *Calendar of State Papers, Venetian*, the *Acts of the Privy Council*, the *Calendar of Treasury Papers* (1557–1728), the *Calendar of Treasury Books* (1660–1714), the *Calendar of Treasury Books and Papers* (1721–45), may all yield much information, and if necessary the original records at the Public Record Office may be traced through them.[113] Also useful are the *Journals of the Board of Trade and Plantations*.

'Maritime History' in W. R. Powell, *Local History from Blue Books: Select List of the Sessional Papers of the House of Commons* (1962).

[110] For references to some, see Jarvis, 'Sources for the History of Ships'.

[111] Another work, containing details of the shipping of various ports, is J. Marshall, *Digest of All the Accounts relating to the Shipping, Colonies, Commerce, etc.* (1833).

[112] N. E. Bang and K. Korst, *Tabeller Over Skibsfart og Voretransport Gennem Øresund, 1497–1660* (2 vols. in 3 parts, 1906, 1922, 1923), with Danish and French introductions. Vol. i is the most useful providing for individual years the total number of ships from different countries (in the case of England individual ports are sometimes distinguished) passing through the Sound. N. E. Bang and K. Korst, *Tabeller Over Skibsfart og Voretransport Gennem Øresund, 1661–1783* (2 vols. in 3 parts, 1930, 1939, 1945), gives similar information for a later period.

[113] For many records at the P.R.O. in this area, not all described in this chapter, see C. M. Andrews, *Guide*, i and ii (1912–14); Davis, *Rise of Shipping*, 408–12. For a valuable list of printed works, see L. A. Harper, *The English Navigation Laws* (1939), 423 sqq.

COMMUNICATIONS

The sources for the history of roads in general are too numerous to be described in any detail.[114] The most obvious sources for modern times are maps, which are dealt with elsewhere.[115] Many of the records covered in the chapters on agriculture may also contain references to roads.[116] Quarter-sessions records, and parish records, particularly vestry minutes and highway surveyors' accounts, are also important, for the parish was responsible to quarter sessions between 1555 and 1835 for the upkeep of the highways within its boundaries.[117] After 1835 the records of highway boards responsible for larger areas than single parishes are to be found among the records of quarter sessions, which were also concerned generally with the oversight of the upkeep of roads and bridges. From 1888 the records of county councils become important. Naturally directories, guides, and local newspapers are useful, especially for carriers and stage-coaches. Road books and itineraries,[118] as well as descriptive

[114] A general bibliography is D. Ballen, *Bibliography of Roadmaking and Roads in the United Kingdom* (1914). For general history of roads, see S. and B. Webb, *English Local Government*, v, *The Story of the King's Highway* (1963 edn); W. T. Jackman, *The Development of Transportation in Modern England* (1962 edn). See W. G. Hoskins, *Fieldwork in Local History* (1967), 136 sqq., for early roads and trackways.

[115] For maps generally, see pp. 30–5. For tithe redemption, enclosure, and estate maps and plans, and ancillary records, see pp. 181–3, 192–5, 201. See also J. B. Harley, *Maps for the Local Historian* (1972), chapter 4.

[116] Especially useful for turnpike and other roads in the later eighteenth and early nineteenth centuries, are the Board of Agriculture, *General Views* (see pp. 183–4).

[117] G. H. Tupling, 'Highway Surveyors' Accounts', *Amateur Historian* i (1952–4). Information on bridges and roads is also found in assize records: see p. 72.

[118] See H. Fordham, *The Road Books and Itineraries of Great Britain, 1570–1850* (1924); D. Paterson, *A New and Accurate Description of All Direct and Principal Cross Roads in Great Britain* (various edns, 1771–1832); H. G. Fordham, 'The Road Books of Wales with a Catalogue, 1775–1850', *Archaeologia Cambrensis* lxxxii (1927); Harley, *Maps*.

accounts by travellers and topographers may also be valuable.[119] Arthur Young and Cobbett, for example, often reported on the state of the roads they used. At the Public Record Office (Class W.O.30) are War Office returns of accommodation for men and horses at inns and alehouses for 1686 and 1756, and these will give some indication of the relative importance of coaching towns in an area.

From the late seventeenth to the mid-nineteenth century the turnpiking of many roads took place. The evidence available for the local historian to trace the history of turnpikes, and of canals and railways[120] consists largely of records concerned with the legal sanction of these enterprises, the business records of the companies, and again maps and plans of various kinds.

All such undertakings (except the most minor canal constructions) required the assent of Parliament. The unpublished petitions and minutes of evidence placed before parliamentary committees on Bills supporting the enterprises may provide the first set of sources.[121] These are to be found in the House of Lords Record Office.[122] There, too,

---

[119] See pp. 26–7, 129.

[120] Many histories of railways have been published. See the monumental reference work: G. Ottley, *A Bibliography of Railway History* (1965). For some local turnpike studies, see E. Pawson, *Transport and Economy: The Turnpike Roads of Eighteenth Century Britain* (1977), 392–3.

[121] They may be traced through the *Commons Journals* and the *Lords Journals*. For details on reports on particular Bills, see the official indexes to the parliamentary papers. See also collections of minutes of evidence in the records of the British Transport Commission: L. J. Johnson, 'Historical Records of the British Transport Commission', *Jnl Transport History* i (1953–4), 91. These records are now in the Public Record Office.

[122] The following is based on : M. Bond, 'The Materials for Transport History Amongst the Records of Parliament', *Jnl Transport History* iv (1959–60), q.v. for official printed records; M. F. Bond, *The Records of Parliament: A Guide for Genealogists and Local Historians* (1964), 10–12, 17–20; E. R. Poyser, *The Private Bill Records of the House of Lords*, House of Lords Record Office, Memorandum no. 16 (1957); H. S. Cobb, 'Sources for Economic History Amongst the Parliamentary Records in the House

are plans of the proposed works and these are accompanied by books of reference giving details of the owners and occupiers of the land likely to be affected. There will also be subscription lists and contracts giving details of sources of capital.

If permission was granted it was done so in the form of an Act setting up a railway or canal company or a turnpike trust.[123] The private and public Acts are, therefore, a prime source.[124] Printed prospectuses and opposing pamphlets and broadsheets may exist in depositories. Large collections are at the library of the Institute of Civil Engineers in London. Many prospectuses are reproduced in local newspapers. For railways they are printed also in the weekly *Railway Times* (1837–1914). Turnpike trusts advertised meetings and the leasing (by auction) of their toll gates in the local press.

The domestic records of railway and canal companies and to a lesser degree those of turnpike trusts are to a certain extent similar to the records of other businesses described in some detail above.[125] Most of the business archives of railway and canal companies are at the Public Record Office, which has absorbed the former British Transport Historical

of Lords Record Office', *Ec.H.R.*, 2nd ser., xix (1966), 161 sqq.; H. S. Cobb, 'Parliamentary Records relating to Internal Navigation', *Archives* ix (1969) (this article deals with records relating to the improvement of river navigation in early modern times).

[123] J. Priestley, *Historical Account of the Navigable Rivers, Canals and Railways throughout Great Britain* (1831), may be useful, though it is not always clear whether canals mentioned were actually built or only authorized. J. Phillips, *General History of Inland Navigation, Foreign and Domestic* (1792), contains preambles to canal Acts. An edition of 1805 was reprinted in 1970.

[124] See Bond, *Records of Parliament*, 1–7; p. 21 above.

[125] See pp. 155–6. See also G. Ottley, *Railway History: A Guide to Sixty-one Collections in Libraries and Archives* (1973).

Records collections,[126] or at local record offices.[127] Turnpike trust records are less prolific and are generally preserved in county record offices or solicitors' offices.[128]

Minute books of canal and railway companies may record meetings of shareholders, directors, committees or subcommittees, and vary as to the extent of the information they contain. Some are scanty, recording only formal discussions, others packed with detail. Some canal minute books incorporate papers and documents including engineers' reports.[129] The minutes of turnpike trustees are largely, but not entirely, formal, tending to be more detailed in the earlier years of existence when the roads were being developed.[130] It should be noted that canal and railway minute books may shed light on turnpike trusts, and railway engineers' reports to

---

[126] See List and Index Society, cxlii, clxxii (1977, 1980), which cover Classes RAIL 800–87 (for canal, dock, harbour, navigation, and steamship companies), and Classes RAIL 410 and 491 (for certain railway companies). The following are useful, but all predate the move of the British Transport Commission records to the P.R.O.: Johnson, 'Historical Records' (which also describes many sources not mentioned here); E. H. Fowkes, 'Sources of History in Railway Records of the British Transport Historical Records', *Jnl Soc. Archivists* iii (1969); J. Simmons, 'The Scottish Records of the British Transport Commission', *Jnl Transport History* iii (1957–8) (contains information relevant to England); L. C. Johnson, 'Records of the British Transport Commission and their Value to the Local and Business Historian', *Amateur Historian* iv (1958–60); E. H. Fowkes, 'The Records of the Railway Clearing House', *Jnl Transport History* vii (1966).

[127] For canals not nationalized or ever owned by a railway company the records are very dispersed: see C. Hadfield, 'Sources for the History of British Canals', *Jnl Transport History* ii (1955–6), 82–3, for some examples.

[128] B. F. Duckham, 'Turnpike Records', *History* liii (1968); Pawson, *Transport and Economy*, 370–9. For physical remains, see E. C. W. French, 'Turnpike Trusts', *Amateur Historian* ii (1954–6); C. Cox and N. Surry, 'The Archaeology of Turnpike Roads., *Jnl Industrial Archaeology* ii (1965).

[129] For details, see Hadfield, 'Sources for Canals', 82–3.

[130] For an example, see Duckham, 'Turnpike Records', 217.

prospective railway promoters sometimes estimate the traffic on local turnpikes.[131]

Financial accounts are a fruitful source of information. Canal accounts usually consist of series of ledgers of two types: those for each toll house or dock recording quantities of goods and types of trade done and the revenue; and those dealing with the accounts of each carrier. Sometimes, however, they are summarized in a single series.[132] The accounts of turnpike trusts are also often in ledger form, and annual balance sheets may also be found amongst the minutes. From 1822 copies of the accounts were required to be filed with the clerk of the peace and are preserved in quarter-sessions records.[133] Since turnpikes were often leased few individual toll bar accounts have survived;[134] where they exist they can be very useful.[135]

Annual company reports were printed by railway companies and the larger canal companies and exist in manuscript for others. They are very helpful to the historian, for they summarize the financial state of the company and give information on the volume of trade and on important events. From them a detailed chronological framework may be built up.

Deeds, contracts, correspondence, engineers' and surveyors' reports and plans as well as, for canals and railways, registers of stocks and shares,[136] will fill out the picture. Parish highway surveyors' accounts[137] may contain some information on turnpike roads. Turnpike records may also include maps, plans of intended improvement, agreements

[131] *Ibid.* 220.

[132] Hadfield, 'Sources for Canals', 84–5.

[133] Annual parliamentary papers provide abstracts of turnpike trust accounts: see below.

[134] Duckham, 'Turnpike Records', 218–19.

[135] J. West, *Village Records* (1962), 159.

[136] For railway shareholders' guides and manuals, see Johnson, 'Historical Records', 93.

[137] See above, p. 79.

with parishes, letters, regulations, and details of charges.[138]

Apart from general maps and plans already touched on above,[139] the maps produced by George Bradshaw in 1830 are considered useful and reliable for canals. There are five of these general maps in two sets covering most English waterways except those of the east and south-west.[140] The early editions of the 1-inch Ordnance Survey maps, and of the 25-inch plans, will be most useful.[141] More detailed plans may be found among the domestic records of companies and trusts. In addition it should be recalled that before Parliament passed a railway or canal Act plans had to be submitted to the Private Bills Office.[142] Promoters also had to deposit plans of turnpikes, canals, and railways with the county, borough, or parish authorities involved, so that quarter-sessions and parish records, often now in local record depositories, should be searched.[143] A good collection for canals is also in the British Library.[144] Estate maps may also be of use, as well as business papers of landed families, often now in local record offices.[145]

[138] West, *Village Records*, 159.

[139] See p. 154.

[140] H. R. de Salis (comp.), *Bradshaw's Canals and Navigable Rivers of England and Wales* (1904, reprinted 1928 and 1969).

[141] See pp. 32–4; and also the *Map of England and Wales showing Railways, Canals, and Inland Navigation*, printed 1852 for the use of the Committee of the Privy Council for Trade.

[142] These are now in the House of Lords Record Office; see above, p. 155.

[143] Duckham, 'Turnpike Records', 220; J. Simmons, 'Railway History in English Local Records', *Jnl Transport History* i (1953–4); M. Robbins, 'Railway History in County Records', *Railway Magazine* xcix (1953). See also, e.g., *Plans and Documents Relating to Roads, Bridges, Canals, Water, Gas, etc. deposited with the Clerk of the Peace for the County of Salop* (Shropshire Record Office, 1969 edn).

[144] B.L. Map Room in three typescript volumes; some, however, are plans of projected canals which were never built. Other canal plans are reprinted in the *Gentleman's Magazine*: Hadfield, 'Sources for Canals', 87. See also P.R.O., *Maps and Plans in the Public Record Office* (1967).

[145] Simmons, 'Railway History', 159 sqq.

Where a canal was owned by a borough,[146] or where a town had a particular interest in canals, railways, or turnpikes they did not own, then the borough records will often yield additional information, particularly on periods of proposal and construction.[147]

Local newspapers often recorded the proceedings of meetings of railway and canal shareholders and annual reports and will contain reference to important events. For railways, trade journals should also be searched. They include such publications as *Herepath's Railway Magazine* (1835–1903), the *Railway Times* (1837–1914), the *Railway Record* (1844–1901), the *Railway News* (1864–1918), the *Railway Fly Sheet* (1870–82) (later the *Railway Official Gazette*, 1882–1914),[148] the *Railway Magazine* (from 1897), and *Bradshaw's Shareholders' Guide and Manual* (1847–1923). All these contain much local information.[149] There are large collections of railway rule books, regulations, and time-tables at the British Library. The time-tables contain not only train schedules and by-laws, but also bus and coach connections and advertisements.[150] The Board of Agriculture's *General Views* may also contain descriptions of communications.[151]

Only a few of the many parliamentary papers dealing with

[146] See e.g., W. B. Stephens, 'The Exeter Lighter Canal, 1566–1698', *Jnl Transport History* iii (1957).

[147] Simmons, 'Railway History', 157.

[148] These later merged into the *Railway Gazette*.

[149] For others, see Fowkes, 'Railway Records', 476–7; E. H. Fowkes, *Railway History and the Local Historian*, E. Yorks. Local History Ser., no. 16 (1963); C. E. Lee, 'Sources of Bus History', *Jnl Transport History* ii (1955–6), 155. Many volumes of these journals may be viewed at the Institute of Transport, the B.L., the Science Museum Library, and the National Railway Museum at York.

[150] *Bradshaw's Time Tables* and *Guides* (from 1839) are most useful. Some of these have recently been republished by David and Charles.

[151] See pp. 183–4. For an example, see J. Farey, *General View of the Agriculture of Derbyshire* (1817) iii, 331 (an early trackway).

railways, canals, and roads can find mention here, so that the indexes should be searched. Very many pertain to individual undertakings or undertakings in a particular area. Of general importance, however, are the reports of select committees on railways published between 1839 and 1844,[152] the report of the Select Committee on Amalgamation,[153] and the annual railway returns (from 1841 under different titles) giving details of traffic, capital, and stock,[154] and the report of the Royal Commission on Railways of 1867.[155]

For canals the most useful are the report from the Select Committee on Canals of 1883,[156] the returns made to the Board of Trade of canal statistics in 1888,[157] and the monumental report in twelve volumes of the Royal Commission on Canals of 1906–11, which contains a great deal of information, including maps.[158]

For turnpikes there are the report of a select committee of 1836,[159] annual returns (1836–1882/3) of income and expenditure,[160] and returns of roads disturnpiked (1871–8).[161]

---

[152] *Rep. Select Committee on Railroads and Turnpike Trusts* (1839) ix; *Reps. Select Committee on State of Communication by Railway* (1839) x; *Reps. Select Committee on Railway Communication* (1840) xiii; *Reps. Select Committee on Railways* (1844) xi.

[153] *Rep. Joint Select Committee on Railway Companies' Amalgamation* (1872) xii.

[154] See indexes.

[155] (1867) xxxviii (I and II). For the twentieth century, see sources cited in D. L. Munby and A. H. Watson, *Inland Transport Statistics of Great Britain, 1900–1970* (1978), 11–16.

[156] (1883) xiii.

[157] (1890) lxiv: showing capacity, length, locks, tunnels, financial details, etc.

[158] (1906) xxxii, (1907) xxxiii (I and II), (1909) xiii, (1910) xii, xiii, (1911) xiii.

[159] (1836) xix.

[160] See indexes.

[161] (1878) lxvi. For other parliamentary papers useful for turnpikes, see Pawson, *Transport and Economy*, 379–80.

The reports of the Royal Commission on Roads of 1840 are also valuable.[162]

At the Public Record Office there are (apart from the former British Transport Commission Historical Records) many classes of records providing details of local railway history.[163] The chief collection is that formerly comprising the records of the railway department of the Board of Trade, now filed under Ministry of Transport records. Of the records embraced in this the most important are the correspondence and papers of the department for the years 1840 to 1919 (Class M.T.6).[164] These contain inspectors' reports and correspondence dealing, among other things, with engineering aspects of the tracks, by-laws, legal matters, and disputes between companies. Also significant are the department's minute books for 1844 to 1857 (Class M.T.13), and its 'out'-letter books for 1840 to 1855 (Class M.T.11).

For turnpikes there are nineteen volumes of correspondence and papers (1872–92) relating to the transfer of turnpike roads and bridges to highway boards, to the ending of trusts, or to the renewal of their powers (Class M.H.28).[165]

The local historian dealing with communications will not overlook the records of tramways and buses.[166] Here local government records, newspapers, directories and guides, the *Stock Exchange Year Book*, and local Acts of Parliament will prove useful. The journals *Modern Transport* (from 1919) and

[162] (1840) xxvii. For expenditure on roads, see (1841) xxvii, and (1849) xlvi.

[163] The following is based on D. B. Wardle, 'Sources for the History of Railways at the Public Record Office', *Jnl Transport History* ii (1955–6), q.v., too, for a large number of other P.R.O. classes of records containing evidence on railways.

[164] See List and Index Soc., cvii, cxiv, cxxiii (1974–6).

[165] *P.R.O. Guide* ii, 175.

[166] Lee, 'Sources of Bus History', which deals with tramways as well as buses; J. A. B. Hibbs, 'Road Transport in *Notices and Proceedings*', *Jnl Transport History* i (1953–4); Pugh, *Parish History*, 41; Munby and Watson, *Inland Transport Statistics*, 228–32, 238–40.

the *Manual of Tramway Companies in the United Kingdom* (later *Duncan's Manual of British and Foreign Tramway (and Omnibus) Companies*) (1877–1905) are particularly fruitful of information. The parliamentary papers should be searched, and here attention is drawn particularly to returns of tramways made between 1877 and 1914.[167]

The development of postal, telephone, and telegraph services are significant in the history of communications, and the local historian may find useful the Post Office records, which date from 1672,[168] and directories, including the *British Postal Guide* (later the *Post Office Guide*) (from 1856).[169] Early references to postmasters are to be found in the *Calendar of State Papers, Domestic*.

[167] See indexes.

[168] Post Office Records, Headquarters Building, St Martin's-le-Grand, London EC1. These include nineteenth-century maps of routes of mail coaches, posts, and foot posts for the period 1791–1843: Harley, *Maps*. They also include treasury letter books (1686–1931), monthly cashbooks (1677–1809), and annual accounts (1678–1850), and contain a good deal of general local material for the economic historian. I am indebted to Professor L. S. Pressnell for this information.

[169] See R. B. Pugh, *How to Write a Parish History* (1954), 41–2.

CHAPTER 6

Agriculture

The technique of writing agricultural history at a local level, particularly that of a village, parish or district, differs from that of dealing on a broader scale with the farming of larger regions.[1] In particular, problems can be investigated and sources searched in a detail not practicable for a county or even a large region. Indeed, it may be felt that only the minute examination of large numbers of individual parishes, villages, or estates can provide the sort of information from which a really reliable picture of agriculture in a larger area may eventually be drawn. Local historians interested in this topic will wish to be able to provide, where possible, various sorts of information at different periods of time. They will wish, for example, to find out the area and composition of the manors in terms of demesne, villein, and freehold land; details of field systems and crop rotations, and the kinds of

[1] This chapter represents a much enlarged version of an article: W. B. Stephens, 'Sources for the History of Agriculture in the English Village and their Treatment', *Agricultural History* xliii (1969). Some minor details and references are not, however, reproduced here, and the article may, therefore, be worth consulting. For medieval records, see also F. G. Davenport, *A Classified List of Printed Original Materials for English Manorial and Agrarian History during the Middle Ages* (1962); R. H. Hilton, 'The Content and Sources of English Agrarian History before 1500', *Ag.H.R.* iii (1953); N. S. B. and E. C. Gras, *The Economic and Social History of an English Village* (1930); H. Hall, 'A Classified List of Agrarian Surveys in the Public Record Office (London)', *Economica* iv (1922) (includes also some modern material). Generally useful are F. A. Buttress, *Agricultural Periodicals in the British Isles, 1681–1900* (1950); and, for many technical terms, I. H. Adams, *Agrarian Landscape Terms: A Glossary for Historical Geography* (1976). For agricultural prices and wages, see pp. 113 sqq., for markets and fairs, see pp. 123–6.

crops and their relative importance;[2] evidence of land farmed in severalty and common, of leys in the open fields, and of consolidation of holdings; and information about common pasture and meadow, stock, woodland, and waste. They may also seek to analyse the class structure of those engaged in agriculture in the village (especially before the nineteenth century) and its relation to conditions of tenure or occupation. They will need evidence about changes in such structure from time to time – for example, the growth of a landless class of wage-earners, the development of a group of substantial small freeholders, and the break-up or build-up of estates.[3] Similarly the effects of enclosure by agreement, of enclosure for pasture farming, and of parliamentary enclosure on occupational and tenurial structure, and any evidence of commercial production and marketing, will need looking into. For modern times the number and size of farms and of their labour force, and the relative importance of ownership and tenancy, will be important. Evidence of prosperity or otherwise may, in a largely agricultural parish, result in poor relief being treated in detail together with the fortunes of agriculture.

The first section of this chapter seeks to describe agricultural sources for the period up to 1750, and the following section deals with those for the years after that. Of course some types of sources are of importance in both periods and since they are not dealt with twice those interested in agriculture only in the modern period should nevertheless read the first section.[4] Some modern records can provide

---

[2] A. R. H. Butler and R. A. Baker (eds.), *Studies of Field Systems in the British Isles* (1973), provides a bibliography covering many parts of the country. See also R. C. Russell, *The Logic of Open Field Systems* (1975).

[3] Useful is A. W. B. Simpson, *An Introduction to the History of the Land Law* (1964 impr.), which has a chapter on medieval conveyancing. See also pp. 301 sqq.

[4] Those interested only in the earlier period should nevertheless consult the second section for estate records (see pp. 200–1).

evidence for earlier times. Thus the study of field names from later maps, such as tithe and Ordnance Survey maps, may throw light on the physical layout of the landscape and land use in medieval and early modern times.[5] In addition it may be noted that many of the records which have been described in the chapters on population and social structure, poor relief, and local government, will be relevant to the agrarian history of the English local community.[6] The records needed to trace the descent of manorial and other landed property are not here described in any detail since they are so well dealt with elsewhere;[7] they may well have to be consulted in order to complete the picture of landownership being built up.

THE PERIOD TO 1750

Apart from class structure the agricultural historian will be interested in the pattern of land-holding and in matters of farming technique. In this section I have sought to distinguish sources for the structure of the community and sources for husbandry, dealing with each in turn. These two aspects of agrarian history are, of course, interlocked and the same sources may be useful for each.

For many places Anglo-Saxon land charters may exist to indicate how land was distributed and what tributes, rents, or services were rendered by peasants to their lords.[8]

Often, however, the first information about local agricul-

---

[5] See, e.g., B. Harrison, 'Reconstituting the Medieval Landscape', in A. Rogers (ed.), *Group Projects in Local History* (1972). J. Field, *English Field Names: A Dictionary* (1972), is useful. See also other books on place names cited on p. 37.

[6] See above.   [7] See p. 76 and n. 23; and pp. 301–4.

[8] P. H. Sawyer, *Anglo-Saxon Charters* (1968), is an up-to-date catalogue. See also A. J. Robertson, *Anglo-Saxon Charters* (1956); M. Gelling, 'Recent Work on Anglo-Saxon Charters', *Local Historian* xiii (1978); H. P. R. Finberg, *The Early Charters of Devon and Cornwall* (1968 edn); H. P. R. Finberg, *The Early Charters of the West Midlands* (1961); H. P. R. Finberg, *The Early Charters of Wessex* (1964); C. R. Hart, *The Early Charters of Eastern England* (1966); C. R. Hart, *The Early Charters of Northern England*

ture will be provided by Domesday,[9] which will often give evidence on the tenurial structure and the state of prosperity in 1066 and 1086. The details of areas of land (meadow, pasture, woodland) and their value provided in the survey will, however, need careful treatment and some special knowledge.[10] The number of plough-teams actually used and the number which the manor could support, and information on mills, fish-ponds, and markets, are also to be found in Domesday. It is not possible here to provide guidance on the interpretation of Domesday, on which so much is already in print, but attention may be drawn in particular to the works of H. C. Darby and his collaborators.[11] The problem of estimating the population involved is treated above.[12]

and the North Midlands (1975); M. Gelling, *The Early Charters of the Thames Valley* (forthcoming). Older works, which must be used with caution since in some cases both genuine and forged charters are included, are: J. M. Kemble, *Codex Diplomaticus Aevi Saxonum* (6 vols., 1839–48), which gives full texts of charters in Latin or Anglo-Saxon; W. de G. Birch, *Cartularium Saxonicum* (3 vols. and index, 1885–99), long the standard work for charters in Anglo-Saxon and Latin to A.D. 957; B. Thorpe, *Diplomatarium Anglicum Aevi Saxonici* (1865); J. Earle, *Handbook to the Land Charters and Other Saxonic Documents* (1888).

[9] For details, see above, pp. 46–8, where information on other early medieval surveys similar in nature to Domesday is also noted.

[10] See R. B. Pugh, *How to Write a Parish History* (1954), 44–5.

[11] H. C. Darby, *The Domesday Geography of Eastern England* (1971 edn); H. C. Darby and E. H. J. Campbell, *The Domesday Geography of South-East England* (1962 edn); H. C. Darby and R. W. Finn, *The Domesday Geography of South-West England* (1967); H. C. Darby and I. S. Maxwell, *The Domesday Geography of Northern England* (1962); H. C. Darby and I. B. Terrett, *The Domesday Geography of Midland England* (1971 edn). A key to this series is H. C. Darby and G. R. Versey, *Domesday Gazetteer* (with an atlas of county maps) (1975): place names arranged alphabetically under counties. See also H. C. Darby, *Domesday England* (1977); R. W. Finn, *The Norman Conquest and its effect on the Economy, 1066–86* (1971), topographically arranged; R. W. Finn, *The Domesday Inquest* (1961), chapter 4, and such works by W. G. Hoskins as *Provincial England* (1963), chapter 2; *Fieldwork in Local History* (1967), 40 sqq.; *Local History in England* (1959), 37–40. [12] See pp. 47–8.

The hundred rolls of the late thirteenth century[13] are an important source for agricultural history,[14] though they do not cover the whole country, and only for some counties are they in very great detail. Nevertheless, the fuller returns of 1279–80 for Bedfordshire, Buckinghamshire, Cambridgeshire, Huntingdonshire, Leicestershire, Oxfordshire, and Warwickshire are the next obvious source for a comparable survey 200 years after Domesday.[15] They may include the extent of the lord's own holding of arable, meadow, enclosed pasture, and woodland, and of the holdings of the peasants, free or servile, together with their obligations and rents. In particular, light may be shed on the progress of commutation. It should be remembered, nevertheless, that the picture given is at best a legalistic one, noting only the holdings of tenants; it is a static impression imposed on the underlying economic reality.[16] It was not intended to record temporary agreement, so information on leasing cannot be deduced from the rolls.[17]

---

[13] Published as the *Rotuli Hundredorum*, ed. W. Illingworth and J. Caley, by the Record Commission (1812–18). Since then other rolls have come to light, as, e.g., that for Coventry (in Shakespeare's Birthplace Library, Stratford-upon-Avon).

[14] Cf. E. A. Kosminsky, 'The Hundred Rolls of 1279–80 as a source for English Agrarian History', *Ec.H.R.* iii (1931).

[15] For their interpretation and the sort of information they contain, see Helen M. Cam, *The Hundred and the Hundred Rolls* (1930), 47 sqq.; J. B. Harley, 'Population Trends and Agricultural Development from the Warwickshire Hundred Rolls of 1279', *Ec.H.R.*, 2nd ser., xi (1958–9); J. B. Harley, 'The Hundred Rolls of 1279', *Amateur Historian* v (1961–3). See also R. H. Hilton, *The Social Structure of Rural Warwickshire in the Middle Ages*, Dugdale Soc. Occasional Paper, no. 9 (1950), based on the Warwickshire hundred rolls.

[16] Cf. A. E. Levett, *Studies in Manorial History*, ed. H. M. Cam, M. Coate, and L. S. Sutherland, (1938), 42–3. For the difficulties involved in using the material, see Kosminsky, 'The Hundred Rolls', 30 sqq.; and E. A. Kosminsky, *Studies in the Agrarian History of England in the 13th Century* (English edn by R. H. Hilton (1956)), 9 sqq., and especially 40 sqq.

[17] Kosminsky, *Studies in Agrarian History*, 38.

For the late sixteenth century some villages have large-scale surveyed plans, which, of course, are extremely valuable for details of the organization of open-field settlements.[18] Such plans are, however, rather rare. Further details of free and servile holdings with their rents and services, and a description of the demesne land, are more likely to be found, especially before the period in which alienation of the demesne became common, in written descriptions – what are known as extents or surveys. Extents attached to inquisitions post mortem[19] are the most common especially for humbler landowners. On the whole these must be used with caution. Some would feel that their use should be confined to indicating the comparative values of free and villein holdings (reflected by the percentages of free and villein rents where distinguished – but it should be noted that generally this will exaggerate the importance of villein land), and how far the demesne was likely to have depended on servile or wage labour (roughly only, by comparing the extent of demesne arable with the labour dues where given).[20] One cannot, however, assume from the absence of details of services that commutation had taken place.[21] On the other hand, as with the hundred rolls, leases are rarely

---

[18] See M. W. Beresford, 'Maps and the Medieval Landscape', *Antiquity* xxiv (1950), 114–15; *The Art of the Map Maker in Essex, 1566–1860* (Essex Record Office, 1947).

[19] P. R. O., Classes C.132–C.142. Calendars for many inquisitions post mortem (indicating which have extents) in the reigns of Henry III to Henry VII have been published by the Record Commission (1806–28) and H.M.S.O. (1904–56). P.R.O., Lists and Indexes, xxiii, xxvi, xxxi, and xxxiii (1907–9), print those for the reigns of Henry VIII to Charles I. For miscellaneous rentals, surveys, extents, etc., see *ibid.* supplementary ser., xiv (1968). See also pp. 51 n. 21, 174 n. 28.

[20] For the difficulties involved, see Kosminsky, *Studies in Agrarian History*, 63–7.

[21] As H. L. Gray did: 'The Commutation of Villein Services in England before the Black Death', *E.H.R.* xxix (1914), 630; cf. Kosminsky, *Studies in Agrarian History*, 55.

recorded in extents though they are known to ·have been common in the thirteenth century.[22]

Extents or surveys described both lands and tenants.[23] Other medieval records, rentals, and custumals (or customaries) give the tenants' names, their holdings and the rents and services due from each, and the customs of the manor. In the early Middle Ages there is no clear distinction between rentals and custumals.[24] In seeking to indicate the tenurial structure it must be recalled that rentals before commutation also tend to present the legal rather than the economic picture, since they disguised fragmentation and accumulation of holdings. More reliable information on services, rents, and commutation, and on leases, may be deduced from manorial court rolls, ministers' accounts,[25] and deeds.[26]

Some of the fiscal sources described in the chapter on population sources (Chapter 2) may be of value to the agrarian historian. The medieval subsidy rolls dating from before 1334[27] can indicate the existence and size of a class of comparatively wealthy free tenants and peasants.[28] Changes in village social structure resulting from the growth of

[22] Cf. P. Vinogradoff, *Villeinage in England* (1927 impr.), 330. For limitations on the use of extents, see also Kosminsky, *Studies in Agrarian History,* 55 sqq.

[23] For further information on extents and surveys, with additional references, see pp. 51–2, 174–5. N.b., too, P.R.O., Lists and Indexes xxv, and *ibid.* supplementary ser., xiv (1908, 1968), for rentals, surveys, and similar records in the P.R.O. (and see also p. 169 n. 19).

[24] Cf. Davenport, *Classified List,* pp. xi–xii. By the sixteenth century rentals were lists of tenants with the payments due from each, while custumals were general statements on the rights and duties of classes of tenants. See G. R. Elton, *England, 1200–1640* (1969), 146 sqq. For alleged distinctions between extents, surveys, rentals, see T. Lomas, 'The Development of the Manorial Extent', *Jnl Soc. Archivists* vi (1980).

[25] For manorial records, see above, pp. 73–5, and also Hilton, 'Content and Sources', 14.

[26] For deeds, see below, pp. 301–4.

[27] See pp. 49–50.

[28] Cf. W. G. Hoskins, *The Midland Peasant* (1957), 71–3.

pasture farming and the break-up of manorial farming may be reflected in the returns of the Tudor subsidy granted in 1523, and collected in 1524 and 1525.[29] This was levied on goods, land, or wages worth £1 or more a year, and in country districts it appears to have applied to almost all householders. The number of persons paying tax only on wages will indicate the size of a landless labouring class. But it must be noted that the adolescent sons of yeomen and husbandmen were assessed on 'wages' though they were not really of the labouring class. Usually, however, they formed only a small proportion of the villagers.[30] Analysis of the other tax-payers (who paid on land or goods) may show the spread of prosperity in the rest of the community, probably reflecting in a rural community the value of the land they farmed. If they paid on goods, this indicated that they did not own land of a greater annual value than their personal estate.[31] Seventeenth-century poll and hearth taxes[32] may similarly indicate the spread of wealth and therefore of agricultural holdings in a farming community in post-Restoration England. Later Tudor and Stuart subsidy returns are, for well-known reasons, generally less useful than the earlier ones. They may, however, suffice to indicate in the later sixteenth century the rise of a yeoman class 'with a disproportionate share of the personal estate or moveable goods'.[33] They can also reflect periods of instability or depression when there was little continuity of tenure and therefore a quick turnover of subsidymen (freeholders and non-freeholders) or impoverishment shown by their fall to lower categories.[34] Similarly the muster rolls, of which those

[29] See p. 59.

[30] W. G. Hoskins, *Essays in Leicestershire History* (1950), 129.

[31] Hoskins, *Midland Peasant*, 143.

[32] See pp. 60–2.

[33] Hoskins, *Midland Peasant*, 141–2.

[34] Cf. L. Marshall, *The Rural Population of Bedfordshire, 1671–1921*, Beds. Historical Records Soc. xvi (1934), 62–3; S. A. Peyton, 'The Village

for 1569, 1573, 1577, and 1580 are considered the most reliable,[35] may also indicate the stability or otherwise of the farming community.[36] Probate inventories can provide much evidence on agricultural matters, and for certain periods exist in large numbers, usually attached to wills.[37] They list farmers' implements, grain and other fruits of the earth in store, and livestock. Sometimes estimates of acreages of growing crops may be given. Even if it is not possible to examine all such documents available for the area being studied, it may be of value to look at some. What may be considered, particularly if other information is sparse, is the examination of inventories belonging to families known (for example from fiscal sources) to be of importance in the parish. Another possibility is to look at those before and after early (non-parliamentary) enclosure has taken place, to see, for example, whether a wealthier group has emerged.[38]

Deeds of various kinds, recording grants, leases, sales, and so on, are of great importance and exist in originals and in

Population in the Tudor Lay Subsidy Rolls', *E.H.R.* xxx (1915), 248–50; E. E. Rich, 'The Population of Elizabethan England', *Ec.H.R.*, 2nd ser., ii (1950), 261.

[35] Rich, 'Population of Elizabethan England', 253. They are to be found among the state papers, domestic; see *ibid.* note.

[36] *Ibid. passim.*

[37] A. J. Camp, *Wills and their Whereabouts* (1974), is useful for tracing inventories as well as wills. O. Ashmore, 'Inventories as a source of Local History', *Amateur Historian* iv (1958–60), is also useful. See, too, p. 63 nn. 67, 68.

[38] For comment on the use of inventories, see J. Thirsk, 'Sources of English Agricultural History after 1500', *Ag.H.R.* iii (1955), 71–3. For examples of their use, see Hoskins, *Essays in Leicestershire History*, 123 sqq.; Hoskins, *Midland Peasant*, 283–310; M. Spufford, 'The Significance of the Cambridgeshire Hearth Tax', *Proceedings of the Cambridge Antiquarian Soc.* lv (1962), which compares the hearth-tax assessment with the size of houses and numbers of rooms as shown in probate inventories; and, among others, F. W. Steer (ed.), *Farm and Cottage Inventories of Mid Essex, 1635–1749* (1950).

copies.[39] It should be recalled that much land has at one time or another been in the hands of the Church, and there is a vast amount of material to be found in monastic, capitular, and other ecclesiastical records, including those of the Church Commissioners.[40] In the sixteenth century the practice of recording sales by fines spread, and changes in the number of those documents called feet of fines and recoveries[41] at different times may indicate changes in the village, for example, the dismemberment of a manor. Alternatively, the accumulation of an estate by a family may be demonstrated.[42] After 1536 and until the early seventeenth century enrolled deeds of bargain and sale may be used to shed light on the land market.[43] The papers of a commission

[39] See pp. 301–4, and, especially for agriculture, P. Roebuck, 'Leases and Tenancy Agreements', *Local Historian* x (1972–3).

[40] Many of the records of the Church useful here are described fully on pp. 266–7. See also p. 175. The Church Commissioners (formerly Ecclesiastical Commissioners) are at Millbank, London SW1.

[41] P.R.O., Class C.P.25. Indexes, transcripts, and calendars have been printed by local societies. There are manuscript indexes in the P.R.O., complete from the beginning of Henry VIII's reign, and transcripts for the periods 28 Henry II to 10 Richard I (Pipe Roll Soc., xvii, xx, xxiii, xxiv), 1195–1214, Bedford – Dorset (Record Commission, *et al.*). For 7 Richard I to John for other counties there are manuscript transcripts in the P.R.O. For an introduction to these records, see Pugh, *Parish History*, 65–6, and works cited there.

[42] See, e.g., Hoskins, *Midland Peasant*, 115 sqq. For the use of fines together with 'common recoveries' and title deeds, see J. Kew, 'The Disposal of Crown Lands and the Devon Land Market, 1536–58', *Ag.H.R.* xviii (1970).

[43] To be found in the P.R.O., in the archives of all the Courts of Record, particularly in the Courts of Chancery and Common Pleas. Bargains and sales could, however, be enrolled before the county J.P.s, and some of these are to be found in the records of most counties, e.g., an extensive collection for Devon: J. Kew, 'Regional Variations in the Devon Land Market, 1536–1558', in M. A. Havinden and Celia M. King (eds.), *The South-West and the Land*, Exeter Papers in Economic History, no. 2 (1969), q.v. for the use of such records. See also S. W. B. Harbin, *Somerset Enrolled Deeds*, Somerset Record Soc. li (1936). See p. 303.

set up to deal with estates of those who fought for the Pretender in 1715 contain evidence of value to local historians interested in particular estates.[44]

Information on agrarian and tenurial matters may also be drawn from details of law suits in proceedings of the prerogative courts, such as Chancery,[45] though since the outcome of so many is not forthcoming it is often difficult to assess the validity of evidence. It may be that the time needed to search this class of record is too great, unless some lead has been obtained.

We may now turn to the investigation of land usage. Much information on such matters as the proportion of arable, pasture, meadow, wood, and waste, and on fisheries, and so on, together with evidence on the division between demesne, free, and villein land, is to be found in Domesday, extents and surveys, ministers' accounts, manorial court rolls,[46] and probate inventories, all already mentioned above.

Court rolls will contain tenurial data such as the alienation of land, and surrenders and admittances, as well as information on the regulation of farming affairs and the interpretation of the customs of the manor. Extents[47] may provide the estimated value of the homestead, court, garden, vineyard, dovecote, etc., and the acreage and estimated value of the arable land, meadow, pasture, woodland, pannage, mills, fisheries, fairs, and markets.[48] The records of Commissioners of Sewers from the mid-sixteenth into the

[44] They are listed in *The Records of the Forfeited Estates Commission* (P.R.O., 1968).

[45] In the P.R.O.

[46] See pp. 167–70.

[47] See also pp. 51, 169.

[48] See Kosminsky, *Studies in Agrarian History*, 47 sqq., for a description of the agrarian content of extents attached to inquisitions post mortem and the difficulties involved in interpretation. See also E. Kerridge, 'The Returns of the Inquisitions of Depopulation', *E.H.R.* lxx (1955), 213–14, for evidence of false returns to inquisitions post mortem.

present century are useful for the history of land drainage.[49]

Between about 1649 and 1653, under the orders of Parliament, surveys of the lands of the Crown and Church were made prior to their sale. These parliamentary surveys form a unique, accurate, and extensive description of virtually every Crown or ecclesiastical property in England and Wales. They provide the quantities of demesne land, annual values, level of rents, actual revenue from feudal dues, and profits of timber, as well as much topographical information. The Church surveys are found among diocesan records, at Lambeth Palace, the House of Lords Record Office, and the British Library. Surveys of Crown lands are mainly in the Public Record Office (Classes E.317, L.R.2, and (transcripts) D.L.32), with full copies or extracts in local depositories and private estate collections.[50]

Some surveys, especially for the period 1550 to 1700, were, of course, not national records but estate ones carried out under the aegis of the manorial courts and now to be found with the manorial records. They were often taken at times when a new lord took possession or when the manor was about to be sold or enclosed.[51] For the period before the Reformation they are also to be found in monastic cartularies.[52]

[49] A. E. B. Owen, 'Records of Commissioners of Sewers', *History* lii (1967).

[50] S. C. Newton, 'Parliamentary Surveys', *History* liii (1968). P.R.O., Lists and Indexes xxv (1908), lists all the E.317 series. See also p. 258.

[51] Thirsk, 'Sources of Agricultural History', 69–71; E. Kerridge, 'The Manorial Survey as an Historical Source', *Amateur Historian* vii (1966–7); F. G. Emmison, 'Estate Maps and Surveys', *History* xlviii (1963); B. M. Evans, 'Sources for the Study of Welsh Agriculture', *Amateur Historian* vii (1966–7). For examples, see E. Kerridge (ed.), *Surveys of the Manors of Philip, First Earl of Pembroke and Montgomery, 1631–2*, Wilts. Archaeological and Natural History Soc., Records Branch ix (1953). For the form of extents, see Hone, *Manor*, 224 sqq. See also pp. 169–70.

[52] For examples, see D. C. Douglas and W. G. Greenaway, *English Historical Documents, 1042–1189* (1953), 813 sqq.; G. Duby, *Rural Economy and Country Life in the Medieval West*, trans. C. Postan (1968), 479 sqq.; C.

The accounts of estate officials (ministers' account rolls or *compoti*) provide statements of the lord's income from fixed rents and farms, sales of works, sales of pasturage and grain, etc., and, on the debit side, expenses of repairs to buildings and implements, payments for farm work, etc. Inventories and other details of the demesne stock may also be included, categorizing working beasts and mature animals and the newly born.[53]

Where a long series of ministers' accounts exists, some selection may have to be made by the investigator. If so it may be better to pick groups of three consecutive years in each ten or twelve (taking into account known periods of dearth or prosperity) and to make general comments based on the averages obtained, rather than to select single years at intervals to provide statistics. In any case it should be made clear what methods have been employed and what accounts, used or not used, exist.[54] Maps and later estate records are dealt with elsewhere in this volume.[55]

D. Ross, *The Cartulary of Cirencester Abbey* (1964) ii, 359. Monastic cartularies contain much information on land tenure and the like. For a list, see G. R. C. Davies, *Medieval Cartularies of Great Britain* (1958).

[53] See Hone, *Manor*, 203 sqq. F. W. Maitland, *Select Pleas in Manorial and Other Seigneurial Courts*, Selden Soc. ii (1889), has a useful introduction, an explanation of technical problems, and examples of pleas in thirteenth-century courts. See also R. Lennard, 'Manorial Traffic and Agricultural Trade in Medieval England', *Jnl of Proceedings of the Agricultural Economics Society* v (1938). Many accounts are in the Public Record Office, especially in Classes S.C.6 and D.L.29; P.R.O., Lists and Indexes, v, xxxiv (1894, 1910).

[54] For the difficulties involved in using ministers' accounts, see R. H. Hilton, *Ministers' Accounts of the Warwickshire Estates of the Duke of Clarence, 1479–80*, Dugdale Soc. publication xxi (1952), esp. pp. xvi sqq.; Levett, *Studies*, chapter 3; D. Oschinsky, 'Notes on the Editing and Interpretation of Estate Accounts', *Archives* ix (1969–70) (2 parts). Many ministers' accounts are to be found among ecclesiastical archives (see pp. 248 sqq.; J. E. Sayers, *Estate Documents at Lambeth Palace Library* (1965)).

[55] See pp. 31–5, 200–2.

Details of land use and area in the hundred rolls must be regarded as incomplete. The majority of estates are there described only in terms of arable land. Normally only those parts of pasture, meadow, and wood which were in the separate use and possession of individuals are recorded.[56]

The so-called Inquisition of the Ninths[57] was in fact an assessment of one-tenth of the agricultural value of each parish in 1341. Jurors were required to explain the discrepancy between it and the valuation at one-tenth in the Tax of Pope Nicholas IV[58] of 1291. Their comments are useful, giving, for example, indication of land falling out of cultivation, dearth of seed, flooding, and so on.[59]

For the sixteenth and seventeenth centuries land use in the open-field manor may be revealed by analysis of glebe terriers. Since glebe land was frequently scattered in strips like other holdings, the terriers give field and perhaps furlong names, and indicate the existence of leys and closes in the open fields. If the glebe strips are concentrated in blocks it will indicate that consolidation has taken place in the village fields.

The terriers, originally found in diocesan and archdiocesan records and parish chests, but now often deposited in local record offices, are specially useful in indicating the extent and possible date of enclosure. If the parson has only strips, then at least part of the village is certainly unenclosed; if he has some strips and some closes, other villagers may well have the same mixture; if he has only hedged closes then some enclosure is likely to have taken place. Some terriers actually

[56] Kosminsky, *Studies in Agrarian History*, 33–4.

[57] Published by the Record Commission as *Nonarum Inquisitiones in Curia Scaccarii* (1807).

[58] Published by the Record Commission as *Taxatio Ecclesiastica Angliae et Walliae, auctoritate Papae Nicholai IV, c. 1291* (1802).

[59] See, e.g., A. R. H. Baker, 'Evidence in the "Nonarum Inquisitiones" of Contracting Arable Land in England during the early 14th century', *Ec.H.R.*, 2nd ser., xix (1966).

give the date of enclosure; and sometimes they provide descriptions of the pre-enclosure pattern along with the newly allocated fields.[60] It has been said of them that 'no single source in one repository sheds as much light on the agricultural pattern of a whole district under the Stuarts as a diocesan collection of terriers'.[61]

For five counties (Devon, Huntingdonshire, Nottinghamshire, Oxfordshire, Yorkshire) the poll tax and census of sheep of 1549 give some indication of the spread of sheep farming.[62] The body of evidence of early (illegal) enclosure, however, must be sought in I. S. Leadam's *Domesday of Inclosures* (1897), and in articles by him in *Transactions of the Royal Historical Society,* NS, vi, vii, viii (returns of Enclosure Commissioners for a large number of counties for 1517 and 1518, and, for Warwickshire, 1548).[63]

[60] Cf. M. W. Beresford, 'Glebe Terriers in Open-Field Leicestershire', *Transactions of the Leics. Archaeological Soc.* xxiv (1948); M. W. Beresford, 'Glebe Terriers and Open-Field Yorkshire', *Yorks. Archaeological Jnl* xxxvii (1948–51). See also D. M. Barratt (ed.), *Ecclesiastical Terriers of Warwickshire Parishes*, Dugdale Soc. publication xxii (1955), introduction, esp. pp. xlvi sqq.; G. H. Tupling, 'Terriers and Tithe and Enclosure Awards', *Amateur Historian* i (1952–4).

[61] D. M. Barratt, 'Glebe Terriers', *History* li (1966), q.v. for a good description and a printed example. For their use in investigating the incidence of tithes, and tithe customs, see E. J. Evans, 'Tithing Customs and Disputes: the Evidence of Glebe Terriers', *Ag.H.R.* xviii (1970). See also p. 261.

[62] M. W. Beresford, 'The Poll Tax and Census of Sheep, 1549', *Ag.H.R.* i (1953–4).

[63] Not, however, complete: M. W. Beresford, *Lost Villages of England* (1954), 106–7, 318; E. F. Gay, 'The Inquisitions of Depopulation in 1517', *T.R.H.S.,* NS, xiv (1900), 238. Information on other cases is in P.R.O., Class C.47/7/2 (indexed, indicating if printed or not; see *Chancery Miscellanea*, List and Index Soc. vii (1966)), in which places are represented in Essex, Glos., Middx., Leics., Lincs., Northants., Shropshire, Staffs., Som., and Cambs., among others; in C.43/2 (MS. calendar in the P.R.O.), which includes a few cases in Oxon., Leics., Northants., and Glos. The Class C.43/3 is not apparently indexed in any way. C.43/28, however, is arranged in bundles by counties and covers common law

Similar returns for 1607[64] are extant for Warwickshire, Leicestershire, Northamptonshire, Buckinghamshire, Bedfordshire, and Huntingdonshire. The appendixes in M. W. Beresford, *Lost Villages of England* (1954), provide Public Record Office references to Exchequer cases against offenders, 1518 to 1558, by year and county, but do not distinguish parishes.[65]

The existence of enclosure by agreement perhaps following consolidation may be inferred from such evidence as is provided by glebe terriers (see above) and other descriptions. Evidence of actual enclosure agreements, however, may perhaps be found in the class of records, Chancery enrolled decrees,[66] where they were confirmed. They may also be traced in Exchequer special commissions[67] and in copies

pleadings (Chancery) concerning depopulation etc. for 10 Henry VIII, for Oxon, (file 7), Glos. (4), Middx. (2), Leics. (5), Northants. (6), and other counties. Other cases are in E.368, memoranda rolls (Lord Treasurer's Remembrancer), but these are unindexed.

[64] P.R.O., Class C.205, not otherwise indexed. E. F. Gay in *T.R.H.S.*, NS, xviii (1904) summarizes the 1607 returns by counties. The Leicestershire return is published in *Transactions of the Leics. Archaeological Soc.* xxiii (1947) ('The Depopulation Returns for Leicestershire in 1607', ed. L. A. Parker); a summary of the missing Lincolnshire return is in the B.L. (Add. MS. 11574, fos. 66 sqq.). For references to a few returns for 1630 and 1631, see E. M. Leonard, 'The Inclosure of Common Fields in the 17th Century', *T.R.H.S.*, NS, xix (1905), 130 sqq.

[65] This work also gives a list of deserted villages county by county with references to evidence. The Deserted Medieval Villages Research Group also provides useful information in its annual reports (from 1953). More recently M. Beresford and J. G. Hurst (eds.), *Deserted Medieval Villages: Studies* (1971), includes a county gazetteer of sites.

[66] P.R.O., Classes C.78 and C.79. M. W. Beresford *et al.*, *P.R.O. Seventeenth Century Chancery Decree Rolls* (3 vols., 1978), (copies at Institute of Historical Research and British Library (Bloomsbury and Boston Spa)), provides references to some 260 enclosure agreements in the rolls. See also M. W. Beresford, 'The Decree Rolls of Chancery as a Source for Economic History, 1547 – *c.* 1700', *Ec.H.R.*, 2nd ser., xxxii (1979). See also *Chancery Decree Rolls (C. 78)*, List and Index Soc. clx (1979).

[67] In P.R.O., Class E.178, indexed in P.R.O., Lists and Indexes xxxvii.

among family papers. There are, of course, a few early Acts for enclosing common land.[68]

THE PERIOD FROM 1750

As indicated in the previous section, some of the types of sources for agricultural history in earlier times described there also exist for the period from 1750, and are not dealt with again.

Many new sources, however, are available in modern times. For the eighteenth century onwards the local historian is more likely to have maps to help him. Topographical maps exist for the eighteenth century for most counties, and these sometimes give evidence of land use, even if only an indication of the extent of woodland and waste.[69] Estate maps, if they exist, will give more reliable and detailed information,[70] the Ordnance Survey maps should always be consulted,[71] and for many parishes enclosure and tithe maps exist.

For the early part of this period the most important matter to be treated will often be parliamentary enclosure, carried out under the terms of private Acts or the general Acts of 1836 and 1845, which had such a great effect on agriculture,[72]

[68] Leonard, 'Inclosure', 108 sqq.

[69] Cf. D. B. Grigg, 'The Changing Agricultural Geography of England: A Commentary on the Sources Available for the Reconstruction of the Agricultural Geography of England, 1770–1850', *Transactions of the Institute of British Geographers* xli (1967), 80, and notes. This is a most important article on sources and is drawn on in what follows without further citation, except in a few cases. See also J. B. Harley, *Maps for the Local Historian* (1972), chapter 6.

[70] See pp. 31, 201.

[71] See pp. 32–5.

[72] Views on the enclosure movement have changed: for a recent summary and bibliography, see G. E. Mingay, *Enclosure and the Small Farmer in the Age of the Industrial Revolution* (1968). See also E. L. Jones, *The Development of English Agriculture, 1815–1873* (1968); J. G. Brewer, *Enclosure and the Open Fields: A Bibliography* (1972); M. Turner, 'Recent Progress in the Study of Parliamentary Enclosure', *Local Historian* xii (1976–7).

social structure, and topography. W. E. Tate's *Domesday of Enclosure Acts and Awards* provides a comprehensive finding list of the main records.[73]

Parliamentary enclosure affected about half the ancient parishes of England, with a concentration in the Midlands. A variety of sources exists for the study of a local enclosure.[74] Notices of a proposed enclosure may be found in local newspapers some years before an Act was passed. The text of the Act will list the commissioners by name and indicate how they were to treat copyholders, tenant farmers, squatters, and so on, and what to do about tithe and glebe land. After the commissioners began work their notices in the local newspaper, including advertisements for tenders for fencing, draining, and so on, will demonstrate the stages of the enclosure. The dates of, for example, the fencing of the tithe allotment, of the commencement of work on new drains and roads, and of the decision regarding general allotments, may well be announced in the press.

The chief records of a parliamentary enclosure, however, are the award and its accompanying map. Two copies of these were made and deposited with the clerk of the peace and in the parish chest. They are thus likely now to be found in local record offices, though the Public Record Office has a

[73] Ed. M. E. Turner (1978). And see *B.I.H.R.* xix (1941–3), 97 sqq. See also P.R.O., Class M.A.F. 1 (inclosure awards, 1847–1936, arranged by counties); Class M.A.F. 13 (orders of exchange of lands under Inclosure Acts, 1846–1964, arranged by counties). The *Agricultural History Review* carries periodic lists of works on agricultural history.

[74] See especially W. E. Tate, 'Enclosure Awards and Acts', *History* li (1966); R. C. Russell, 'Parliamentary Enclosure and the Documents for its Study', in A. Rogers and T. Rowley (eds.), *Landscapes and Documents* (1974); Harley, *Maps,* chapter 3; W. E. Tate, *The English Village Community and the Enclosure Movements* (1967), esp. 117–20; F. G. Emmison, *Archives and Local History* (1966), 25–7; W. E. Tate, *The Parish Chest* (1960 edn.), 268–9; Hoskins, *Fieldwork* (1967), 74–5, 122; J. West, *Village Records* (1962), 137 sqq.

large collection.[75] The award in its preamble lists the main provisions of the Act, describes the new paths, roads, drains, and watercourses, and outlines the special allotments. These include allotments in lieu of tithe rights and glebe land and in lieu of manorial rights, and allotments to the overseers of the highway of gravel and sand pits and quarries, and perhaps to local endowed institutions. The main part of the award will be a schedule of the general allotments. The position, acreage, and ownership of each new plot awarded in lieu of holdings and rights in the common fields, commons, and so on, are described, and usually the exchange of old enclosures noted. Also in the award will be instructions for fencing, hedging, and draining the new allotments, and sometimes the allocation of the costs of enclosure to the allotment holders. Accompanying the award is a large-scale map or plan which identifies the allotments named in the award, together with the lines of the new roads, paths, sand pits, hedges, fences, and so on, as well as other topographical features. Occasionally, particularly after 1830, draft enclosure plans of the area before enclosure may have survived, with the layout of the commons and open fields and with the strips shown and tenants' names marked in. In such cases there is provided material for a clear comparison of the pre- and post-enclosure arrangements. The official post-enclosure map will, however, show on it ancient enclosures and some pre-enclosure features, so that it is often possible to reconstruct the pattern existing before enclosure from it and other evidence (not excluding modern Ordnance Survey maps and physical features on the ground).

Other enclosure records, if they exist, may provide fuller details. The minutes of the commissioners' meetings, for example, fill out the details of the progress of the enclosure arrangements, and, though usually rather formal, sometimes give details of the use of agricultural land and the appor-

---

[75] See above, p. 34 n. 106.

tionment of costs. The distribution of financial charges to the allotment holders, however, quite often forms distinct accounts. Other commissioners' records include surveys and field books, valuations made prior to redistribution, notes and correspondence, and documents containing particulars of the course of farming during the enclosure operation. Occasionally some early estate maps are to be found with the commissioners' records.[76]

It should be noted that not all parliamentary enclosures were of whole villages; some were only of a few acres of waste, and two major groups may be distinguished: those embracing common arable fields and meadow; and those concerned with the commons such as heath, marsh, forest, and moor. The enclosure of common land may be of significance in urban development, as at Nottingham, or provide information on the settlement and exploitation of previously unused or barely used land. Where large-scale enclosure of arable and meadow occurred, the enclosure records shed much light on the distribution of the ownership and tenure of land before and after enclosure, and provide information on the nature of the agriculture of the locality, the existence of local industry, and, of course, on local topography generally.

Whether or not there was an 'agricultural revolution' in the late eighteenth and early nineteenth centuries, it is true that a great deal of energy went into the publication of works relating to farming. Some of the chief sources for the history of agriculture in these times are printed; here it is possible to cite only the more important of them.

Of all the contemporary descriptions of agricultural practice the best known are the *General Views* sponsored by the Board of Agriculture (which was founded in 1793 and lasted

[76] W. E. Tate, 'Some Unexplored Records of the Enclosure Movement', *E.H.R.* lvii (1942); M. W. Beresford, 'Minutes of Enclosure Awards', *B.I.H.R.* xxi (1946–8); R. C. Russell, 'Parliamentary Enclosure'.

until 1821).[77] There are usually two reports for each county, one published within the period 1793 to 1796, and a second edition, often by a different writer, between *c.* 1805 and 1817. William Marshall, the agriculturalist and philologist, published between 1808 and 1817 in a number of volumes a *Review and Complete Abstract of the Reports of the Board of Agriculture* which contains also information on more recent developments. The *General Views* are important not so much for their accuracy (for they were subjective accounts laying stress more on the 'improving' farming than on the average state of husbandry, and not always reliable),[78] but because of the paucity of other evidence at this time.

Some of the *General Views* were written by Arthur Young, the Secretary to the Board, and other works by Young, especially his *Tours* of the 1760s and 1770s,[79] are an important source, as are other works by William Marshall.[80] Other surveys also exist. *Communications to the Board of Agriculture relative to the Husbandry of the Country* (7 vols., 1797–1811) contains information on local topics. Volume v, for example, has tables showing the rise of rent, tithes, rates, and labour costs in each county, and the replies of correspondents to a

[77] Published under the titles *A General View of the Agriculture of* [name of county] and listed in Lord Ernle (R. E. Prothero), *English Farming Past and Present*, ed. Sir D. Hall (1961 edn), pp. xcix–c, in W. F. Perkins, *British and Irish Writers on Agriculture* (1939 edn), and in Grigg, 'Changing Agricultural Geography', 92 n. 27.

[78] For strictures on the *General Views*, see Grigg, 'Changing Agricultural Geography', 76–7.

[79] *A Six Weeks' Tour through the Southern Counties of England and Wales* (1768); *A Six Months' Tour through the North of England* (4 vols., 1770); *A Farmer's Tour through the East of England* (4 vols., 1771).

[80] *The Rural Economy of Norfolk* (2 vols., 1787); *The Rural Economy of Yorkshire* (2 vols., 1788); *The Rural Economy of Gloucestershire* (2 vols., 1789); *The Rural Economy of the Southern Counties* (2 vols., 1789); *The Rural Economy of the Midland Counties* (2 vols., 1790); *The Rural Economy of the West of England* (2 vols., 1796); *General Remarks on Agriculture in the Southern Counties* (2 vols., 1799).

questionnaire on the comparative expenses of arable cultivation in the late eighteenth century. Another Board of Agriculture report, *The Agricultural State of the Kingdom in February, March, and April 1816* (1816),[81] gives details for a few parishes in each county of replies to queries about agricultural distress and poverty. The details vary from county to county and perhaps paint too black a picture. William Cobbett's *Rural Rides* are more polemical than technical, but there are a number of important books from the mid-century which must now be regarded as primary sources. The Society for the Diffusion of Useful Knowledge published in 1840 its third volume of *British Husbandry* which contains a series of first-hand reports on a few select farms in several counties including Yorkshire, Hampshire, Cumberland, and Gloucestershire. James Caird's *English Agriculture in 1850–1* (1852) has county descriptions (some much more detailed than others), including a few detailed accounts of individual farms.

Another work of this period, L. de Lavergne's, *The Rural Economy of England, Scotland and Ireland* (1855), draws heavily on Caird. Sir H. Rider Haggard's *Rural England* (1902; 2nd edn 1906) gives a county by county picture of English farming at the beginning of the twentieth century, with some details of a few individual farms.

County histories and topographies are of limited use to the agricultural historian, though they must be searched, particularly for the eighteenth and early nineteenth centuries when other evidence is lacking. Those published later in the nineteenth century often repeat, without acknowledgement, the information found in the *General Views* even though it may by then have been out of date.[82]

Certain journals also contain useful information. The *Annals of Agriculture* (annually, 1784–1815), edited by Arthur

---

[81] Reprinted 1970, with introduction by G. E. Mingay.
[82] Grigg, 'Changing Agricultural Geography', 77.

Young, is a most important source which has been too little used by local historians. It contains a wide variety of materials difficult to describe briefly, but much of it pertaining to particular areas, counties, or even individual farms and estates. Its volumes will often prove a mine of information.[83]

The *Farmers' Magazine* (1800–25) has accounts of farming practice in England and quarterly reports from local correspondents.[84] The *Gardener's Chronicle and Agricultural Gazette* for 1867 has a national survey of harvesting methods.[85] Newspapers, rather a neglected source for agricultural history, contain much information, including reports on the progress of seasonal work, the state of the crops and of local markets, and the price of labour. In periods of depression correspondence from farmers (often unsigned) gives an insight into relations with landlords, while local meetings of agricultural interest will usually be reported.

Of particular significance is the *Journal of the Royal Agricultural Society* which first appeared in 1839 and is still being published. Throughout its volumes is to be found much information on agriculture in different parts of the country. In particular between 1845 and 1869 a series of prize essays was published, each describing the agriculture of an individual county.[86] Detailed descriptions of particular parishes are sometimes to be found. On the whole the prize essays are of a higher quality than the *General Views*, distinguishing better between the average and the progressive.[87]

[83] To quote a single example, vol. xxiv (1795) prints a large number of replies from parishes to a questionnaire sent out by Arthur Young concerning agricultural prices and the state of certain crops.

[84] Grigg, 'Changing Agricultural Geography', 78.

[85] E. J. T. Collins, 'Harvest Technology and Labour Supply in Britain, 1790–1870', *Ec.H.R.*, 2nd ser., xxii (1969), 458n.

[86] All the counties are covered. For a complete key to the volumes of the *Journal* containing these essays, see Ernle, *English Farming*, pp. cii–ciii, and Grigg, 'Changing Agricultural Geography', 92–3, n. 40. Some other reports on counties were published; e.g., H. Wright on Yorkshire (vol. xxii (1861)). [87] Grigg, 'Changing Agricultural Geography', 78–9.

The value of the records of the land tax to the local agricultural historian is controversial.[88] They are considered most likely to be useful for the period between 1780 and 1832,[89] for during those years duplicates of the annual assessments for each parish were deposited with the clerk of the peace and are now to be found, if they still exist, with the quarter-sessions records.[90]

The assessments and returns were usually presented in four columns: (a) names of landowners, (b) names of occupiers of the land (though up to 1780 little effort was made to distinguish between owners and tenant occupiers), (c) the rateable value, and (d) the amount assessed or paid. In some cases the name of the property is given, and it may be stated that it was a close, garden, cottage, etc. Sometimes there was a fifth column of (e) sums exonerated (see below). The pitfalls of using the land-tax documents have been described by G. E. Mingay[91] and an assessment of how, given local knowledge, they may be used with caution has been made by J. M. Martin.[92] Martin elsewhere illustrates how the records can be used effectively in conjunction with enclosure records to indicate significant trends in local landownership.[93]

[88] For the land tax as a source, see E. Davies, 'The Small Landowner, 1780–1832, in the Light of the Land Tax Assessments', *Ec.H.R.* i (1927); D. B. Grigg, 'The Land Tax Returns', *Ag.H.R.* xi (1963); G. E. Mingay 'The Land Tax Assessments and the Small Landowner', *Ec.H.R.*, 2nd ser., xvii (1964); J. M. Martin, 'Landownership and the Land Tax Returns', *Ag.H.R.* xiv (1966); H. G. Hunt, 'Land Tax Assessments', *History* lii (1967). See also letter by G. E. Mingay in *Ag.H.R.* xv (1967), 18.

[89] Between these dates the payment of land tax was regarded as an indication of the right to claim a parliamentary vote. For a brief description of the history of the tax, see West, *Village Records*, 144–5.

[90] Some land-tax returns, of course, exist outside these dates. For an indication of the years for which they are available for different counties, see list in Davies, 'Small Landowner'. This list is, however, considerably out of date. See also *P.R.O. Guide* ii, 197 (Class I.R.2).

[91] Mingay, 'Land Tax Assessments'.   [92] Martin, 'Landownership'.

[93] J. M. Martin, 'The Parliamentary Enclosure Movement and Rural Society in Warwickshire', *Ag.H.R.* xv (1967).

In general the land-tax records have been used by historians to throw light on two matters – the size of farms, and the structure of landownership. It is now believed that parliamentary enclosure has been exaggerated as a factor in the disappearance of the small landowners (the owner-occupiers) who still remained numerous until the 1870s. What is less certain is the regional distribution of farm size, and it is here that the study of the land-tax and other records by the local historian may make a contribution to agricultural history generally. As D. B. Grigg points out, 'the relative importance of tenants may well help to explain regional differences in farm improvement'. The distribution of large estates may have been significant in the rate of agricultural advance.[94]

There are certain problems in the use of the land-tax records of which the investigator must be aware. In attempting to assess the distribution of farms of different sizes one is faced with the difficulty of relating the tax paid to acreage. The tax was based on the value of the land not at the time, but in 1692, and caution is needed in relating this to acreage. A simple division of the total acreage of a parish into the total land tax paid may often, however, indicate a rough pattern of farm size, except where the parish contains soils of widely contrasting worth, or where there is urban development. But it must be remembered that the returns include assessments on occupiers of tiny pieces of land who were not farmers but inn-holders, blacksmiths, and so on. The names of such men may, however, be recognized by the historian with local knowledge. When comparing one parish with another it must be recalled that, whereas the incidence of the tax burden was roughly the same within counties, it might vary from county to county.

There are also difficulties in using the land-tax records to compare the extent of owner-occupation as opposed to

[94] Grigg, 'Changing Agricultural Geography', 88–9.

farming by tenants. The relative numbers of owner-occupiers and landlords who let to tenants can be found from year to year by addition, and this can be related to the tax they paid. It would be dangerous, however, to assume that, over an area of any size, a number of, say, owner-occupiers each paying the same amount of tax owned farms of equivalent size – for the reasons noted above. Moreover, the value of buildings may lead to distortions, for the tax was paid on some buildings and also on some offices of profit, and on tithes.[95] Nevertheless, taking into account such caveats, the expression of the tax paid by owner-occupiers as a percentage of the parish's total tax will indicate roughly the proportion of land farmed by them.[96]

Other matters of which the historian should be aware are that in the early returns owners and tenants sometimes get placed in the wrong columns (for the actual occupier was then responsible for the tax) or the columns have no headings so that which is which has to be determined. Some documents are quarterly returns, some are annual, and this again must be determined, for it is not always stated. Again, many occupiers of tiny pieces of land and rights of common escaped the tax before enclosure but were subsequently returned. Thus an apparent increase in the number of small owner-occupiers may be due solely to the legalization of their ownership in this way. Another complication arises from the fact that from 1798 owners of land were permitted to redeem their tax commitment for a lump sum. Those thus

[95] Earlier returns do not distinguish these, but they can sometimes be recognized (e.g. payment by a clergyman may be suspected of being on tithe) or they may be traced back from later returns where (from 1815) they were distinguished.

[96] Grigg, 'Land Tax Returns', shows, for two Lincolnshire parishes, that a satisfactory picture of the distribution of landownership can be extracted from the land-tax records. He emphasizes, however, that it is more revealing to examine the distribution in small units (like the parish) than to consider the county as a whole.

exonerated were omitted from some assessments, the value of which to the historian is thus diminished. Often, however, they remain in the assessment with an indication of the payment they would otherwise have had to make. Mingay has suggested that there were many illegal avoidances of the tax, but Martin finds no evidence for this in Warwickshire. It is a possibility, however, of which the local historian must be aware.

Finally, it must be realized that in any classification of owners or occupiers a tenant in one parish may well be an owner-occupier in another, so that conclusions about the importance of the owner-occupier in any area must be made with caution if based upon the investigation of only one or two parishes.

Returning to matters of husbandry, a useful exercise is to compare the findings in the two county reports in the *General Views* with the more detailed evidence provided by the Home Office crop returns of the period of the Napoleonic Wars. There were a number of these and only the more important can be noted here.[97]

Crop returns for 1794 and 1795 do not exist for everywhere and they vary in content. Some give information by parishes, others by hundreds, some even by individual holdings. They rarely exist for a whole county.[98] Some provide yields in bushels per acre, others acreages of various crops, and others impressionistic reports. It is not clear how

[97] For some others, see Grigg, 'Changing Agricultural Geography'.

[98] They are to be found in the Home Office papers: P.R.O., Class H.O.42/36 and 37, and in local collections (e.g. for Glos. and Leics.). Some counties may be mentioned in detail: H.O.42/36 includes parish information for a few parishes in Middx, Corn., and Sussex, and very detailed information for Northants. parishes. H.O.42/37 includes information for Middx, Northants., Ches., Wilts., Glos., Essex (details by hundreds), and Shropshire (general account for county). For further details, see also Grigg, 'Changing Agricultural Geography', 81.

useful they are: evidently they vary in accuracy and must be used with caution.[99]

The so-called livestock returns for 1796, 1798, 1801, and 1803 exist for parishes in a few counties, including Essex, Sussex, Lincolnshire, Dorset, Somerset, and Gloucestershire, in local depositories and some give details, by parishes, of crops and grain in store as well as livestock.[100]

Returns to an enquiry of 1800 exist for most dioceses.[101] They were intended to be arranged by counties and districts and not parishes,[102] but in fact some definitely relate to specific parishes; others are clearly useful in giving a picture of agriculture in the parish of the incumbent making the return and its surrounding area. They provide details of crops, prices of agricultural produce, and general remarks covering the years 1798, 1799, and 1800.[103]

The returns for 1801[104] are the most generally useful and best known of the crop returns of this period. They are arranged by dioceses and parishes and most counties are represented. They provide acreage returns, on a printed form, for specific crops (wheat, barley, oats, potatoes, peas, beans, and turnips or rape) and often useful general remarks which at times give information on marketing and other matters. A list of those in print is in *Agricultural History*

[99] Cf. W. E. Minchinton, 'Agricultural Returns during the Napoleonic Wars', *Ag.H.R.* i (1953), 35, 41, 42.

[100] See Grigg, 'Changing Agricultural Geography', 83–4, and sources entered therein.

[101] In P.R.O., Class H.O.42/52 5.

[102] Minchinton, 'Agricultural Returns', 37.

[103] They are particularly worth consulting for Lincs. (H.O.42/52, 53), Northants. (H.O.42/53, 54), Corn. (H.O.42/53), Staffs., Eccleshall district (H.O. 42/53), East Riding of Yorks. (H.O. 42/54), Ches. (*ibid.* very detailed), Som. (*ibid.* nos. 326 sqq.), Dorset (*ibid.*), Cambs. (*ibid.* esp. 502 sqq.), Lincs. (*ibid.*). Wilts (*ibid.* 405 sqq.), and perhaps Essex (H.O.42/55, no. 274). Only one diocese (Peterborough) is completely unrepresented.

[104] In P.R.O., Class H.O.67. Some are found locally; the Dorset returns, e.g., are in the Dorset County Record Office.

Review i (1953), which also contains a critical assessment.[105] It is generally considered that the returns tend to err on the side of understatement, but information on proportions of crops are probably significant and the detailed comments may be very valuable. They provide more concrete data to supplement the rather more impressionistic accounts of the *General Views*. The accuracy of the returns may, however, vary from county to county. W. G. Hoskins, on grounds he explains in detail, believes the returns for Devon, for example, to be largely useless, but those for Leicestershire, and probably some other counties, substantially accurate.[106] It should be noted, however, that no return of fallow land or land permanently or temporarily under grass was required.

For the eighteenth century there may be tithe surveys to indicate the usage of land subject to tithe. These are to be found in private papers or among the ecclesiastical records.[107] More generally important are tithe commutation records. Before 1836 tithes in some places had been converted to money payments, often by agreement between the tithe owners and farmers, or had disappeared when, under terms of a parliamentary enclosure Act, the owner received an allotment of land in its place. Following the tithe commutation Acts of 1836–60 all remaining tithes (for some 12,000 parishes) were converted to a fluctuating annual money payment, known as 'corn rents' or 'tithe rent charge'. Most of the surveys resulting from this legislation were made

[105] For articles based on these returns, see Grigg, 'Changing Agricultural Geography', 94, n. 60. See also H. C. K. Henderson, 'Agriculture in England and Wales in 1801', *Geographical Jnl* cxviii (1952).

[106] W. G. Hoskins, 'The Leicestershire Crop Returns for 1801', *Transactions of the Leics. Archaeological Soc.* xxiv (1948), 128 sqq.

[107] E. J. Evans, *Tithes and the Tithe Commutation Act, 1836* (1978); J. H. Clapham, 'Tithe Surveys as a Source of Agrarian History', *Cambridge Historical Jnl* i (1923–5). Exhibits in tithe suits at ecclesiastical courts may also contain useful information: E. R. Brinkworth, 'The Study and Use of Archdeacons' Court Records: Illustrated from the Oxford Records, 1566–1759', *T.R.H.S.*, 4th ser., xxv (1943), 115–16.

before 1841 and almost all by 1851. Valuable information may be obtained from the apportionments and maps which resulted from the surveys. Copies are normally to be found at the Public Record Office[108] and, if they survive, in diocesan registries, and among parish records.[109]

The tithe maps are large-scale maps (varying between about 27 inches and 13 inches to the mile) showing in great detail all the physical features of the parish including field boundaries, woods, roads, streams, and buildings. Some indicate land use by means of colours. Each field or plot of land bears a number which allows identification in the apportionment.[110]

The tithe apportionments comprise, first, the articles of agreement, which include details of the area of the parish, and the area subject to tithe, indicating how much was arable, grass, or other kinds of land; and, secondly, the schedule, which is more useful for the agricultural historian. The schedule consists of a number of columns indicating alphabetically the names of landowners in the parish, the

[108] These records were formerly held by the Tithe Redemption Commission, East Block, Barrington Road, Worthing, Sussex, which retains microfilm copies. They are now P.R.O., Classes I.R.29 (apportionments) and I.R.30 (maps). See also *Inland Revenue, Tithe Maps and Apportionments (Bedford to Northumberland)* and *(Nottingham to Yorkshire, Wales)*, List and Index Soc., lxviii, lxxxiii (1971–2), and also *Index to the Tithe Survey* (a special printing of the 1st edn of the 1-inch O.S. maps showing parishes for which a tithe survey was made: R. Douch, *Local History and the Teacher* (1967), 38. A parliamentary paper, *Return of all Tithes Commuted* (1887) lxiv, 239–533, provides a convenient list of all parishes for which records should exist.

[109] For the procedure involved in their compilation, see H. C. Prince, 'Tithe Surveys of the Mid 19th Century', *Ag.H.R.* vii (1954); and P. Walne, 'The Records of the Tithe Redemption Commission', *Jnl of the Society of Archivists* i (1957) (reprinted by the Board of Inland Revenue under the title *Records of the Tithe Redemption Office* (n.d.)). The following description draws much on these.

[110] Harley, *Maps,* chapter 3; L. M. Munby, 'Tithe Apportionments and Maps', *History* liv (1969).

occupier of each piece of land, with its number on the map, the name or a description of the premises (as, for example, croft, barn and fold, garden, stable, plantation, or the name of a field), usually its state of cultivation (as arable, meadow, pasture, wood) if appropriate (sometimes actual crops may be noted), its area, and the rent charge approved in lieu of tithe. Sometimes additional remarks are made in a final column. A summary at the end provides the total areas of each landowner and occupier. The copies of the tithe records kept at the Public Record Office have been kept up to date so that changes in the tithe areas resultant on such events as the construction of roads and railways or reallocation consequent on enclosure are documented.

Together the maps and apportionments have been said to 'rank as the most complete record of the agrarian landscape at any period'.[111] They may give information not only on landownership and occupation, but also on size of farms, use of land, and extent of still unenclosed land and of heath, waste, or other unproductive land (exempt from tithe).[112] Where tithe redemption preceded the enclosure the maps will provide a valuable record of the previous topography and field system.

Less well known, but very valuable, are the tithe files, also to be found at the Public Record Office.[113] They exist for each tithe district (generally a parish), and the most important of the documents contained in them are the correspondence, consisting of replies to a printed questionnaire (ap-

[111] Prince, 'Tithe Surveys', 14.

[112] For the investigation of landownership by computer techniques using tithe apportionments, see R. J. P. Kain, 'Tithe Surveys and Landownership', *Jnl of Historical Geography* i (1975).

[113] P.R.O., Class I.R.18. For a description and examples of content, see E. A. Cox and B. R. Dittmer, 'The Tithe Files of the Mid 19th Century', *Ag.H.R.* xii (1965). Files concerning tithes in the City of London are in P.R.O., Class M.A.F.8; papers on payment of tithe by local authorities are in Class H.L.G.35.

parently varying from county to county) giving information on areas of arable, pasture, and common, courses of crop rotation, kinds of soil, and estimates of livestock. Sometimes attached remarks include information on yields of crops and markets. Occasionally a report on agricultural matters by the assistant commissioner is included and sometimes there are also minutes of meetings held where agreement was not easily obtained. These may contain, in evidence, detailed information on individual farms.

Annual parish agricultural summaries exist in manuscript[114] for most counties for years from 1866 (except 1868, 1871, 1872, 1892, 1893), and these must often be regarded as a prime source for the local historian for agricultural matters in recent times. They must, however, be used with caution. For various reasons, however, these are ruled out as a source universally useful for all parishes, and have defects which should be understood if they are studied at all.[115] The returns are not strictly comparable year against year over the whole period. New categories of information were added from time to time; old categories were subdivided, otherwise amended, or occasionally dropped. The basic area of the holding required or requested to make a return varied from time to time,[116] and not all who should have made a return did so, with the result that officials made

[114] At the P.R.O. in Class M.A.F.68.

[115] These documents are described and criticized in three articles by J. T. Coppock: 'The Statistical Assessment of British Agriculture', *Ag.H.R.* iv (1956); 'The Agricultural Returns as a Source for Local History', *Amateur Historian* iv (1958–60); 'The Cartographic Representation of British Agricultural Statistics', *Geography* l (1965); and in J. M. Ramsay, 'The Development of Agricultural Statistics', *Jnl of the Proceedings of the Agricultural Economics Soc.* vi, no. 2 (1940), which also gives details of other recent statistical investigations into farming matters. See also P. G. Craigie, 'Statistics of English Agricultural Production', *Jnl Royal Statistical Soc.* xliv (1883).

[116] 1866: holdings of 5 acres and over; 1867–8: all holdings; 1869–91: ¼ acre and over; 1891 to present: 1 acre and over.

estimates to fill gaps.[117] The unit of the summary is the parish, but in fact includes all land belonging to holdings of which the homesteads lay within the parish boundary. Changes in farm and parish boundaries also affect comparability.[118]

Local knowledge and the extent of alternative sources of information will no doubt guide the historian in deciding whether these returns should be used or not for the history of any particular local region. They are clearly most useful where parishes are large and farms small, or where other information is particularly sparse. Where farms are large and parishes small it is more likely that significant areas outside the parish are included in the summary. Even then, however, if very little other information is available they may be worth looking at.

If it is intended to search these records, then the following points may be helpful. Returns for the years up to 1871 are perhaps the least reliable and should probably be ignored altogether. Comparisons from year to year for later years can only be made with caution. Rises of acreages etc. in returns in the initial years of collection are likely to be due to increased accuracy rather than an increase in the area cropped etc. Most crop and livestock figures are considered, however, sufficiently comparable over long periods to be valuable.

Nevertheless, when attempting comparisons, ratios of different crops and animals provide the only safe basis (especially when based on mean figures for a number of years – say blocks of four).[119] Analysis of the relative importance of, for example, different types of crops, rather than

[117] Estimated figures are, however, distinguished. Returns were compulsory only from 1918 to 1921, and from 1925.

[118] For this topic, see J. T. Coppock, 'Changes in Farm and Field Boundaries in the 19th Century', *Amateur Historian* iii (1956–8).

[119] These should be carefully selected and perhaps spaced roughly every 20–25 years.

emphasis on actual acreages, is perhaps the most satisfactory approach.[120] It may be noted that some twentieth-century summaries include the numbers of men and women employed on the land both full-time and part-time.

The parish summaries form the basis for annual parliamentary papers from 1866 conflating the information on a county basis.[121] There are, of course, a multitude of other parliamentary papers from which the local historian may extract detailed evidence on agrarian matters in the locality he is studying. These are, however, so numerous that only a few can be mentioned here.[122] Particularly important are the reports of committees on agricultural distress in the 1820s and 1830s,[123] and similar investigations for the 1880s and 1890s.[124] Also useful are the reports of the Select Committees on Agricultural Customs published in 1847–8 and 1866,[125] the reports on the employment of women and children in

---

[120] Acreages of woodland (collected 1872, 1880, 1888, 1891, 1895, 1905, 1913) are thought to be particularly unreliable.

[121] *Agricultural Returns* (from 1866; called *Agricultural Statistics* from 1907).

[122] But see W. R. Powell, *Local History from Blue Books: Select List of Sessional Papers of the House of Commons* (1962), 22–45, Grigg, 'Changing Agricultural Geography', 93 nn. 43–9.

[123] *Rep. Select Committee on Agricultural Distress* (1820) ii (mainly important for agricultural prices); *Reps. Select Committee on Petitions Complaining of the Depressed State of the Agriculture of the U.K.* (1821) ix; (1822) v (list of places from which petitions came, 1820–22); *Rep. Select Committee into the Present State of Agriculture and of Persons Employed in Agriculture in the U.K.* (1833) v (important because indexed); *First, Second, and Third Reps. Select Committee on the State of Agriculture and the Causes of Distress* (1836) viii (I and II) (indexed): *Rep. Select Committee of the House of Lords on the State of Agriculture* (1837) v (indexed).

[124] *Rep. R. Commission on Depressed Condition of the Agricultural Interests* (1881) xv–xvii; (1882) xiv (extremely detailed but not indexed); *First and Second Reps. R. Commission on the Agricultural Depression* (1894) xvi (I–III); (1896) xvi, xvii (descriptions of witnesses provides a topographical key); *Final Report* (1897) xv (information on rateable values of land in poor-law unions). See also list in Ernle, *English Farming*, pp. cv sqq.

[125] (1847–8) vii (indexed); (1866) vi (indexed).

agriculture in 1843,[126] and later in the century,[127] various reports on agricultural wages,[128] the return of owners of land in 1874,[129] and reports on stock, corn trade, wool trade, markets, hops, allotments, and smallholdings. The likelihood of bias and of interested presentation of material in reports and evidence must, of course, be taken into account in using such material.

A report of a select committee on real property[130] contains appendixes giving the number of occupiers of land in six tithe districts in each county, subdividing them into four groups according to the area of land occupied, and also of acreages in a number of districts in several counties including Cornwall, Devon, Norfolk, Suffolk, and Somerset.

The published censuses of population, of course, provide evidence on agricultural occupations and the numbers engaged in them. The 1831 census gives the number of farmers in each parish, from which average farm size can be worked out.[131] The original census enumerators' schedules for 1851 (at the Public Record Office) include the names of farmers, indicating how many acres they farmed and how many labourers they employed.[132] The schedules can also be used very easily to show how many people in the parish were engaged in agriculture and often in what capacity, and are certainly worth searching for this purpose.

---

[126] (1843) xii (for twelve counties) (reps. assistant poor law commissioners, and evidence).

[127] *Rep. R. Commission on Children and Women in Agriculture* (1867–8) xvii; (1868–9) xiii; (1870) xiii. Last vol. contains index.

[128] *Rep. Select Committee on Labourers' Wages* (1824) vi; *Returns of Agricultural Labourers' Average Weekly Earnings* (1861) l; (1871) lvi; (1873) liii (provide data by poor-law unions); *First and Second Reps. Board of Trade on Agricultural Labourers' Wages* (1900) lxxxii (for a few farms, information over half a century); (1905) xcvii. For prices and wages, see also p. 115 n. 84.

[129] *Return of Owners of Land in Each County* (1874) lxxii (I and II).

[130] (1846) vi (2).

[131] Grigg, 'Changing Agricultural Geography', 88.

[132] Class H.O.107.

It has been suggested that the records of the income (property) tax (levied between 1799 and 1816), of the county rate of the nineteenth century, and of the income tax (for 1842–3 and 1859–60) can provide for any area in England a means for comparing the changing relative values of agricultural land, and therefore of relative progress or decline in local farming.[133] Schedule A property-tax assessments for every English parish were published for the year 1815,[134] and Schedule A income-tax assessments for every parish for the years 1842–3 and 1859–60.[135] County rate assessments may exist locally for 1815, 1840, and 1847. The property tax and the county rate assessments were on buildings as well as on land, and are therefore of value for the purpose suggested only for agricultural areas where no great expansion of building took place. They can then be used to show the average rent per acre in various parishes. The income-tax assessments distinguished between land not built on (based on annual value) and other items. Bearing in mind that the 1842–3 income-tax assessment was held to have undervalued land, it should be possible from these sources to construct for any agricultural area tables or maps showing the rent per acre in 1815, 1842–3, and 1859–60, and the percentage change in rent per acre between 1815 and 1840–7, and between 1842–3 and 1859–60. Such information may be augmented by other evidence such as that culled from estate records.

Collections, now often in local record offices, of estate

[133] D. B. Grigg, 'The Agricultural Revolution in South Lincolnshire', *Transactions of the Institute of British Geographers* xxx (1962). This article should be consulted for full details, and further references.

[134] (1818) xix. The original income- and property-tax returns, however, exist for most parishes for the period 1799–1816 in P.R.O., Class E.182. They are listed by counties with other records in E.181, in A. Hope-Jones, *Income Tax in the Napoleonic Wars* (1939), appendix I.

[135] (1844) xxxii; (1860) xxxix. P.R.O., Class I.R.14, contains surviving returns by parishes of land and house values for 1842–3 and 1888–9. *Parliamentary Constituencies (Population)* (1882) lii lists assessments and tax paid for each constituency in 1879–80. See also p. 69, above.

agents' records may also be useful for the modern period. They include sale and valuation books, property registers, sale catalogues, accounts books, and correspondence. The prosperity of agriculture in an area at a particular time may be made apparent from these records.[136]

The reports of the Land Utilization Survey of Britain of the 1930s[137] treat agriculture in each county or region as a whole. Many, however, have a good survey of the history of agriculture in the county which may serve as a useful starting point. In some, detailed information on individual farms or places may be included, either because they are unusual or as examples of the typical. The East Riding survey, for example, prints maps of typical parts of each region showing what crops are in the fields; the surveys for Devon and Cornwall give details of specimen farms and these could be identified from accompanying maps. A land utilization map accompanies each county survey, and can be of use for the individual place.

The National Farm Survey of 1941–3 formed the basis of a government publication of that name.[138] The conclusions there contained derive from a 15 per cent sample of information culled from every farm in the country.

Estate and farm records are, of course, a prime source for the local history of agriculture, both before and after 1750, but they vary very much in content and type.[139] Some have already been touched on in the previous section. Deeds and leases[140] are important for individual farms and estates, and

---

[136] B. S. Smith, 'The Business Archives of Estate Agents', *Jnl Soc. Archivists* iii (1967).

[137] Published in a number of volumes under the general title of *The Land of Britain* followed by county name and part no. Parts 1–92 published 1937–40. An extra volume on the Channel Islands was published in 1950.

[138] Ministry of Agriculture and Fisheries, *National Farm Survey of England and Wales (1941–1943): A Summary Report* (1946).

[139] See Hoskins, *Fieldwork* 111 sqq. For extents, see above, pp. 51–2, 169–70, 174, and, for manorial accounts, above, p. 176.

[140] See pp. 301–4.

among other records of particular value are account books and other business records[141] and estate maps.[142]

It may be noted that there is now a large new collection of farm records at the University of Reading Library. This consists mainly of farm account books, but also includes diaries, letters, sale catalogues,[143] labour books, leases, registers, and valuations. There are also a certain number of maps, photographs, and printed items. The records so far collected come mostly (but not entirely) from the south of England and the Midlands. Chronologically the records fall mainly in the period from the eighteenth century, but there are some earlier ones.

Newspaper advertisements of farms for sale and to let can throw light on the state of agriculture and the local land market.[144] Advertisements for sale of crops and stock can also shed light on the nature and fortunes of farming in a district. The agricultural historian may also cull from recent farm records such as accounts, day books, labour books, cropping books, granary books, herd and flock books,

---

[141] R. J. Colyer, 'The Use of Home Farm Accounts as Sources for Nineteenth Century Agricultural History', *Local Historian* xi (1974–6); E. L. Jones and E. J. T. Collins, 'The Collection and Analysis of Farm Record Books', *Jnl Soc. Archivists* ii (1965). For examples in print, see, e.g., Eleanor C. Lodge (ed.), *Account Book of a Kentish Estate, 1616–1704*, Records of Social and Economic History of England and Wales vi (1927); G. E. Fussell (ed.), *Robert Loder's Farm Accounts, 1610–20*, Camden Soc., 3rd ser., liii (1936). N.b., also, E. J. Willson, 'Commercial Gardening Records', *Archives* xii (1976).

[142] For much bibliographical information on estate maps, their content, and how to trace them, see Harley, *Maps*, chapter 2; F. G. Emmison, 'Estate Maps and Surveys', *History* xlviii (1963); A. R. H. Baker, 'Local History and Early Estate Maps', *Amateur Historian* v (1961–2). See also p. 31.

[143] Many of these are to be found in local record offices, and there is a collection at the B.L.

[144] For greater detail, see P. Parry 'A Source for Agricultural History: Newspaper Advertisements', *Local Historian* ix (1970–1).

diaries and memoranda, information on the financial fortunes of the farmer, how the farmer raised capital and invested it, crop and milk yields, lambing and calving rates, livestock weights, the amount of the wool-clip, farming practice, tools and implements, land usage, marketing methods, and so on.[145]

[145] E. J. T. Collins, 'Historical Farm Records', *Archives* vii (1966), esp. 145; cf. L. J. Redstone and F. W. Steer, *Local Records* (1953), 200–1.

CHAPTER 7

Education

Educational records are here dealt with, for the sake of convenience, in three sections.[1] The first treats records relating to those schools which were intended to provide mainly elementary education. The second section describes the sources for schools providing what would now be considered secondary education. A third section deals with adult education, loosely embracing the formal institutional education, elementary or otherwise, and the less formal

[1] Reference books useful for the whole field of educational sources include: A. Christopher, *An Index to Nineteenth Century British Educational Biography*, Education Libraries Bulletin, supplement no. 10 (1965); P. H. J. H. Gosden, *Educational Administration in England and Wales: A Bibliographical Guide*, University of Leeds, Institute of Education, Paper 6 (1967); C. W. J. Higson, *Sources for the History of Education* (1967) and *Supplement* (1976) (lists published primary material, indicating its whereabouts in (mainly) university Institutes of Education libraries); S. H. Atkins, *A Select Check List of Printed Material on Education Published in English to 1800* (1970); S. K. Kimmance, *A Guide to the Literature of Education*, Education Libraries Bulletin, supplement no. 1 (1961); D. W. Sylvester, *Educational Documents, 800–1816* (1970); J. S. Maclure, *Educational Documents, England and Wales, 1816–1967* (1965). For guidance on parliamentary papers concerned with education, see W. R. Powell, *Local History from Blue Books: Select List of the Sessional Papers of the House of Commons* (1962); M. Argles, 'British Government Publications in Education during the Nineteenth Century', *History of Education Soc. Bulletin* v (1970); J. E. Vaughan and M. Argles, *British Government Publications Concerning Education: An Introductory Guide* (1968 edn); G. Sutherland (ed.), *Government and Society in Nineteenth Century Britain: Commentaries on British Parliamentary Papers: Education* (1977). Very useful is V. F. Gilbert and C. Holmes (eds.), *Theses and Dissertations on the History of Education at British and Irish Universities between 1900 and 1976* (1979).

cultural activity of those of post-school age. The records for the history of universities and teacher-training establishments are not considered in this book although in the nineteenth century some of them were to a certain extent 'local' institutions.[2]

A division into elementary and secondary is necessarily artificial since, for example, some endowed 'grammar schools', despite the intention of their founders, were by the nineteenth century providing mainly or entirely elementary education,[3] and for early periods the nature of the instruction is sometimes difficult to determine. In middle-class education, in particular, there was no clear-cut distinction between elementary and secondary. For that reason sources for all 'grammar' and for some other schools before the eighteenth century are dealt with in the second section, as, too, are the records of nineteenth- and twentieth-century private schools,[4] although some of these may have been elementary

---

[2] Teacher-training institutions were often diocesan, and in that sense local; diocesan records may therefore be of use. There is, too, information in the P.R.O. Class Ed.40 (teacher-training colleges, endowment files, 1858–1938): see *Department of Education and Sciences, Class List, Part IV*, List and Index Soc. lxii (1971). See also N. R. Tempest, 'Some Sources for the History of Teacher Training', *British Jnl Educational Studies* ix (1960). Pupil-teacher centres established by the school boards on a large scale were entirely local; some became local authority training colleges after 1902; many became girls' high schools in the early years of this century. Their early history, therefore, is to be sought in the records of the school boards and l.e.a.s dealt with below. See also M. Berry, *Teacher Training Institutions in England and Wales: A Bibliographical Guide to their History* (1973).

Some provincial universities and university colleges in the nineteenth century were essentially local, some being subsidized by the local technical instruction committees whose records are mentioned below (pp. 237,246). See also H. Silver and S. J. Teague, *The History of the British Universities, 1800–1969: A Bibliography* (1971), for the provincial universities.

[3] Cf. M. Sanderson, 'The Grammar School and the Education of the Poor, 1780–1840', *British Jnl Educational Studies* xi (1962–3), *passim*; W. A. L. Vincent, *The Grammar Schools: Their Continuing Tradition, 1660–1714* (1969), 16. [4] See pp. 239–40.

in nature. Much adult education in the nineteenth century, the sources for which are described in the third section, was also largely elementary.

ELEMENTARY EDUCATION

Apart from local monographs on the history of elementary education, of which there are a large number,[5] the most obvious general starting point is the volumes of the *Victoria History of the Counties of England*, if they cover the area concerned. Older volumes in this series may contain in their general sections brief histories of older elementary, particularly charity, schools.[6] Since the early 1950s the *V.C.H.* has attempted in its topographical volumes to deal with the history of every 'primary' school within the history of the parish or town concerned,[7] and there may also be general articles dealing with education in the town or county without particularly dealing individually with each school.[8]

Early 'petty' or parish schools of an elementary nature may be traced through the ecclesiastical sources noted below for secondary schools.[9] The first general movement for public popular education is, however, to be found in the charity-

[5] See P. Cunningham, *Local History of Education in England and Wales: A Bibliography* (1976).

[6] E.g., A. F. Leach, 'Elementary Schools founded before 1750', in *V.C.H., Warwickshire* ii, ed. W. Page (1908).

[7] R. B. Pugh, 'Sources for the History of English Primary Schools', *British Jnl Educational Studies* i (1952), 43. This article is extremely valuable and has been drawn on extensively in the ensuing account.

[8] E.g., Asa Briggs, 'Public Education: Introduction', in *V.C.H., Warwickshire* vii, ed. W. B. Stephens (1964); E. E. Butcher, 'Education', in *V.C.H., Wiltshire* v, ed. R. B. Pugh and E. Crittall (1957).

[9] See also, e.g., J. S. Purvis, *Educational Records* (1959), 4; R. O'Day, 'Church Records and the History of Education in Early Modern England, 1558–1642', *History of Education* ii (1973). For sources for the local extent of literacy in the early modern period, see references in L. Stone, 'Literacy and Education in England, 1640–1900', *Past and Present* xlii (1969); D. Cressy, *Literacy and the Social Order* (1980); and pp. 214–15.

school movement.[10] Not all charity schools were elementary in character at all periods,[11] but most were. Although not all were connected with the Society for the Promotion of Christian Knowledge, again, many were, and the records of the society are therefore of importance to the local and educational historian.[12]

The society's printed *Reports* (from 1720 *Reports and Accounts*)[13] for the period 1705 to 1732 contain to a varying degree lists of those schools (topographically arranged from 1715) which had a connection with the society. These lists may provide such details as the numbers and sexes of pupils and information as to the curriculum, together with financial details.[14] Some of the information was reproduced in contemporary annual publications, as, for example, in the earlier volumes of Chamberlayne's *Angliae Notitia* (from 1708 *Magnae Britanniae Notitia*),[15] published 1704–1811 (but from 1732 of little value to the local historian).

The manuscript records of the society include volumes of 'in' letters (1699 to 1729) and 'out' letters (1711 to 1729), as well as other correspondence; the minutes of the general board (from 1699)[16] and of the standing committee (1705 to

[10] The standard work on the subject is M. G. Jones, *The Charity School Movement* (1938).

[11] Cf. W. B. Stephens, 'Early Victorian Coventry: Education in an Industrial Community, 1830–1851', in A. Everitt (ed.), *Perspectives in English Urban History* (1973).

[12] See, especially, W. E. Tate, 'S.P.C.K. Archives', *Archives* iii (1957).

[13] The society has two incomplete sets. Its records are kept at Holy Trinity Church, Marylebone Road, London NW1. Tate, 'S.P.C.K. Archives', 108–9, lists the whereabouts elsewhere of copies of these volumes.

[14] For further information, see Tate, 'S.P.C.K. Archives', 108–9; Pugh, 'English Primary Schools', 43–4. The table for 1724 is reproduced in Jones, *Charity School Movement*, 364–71.

[15] Tate, 'S.P.C.K. Archives', 109; W. E. Tate, 'Some Sources for the History of English Grammar Schools', *British Jnl Educational Studies* ii (1954), 146. From 1707 Chamberlayne gives a report of the schools, and to 1716 reprints the topographical list.

[16] Draft minutes also exist.

1722, and from 1825); and 'miscellaneous abstracts' (1709 to 1733), which include several relating to charity schools.[17]

Miscellaneous sources for charity schools include the anonymous *Account of Several Workhouses, as also of Several Charity Schools* (1725; 2nd edn 1732).[18] Local charity records often exist among the parish archives, the archives of trustees, or, where borough councils had control of such schools, in the borough archives.[19] Many village and town charity schools have left their own records,[20] such as account and minute books,[21] and even printed material.[22]

Among the parliamentary papers the volumes of the *Reports of the Charity Commissioners* (1819–40)[23] contain information on elementary endowed (charity) schools. For certain places[24] later investigations into charities (1896–1907) bring the information in the earlier reports up to date.[25] Reports on endowed elementary schools are also to be found in the Taunton Commission's reports.[26]

[17] For details, see Tate, 'S.P.C.K. Archives', 110–15.

[18] Cited in *ibid.* 109–10.

[19] E.g., 'Newcastle Common Council Book, 1699–1718, 18 Dec. 1705' (reproduced in *Popular Education, 1700–1870*, University of Newcastle-upon-Tyne Archive Teaching Units, no. 4 (1969).

[20] E.g., in *ibid.*: 'Account Book of Durham Blue-Coat Charity School, 1718–1808'. Similarly the so-called '*Pietas Leodiensis*' consists of a collection of records, compiled *c.* 1835, concerning the charity school in Leeds: see Sylvester, *Educational Documents*, 187–9. Cf. 'Education in London before 1870: A Handlist of Selected Items in Guildhall Library', *Guildhall Miscellany* (Oct. 1970), 231–2.

[21] For a detailed list which may serve as an example, see *Records of Schools and other Endowed Institutions* (Surrey County Council, 1930) (some of the records pertain to grammar schools).

[22] E.g., *Short Account of the Blue-Coat Charity School (Birmingham): 1724 to 1784* [1784]; *1724–1830* (1832): in Birmingham City Reference Library.

[23] See the following section. These volumes begin in reports as *Charities for the Education of the Poor* but are later concerned with all charities.

[24] Berks., Devon, Co. Durham, Lancs., Wilts., most Welsh counties, London, and some other towns.

[25] Pugh, 'English Primary Schools', 44.

[26] See below, pp. 228–9.

Provision for elementary education in the late eighteenth and the nineteenth centuries included, apart from the charity schools, Sunday schools, private schools of one sort and another, the so-called voluntary (church and chapel) schools, ragged schools, poor-law or workhouse schools, and factory and colliery schools.

Sunday schools were, particularly at the beginning of this period, important not only for religious instruction but for the elementary education both of the young and of adults. Their extant records, however, are few and are to be found mainly among the general records of the church and chapel with which they were associated,[27] as well as in the records cited below relating to the voluntary schools and ragged schools. There is, however, much information to be found in various journals, periodicals, and parliamentary papers.[28]

Most important in the nineteenth century were the voluntary schools,[29] particularly those established by Anglican congregations. Often these were associated at some time or other with the National Society for Promoting the Education of the Poor in the Principles of the Established Church (now the National Society for Promoting Religious Education). The records of the National Society are thus of great significance. For any individual school which ever received a grant from the society (some 10,000 schools) there exists a file of papers in the society's archives.[30] There are also annual printed *Reports* which contain references to, lists of, and

[27] For examples, see K. Dawson and P. Wall, *Society and Industry in the 19th Century*, iv, *Education* (1969), 4–5. For Methodist Sunday schools, see also reports listed in H. F. Mathews, *Methodism and the Education of the People, 1791–1851* (1949), 208–9. The useful minutes and other records of the Sunday School Union are at the National Christian Education Council, Robert Denham House, Nutfield, Redhill, Surrey.

[28] See those listed in T. W. Laqueur, *Religion and Respectability* (1976), 255, 262 sqq.

[29] The following is based largely on Pugh, 'English Primary Schools', 44–6.

[30] At Church House, Dean's Yard, London SW1P 3NZ.

reports on National schools (i.e. schools in union with the society); these vary in content and nature from time to time.[31] Two general surveys of National schools made by the society exist in print—one for 1846–7,[32] and another for 1866–7.[33] For some areas there are for the society local published records, as, for example, the annual reports of the National Society in the Archdeaconry of Coventry,[34] and the annual reports of the Birmingham Archdeaconry Church Schools Association.[35] Diocesan registries may contain records of diocesan boards of education and their inspectorates.[36] Often the annual reports of these bodies were substantial volumes and could provide much material for the historian for the years from 1839.

Episcopal visitation records may also contain evidence about Anglican schools and also general information on the availability of schooling in parishes. Parish magazines, a commonly ignored source, often published detailed reports, including financial information, on the National schools, and parish records may contain correspondence between the National Society and incumbents.

A survey of Roman Catholic voluntary schools returned in 1845[37] was published as an appendix to the *Report of the*

[31] The society possesses a set. For details, see Pugh, 'English Primary Schools', 45.

[32] Copy with the society; another is in the library of the Department of Education and Science.

[33] Published as *Statistics of Church of England Schools for the Poor in England and Wales* (information on county basis only). For abstracts of answers to an enquiry of 1815, see the society's fifth report (cf. *History of Education Soc. Bulletin* ii (1968), 54–5; iii (1969), 58–60). For details of the 1846–7, 1866–7, and other surveys, see also C. K. F. Brown, *The Church's Part in Education, 1833–1941* (1942), *passim*.

[34] See *V.C.H.: Warwickshire* viii, 315.   [35] *ibid.* vii (1964), 547.

[36] D. M. Owen, *The Records of the Established Church in England* (1970), 30.

[37] Pugh, 'English Primary Schools', 46, incorrectly gives 1843, but it is certain that the returns pertain to 1845: I am grateful to Dr J. Kitching and Miss E. R. Poyser for this information.

Catholic Poor School Committee for 1849. Other published annual reports of this body (established 1847), and the manuscript records of the committee, are the main source for Roman Catholic schools in the later nineteenth century,[38] apart from general sources cited below.[39]

Similar manuscript records for Methodist schools are held by the Methodist Education Committee.[40] The Wesleyan Committee of Education published annual reports (1837–1932) and copies of these are held by the Methodist Church Division of Education and Youth.[41]

The British and Foreign School Society, nominally non-denominational but in fact associated with nonconformist schools, however, was, after the National Society, the most important sponsor of voluntary schools in the nineteenth century. Its manuscript records include minute books, information on its colleges, correspondence with local schools and committees, and other documents. The society's published annual reports contain information on many individual schools.[42]

[38] Held by the Catholic Education Council (which succeeded the Committee in 1905), 41 Cromwell Road, London sw7. Sets of the *Reports* (not all complete) are also at the B.L.; Bishop's House, Leeds; Ushaw College, Durham; and Archbishop's House, Westminster.

[39] For Roman Catholic periodicals and reference to diocesan archives which may be of use, see the notes to J. Kitching, 'The Catholic Poor Schools, 1800 to 1845', *Jnl Educational Administration and History* i, no. 2, and ii, no. 1 (1969).

[40] At 25 Marylebone Rd, London NW1.

[41] A complete set (except vol. xxxii (1871)). The series was continued by the Methodist Committee of Education (1933–73) and then by the Division of Education and Youth (2 Chester House, Pages Lane, Muswell Hill, London, N10 1PZ). See also reports and periodicals listed in Mathews, *Methodism*, 208–9.

[42] The records of the society and a complete set of the annual reports are at the West London Institute of Higher Education, Borough Road, Isleworth, Middlesex. See G. F. Bartle, 'The Records of the British and Foreign School Society at Borough Road', *Jnl Educational Administration and History* xii (1980); Pugh, 'English Primary Schools', 44–5.

For the nineteenth century the parliamentary papers provide an extremely fruitful source of information for the history of elementary education in any area. All those which might be used cannot be mentioned here, and the investigator will need to search the official indexes assiduously. There are certainly parliamentary papers, however, which are of prime importance as starting points for local investigation into educational provision, and which cannot be overlooked. It should, of course, be borne in mind that education was a particularly controversial matter and that official reports and evidence attached to them should always be viewed with some circumspection.

The *Abstract of the Answers and Returns Relative to the Poor* (1803–4) provides by parishes the number of children in schools of industry and information on the state of the parochial schools.[43] A select committee to enquire into the 'education of the lower orders' produced not only general reports in 1817 and 1818 which contain local evidence and are indexed,[44] but also a *Digest of Parochial Returns*[45] listing from the returns made by incumbents statements of the educational provision of every parish, topographically arranged under counties. Scotland and Wales are also covered. The *Digest* gives the capacity of the schools in each parish, and distinguishes endowed and non-endowed schools, and dame and Sunday schools. There are also 'observations' which in some cases are particularly illuminating.

Further official surveys took place in the 1830s and in

[43] (1803–4) xiii, not housed with the other parliamentary papers in the B.L. Official Publications Room, but at call mark 433, i, 12 (2).

[44] *Reps. Select Committee on the Education of the Lower Orders* (1817) iii; (1818) iv.

[45] (1819) ix. *Tables showing the State of Education in England, Scotland and Wales* (1820) xii summarizes by counties the information in the 1819 digest. See also for this period: *Abridgement of the Abstract of Returns Relative to the Poor* (1818) xix, which contains information on education and schools.

1851.[46] The surveys of the 1830s resulted in volumes of evidence which are indexed,[47] and also an *Abstract of Education Returns: 1833*.[48] This latter gives information similar to that of the *Digest* of 1818 but also includes the numbers of pupils and indicates the foundation date of schools established or revived since 1818. Where there was no school in the parish the location of schools attended by local children is sometimes given.

The 1851 survey (a voluntary return made as part of the 1851 census)[49] differs from the earlier ones in not being concerned with individual schools. It is, however, of enormous value to the local historian, providing detailed analysis of numbers and types of schools (day and Sunday), attendance of pupils, ages of pupils, capacity of schools, religious affiliation of schools, and so on, arranged in registration districts or poor-law unions. It is particularly useful for education in the larger towns.

[46] A Royal Commission report on education in Wales, topographically arranged, was published in 1847.

[47] *Rep. Select Committee on the State of Education of the People in England and Wales* (1834) ix; *Rep. Select Committee on Education in England and Wales* (1835) vii; *Rep. Select Committee on Education of the Poorer Classes* (1837–8) vii.

[48] (1835) xli–xliii. For reflections on the accuracy of this return and of nineteenth-century educational statistics generally, see E. G. West, *Education and the State* (1965), 145–6, and E. G. West, 'Resource Allocation and Growth in Early Nineteenth Century British Education', *Ec.H.R.*, 2nd ser., xxiii (1970), *passim*, and works cited by this writer.

[49] It is to be found in *Rep. Commissioners for Taking a Census of Great Britain on Education* (1852–3) xc; and in *Day Schools and Sunday Schools in Cities and Municipal Boroughs* (1852–3) lxxix; also separately published, 1854. See also J. M. Goldstrom, 'Education in England and Wales in 1851: the Education Census of Great Britain, 1851', in R. Lawton (ed.), *The Census and Social Structure* (1978); and, for examples of work based on the census, W. B. Stephens, *Regional Variations in Education during the Industrial Revolution, 1780–1870* (1973); W. B. Stephens, 'Illiteracy and Schooling in the Provincial Towns, 1640–1870' in D. Reeder (ed.), *Urban Education in the 19th Century* (1977).

For the latter part of the century there are surveys to be found among the parliamentary papers including ones for 1871, 1893, and 1899. The 1871 publication (*Returns Relating to Elementary Education (Civil Parishes)*)[50] covers civil parishes outside the London area[51] giving, as well as other information, the numbers of schools at which fees were less than 10*d.* a week, their capacity and actual attendance on a particular date, distinguishing public and private schools and indicating religious connections. It also indicates parishes where the schools were attended by children living in other parishes where there were no schools. A return of 1867–8 gives average attendance at schools by parishes.[52]

The later surveys (*Returns for each Public Elementary School Examined (Inspected) in England and Wales*)[53] give somewhat similar information for those public elementary schools examined (including London schools), with financial particulars for 1892–3 and 1898–9 respectively. They show the sources from which schools obtained financial support, and their expenditure on various items (such as salaries, equipment, rates, and so on). A less full return, giving only attendance figures and sources of income, exists for 1888–9.[54] A return for London and the larger municipal boroughs showing school accommodation, attendance, and half-timers in board and voluntary schools exists for 1878–9, and there is a somewhat similar return for 1887–8.[55]

The *Returns of Tenures and Trusts of Voluntary Schools* (1906), another parliamentary paper,[56] is useful for information on voluntary schools in the early twentieth century, particularly for their foundation dates.

[50] (1871) lv.
[51] For the original returns for London, see P.R.O., Class Ed.3.
[52] *Parishes of England and Wales* (1867–8) liii.
[53] (1894) lxv; (1900) lxv (ii).
[54] *Return of Public Elementary Schools Examined* (1890) lvi.
[55] *Elementary Schools (Attendance)* (1880) liv; (1889) lix.
[56] (1906) lxxxvii, lxxxviii.

The volumes of the Report of the Royal Commission on the State of Popular Education (the Newcastle Commission), published in 1861,[57] do not attempt a comprehensive topographical survey like the investigations of the early part of the century. Nevertheless for certain places extremely detailed evidence is embedded in their pages. There are reports by commissioners on agricultural districts in the south and east, textile manufacturing districts in Lancashire and Yorkshire, centres of the iron, coal, and pottery industries in Warwickshire and Staffordshire, maritime areas around Bristol, Plymouth, Hull, Yarmouth, Ipswich, and parts of London, and a report on Liverpool. There are also special reports on educational charities and teacher-training colleges.

Similarly the reports of the Royal Commission on the Working of the Elementary Education Acts in England and Wales[58] (the Cross Commission), published 1886–8, is a general investigation but has very detailed information on individual places and even on individual schools. The contents pages should be searched carefully.

For information on the extent of basic literacy in the eighteenth and nineteenth centuries parish registers (from 1754 all brides and grooms except Quakers and Jews were required to sign their names), the 1723 Test Oath rolls and gaol lists (in quarter-sessions records),[59] marriage licence records (in diocesan records),[60] and, for the years 1838–9 onwards, the published annual reports of the Registrar General are useful.[61] Local surveys of ability to read and

---

[57] *Rep. R. Commission on the State of Popular Education in England* (1861) xxi; and see (1861) xlviii, for dissenters' schools.

[58] (1886) xxv; (1887) xxix, xxx; (1888) xxxv, xxxvi, xxxvii.

[59] R. S. Schofield, 'The Measurement of Literacy in Pre-Industrial England', in J. Goody (ed.), *Literacy in Traditional Societies* (1968), 319.

[60] Stone, 'Literacy and Education'.

[61] *Ibid.* See also G. R. Lucas, 'The Diffusion of Literacy in England and Wales in the Nineteenth Century', *Studies in Education* iii (1958–63) (not cited by Stone); and see p. 205 n. 9.

write were often undertaken by local statistical societies and published by them or the Statistical Society of London, and similar information is to be found in parliamentary papers concerned with the employment of women and children, and in the *Minutes (Reports) of the Committee of Council on Education.*[62]

Some large towns have had special government investigations of their educational facilities, the results of which have been published as parliamentary papers. For example, a select committee reported on popular education in the Metropolis in 1816–17; there was a report on schools for the poorer classes in Birmingham, Leeds, Liverpool, and Manchester in 1869 (published 1870); and an investigation of education in Manchester and Salford resulted in a parliamentary paper in 1852. Reference should also be made here to the *Report of the Select Committee on Education for the Children of the Poorer Classes in Large Towns* (1837–8).[63]

If a town of any size is being investigated it is worthwhile consulting any parliamentary paper devoted to that place or devoted to an industry dominant there. The *Report from the Assistant Handloom Weavers' Commissioners* (1840), for example, gives an extremely detailed description of education in Coventry and its environs for 1838.[64] The reports of the Commissioners on Municipal Corporations of 1835 include information on such education as concerned the councils of some of the boroughs investigated.[65]

Reports such as those of investigations into the employ-

---

[62] For some references, see R. K. Webb, 'Working Class Readers in Early Victorian England', *E.H.R.* lxv (1950).

[63] (1816) iv; (1817) iii; (1870) liv; (1852) xi; (1837–8) vii.

[64] *Reps. from Assistant Handloom Weavers' Commissioners*, IV (1840), xxiv. For detailed analysis, see Stephens, 'Early Victorian Coventry'.

[65] These include grammar schools. For some towns it is merely indicated that the town council was taking no active part in education. The index volume lists the places worth looking at (under 'Free Schools', and 'Local Acts (Schools)').

ment of children in factories and mines,[66] and (especially) in
agriculture,[67] and factory inspectors' reports,[68] may contain
much general and particular evidence about children and
schooling in the area being studied. These are important
sources which have not been fully utilized by local and
educational historians. They may include, for example,
information on schools set up by colliery and factory
owners, as well as on the workings of the educational clauses
of the Factory Acts. Details of mine, factory, and similar
schools may also be found in the relevant records of the
business enterprise concerned.[69]

In addition to the parliamentary papers deriving from
specific government investigations, and factory and mine

[66] See J. Benson, 'Some Sources for the Study of Nineteenth-Century
English Colliery Schools', *History of Education Soc. Bulletin* iii (1969),
37–41.

[67] E.g., *Rep. R. Commission on Employment of Children in Factories* (1833)
xx, xxi; (1834) xix, xx. See also *Reps. Select Committee on the Working of the
1833 Act* (1840) x; (1841) ix; *Rep. R. Commission on Children's Employment*
(1842) xv, xvii; (1843) xiii–xv; 1845 xlii (index); *Reps. Special Assistant Poor
Law Commissioners on the Employment of Women and Children in Agriculture*
(1843) xii; *Rep. R. Commission on Children and Women in Agriculture*
(1867–8) xvii; (1868–9) xiii; (1870) xiii; *Reps. R. Commission on Children's
Employment* (1863) xviii; (1864) xxii, xxix; (1865) xx; (1866) xxiv; (1867)
xvi. A useful topographical and subject index is: *Index to British Parliamentary Papers on Children's Employment* (Irish Universities Press, 1973). For
mining areas, see *Reps. of Commissioners appointed to enquire into State of
Population, and as to Education of Schools in Mining Districts* (annually,
1844–59) (for volume references, see official indexes to the parliamentary
papers).

[68] For these, see official indexes to the parliamentary papers.

[69] See, e.g. W. G. Rimmer, *Marshalls of Leeds, Flax-Spinners, 1788–1886*
(1960), 105, 216–17. For a general introduction to this subject, see D. H.
Robson, *The Education of Children Engaged in Industry in England, 1833–76*
(1931); M. Sanderson, 'Education and the Factory in Industrial Lancashire,
1784–1840', *Ec.H.R.*, 2nd ser., xx (1967), and works cited therein; L.
Wynne-Evans, 'Ironworks Schools in South Wales, 1784–1860', *Sociological Review* xliii (1951); L. Wynne-Evans, *Education in Industrial Wales,
1700–1900* (1971).

inspectors' reports, there exists a most important series, for the history of elementary education in any area, in the government's annual reports on education. These are from 1840–1 onwards the *Minutes of the Committee of Council on Education* (from 1858–9 called *Reports*).[70] They contain a wealth of information both on particular areas, counties, and towns, and also on individual schools. Although the content varies from one part of the period to another,[71] they are important for the local historian throughout, but are particularly useful in the earlier years for detailed inspectors' reports on individual schools. Among other things the series provides information about the government's financial assistance to schools (for buildings, equipment, pupil teachers, etc.), and attendance and accommodation figures. After the Education Act of 1870 and until 1879 they include details of school boards.[72]

For the years immediately preceding those covered by the *Minutes* some information on individual schools may be obtained from those parliamentary papers (1834–9) which list schools which had received treasury grants.[73] From 1895–6 to 1902–3 parliamentary papers known as *Schools in Receipt of Parliamentary Grants* (1895–1900) and *Schools under the Administration of the Board of Education* (1901–3) give the information on individual schools as to grants, accommodation, and attendance, which formerly formed part of the *Reports* (which ceased to be published, 1898). Lists of public element-

---

[70] For a list of these with their parliamentary paper references, see *V.C.H.: Warwickshire* vii, 546–7; or *V.C.H.: Warwickshire* viii, 314–15.

[71] For a more detailed description, see Pugh, 'English Primary Schools', 48–9.

[72] Lists of school boards and attendance committees were published as separate parliamentary papers, 1880–90, 1893–1902 (see official indexes).

[73] *Accounts of Sums granted in Aid of Erection of Schools* (1834) xlii; (1835) xl; (1836) xlvii; (1837) xli; *Returns of Parliamentary Grants, 1834–7* (1937–8) xxxviii (also provides an index to the above *Accounts*); *Returns of Application for the Sum granted in 1839* (1840) xl.

ary schools covering the years 1905–7 were published as parliamentary papers, providing accommodation and attendance figures. A non-parliamentary government publication, *Board of Education, List 21*, periodically produced, continued the provision of this sort of information until 1938.[74]

Some isolated parliamentary papers provide less comprehensive lists, which may nevertheless be of use, such as *Returns of Schools to which Annual Grants have been Refused* ((1878) lx) (covering each year from the 1870 Act), a *Return showing Public and Elementary Schools which have not received Building Grants, Closed since 1870* ((1898) lxx), and a *Return of Voluntary Schools Closed or Transferred since 1897* ((1899) lxxv).

Details of poor-law schools,[75] which became common after the Poor Law Amendment Act of 1834, may be found among the records of the boards of guardians, especially their minute books,[76] and also in some of the general government investigations mentioned above (e.g., the 1851 educational census). In addition a few reports on some of the schools are to be found in the Reports of the Poor Law Commissioners prior to 1847.[77] For the years 1847 to 1858 the schools came under the inspection of the school inspectors of the Committee on Education, and separate parliamentary papers are devoted to them.[78] From 1858 until 1865 inspectors' reports

---

[74] See Pugh, 'English Primary Schools', 49.

[75] For leads to sources here, see W. Chance, *Children under the Poor Law* (1897); R. Palliser, 'Workhouse Education in County Durham, 1834–1870', *British Jnl Educational Studies* xvi (1968); F. Duke, 'The Poor Law Commissioners and Education', *Jnl Educational Administration and History* iii (1970).

[76] See pp. 108–9.

[77] Unfortunately the reports are not indexed. See also a very useful *Rep. on the Training of Pauper Children*, H.L. (1841) xxxiii.

[78] *Minutes of the Committee of Council on Education (Schools of Parochial Unions)*: 1847–9 (1849) xlii; 1848–50 (1850) xlii; 1850–2 (1852) xxxix;

on pauper and industrial schools are to be found in the ordinary *Reports of the Committee of Council on Education*,[79] but in an abbreviated and less useful form. Reports appear again in 1867 and subsequently in the Reports of the Poor Law Board,[80] and later those of the Local Government Board.[81]

In addition a return made to the Commons in 1851 comprises reports made to the Poor Law Board by its inspectors on the education and training of pauper children in their districts in 1850,[82] and there are other reports in parliamentary papers of 1862 and 1878.[83] There are many other parliamentary papers devoted to pauper children and their education, and the indexes should be searched for these. The report of a select committee of 1861 on poor relief contains information on workhouse schools.[84] *Shaw's Union Officers and Local Boards of Health Manual* (annually from 1846) provides periodic details of such schools.[85]

At the Public Record Office various classes of records are useful for pauper education. In particular may be mentioned the poor law union files (Class Ed.6), the correspondence and papers of the central authority for the poor law (M.H.19), correspondence and other materials particularly

1852–3 (1852–3) lxxix; 1853–4 (1854) li; 1854–5 (1854–5) xlii; 1855–6 (1856) xlvii; 1856–7 (1857) (2) xxxii; 1857–8 (1857–8) xlv.

[79] See above. Some schools are mentioned in the minutes before 1847: e.g., Norwood, Swindon, and Kirkdale schools in 1842, 1843, 1846. I am grateful to Mr F. Duke for this information.

[80] The Poor Law Board reports overlap the *Reports of the Committee of Council* and give additional information.

[81] See, e.g., *Fifth Rep. Local Government Board* (1876) xxxi.

[82] *Reps. Poor Law Board on the Education and Training of Pauper Children* (1851) xlix. See also Newcastle Comm. Rep. (p. 214, above) i, 352 sqq.

[83] *Rep. Poor Law Board on Education of Pauper Children* (1862) xlix (1) (extremely detailed); *Reps. on the Education of Pauper Children* (1878) lx. For London, see *Rep. on the Education of Pauper Children in the Metropolis*, vols. viii and ix (1869) xliii.

[84] (1861) ix (indexed).

[85] For details of this publication, see p. 110.

relating to the administration and control of poor-law education, arranged under school districts (M.H.27), and the correspondence of the assistant poor law commissioners and inspectors (M.H.32). For more recent times (1929–45) the poor-law children files (Ed.95) may contain local information.

There are also parliamentary papers which deal with vagrant children and 'ragged' schools.[86] One important source for ragged schools, however, is the magazine issued by the Ragged School Union under various names (*Illustrated Ragged School Magazine and Sunday Teachers' Mirror* (1848); *Ragged School Union Magazine* (1849–75); *Ragged School Union Quarterly Record* (1876–87); *In His Name* (1888–1907); *Shaftesbury Magazine* (1908 to date)).[87] The other major source for ragged schools is the published annual reports of the Ragged School Union,[88] though detailed summaries of these reports and of those of individual schools (including financial accounts) are printed in the *Ragged School Union Magazine*. The manuscript minute books of the Ragged School Union, held by the Shaftesbury Society[89] from 1846, do not add greatly to the copious information found in the magazines and annual reports. It is important to realize, however, that these Ragged School Union sources are all mainly concerned with the London ragged schools. However, provincial and Scottish ragged schools do receive some attention, particularly in the magazines of the 1840s and 1850s. The *School Board Chronicle* (mentioned below) is a useful source for provincial ragged schools after 1870. Sunday-school magazines, too,

[86] See, e.g., *Rep. Select Committee on the Education of Destitute Children* (1861) vii (indexed).

[87] An almost complete set is at B.L. Vol. i is at Shaftesbury Soc.'s Office; vol. ii at Goldsmiths' Library of Economic Literature, University of London.

[88] Available from 1846 (2nd annual report) in Shaftesbury Soc.'s Office; broken set at B.L. 1847–56, 1868.

[89] Shaftesbury House, 112 Regent Street, London sw1.

may provide information on ragged schools.[90] Some ragged schools were absorbed into industrial or reformatory schools, and information on these is to be found among other places in the parliamentary papers.[91]

The unpublished records of the central government are, of course, essential for the detailed examination of local elementary education generally in the nineteenth and twentieth centuries. There are many classes at the Public Record Office which might fruitfully be searched,[92] and only the more obviously useful can be cited here.

A very important source for elementary schools since 1870 are the files, topographically arranged, which are to be found in Classes Ed.16 (for municipal boroughs and Part III authorities from 1870, and for all l.e.a.s from 1903), Ed.3 and Ed.4 (London, 1871–1901), Ed.2 (parishes not in London or municipal boroughs, with more than one school, 1871–1904), and Ed.21 (1871–1906: elementary schools which had received a treasury grant but had closed before 1906, and

---

[90] There is a large collection at the B.L. I am grateful to Dr E. A. G. Clark for the information on ragged school sources given here. For some parliamentary papers and other miscellaneous material relating to these schools, see Dr Clark's 'The Early Ragged Schools and the Foundation of the Ragged School Union', *Jnl of Educational Administration and History* i, no. 2 (1968), and also his 'The Ragged School Union and the Education of the London Poor' (London Univ. M.A. thesis, 1967).

[91] See the official indexes, and also B. E. Elliott, 'Sources for a study of 19th-century Juvenile Delinquency', *Local Historian* xiii (1978).

[92] See *P.R.O. Guide*, ii, iii; List and Index Soc., xxi, xlviii, lv, lxxi, lxxviii, xciv, cii, cxi: *Department of Education and Science, Class List, Part I* (1967) (details of Classes Ed.1–Ed.20, omitting Classes Ed.13, Ed.15); *Part II* (1969) (Ed.21–Ed.31, omitting Ed.24, Ed.27); *Part III* (1970) (Ed.24); *Part IV* (1971) (Ed.32–Ed.40, omitting Ed.34, Ed.35); *Part V* (1972) (Ed.41–Ed.53, omitting Ed.42, Ed.49, Ed.52: some are concerned with secondary and further education); *Part VI* (1973) (Ed.54–Ed.69: some concern further education); *Part VII* (1974) (Ed.83–Ed.110, omitting Ed.85, Ed.94, Ed.104, Ed.109: some concern secondary education); *Part VIII* (1975) (various classes, not all on elementary education).

parishes not in Ed.2 with only one school).[93] The information to be obtained from one of these files may include a school history sheet showing attendance figures at different times; details of the organization of the school by ages and sexes; details of buildings; inspectors' reports; and much miscellaneous material including correspondence.[94]

Class Ed.1 provides the number and sizes of schools existing in each school district for the years 1872 to 1902. Another important class, Ed.7 (public elementary schools: preliminary statements), contains details (submitted by promoters of schools seeking grants, 1846–1924) of foundation dates, building history, accommodation, and staffing. Sometimes information is given about the character of the area and the sort of schools generally available there. The statements are arranged under the school numbers used in the Board of Education *Lists* (see below). Class Ed.49 consists of files on endowed elementary schools for the period 1853 to 1935.[95] Class Ed.9 contains miscellaneous material including (Ed.9/14) confidential reports by the inspectorate on the efficiency of Roman Catholic schools in 1875.

For detailed examination of a district the census enumerators' books for 1851, 1861, and 1871 (Classes H.O.107; R.G.9, 10) will indicate which children were at school (as 'scholars') or at work, and their ages. Many voluntary and board schools, of course, will still possess their own internal records, or these may be housed in the local record office, the local education authority's offices, in a school which in some way is the successor of an older institution, or, for the voluntary schools, as has already been noted, among parish or chapel records. The most useful of these are school log books, attendance registers, letter-books, and files, copies of

[93] For full details, see *P.R.O. Guide* ii, 111–13.

[94] See Pugh, 'English Primary Schools', 49–50.

[95] See P. Gordon, 'Some Sources for the History of the Endowed Schools Commission, 1869–1900', *British Jnl Educational Studies* xiv (1966) for further details.

returns, and children's exercise books.

School log books often derive from a government requirement for schools seeking grants and thus generally date from the 1840s. Some, however, were kept before legally required. Log books were day books kept by the head teacher and containing a great deal of useful but very miscellaneous and varied information, but including details of attainments and attendance of children, the curriculum, assistant teachers, inspections, relations with school managers and inspectors, and so on. Managers' minute books sometimes exist to supplement the log books. Registers are important for an indication not only of attendances but also of catchment areas, occupations of parents, reasons for leaving, ages of pupils, and the like. Pupils' exercise books may give intimate details about the curriculum and standard of attainment.

Educational periodicals, of which there are many, often contain references to schools and education generally in individual places.[96] For the years after 1870 the *School Board Chronicle* is of use; it gives, for example, the results of school board elections, and is indexed.[97] The *Municipal Corporations Companion* (annually from 1877) gives details of school boards.[98] The *Builder* (from 1843), though not an educational journal, nevertheless contains much on specific nineteenth-century school buildings.[99]

There are also the records of school boards, of which the most important are minute books, ledgers, letter-books, correspondence, circulars, plans, election posters, public loan

[96] For references to many of these, see L. Fletcher, *The Teachers' Press in Britain, 1802–1880* (1978). See also *An International List of Educational Periodicals* (UNESCO, 1963 edn).

[97] Copies in B.L. Newspaper Library and elsewhere.

[98] For details of this publication, see p. 93.

[99] For sources for school buildings, see M. Seaborne, *The English School: Its Architecture and Organization:* i, *1370–1870* (1971); M. Seaborne and R. Lowe, ii, *1870–1970* (1977), *passim*.

accounts, teachers' salary books, school returns, photographs, and school attendance committee minute books.[100] These records will probably exist in local record offices or with the l.e.a., and, of course, are important for the period 1870–1903. Some school boards, particularly those in larger cities, issued intermittent reports, often at election times; the Leicester board, for example, did so triennially.[101] From 1903 the records of the l.e.a.s are the chief source. Some of these will be published as part of the county or borough council's annual reports. Other records will be similar to those noted for the school boards. In addition records of school meals, school medical officers' reports, and managers' minute books may be important. Records of other departments of the council, such as treasurers' reports, architects' and surveyors' plans, and so on, may also be significant.[102]

The London Statistical Society and provincial statistical societies made public the results of many investigations into education in certain towns and areas in the nineteenth century, and these must be considered as primary sources,[103] as also must the *Transactions of the National Association for the Promotion of Social Science*.

For the twentieth century there is much statistical informa-

---

[100] For an administrative outline of these, see *Preservation of School Records*, British Record Association, Memorandum no. 12 (1950), 2. For a monograph quoting many of these records, see J. H. Bingham, *The Period of the Sheffield School Board, 1870–1903* (1949). See also B. V. Spence, 'School Board Records in County Durham', *Archives* x (1971).

[101] M. Seaborne, *Recent Education from Local Sources* (1967), 6.

[102] *Ibid.*

[103] They are generally to be found in the *Jnl Statistical Soc. of London*, which published not only its own investigations but those of other such societies; see especially the index to vols. i–xv. The Manchester Statistical Society published its own *Transactions*. See also *Report of 8th Meeting* (British Association, 1838) (on Ramsbottom, Lancs.); *First Publication* and *Second Publication* (Central Soc. of Education, 1837, 1838) (on St Marylebone); T. Kelly, *George Birkbeck* (1957), appendix x; R. K. Webb, 'Working Class Readers in Early Victorian England', *E.H.R.* lxv (1950).

tion to be found in government and other official publications. Only the more important can be mentioned here, and those interested should search, especially, the indexes to the parliamentary papers and the periodical (now annual) *Government Publications* (which includes the non-parliamentary publications emanating from the Board of Education).

Very useful for the earlier years of the century[104] are the *Statistics of Public Education* published as parliamentary papers from 1905 (covering 1903–5) until 1915 (covering 1912–13). These provide financial and other educational statistics for elementary, secondary, and further education for each individual local education authority. After the First World War the *Statistics of Public Education* appeared again until 1926 (covering 1924–5) as a non-parliamentary publication and without the detailed local financial statistics.[105] *Board of Education, List 43* (annually, 1928–38)[106] and *Board of Education, List 65* (1926–7, 1927–8, 1936–7), however, respectively analyse the costs of elementary and secondary education, and *Board of Education, List 50* analyses costing statistics for primary and secondary schools for each local education authority in 1946–7 and 1947–8. Similar financial statistics are published annually by the Institute of Municipal Treasurers and Accountants (Inc.) and the Society of County Treasurers, and a number of local authorities also prepare annual statistics including educational statistics.[107]

Other publications providing individual local education authority statistics include the periodic *Board of Education,*

[104] The following is partly based on Interdepartmental Committee on Social and Economic Research, *Guides to Official Sources, no. 3: Local Government Statistics* (1953), 22.

[105] But see *Statistics Relating to the Receipts and Expenditure of Local Education Authorities, in respect of Elementary Education for 1918–19* (1920) xxxvi; *Estimates of the Expenditure of Local Education Authorities in 1921–2* (1921) xxvii.

[106] Similar lists, not so named, were published in 1923 and 1926.

[107] For details, see *Guides to Official Sources, no. 3*, 32–4.

List 54, which gives the size of classes in public elementary schools for every second year from 1926 to 1938 (except for 1930) and *Board of Education, List 45*, which gives the age-distribution of pupils in these schools every other year from 1927 to 1937 (except 1931). *Board of Education, List 46* provides statistics of teachers in the elementary schools of individual local authorities, for every other year from 1929 to 1937. After the Second World War the unpublished Ministry of Education 'Statistical Returns' continued to produce information similar to the Board of Education *Lists*.[108]

SECONDARY EDUCATION

As has been explained in the beginning of the chapter, the division of schools into elementary and secondary is less easy for former times than it is today. For that reason some of the sources for secondary education may well be found in the previous section, particularly with regard to some charity schools.[109] Likewise some of the information which is treated below may also be of use for those interested in elementary education. In addition, adult education, the sources for which constitute the third section of this chapter, embraces institutions which gave not only post-school education but also those providing what would now be regarded as elementary and secondary schooling.

The initial task of the investigator of secondary education will be to establish what is already known about such schools in the locality being studied. Apart from individual school histories, of which there are many for the public and grammar schools,[110] there are several obvious places where a

---

[108] Available to research students: for details, see *ibid.* 22. These are not to be confused with Ministry of Education, *Statistics of Education*, annually from 1961 (1962), which contain little of use to the local historian.

[109] Particular attention is drawn to p. 203 n. 1, above, which provides bibliographical information applicable to this section, too.

[110] See P. J. Wallis, *Histories of Old Schools: A Revised List for England and*

preliminary search may be made.[111] The *Victoria History of the Counties of England* contains in the general volumes of each county so far published brief histories of many of the endowed grammar schools and sometimes of other schools of note.[112] Many of the articles in the earlier volumes are by A. F. Leach, the pioneer historian of the grammar schools. It cannot, however, be guaranteed that the *V.C.H.* covers all the schools modern educational historians would have felt merited inclusion, and the selection in some counties appears somewhat random.[113] More recent topographical volumes of the *V.C.H.* (particularly those dealing with towns) have sought to make good these deficiencies and also include histories of secondary schools of more recent date.[114]

Another readily available printed source is Nicholas Carlisle's *Concise Description of the Endowed Grammar Schools in England and Wales*, published in two volumes in 1818; this prints information about the then state and the history of the many grammar schools which replied to the 18-point questionnaire sent out by Carlisle.[115] Not all such schools in

Wales (1966) (an expansion of a list originally published in *British Jnl Educational Studies* xiv, nos. 1, 2, 3 (1965, 1966)).

[111] For a general survey, see W. E. Tate, 'Some Sources for the History of English Grammar Schools', *British Jnl Educational Studies* i (1953), 164–75; ii (1953), 67–81; iii (1954), 145–65 (3 parts, subsequently cited as Tate, 'English Grammar Schools', i, ii, or iii).

[112] For lists (not now up to date) see Tate, 'English Grammar Schools' i, 166–7; and W. A. L. Vincent, *The Grammar Schools: Their Continuing Tradition, 1660–1714* (1969), 273.

[113] For Leach, see W. E. Tate, 'A. F. Leach as a Historian of Yorkshire Education', *St Anthony's Hall Publications* xxiii (1963); J. Simon, 'The Reformation and English Education', *Past and Present* xi (1957); J. Simon, 'A. F. Leach on the Reformation', *British Jnl Educational Studies* iii (1954–5), iv (1955–6). J. Simon's strictures on Leach as a historian are by no means entirely acceptable: W. N. Chaplin, 'A. F. Leach: A Re-Appraisal', *ibid.* xi (1962–3); J. Simon, 'A. F. Leach: a reply', *ibid.* xii (1963–4).

[114] E.g., *V.C.H., Warwickshire* vii, 501.

[115] The questions related to the founder and the foundation date, details of the endowment, statutes and ordinances, whether attendance was free,

existence in 1818 are, however, to be found in this book, and the information about those that are is not always accurate.

The next place to search is the *Reports of the Charity Commissioners* of the earlier nineteenth century, often known as the reports of the Brougham Commission.[116] These, published from 1819 in 32 volumes, include county reports and an index volume and are a major source of information on all endowed schools then existing, whether providing secondary or elementary education. The *Digest of Parochial Returns* (1819) and the *Abstract of Education Returns* (1835)[117] also include details on some endowed grammar schools.

The *Reports of the Schools Inquiry Commission* (the Taunton Commission) (1868–9), index all the references to grammar schools in the earlier Charity Commissioners' reports. The Taunton Commission volumes are themselves, however, a mine of information on the grammar schools, for the Commission was specifically established to investigate the state of education for 'those classes of English society which are comprised between the humblest and the very highest'.[118] Much of the material to be found here is arranged topographically and, while the bulk of the schools reported on were endowed grammar schools, some other schools offering

or in what ways it was limited, numbers of foundationers and other pupils, ages of pupils, Latin and Greek grammars in use and mode of instruction, exhibitions at the universities, the headmaster and his salary, charges for fee-paying, eminent past pupils. Information on other matters was invited.

[116] They begin as reports on charities for the education of the poor (first two volumes) but then extend to all charities. See also a digest of the reports: *Digest of Schools and Charities for Education* (1843) xviii. The former P.R.O. Class, Charity 2 (now at the Charity Commission), on which these reports are based, contains much fuller information.

[117] See above, pp. 211–12.

[118] (1867–8) xxviii (in 21 vols.). There is also a topographically arranged list of endowed grammar schools in *Return of Endowed Grammar Schools* (1865) xliii. For the nine great public schools, see the *Rep. R. Commission on Revenues and Management of Certain Colleges and Schools* (1864) xx, xxi (the Clarendon Commission).

secondary education, such as private schools and academies, are also included.[119]

Later in the century the *Reports of the Royal Commission on Secondary Education* of 1895 (the Bryce Commission)[120] provides further information on then existing grammar schools and also on other schools offering secondary education. Apart from the volumes of evidence which have information on schools in different places, volumes vi and vii include reports on the counties of Bedford, Devon, Lancaster (part of), Norfolk, Surrey, Warwick, and York (W.R.).

Investigators may be given a lead to the existence of early grammar schools by reference to A. F. Leach's *English Schools at the Reformation, 1546–8* (1896), which tabulates all the schools mentioned in the chantry certificates of 1546 and 1548 and derivative documents,[121] W. A. L. Vincent's, *The State and School Education in England and Wales, 1640–1660* (1952), which lists topographically those grammar schools in existence in the period 1600 to 1660,[122] the works of W. H. Jordan on charities in the early modern period,[123] and such

---

[119] The Commission dealt with some 700 endowed grammar schools and about 80 other schools. General reports are in vols. vii (S. counties), viii (Midland counties, Northumberland), ix (N. counties); special reports in vols. x (London), xi (S.E. counties), xii (S. Midland counties), xiii (E. counties), xiv (S.W. counties), xv (W. Midland counties), xvi (N. Midland counties), xvii (N.W. counties), xviii (Yorks.), xix (N. counties). Vol. xxi has tabular summaries.

[120] (1895) xliii (general rep.); xliv, xlv, xlvi (minutes of evidence); xlvii (memos etc.); xlviii (Beds., Devon, Lancs. (part of), Norfolk) (vol. vi); xlviii (Surrey, War., Yorks. (W.R.)) (vol. vii); xlix (index and appendix).

[121] Part II, pp. 321–7. See also A. F. Leach, *Educational Charters and Documents, 598–1909* (1911); A. F. Leach, *The Schools of Medieval England* (1915, reprinted 1969).

[122] Pp. 120–35. See also the same author's *The Grammar Schools: Their Continuing Tradition, 1660–1714* (1969), for a good bibliography of printed sources.

[123] *Philanthropy in England, 1480–1660* (1959); *The Charities of London, 1480–1660* (1960); *The Charities of Rural England, 1480–1660* (1961).

contemporary sources as, for example, the writings of travellers and topographers.[124]

Later grammar and secondary schools may be traced through the reports of the Commissions already cited, and, for the mid-nineteenth century, through the *Educational Register* (1851–5), which often gives the names of staff, numbers of pupils, date of foundation, details of buildings, endowments, and scholarships.[125] For the present century the periodic lists issued by the Board of Education between 1907–8 and 1939,[126] the *Education Committees' Year Book*, and the *Education Authorities' Directory and Annual* may be consulted.

The sources for more detailed investigation of secondary education in a locality will depend on the period and on the type of school. For early schools which originated under the aegis of cathedrals and collegiate churches, the diocesan or chapter records, such as, in particular, the episcopal registers and the chapter act books, may contain information. For ancient schools connected with monasteries and those connected with Oxford and Cambridge colleges, references may be found in cartularies and college records.[127] Of the 400-odd

[124] See W. E. Tate and P. J. Wallis, 'The English Topographers, *c.* 1545–1789, and Ancient English Schools', *Researches and Studies* xviii (1958); and see pp. 26–7.

[125] See P. J. Wallis, 'The Educational Register, 1851–5', *British Jnl Educational Studies* xiii (1964), which indexes, under counties, the schools there found.

[126] The 1939 issue was called *List 60. List 70* (published approximately every two years) lists all independent secondary (and primary) schools recognized as efficient, and gives tuition fees, boarding fees, number, sex, and age-range of pupils, and numbers of boarders. For comment on reliability, see H. Glennerster and G. Wilson, *Paying for Private Schools* (1970), 148. *Board of Education, List 61* provided, for each local education authority, figures of pupils in grant-aided secondary schools in 1926–7, 1928–9, and 1937–8. *List 62* gave figures for these schools for 1924–8 and 1936–7. For other statistical sources, see p. 225.

[127] For fuller information on schools connected with monasteries, see Tate, 'English Grammar Schools' i, 168–71; J. S. Purvis, *Educational*

oaly 'grammar schools', however, about a quarter were chantry schools, and these (and gild schools) can be traced through the chantry certificates of the 1540s.[128] Earlier references may be found in copies of the chantry founder's deed and licence sometimes recorded in episcopal registers, or, after 1391, in the patent rolls.[129] Later references (deriving from the Crown's obligation to make educational provision from the confiscated chantry estates) may be found in the Court of Augmentations (from 1554 the Augmentations Office of the Exchequer) records,[130] the Exchequer Q.R. decrees and orders,[131] the Exchequer L.R. receivers' accounts,[132] the Duchy of Lancaster ministers' accounts,[133] and the Exchequer special commissions. The last named may provide the name of the schoolmaster and information about the school.[134]

Records (1959), foreword. For schools connected with colleges, see examples in Leach, *Educational Charters*.

[128] P.R.O., Class E.301. There are also ancillary records: e.g. warrants for the continuance of schools; 'particulars' of schools (for letters patent of refounding). See Tate, 'English Grammar Schools' ii, 67–70, for a more detailed description. The chantry certificates for some counties have, of course, been published: see E. L. C. Mullins (ed.), *Texts and Calendars: An Analytical Guide to Serial Publications*, Royal Historial Soc., Guides and Handbooks, no. 7 (1958). Leach's analysis of the schools mentioned in the chantry certificates has been cited above (p. 229).

[129] P.R.O., Classes C.66, C.67; calendars for some exist in print: see *P.R.O. Guide* i, 23–4, for details. For 1509–47, the patents calendared are included in the *Letters and Papers, Henry VIII*. Even if the school existed, however, it was not necessarily mentioned in references to the chantry.

[130] Especially P.R.O., Class F.319.

[131] P.R.O., Class E.123, etc.

[132] P.R.O., Classes L.R.6, 7, 12.

[133] P.R.O., Class D.L.29.

[134] P.R.O., Class E.178. For a descriptive list arranged chronologically under counties, see P.R.O., Lists and Indexes xxxvii (1912). For fuller details of these sources, see Tate, 'English Grammar Schools' ii, 69–70, on which this description is largely based.

The proceedings of the Commissioners for Charitable Uses have also left records of value to the educational historian. Under an Act of 1601 Commissioners could be appointed to investigate alleged misemployment of lands left for charitable purposes (including provision of grammar schools) and decrees for the correction of abuses were issued. P.R.O., Lists and Indexes x (1899), tabulates the decrees under counties; most are for the early seventeenth century.

For the early 1670s there exist the results of an enquiry into the grammar schools instituted by Christopher Wase. In the Wase manuscripts 704 schools are mentioned, and details of their foundations and endowments, governors and patrons, libraries, and so on are to be found.[135] Indexes to the schools are in print.[136]

Many of the educational records of the sixteenth and seventeenth centuries pertain rather to 'a highly mobile body of schoolmasters and of curates who taught part-time rather than to established schools',[137] but they cannot be ignored by local historians, and sometimes schools of some substance are mentioned. From early times schoolmasters were subject to licensing by the church authorities, and records concerning this process are to be found in episcopal, archdiaconal, and parish archives.[138] Visitation exhibits books record the

[135] This collection is bound in four volumes and housed in the Bodleian Library, Oxford. See Vincent, *The Grammar Schools, 1660–1714*, esp. chapter 2.

[136] P. J. Wallis, 'The Wase School Collection', *Bodleian Library Record* iv, no. 2 (1952); A. M. d'I. Oakeshott, 'The Education Inquiry Papers of Christopher Wase', *British Jnl Educational Studies* xix (1971).

[137] Seaborne, *The English School: 1370–1870*, 43.

[138] See Purvis, *Educational Records*, 2–6, and relevant plates, for a great deal of detailed information. See also W. E. Tate, 'The Episcopal Licensing of Schoolmasters in England', *Church Quarterly Review* clvii, 325 (1956). For further details of these church records, see chapter 8, and for reasons for their incompleteness, see R. O'Day, 'Church Records and the History of Education in Early Modern England, 1558–1642', *History of Education* ii (1973).

dates of the licences of schoolmasters in the diocese (they were required to attend and exhibit their licences), and the visitation act books sometimes record examinations of the academic qualifications of masters before and after licensing.[139] Nomination forms and testimonials declaring the moral, religious, and political integrity of the would-be schoolmasters are also to be found among the episcopal records.[140] Archdeacons' fee books record fees for schoolmasters' licences with dates and names.[141] Infrequently, cases heard before the ecclesiastical courts may shed light on the actual curriculum and other internal details of the early schools.[142] A specific episcopal return of 1665 gives, for certain dioceses, the names of unlicensed or suspected schoolmasters at that date.[143]

For politico-religious reasons, too, schoolmasters were from time to time required to swear certain oaths (e.g. of allegiance, of non-resistance, of acceptance of supremacy, and of uniformity), and these are recorded in diocesan subscription books.[144] Civil certificates deriving from the Test Act of 1673 (repealed 1828) had to be obtained within six months of appointment by those schoolmasters who could be regarded as Crown officers (for example, where the school received a Crown payment stemming from former

---

[139] E. R. C. Brinkworth, 'The Records of Bishops' and Archbishops' Visitations', *Amateur Historian* ii (1954–6). For examples, see J. S. Purvis, *Tudor Parish Documents in the Diocese of York* (1948), 103–9.

[140] See F. G. Emmison, *Archives and Local History* (1966), plate 5.

[141] E. R. Brinkworth, 'The Study and Use of Archdeacons' Court Records: Illustrated from the Oxford Records, 1566–1759', *T.R.H.S.*, 4th ser., xxv 1943), 101.

[142] See pp. 262–3.

[143] Exeter, Bristol, St David's: printed in G. Lyon Turner, *Original Records of Nonconformity* (1911) ii, 178.

[144] Purvis, *Educational Records*, 3; Tate, 'English Grammar Schools' ii, 77–9. For published examples, see E. H. Carter, *The Norwich Subscription Books* (1937); C. W. Foster, *The State of the Church in the Diocese of Lincoln*, i, Lincoln Record Soc. xxiii (1926).

monastic or chantry property). These are to be found among the quarter-sessions records.

The biographies of the clergy who became schoolmasters when unable to follow their primary calling may again shed light on local grammar schools, if only their existence. A. G. Matthews, *Calamy Revised* (1934) (for Puritan clergy), and the same author's *Walker Revised* (1948) (for Anglican clergy during the Interregnum) are useful. The first has a topographical index and in the second names are arranged under counties.

From Tudor to recent times some grammar schools, particularly in boroughs, were owned by the towns, whose councils appointed and paid the schoolmasters, maintained the buildings, and laid down regulations for discipline and curriculum.[145] Details of the history of such schools may, therefore, be culled from the minute books of the town council and from the borough treasurers' accounts.[146]

Particularly for the period after the Revolution of 1688, Acts of Parliament, especially private and local Acts, have been concerned with the foundation and structures of individual schools, and these should be searched.[147]

In the last thirty years of the nineteenth century the revitalization of the endowed grammar schools by the revision of their endowments followed the Endowed Schools Act of 1869. The records of the Endowed Schools Commission are important for the subsequent history of the schools. The Commission, established in 1869,[148] was entrusted with the tasks of redistributing endowments which were not being fully utilized, of establishing sound administrative and financial arrangements for schools, and of making provision

---

[145] See, e.g., W. B. Stephens (ed.), *History of Congleton* (1970), 273–4.

[146] For such records, see pp. 85–7.

[147] Consult M. Bond, *The Records of Parliament: A Guide for Genealogists and Local Historians* (1964); see also Tate, 'English Grammar Schools' iii, 147–8.

[148] Its duties were taken over by the Charity Commissioners in 1874.

for the education of girls and for schemes for scholarships for able pupils.[149]

The minutes of the Commission no longer exist but the 6,700-odd endowment files in the Public Record Office covering the years 1850 to 1903, relate to individual schools.[150] These files are arranged topographically by counties and contain much information. They include correspondence between schools and the Commissioners, reports on schools by the Commissioners and their assistants, correspondence between the Commissioners and the Education Department of the Privy Council, cuttings from local newspapers, and decisions or Schemes for particular schools.[151]

Among the many parliamentary papers relating to grammar schools are the *Reports of the Endowed School Commissioners* for 1872 and 1875,[152] the *Reports of the Select Committee on the Endowed Schools Acts* published in 1873, 1886, and 1887,[153] the *Reports of the Charity Commissioners' Proceedings on Endowed Schools*,[154] and the details of the Schemes laid before Parliament under the Acts.[155] Two returns of endowed schools, published in 1865 and 1891, are also useful.[156]

The Public Record Office Class Ed.9 contains for the years

---

[149] See P. Gordon, 'Some Sources for the History of the Endowed Schools Commission, 1869–1900', *British Jnl Educational Studies* xiv (1966), 59.

[150] Class Ed.27. There is an index in the P.R.O.

[151] Gordon, 'Endowed Schools Commission', 61–2.

[152] (1872) xxiv; (1875) xxviii.

[153] (1873) viii; (1886) ix; (1887) ix (indexed).

[154] (1894) xxx (1), etc. (see indexes). These list Schemes published, submitted, approved, and give the income of the schools. See also *Rep. Select Committee on Charitable Trusts Acts* (1884) ix and the annual *Reps. Charity Commissioners*.

[155] Listed under names of schools in the official index to the parliamentary papers.

[156] *Return of Each Endowed Grammar School* (1865) xliii (names of founders and other particulars); *Return of Endowed Schools Foundations* (1892) lx (dates and details of Schemes, and gross incomes for 1890).

1879 to 1905 some inspectors' reports on science and art day classes in certain grammar and private secondary schools.

In the early 1880s a parliamentary paper (known as the Fortescue Return) contains for 166 endowed schools, information about provision of scholarships and exhibitions.[157] The Bryce Commission of 1895 analyses similar information for a number of counties.[158] Since the revision of endowments caused much public controversy, the files of local newspapers may also reveal a great deal in this period, as, too, may the pages of *Hansard* which record debates on new Schemes proposed by the Commissioners.[159] A number of girls' schools originated from Schemes to make use of endowments previously applied only to the education of boys.

In the later nineteenth century higher-grade elementary schools, which were in fact public secondary schools, emerged from the existing system of board schools. Records of these schools are to be found with those of the school board concerned,[160] and also in the Public Record Office.[161] For secondary schools established under the 1902 Act the records of the local education authority must be searched.[162] Between 1903 and 1906 Michael E. Sadler undertook local surveys of Sheffield, Huddersfield, Birkenhead, Liverpool,

---

[157] *Return of Scholarships and Exhibitions*, H.L. (1884) x.

[158] See above, p. 229.

[159] Tate, 'English Grammar Schools' iii, 149–50.

[160] See pp. 223–4. There is also a parliamentary paper: *Return of Higher Grade Board Schools* (1898) lxx.

[161] P.R.O., Class Ed.20 (higher elementary school files, 1896–1926). See also Class Ed.7 (no. 168), for 'Preliminary Statements for Higher Elementary Schools'; and the parliamentary paper, *Abstract of Accounts of Secondary Schools on the Grants List in England, 1911–12* (1913) l.

[162] And P.R.O., Class Ed.35 (secondary educational institution files), and Class Ed.53 (l.e.a. files), which include also information on some grammar schools before 1902; and Class Ed.109 (inspectors' reports on secondary schools). See also some classes cited in p. 221 n. 92 above, with reference to List and Index Soc. vols.

Newcastle-upon-Tyne, Exeter, and Essex, and these are likely to be in local libraries. They cover secondary and higher education.

In the late nineteenth and early twentieth centuries it is not always easy to distinguish between secondary and adult education, and the next section of this chapter should, therefore, be consulted by those interested in secondary education. In particular it should be noted that the records relating to the Technical Instruction Committees of county councils and boroughs[163] contain evidence on secondary education, since these committees administered funds which went to promote technical education in existing secondary schools.

Miscellaneous sources for different periods include the *Calendar of State Papers, Domestic,*[164] the parliamentary paper, *Return of Owners of Land, 1872–3,* which gives information on landowners, including schools which owned land,[165] the volumes of the Historical Manuscripts Commission,[166] local newspapers and directories, and the reports of the Cathedral Commissioners.[167] The census enumerators' books for 1841, 1851, 1861, and 1871 will list by name resident staff and pupils. Any boy living near the school described as 'scholar' may be a day boy.[168]

Many secondary schools will, of course have their own

---

[163] See p. 246. The official government publications cited there are also relevant. The *Record of Technical and Secondary Education* (p. 245 n. 206) often has lengthy articles about work in particular schools.

[164] E.g., *Cal. S.P.D., 1655–6,* 387–8 (Grimstone, Norfolk), *inter multa alia.*

[165] (1874) lxxiii. See W. E. Tate, 'The "New Domesday Book" of 1873 as a Record of Schools and Educational Endowments in Yorkshire', *Researches and Studies* ix (1954).

[166] There is an index of places (1914) but it covers only the first 118 volumes (1870–1911) and an index of persons (1935, 1938, 1966) covering the volumes to 1957; a subject index is being prepared.

[167] (1854) xxv; (1854–5) xv.

[168] A. T. Wicks, 'School Registers', *Amateur Historian* iv (1958–60), 30.

records, either still kept in the school, housed in the local record office, or occasionally among the records of an Oxford or Cambridge college with which the school is connected. Many of the records of the older endowed schools are financial and legal rather than educational, pertaining to the school's property (particularly deeds of land), though there may be records of use to the purely educational historian.[169] These may include foundation deeds, letters patent, inspeximuses, statutes, correspondence, governors' minute books, account books, punishment books,[170] school registers, and, in recent times, school magazines. Governors' minute books may include information on a variety of matters including perhaps some on the names of boys, and details of free and fee-paying pupils and the social background of their parents. Disagreements between parents and masters or between the head and governors will often be noted. School 'registers' may be either documents compiled as admission registers, or they may be lists of former pupils.[171] Some will include lists of governors, heads, and assistants, captains of the school and of athletics and so on.[172] Since the grammar schools supplied scholars for the universities a source of information on pupils is the *Alumni Cantabri-*

---

[169] Tate, 'English Grammar Schools' iii, 160–5; Purvis, *Educational Records,* 5. For some of the more important schools there are considerable collections of records. For some in print, see G. A. Stocks (ed.), *Records of Blackburn Grammar School,* Chetham Soc., NS, lxvi, lxvii, lxviii (1909); *Records of King Edward's School, Birmingham* (Dugdale Soc., various vols.). See also p. 207, n. 21.

[170] E.g., Hull Corporation, Town Clerk's Department Records, Section 150: Punishment Book of William Street School, Girls' Division, 1900–1932; Leeds University Museum of the History of Education: Batley Carr S.M. School, Record of Cases of Corporal Punishment, 1912–61 (boys and girls).

[171] For both, see the bibliographies in *B.I.H.R.* ix (1931–2), x (1932–3) (which, however, tend to be confined to public schools); P. M. Jacobs (comp.), *Registers of the Universities, Colleges, and Schools of Great Britain and Ireland: A List* (1964).

[172] Wicks, 'School Registers'.

gienses and the *Alumni Oxonienses*. The former notes the school and the master of the person concerned.[173] The *Schoolmaster's Yearbook and Directory* (from 1903 to the early 1930s) is useful for its 'directory of masters in secondary schools' (which lists, with varying degrees of detail, biographical information) and for its list of boys' and mixed secondary schools (including public and grammar schools) which provides names of teachers, numbers and ages of pupils, and details of fees and sometimes of salaries.

Information on private schools is difficult to come by since these establishments were often ephemeral. Evidence must be sought in many miscellaneous sources difficult to classify.[174] Comments on dame and other private adventure schools are to be found in the general investigations of education of the early nineteenth century, as, for example, that of 1833, and for private secondary schools the reports of the Schools Inquiry Commission and the Bryce Commission have some information. A very useful parliamentary paper of 1897, *Return of the Pupils in Public and Private Secondary and Other Schools in England*, provides a great deal of information on numbers of schools and pupils and ages of pupils, in different counties and county boroughs (excluding public elementary and technical schools), and on the qualifications of the teachers.[175] Advertisements appeared in local newspapers, and lists of schools catering for the middle classes in local and other directories. The *Monthly Preceptor or Juvenile*

[173] *Ibid.* 30–3, q.v. for other similar sources. See also above, p. 233 n. 141.

[174] For an excellent example of the multifarious nature of the sources, see M. E. Bryant 'Private Education [in Middlesex] from the Sixteenth Century', *V.C.H., Middlesex* i, ed. J. S. Cockburn, H. P. F. King, K. G. T. McDonnell (1969). See also E. L. Greenberg, 'The Contribution made by private academies in the first half of the 19th century to modern curricula and methods' (London Univ. M.A. thesis, 1953); J. A. Harrison, *Private Schools in Doncaster in the Nineteenth Century* (5 parts, Doncaster Museum and Art Gallery, 1958–65).

[175] (1897) lxx. I am indebted to Professor W. H. G. Armytage for this reference.

Library (later *Juvenile Encyclopaedia*), published 1800–3, is a source of miscellaneous information on private education at the beginning of the century.[176] Later there are other periodicals such as the *Preparatory Schools Review* (published from 1895), the *Public Schools' Year Book* (later the *Public and Preparatory Schools' Year Book*) (from 1890), the *Girls' School Year Book* (from 1906), *Schools of England, Wales, Scotland and Ireland* (from 1912), *Paton's List of Schools and Tutors* (from 1888–9, schools from 1924), the *Directory of Catholic Schools and Colleges in Great Britain* (from 1935), and *Catholic Schools in England and Wales* (from 1954).[177] Some information on private schools is to be found in the records of the Department of Education and Science[178] and in those of the College of Preceptors.[179]

ADULT EDUCATION

Today adult education is virtually synonymous with further education. In the nineteenth century it embraced not only further education but, for much of the period, elementary education for those who had had little or no schooling as children. This distinction is worth keeping in mind when investigating the local history of adult education. In addition it should be recalled that partaking of 'adult' education in the nineteenth century were many adolescents who would now

[176] C. W. J. Higson, 'Early 19th Century Private Schools', *History of Education Soc. Bulletin* iii (1969), 53.

[177] See also F. S. D. de Carteret-Bisson, *Our Schools and Colleges* (1872 and later edns). For Jesuit records throwing some light on Roman Catholic schools in the London area, see F. O. Edwards, 'The Archives of the English Province of the Society of Jesus', *Jnl Soc. Archivists* iii (1966).

[178] E.g., P.R.O., Class Ed.15 (private schools not recognized for grant or efficiency, returns, 1919–44); Ed.33 (certified efficient schools files, 1871–1936). See also *Department of Education and Science, List 70* and *List 73* (and above, pp. 221 n. 92, 230 n. 126).

[179] 130 High Holborn, London WC1: official lists of examination results for private schools from *c.* 1860.

be of school age and the instruction they received might at best be described in modern terms as 'secondary'.

The field is so immense that I must concentrate almost entirely on the main sources for the nineteenth century.[180] The multitude of musical, scientific, philosophical, and literary clubs and societies, circulating libraries, and book clubs, through which the middle classes carried out an exercise in self-education, have sometimes left useful records which are often to be found in local libraries and record offices. They include minute and account books, usually in manuscript, and for the larger societies some published papers, prospectuses, and rules and regulations, library catalogues, and the like. Their activities were frequently recorded in the local press and in directories. Occasionally they find mention in the general parliamentary papers dealing with education.

The mechanics' institutes were the first important national movement in adult education and most large towns and many smaller ones had mechanics' institutes from the 1820s onwards. Their records are therefore worthy of attention.[181] The larger institutes produced printed material such as annual reports (often also reproduced in the local newspapers), handbooks, periodicals, special addresses and lectures,

[180] For general guides, see W. H. G. Armytage, 'Some Sources for the History of Technical Education in England', *British Jnl Educational Studies* v (1956–7), vi (1957–8); J. F. C. Harrison, 'The Materials for the Early History of Adult Education', *Adult Education* xxiii (1950–1); T. Kelly (ed.), *A Select Bibliography of Adult Education in Great Britain* (2nd edn, 1962). For the eighteenth-century dissenting and other academies, important scientific societies, leisure-time lectures, and classes for adults in scientific and religious subjects common in the eighteenth century, see such sources as those cited in N. Hans, *New Trends in Education in the Eighteenth Century* (1951); J. W. A. Smith, *The Birth of Modern Education* (1954); H. McLachlan, *English Education under the Test Acts* (1931); Sylvester, *Educational Documents*, 233 sqq. For universities and teacher-training colleges, see above, p. 204 n. 2.

[181] For a general account, see C. M. Turner, 'Mechanics' Institutes: A Topic for Local Study', *Amateur Historian* vii (1966–7).

rules and regulations, and prospectuses. Their manuscript records include minute books (most valuable for tracing the policy pursued by the committee, the leading members and their social class, and the reasons for their actions), reports of committees, and account books. Since finance was such an important factor in adult education these last are most useful. All these records are likely to be found in local depositories.[182]

Certain contemporary works must also be considered as primary sources; in particular T. Claxton's *Hints to Mechanics on Self Education* (1839), Thomas Coate's *Report of the State of Literary, Scientific, and Mechanics' Institutions in England*, published for the Society for the Diffusion of Useful Knowledge in 1841, and J. W. Hudson's *History of Adult Education* (1851) and J. Hole's *History and Management of Literary, Scientific and Mechanics' Institutes* (1853),[183] which give detailed information on specific institutions. The *Mechanics' Magazine*,[184] the organ of the movement, contains much local material. The Brougham MSS. and the S.D.U.K. MSS. at University College London, may also yield evidence on individual institutes.[185]

A parliamentary paper particularly relevant to adult education is the *Report from the Select Committee on Public Libraries* (1849),[186] which investigated the state of adult education in

---

[182] For a valuable list of the location of known records, see T. Kelly, *George Birkbeck* (1957), appendix vi. For the scattered letters of Birkbeck, containing much about individual institutes, see *ibid.* appendix iv. This book also contains a large bibliography of printed material on mechanics' institutes and adult education generally. See also the bibliography in M. Tylecote, *The Mechanics' Institutes of Lancashire and Yorkshire before 1851* (1957).

[183] Coate and Hole have recently been republished.

[184] Weekly, 1823–72. For local journals, see Kelly (ed.), *Select Bibliography*, 37, q.v., too, for a list of printed histories of individual institutes.

[185] Cited Turner, 'Mechanics' Institutes', 64–5.

[186] (1849) xvii (indexed).

various places.[187] The 1851 Education Census[188] contains much on adult education, including information about evening schools and literary, scientific, and mechanics' institutes, arranged in registration districts or poor-law unions.

Other sources derive from the growing interest of the government in the promotion of technical and scientific education. Details of the early government schools of design may be found in *Reports on the State of Head or Provincial Schools of Design, 1849*.[189]

Information on the subsequent schools of art and science is to be traced in the *Report of the Select Committee on Schools of Art* (1864),[190] and in the annual reports of the Department of Practical Art and of the Department of Science and Art which immediately followed it.[191] The last form a series which is of the utmost value in the local study of adult education generally. Many of the schools of art have left their own records which are to be found in local depositories. Some of these schools developed into technical institutes and colleges and may still retain their own records. These, which may be extensive, are similar in nature to the records of the larger mechanics' institutes noted above, with more printed material and also correspondence with the Department. This last is most useful since the Department's own records of correspondence with the schools is not to be found in the Public Record Office.[192]

---

[187] It has a list of mechanics' institutes (pp. 310–17).

[188] See above p. 212.

[189] (1850) xlii.

[190] (1864) xii.

[191] *First Rep. Department of Practical Art* (1852–3) liv; Reports of the Department of Science and Art, annually from 1854 to 1899. See W. B. Stephens, 'The Victorian Art Schools and Technical Education: A Case Study, 1850–1899', *Jnl Educational Administration and History* ii, no. 1 (1969).

[192] For information on science, art, and technical education in the P.R.O., see Class B.T.1, and, for the late nineteenth and the twentieth centuries, Classes Ed.82, Ed.83, Ed.90 (see p. 221 n. 92).

There are also specific parliamentary papers which may be searched.[193] Especially important here are the *Report of the Select Committee on the Provisions for giving Instruction in Theoretical and Applied Science to the Industrial Classes* (1868) (the Samuelson Committee),[194] the reports of the Royal Commission on Scientific Instruction and the Advancement of Science (the Devonshire Commission) 1871–5,[195] and, especially, the reports of the Royal Commission on Technical Instruction (1881–4)[196] and of the Royal Commission on Secondary Education (1895–6).[197] A Canadian Royal Commission report on technical education for 1913 contains much useful information on secondary and technical education in parts of Britain.[198] Ministry of Reconstruction report of 1919 provides much local evidence on university extension and tutorial classes and other non-vocational adult education courses carried on by universities, local education authorities, voluntary associations (as the adult-school movement, W.E.A., working-men's colleges), co-operative societies, literary and scientific societies, and so on.[199] For the period 1903 to 1925 the volumes of *Statistics of Public Education* provide statistics for each local education authority.[200]

During the later nineteenth century other important bodies

---

[193] Many of the parliamentary papers relating primarily to children's education (e.g. the *Minutes and Reps. of the Committee of Council on Education,* the *Rep. R. Commission on Popular Education*) cited above may contain information on adult education. Those particularly relevant to adult education are too numerous to cite here.

[194] (1867–8) xv.

[195] (1871) xxiv; (1872) xxv; (1873) xxviii; (1874) xxii; (1875) xxviii.

[196] (1882) xxvii; (1884) xxix, xxx, xxxi, xxxi (1).

[197] See above.

[198] Dominion of Canada, *Rep. R. Commission on Industrial Training and Education* (1913), sessional paper 191d.

[199] *Final Rep. Adult Education Committee of the Ministry of Reconstruction* (1919) xxviii.

[200] See p. 225.

also helped to promote technical education.[201] In particular the Royal Society of Arts developed examinations and syllabuses for schools of art and science, and mechanics' and other institutes. The manuscript and printed records of the R.S.A.[202] are, therefore, valuable, and tell much of the institutes which entered the union with it.[203] An investigation into technical education undertaken by the Society and published in 1853 may also be useful.[204] The transactions, proceedings, and occasional papers of bodies such as the National Association for the Promotion of Social Science (annual transactions, 1857–86), the Society for the Diffusion of Useful Knowledge,[205] the Manchester Statistical Society, the London Statistical Society, the Union of Lancashire and Cheshire Institutes, and the Yorkshire Union of Mechanics' Institutes, can also yield information.

For the later part of the century the National Association for the Promotion of Technical and Secondary Education published reports and the results of local investigations.[206] Local branches of the Association held meetings which were often reported in the provincial newspapers. Acts of Parliament passed between 1889 and 1901 established a new system of locally administered rate-provided technical educa-

[201] See p. 237.

[202] D. G. C. Allan, 'The Archives of the Royal Society of Arts, 1754–1847', *Archives* iv (1959–60) (an almost identical article appears in *Jnl Royal Soc. of Arts* cvi (1958)).

[203] See, e.g., W. B. Stephens, 'The Society of Arts and the Warrington Mechanics' Institution', *Jnl Royal Soc. of Arts* cxi (1963) (2 parts). The *Second Rep. Commissioners on the Exhibition of 1851* (1852–3) liv, includes a list of institutions in union with the Soc. of Arts.

[204] *Rep. Committee of the Society of Arts to Enquire into the Subject of Industrial Instruction* (1853).

[205] E.g., *A Manual for Mechanics' Institutions* (S.D.U.K., 1839).

[206] See its *Annual Reports* and *Miscellaneous Publications* (1887–91), cited Armytage, 'Technical Education' vi, 70; also, especially, its publication, the *Record of Technical and Secondary Education*, published from the 1890s and containing an enormous amount of local information.

tion. The technical institutes which were established had, of course, their own records, but particularly important are the records (especially minutes, reports, financial accounts) of the technical instruction committees set up by county councils and county boroughs to administer local technical education.[207]

For adult instruction of a more elementary kind, the records of evening classes, adult schools, co-operative societies, the Y.M.C.A., and the like are valuable. In addition, since Quakers were so active in the adult school movement, the records and publications of the Society of Friends are significant.[208] Anglican records, especially visitation returns, may report on adult classes. Parish magazines in the later years of the century sometimes list lectures and mention adult education available.

Material in the Public Record Office relating to adult education includes, apart from that already cited, junior technical schools files (1913–35) (Class Ed.98), and evening

[207] For a general introduction to this field, see P. Gosden, 'Technical Instruction Committees', in *Studies in the Government and Control of Education since 1860* (History of Education Society, 1970); P. R. Sharp, 'The Entry of County Councils into Educational Administration, 1889', *Jnl Educational Administration and History* i, no. 1 (1968). See *Rep. R. Commission on Secondary Education* (1895) ii, for accounts of the work of some technical instruction committees. *Returns of Counties and Boroughs using Funds for Technical [later Higher] Education*, published in parliamentary papers, 1893–4 to 1908, should be consulted, and information is to be found, too, in some apparently unlikely parliamentary papers, e.g., the reports of assistant commissioners on various counties to the R. Commission on the Agricultural Depression (the report on North Devon, e.g., quotes grants and scholarships awarded to adult institutions and secondary schools: (1895) xvi).

[208] Cf. Harrison, 'Adult Education', 275–6. See also: T. Pole, *A History of the Origin and Progress of Adult Schools* (1814; 2nd edn 1816); *Monthly Record* (1882–91); *Adult School* (1857–92); *Adult School Year Book and Directory* (periodically since 1901); J. W. Rowntree and H. B. Binns, *A History of the Adult School Movement* (1903); G. C. Martin, *The Adult School Movement: its Origin and Development* (1924).

institute files (1901–54) (Class Ed.41). Local education authority files (1921–35) (Ed.51) include reports on further education in authorities' areas and on individual institutions. Endowment files (1854–1944) (Ed.37) relate to institutions concerned with domestic, general, and art subjects.[209] Statistical material in print for the present century to be found in official publications is dealt with in the first section of this chapter.[210]

[209] For references to other P.R.O. classes of use for further information, see *Public Record Office: Records of Interest to Social Scientists, 1919 to 1939, Introduction*, ed. B. Swann and M. Turnbull (H.M.S.O., 1971); p. 221 n. 92.

[210] See pp. 225–6.

CHAPTER 8

Religion

This chapter deals successively with sources for the history of the Church in and of England, of Protestant nonconformity, and of Roman Catholicism. Those who seek to deal at a local level with the history of the Church will find the path well trodden and for that reason it has been possible to deal with it here more briefly than might otherwise have been the case.

THE CHURCH

Over the centuries the essential local ecclesiastical unit has remained the parish and it is the church history of parishes, which, therefore, often forms our main object of investigation.[1] For places covered in the topographical volumes of the *Victoria History of the Counties of England* the essential outlines will be available in print, and other parishes may also have respectable histories. Where this is not so the local historian

---

[1] The best introductory works are: A. Hamilton Thompson, *Parish History and Records*, Hist. Assoc., Leaflet 66 (1926 edn); R. B. Pugh, *How to Write a Parish History* (1954), 69 sqq.; W. G. Hoskins, *Local History in England* (1959), 60 sqq.; D. M. Owen, 'How to Study your Parish Church from Documents', *Amateur Historian* vii (1966–7). The following account owes much to these. Useful, too, are: S. G. Ollard, G. Cross, and M. F. Bond, *Dictionary of Church History* (1948 edn); the bibliography in *English Local History Handlist* (Hist. Assoc., various edns); W. O. Chadwick, *The History of the Church: A Select Bibliography*, Hist. Assoc., Helps for Students of History, no. 66 (1966 edn); J. S. Purvis, *Dictionary of Ecclesiastical Terms* (1962); and F. R. H. Du Boulay, *A Handlist of Medieval Ecclesiastical History* (1952). See also, for an account of local ecclesiastical records, *Third Rep. R. Commission on Public Records* (1919), 14 sqq.

will have the task of discovering what he can of the church as a building, of the incumbents and patrons, and of the spiritual life of the parish community both before and after the Reformation. On these topics, except the spiritual life, much will be found in the books of the older topographers, though strict accuracy there should certainly not be assumed.

In his investigation the parochial historian will need to establish whether the incumbent was a vicar or a rector. Originally the parish priest was its rector (parson), but during the Middle Ages many rectories were appropriated by monastic houses which enjoyed the rectorial revenue and appointed vicars (clerical deputies) to carry out the parochial duties. From the early thirteenth century, however, vicars were usually guaranteed an adequate stipend and in effect they had security of tenure as 'perpetual vicars'. With the Reformation these monastic appropriations passed into lay hands so that lay rectorship emerged. Other vicarages re-sulted from the non-residence of individual clerical rectors; in such cases the parish had both vicars and clerical rectors at the same time, and the investigator will need to distinguish which is which if he seeks to trace the history of the benefice and the incumbents. Thus he may wish to compile 'parallel lists of rectors and vicars, the rectors being presented to the bishop by the original patrons, while they themselves were patrons of the vicarage and presented the vicars'.[2]

It will also be necessary to trace the history of the advowson, that is, to list the successive patrons who had the right to present to the living. This generally derived from the original lay founder of a church and was a piece of heritable property. Where, as often, it went with the lordship of the manor, the descent of the advowson followed that of the manor.[3] Where, however, the church was made over to a

[2] A. Hamilton Thompson, 'Ecclesiastical Benefices and their Incum-bents', *Transactions of the Leics. Archaeological Soc.* xxii (1941–5), 4.
[3] For the descent of manors, see p. 76.

religious house, the monastery usually became both patron and rector until the Reformation.[4]

The foundation of ecclesiastical buildings and the history of their fabric will also form part of the history of the parish. Not all such places of worship were parish churches; some were subsidiary chapels served by chaplains, often deriving from chantries. Other 'free' chapels (usually in large parishes) had separate endowments and had their own rectors. Usually in such cases the 'cure of souls' was not involved; some such chapels, however, acquired rights which rendered them barely distinguishable from parish churches.[5]

Those sufficiently knowledgeable and skilled will be able to make use of the church building itself to deduce something of its structural history, but this is a specialism[6] which cannot be explored here, and most will need to rely largely on written evidence for this as well as other aspects of local church history. The parish history volumes of the *Victoria History of the Counties of England*, the volumes of inventories of the Royal Commission on Historical Monuments, Sir

---

[4] Thompson, 'Ecclesiastical Benefices', 4–5. For the Dissolution suppression papers in the P.R.O., see *Letters and Papers of Henry VIII*, and, e.g., J. W. Clay (ed.), *Yorkshire Monasteries: Suppression Papers,* Yorks. Archaeological Soc., Record Ser. xlviii (1912); *P.R.O. Guide* i, 17, 28, 85, 193.

[5] Thompson, 'Ecclesiastical Benefices', 8 sqq., q.v. for further details. A chantry foundation could, of course, be in a parish church.

[6] For an introduction, see A. Hamilton Thompson, *The Historical Growth of the English Parish Church* (1911); G. W. Addleshaw and F. Etchells, *The Architectural Setting of Anglican Worship* (1948); A. Needham, *How To Study an Old Church* (1948 edn); M. D. Anderson, *Looking for History in British Churches* (1951); H. Braun, *An Introduction to English Medieval Architecture* (1951); G. H. Cook, *The English Medieval Parish Church* (1954); P. Eden, 'Studying Your Parish Church – from the Building', *Amateur Historian* vii (1966–7); H. Braun, *Parish Churches: Their Architectural Development in England* (1970); P. Addyman and R. K. Morris (eds.), *The Archaeological Study of Churches* (Council for British Archaeology, 1976).

Nikolaus Pevsner's *Buildings of England* series, and the volumes of the *Survey of London* are authoritative secondary sources.

Before Henry VIII's reign the sources are limited, and the first place to seek information will be certain published records which may be used to build a framework. There are references to churches in Anglo-Saxon charters.[7] These apart, however, the earliest reference to an *ecclesia* may be in Domesday,[8] which will also record the existence of priests in a manor. It must be noted, however, that in medieval documents the word *ecclesia* does not necessarily indicate a building; it may, and often does, refer to the advowson. Also the absence of the mention of an *ecclesia* in Domesday does not rule out the existence of a church building, for the commissioners were primarily concerned with the financial relations of the church to the manor. Physical evidence will sometimes suggest whether the Domesday entry refers to an actual building. The mention of a priest does not necessarily imply the existence of a church.

Other medieval sources now in print are the Taxation of Norwich,[9] the Taxation of Pope Nicholas IV,[10] and the Inquisition of the Ninths,[11] which respectively provide a rough idea of the relative prosperity of benefices in 1254, 1291, and 1341. They must, however, be used with caution

---

[7] For details of how to find these, see pp. 166–7. See also J. Godfrey, *The English Parish, 600–1300* (for a good survey of the early church in England, with bibliographies); G. Ward, 'The List of Saxon Churches in the Textus Roffensis', *Archaeologia Cantiana* xliv (1932).

[8] See pp. 46–8; W. Page, 'Some Remarks on the Churches of the Domesday Survey, *Archaeologia* lxvi (1914–15); the works on Domesday by H. C. Darby and his collaborators (see p. 167 n. 11).

[9] W. E. Lunt (ed.), *The Valuation of Norwich* (1926).

[10] S. Ayscough and J. Caley (eds.), *Taxatio Ecclesiastica Angliae et Walliae auctoritate Papae Nicholia IV, c. 1291* (Record Commission, 1802).

[11] G. Vanderzee (ed.), *Nonarum Inquisitiones in Curia Scaccarii* (Record Commission, 1807).

for their basis is vague and it is not known, for example, whether the values are gross or net.[12]

The Taxation of Norwich consists of returns for parishes in eight dioceses in England and Wales (Bangor, Durham, Ely, Lincoln, Llandaff, London, Norwich, St Asaph) for a clerical tax, indicating the value of the benefice and whether or not it was a rectory or a vicarage.

The Taxation of Pope Nicholas of 1291 lists benefices the value of which was greater than six marks (£4). Though it is thus limited and, moreover, the returns for the whole country are not extant, it is nevertheless in Professor Pugh's words 'the most comprehensive directory of medieval benefices in existence',[13] forming the basis for later clerical taxes both royal and papal. It mentions some 8,500 churches and chapels, listing separately spiritualities and temporalities and showing the appropriation of the latter.[14]

The Inquisition of the Ninths of 1341 covers much of the area of 27 counties,[15] and indicates where and why income from tithes differed from that of the assessment of 1291.[16]

On the eve of the breakaway from Rome a much more detailed and exact valuation of ecclesiastical benefices was undertaken. The information collected formed the monumental *Valor Ecclesiasticus* of 1535, also available in print.[17]

[12] Pugh, *Parish History*, 74–5; R. Graham, *English Ecclesiastical Studies* (1929), 271. [13] Pugh, *Parish History*, 73.

[14] For comment and warnings on too facile a use of this source, see Graham, *English Ecclesiastical Studies*, 271 sqq. See also *P.R.O. Guide* i, 37, 66–7.

[15] In the order printed: Berks., Beds., Northants., Lancs., Dorset, Suffolk, Hants., Staffs., Oxon., Herefordshire, Wilts., Shropshire, Middx., Kent, Yorks., Lincs., Notts., Worcs., Essex, Bucks., Corn., Sussex, Glos., Hunts., Herts., War., Rutland.

[16] See p. 177; see also Graham, *English Ecclesiastical Studies*, 283 sqq. For other surviving taxation lists which may be of use to the historian, see W. E. Lunt, *Financial Relations with the Papacy* (2 vols., 1939, 1962).

[17] J. Caley and J. Hunter (eds.), *Valor Ecclesiasticus temp. Henrici VIII, Auctoritate Regia Institus* (Record Commission, 1810–34). See *P.R.O. Guide* i, 88.

These publications will provide an outline for the student of medieval parish church history in many places in England and Wales to which he will need to add from more miscellaneous, often manuscript, records.[18] Details about the parish church, its clergy, and the spiritual life of the parishioners may be traced through many records, the more important of which I now go on to describe.

Clerical subsidy (tax) rolls are to be found in the Public Record Office (Class E.179) and consist chiefly of the accounts of collectors, indicating the amount at which each benefice was assessed and at times the names of the priests who paid.[19] There may also be diocesan subsidy books (the local compilations from which the assessments were made and sent to the Exchequer), some of which have been

---

[18] For an analysis of ecclesiastical records, see H. Hall, *Repertory of British Archives* (1920), 134–44. The most detailed survey of the records in the possession of the Established Church is the Pilgrim Trust, *Survey of Ecclesiastical Archives, 1946* (1951) (henceforward referred to as *Pilgrim Trust Survey*), produced in typescript and deposited in important libraries; a copy is in the library of the Institute of Historical Research. The first volume of this work notes the whereabouts of the different classes of ecclesiastical records; the second volume (in three parts) lists individual documents by province and diocese in great detail. See also *The Central Records of the Church of England: A Report and Survey presented to the Pilgrim and Radcliffe Trustees* (1976); J. S. Purvis, 'The Archives of York', *Studies in Church History* iv (1967); C. R. Cheney, *English Bishops' Chanceries, 1100–1250* (1950); D. M. Owen, *The Records of the Established Church in England, excluding Parochial Records*, British Record Assoc., Archives and the User, no. 1 (1970). The last named has (pp. 58–60) a list of the location of those ecclesiastical records regularly available to searchers, and a note of catalogues of church records (p. 10n).

[19] *P.R.O. Guide* i, 66–7. For examples in print, see T. M. Fallow (ed.), 'The Fallow Papers', *Yorks. Archaeological Jnl* xxi (1910–11), 243 sqq.; T. M. Fallow (ed.), 'The East Riding Clergy in 1525–6', *ibid.* xxiv (1916–17). Names of priests occur only in the poll taxes of Richard II's reign and then in the early sixteenth century; names of chaplains only in 1450 and 1468: I am indebted to Dr R. W. Dunning for this information.

published.[20] Another source for clerical names are the Chancery significations of excommunication at the Public Record Office (Class C.85).[21] For certain places there are medieval *matriculae* or *scrutinia*, surveys of churches and livings in religious districts.[22] Medieval wills, including those of clerics and laymen, to be found in bishops' registers, registers of cathedral chapters, and the records of ecclesiastical courts, are full of information about altars, church plate, vestments, and church buildings, and there are some early clerical accounts.[23] They also contain references to chantries (see below) and religious gilds[24] and their chaplains, and aspects of church services.[25]

Since in medieval times many benefices were appropriated to religious houses, monastic cartularies may provide a record of such appropriations and of the ordination of vicarages. These may also provide evidence of the value of the income involved. Dugdale's *Monasticon*[26] prints many deeds and charters or grants of land to monastic houses, and a

[20] E.g., H. E. Salter (ed.), *A Subsidy Collected in the Diocese of Lincoln in 1526*, Oxford Historical Soc. lxiii (1909); *Somerset Record Soc.* lv (1940), 159–63.

[21] Cf. R. W. Dunning, 'Somerset Parochial Clergy, 1373–1404', *Proceedings of the Somersetshire Archaeological and Natural History Soc.* cxiv (1970). See also *P.R.O. Guide* i, 42.

[22] See Cheney, *English Bishops' Chanceries*, 110 sqq.

[23] For the whereabout of wills generally, see pp. 63–5. For clerical accounts, see P. Heath, *Medieval Clerical Accounts* (1964).

[24] For these gilds, see also J. Toulmin Smith, *English Gilds* (1870); Pugh, *Parish History*, 76–7; and pp. 126–8, above.

[25] For examples of the kind of information which may be culled from wills, see R. M. Serjeantson and H. I. Longden, 'The Parish Churches and Religious Houses of Northamptonshire', *Archaeological Jnl* lxx (1913); I. Darlington (ed.), *London Consistory Court Wills, 1492–1547*, London Record Soc. iii (1967).

[26] W. Dugdale, *Monasticon Anglicanum*, ed. J. Caley, H. Ellis, and B. Bandinel (1817–30).

large number of cartularies have been published.[27] After 1279 licences for the appropriation of benefices or alienation of advowsons are to be found on the patent rolls (P.R.O., Class C.66).[28] Episcopal registers may record the appropriation of benefices to monasteries and the ordination of vicarages for clerks serving such benefices.[29]

Episcopal registers, which date from the thirteenth century, can be of great value for the Middle Ages and later,[30] though some contain much more information than others. The historian may, however, hope to find the record of the institution[31] of rectors and vicars, giving the date and place of institution, the name, orders, and degree of the incumbent, and the name of the patron. Professor Hamilton Thompson with reason recommended the registers as 'the only real foundation for a trustworthy and continuous list of medieval incumbents'.[32] Sometimes the name of the previous incumbent and his reason for leaving is there, too, and details of the

[27] For a finding aid, see G. R. C. Davis, *The Medieval Cartularies of Great Britain* (1958).

[28] Pugh, *Parish History*, 73.

[29] Thompson, 'Ecclesiastical Benefices', 13; Owen, *Records of the Established Church*, 15. Most appropriations, however, had taken place before the compilation of the earliest surviving records.

[30] Cheney, *English Bishops' Chanceries*, 100 sqq.; C. Jenkins, 'Some Thirteenth-Century Registers', *Church Quarterly Review* xcix (1924); R. C. Fowler, *Episcopal Registers of England and Wales*, S.P.C.K., Helps for Students of History, no. 1 (1918); J. S. Purvis, *An Introduction to Ecclesiastical Records* (1953), 9 sqq.; G. R. Elton, *England, 1200–1640* (1969), 95–8. A. D. Frankforter, 'The Episcopal Registers of Medieval England: An Inventory', *British Studies Monitor* vi (1976), and D. M. Smith, *Guide to Bishops' Registers of England and Wales: A Survey from the Middle Ages to the Abolition of Episcopacy in 1646* (1981), indicate the existence of registers and whether they have appeared in print.

[31] For definitions of this and other ecclesiastical terms, see Purvis, *Introduction*.

[32] *Parish History*, 27. For detailed advice, see Thompson, 'Ecclesiastical Benefices'.

results of litigation concerning the advowson and the reasons for any vacancy of the benefice may also be recorded. Occasionally the award of a pension to a retiring incumbent may be included. Episcopal registers may also reveal other aspects of parish church history such as alterations of dedication festivals, and rededications after rebuilding or after bloodshed in church or churchyard.

Gaps in the records of institutions may sometimes be filled by reference to the registers of neighbouring bishops, for cases of exchange of benefices were frequent in the late Middle Ages,[33] or perhaps to archiepiscopal registers, for the archbishop had the right to institute when sees were vacant and during visitations. Certain archidiaconal registers also contain such information, but these survive only rarely.[34] From the fifteenth century, too, some archdeacons kept separate registers of induction (the act of giving the clerk charge of the temporalities of his church).[35]

From the late fifteenth century episcopal records may also include the formal records of presentation of clerks to livings by patrons (presentation deeds) and deeds of resignation from benefices.[36] Presentations to livings by the Crown by letters patent were numerous at certain times, and these are to be found on the patent rolls (P.R.O., Class C.66) which, it has been said, 'no compiler of a list of incumbents can afford to neglect'.[37]

Occasionally more personal details about parish clergy in

[33] R. L. Storey, *Diocesan Administration in the Fifteenth Century* (1959), 23.

[34] Thompson, *Parish History*, 29–31; Thompson, 'Ecclesiastical Benefices', 24. See also A. Hamilton Thompson, 'Diocesan Organization in the Middle Ages: Archdeacons and Rural Deans', *Proceedings British Academy* xxix (1943).

[35] Owen, *Records of the Established Church*, 47–8; Purvis, *Introduction*, 17; L. J. Redstone and F. W. Steer, *Local Records* (1953), 169–70.

[36] Owen, *Records of the Established Church*, 15–16.

[37] Thompson, 'Ecclesiastical Benefices', 26–8 (q.v. for difficulties which arise in the use of this source). See also Thompson, *Parish History*, 26–7.

the Middle Ages can be found. Apart from their wills, mentioned above, they sometimes witnessed deeds. The P.R.O., *Calendar of Papal Registers relating to Great Britain and Ireland*, and the P.R.O., *Calendar of Petitions to the Pope*,[38] contain dispensations for plurality of benefices, petitions for preferment, for temporary absence, and for non-residence, and additional information on the rectors of well-endowed churches, though their accuracy is not always to be relied on.[39] These registers and petitions also mention many chapels. From 1400 the universities' records of matriculation and graduation will provide personal information on the clergy.[40]

For the later Middle Ages the local historian of many parishes will need to deal with permanent or temporary chantry foundations and property.[41] Wills will mention some chantries, and the patent rolls record the licences necessary for such foundations from 1279. In a few cases bishops' registers (as noted above) have the details of foundations and endowments. The most obvious source, however, is the chantry certificates of 1545 and 1547[42] which though concerned with the winding up of the chantries may serve as a starting point from which to move backwards.[43] At the Public Record Office, where these are housed, there is a topographical catalogue.[44]

Many of the types of record already described are also useful for the post-Reformation period, often being more

---

[38] Covering the years 1198–1492, and 1342–1419 respectively.

[39] Thompson, 'Ecclesiastical Benefices', 28–9.

[40] Elton, *England, 1200–1640*, 96–7.

[41] Thompson, *Parish History*, 35 sqq.

[42] See pp. 56–7.

[43] For other records concerning chantries at the P.R.O., see Thompson, *Parish History*, 37–8; P.R.O. *Guide*, i 80 sqq., 184. For examples in print, with a good introduction on chantries, see A. Hamilton Thompson, 'Chantry Certificate Rolls for the County of Nottingham', *Transactions of the Thoroton Society* xvi, xvii, xviii (1913, 1914, 1915).

[44] Pugh, *Parish History*, 76.

varied and extant in larger numbers. Other evidence, however, is available too.

Often to be found in diocesan registries and elsewhere are
special valuations of livings for the seventeenth and eighteenth centuries.[45] Some were undertaken as a result of a
parliamentary order of 1649, and these also provide names of
incumbents during the Interregnum. The records of these
particular surveys are at the Public Record Office (Classes
C.94; D.L.32), and there are nearly contemporary copies
(sometimes filling gaps in the originals) at Lambeth Palace
and other ecclesiastical depositories.[46] Other surveys of
clergy and churches for the sixteenth and seventeenth centuries are to be found in the *Carte Antique et Miscellanee* at
Lambeth Palace[47] where there are also returns of clergy to an
enquiry of 1705 which provide details of the value of the
livings and the names of patrons.[48] The records of other
ecclesiastical surveys for the sixteenth and seventeenth centuries are described in the next section of this chapter.[49]

[45] *Ibid.* 78–9.

[46] In MSS. 902–22, 944–50, 968, 983, 996–9: D. M. Owen, 'Canterbury
Episcopal Archives in Lambeth Palace Library', *Jnl Soc. Archivists* ii
(1960–4), 147; *P.R.O. Guide* i, 42. Some of these are listed in an N.R.A.
report; *Lambeth Palace Library – Commonwealth Records*, 114 sqq. See also
S. C. Newton, 'Parliamentary Surveys', *History* lii (1968); *Pilgrim Trust
Survey* i, 21.

[47] MSS. 889–901: C. Jenkins, *Ecclesiastical Records*, S.P.C.K., Helps for
History Students, no. 18 (1920), 70. See also Dorothy M. Owen, *A
Catalogue of Lambeth Manuscripts 889 to 901 (Carte Antique et Miscellanee)*
(1968).

[48] In MSS. 960–5, for which there is a manuscript index. The questions
answered are to be found in the *Catalogue of the Library at Lambeth Palace*
(1812), 269–70. For examples in print, see A. R. Bax, 'On the State of
Certain Parish Churches in Surrey in 1705', *Surrey Archaeological Collections*
xii (1895); R. W. Dunning, 'Some Somerset Parishes in 1705', *Proceedings
of the Somerset Archaeological and Natural History Soc.* cxii (1968).

[49] N.b. also at Lambeth a recently acquired seventeenth-century account
of parochial clergy in Essex (MS. 2442): I am grateful to Mr E. G. W. Bill
for this reference.

Described as 'the most convenient means of tracing the names of incumbents and patrons'[50] for modern times are the manuscript institution books' at the Public Record Office, which index bishops' certificates of institutions to benefices (1544–1912) returned to the Exchequer (Class E.331) and taken from episcopal registers. There are also certificates of readmission to benefices mainly following the Restoration (Class E.333), and presentation to benefices in the gift of the Duchy of Lancaster (Elizabeth I to George I) (Class D.L.16).[51]

The appropriation by the Crown of annates or first fruits resulted not only in the *Valor Ecclesiasticus*, described above, but in other records now housed in the Public Record Office.[52] They include composition books (1535–1794) (Class E.334; indexes at P.R.O.) and controller's state books (1688–1783) (E.335) recording compositions for the payment of annates and the names of incumbents; process books (1540–1822) (E.338) containing details of payments and incumbents; returns of benefices and incumbents (1651–8) (E.339); and remembrancer's constat books (1709–13; 1793–1838) (E.340), again naming incumbents and showing the value of benefices. At the same depository are the inventories of 1552 of church goods, vestments, and ornaments,[53] some of which have been published.[54] Published lists of benefices and their values (deriving from the activities of Queen Anne's Bounty) include[55] John Ecton's *Liber Valo-*

---

[50] Hoskins, *Local History*, 65.

[51] *P.R.O. Guide* i, 186. See also Classes D.L.37, D.L.42, for earlier duchy presentations.   [52] *P.R.O. Guide* i, 86–88.

[53] *Ibid.* 56; *Exchequer K.R., Church Goods*, List and Index Soc., lxix, lxxvi (1971–2) (topographically arranged).

[54] E.g., S. C. Lomas (ed.), *The Edwardian Inventories for Huntingdonshire*, Alcuin Club, Collections vii (1906); W. Page (ed.), *The Inventories of Church Goods for the Counties of York, Durham, and Northumberland*, Surtees Soc. xcvii (1897).

[55] Pugh, *Parish History*, 78; *P.R.O. Guide* i, 87–88, x88; ii, 118. For other records of Queen Anne's Bounty, see below, p. 267.

rum et Decimarum (1711) and a revised edition of the same work, J. Bacon's *Liber Regis* (1786).

For the post-Reformation period church records remain important. Apart from the episcopal registers which continue to record ordinations and institutions, there are sometimes, as at York, separate institution books at first duplicating the entries in the registers and then supplanting them for this purpose.[56]

Various ecclesiastical surveys and returns assessing the prevalence of dissent, both protestant and Roman Catholic, and the number of Anglican communicants in parishes, are described elsewhere in this volume, as are records dealing with early puritanism.[57] Visitation records of bishops and of archdeacons[58] throw light on these matters too,[59] but also on much else. Visitation books, of various kinds, and papers include returns to visitation articles and churchwardens' presentments which reflect the spiritual life of the parish, the particular outlook of the incumbent (such as puritanical leanings), the number and nature of services, the state of lay morality, of church buildings, goods, and furnishings, and of popular education.[60] In the eighteenth century archdeacons' visitation records contain much about the fabric of chur-

---

[56] Thompson, 'Ecclesiastical Benefices', 19–20; *Pilgrim Trust Survey* i, 13.

[57] See p. 269 sqq.

[58] For archdeacons' records, see E. R. Brinkworth, 'The Study and Use of Archdeacons' Court Records: Illustrated from the Oxford Records (1566–1759)', *T.R.H.S.*, 4th ser., xxv (1943); Redstone and Steer, *Local Records*, 169–71; Jenkins, *Ecclesiastical Records*, 70.

[59] See p. 271.

[60] D. M. Owen, 'Episcopal Visitation Books', *History* xlix (1964); Owen, *Records of the Established Church*, 30–5; Redstone and Steer, *Local Records*, 167–8. For examples of visitation articles and books, see J. S. Purvis, *Tudor Parish Documents of the Diocese of York* (1948), q.v. also (pp. 96 sqq.) for records of examinations of the clergy; S. L. Ollard and P. C. Walker (eds.), *Archbishop Herring's Visitation Returns, 1743*, Yorks. Archaeological Soc., Record Ser., lxxi, lxxii, lxxv, lxxvii, lxix (1928–31); H. Johnstone, *Churchwardens' Presentments, 17th Century*, Sussex Record Soc., xlix, l (1949–50).

ches.[61] It should be emphasized, however, that visitation material is often difficult to use, particularly for early periods.

Other episcopal records will include subscription books which will record the subscription of those licensed to benefices and curacies to conform to the Thirty-Nine Articles and the Prayer Book; presentations to and resignations from benefices; letters testimonial and other ordination papers; and nominations of curates. Benefice papers may provide information on revenues, ordinations to vicarages, and augmentations.[62] Faculty petitions and faculty books among diocesan judicial records contain evidence of changes to the fabric and furniture of churches requiring the bishop's permission, and archdeacons' records may include inspection books setting out what repairs to the church were required or undertaken.[63]

Very occasionally glebe terriers hold evidence of the state of the church fabric and its endowments, and sometimes lists of fittings and plate. They often have details of the parsonage worth noting, and are to be found among the visitation papers of bishops and archdeacons[64] and in parish chests.[65] If they are detailed enough they can on occasion be used with tithe books to calculate the revenue of a benefice.[66] The collection of tithes and the right to tithes led to legal disputes which may be recorded in the archives of ecclesiastical courts

[61] Purvis, *Introduction*, 47.

[62] Redstone and Steer, *Local Records*, 164 sqq.; *Pilgrim Trust Survey* i, 14.

[63] Redstone and Steer, *Local Records*, 167; Hoskins, *Local History*, 167; W. E. Tate, *The Parish Chest* (1960 edn), 153 sqq. For the types of modern documents to be found in diocesan registries, see Owen, *Records of the Established Church*, 28–30.

[64] *Pilgrim Trust Survey* i, 14.

[65] See pp. 177–8.

[66] Pugh, *Parish History*, 79. For later awards by the tithe commissioners of exchange of glebe lands for other lands, arranged by counties, 1841–1935, see P.R.O. Class. M.A.F. 14.

(see below) and in those of lay courts, particularly the Exchequer of Pleas.[67]

Sometimes tithes were extinguished by the allotment of a plot of land under an enclosure Act; more often they were commuted. The tithe commutation Acts of 1836–60 converted all tithes in kind into 'corn rent' or 'tithe rent' charges. The records of enclosure, tithes (including glebe terriers), and tithe commutation have been described fully under agricultural sources.[68] Naturally they contain much material on the profits of livings and tithing customs.[69] There are several parliamentary papers which are useful for tithes.[70]

The records of ecclesiastical courts may contain much that is pertinent to the work of the local historian. The diocesan and archidiaconal courts for the area concerned, particularly the consistory courts, are naturally likely to yield the most useful material.[71] Cause (case) books or papers contain the detailed documents concerning the case – arguments, evidence – while act books summarize the actual procedure of

---

[67] *P.R.O. Guide* i, 92–4. For a calendar of tithe suits on the plea rolls (Class E.13) (Edward IV to George IV), topographically arranged, see P.R.O., *Deputy Keeper's Report* ii (1841), appendix ii, 249–72.

[68] See pp. 180–3, 192–5; and also Tate, *Parish Chest*, 139–42.

[69] Cf. E. J. Evans, 'Tithing Customs and Disputes: the Evidence of Glebe Terriers', *Ag.H.R.* xviii (1970); Tate, *Parish Chest*, 129–30; Pugh, *Parish History*, 80.

[70] See the official indexes, and above p. 17 n. 42. *A Return of Tithes Commuted or Apportioned* (1887) lxiv includes within it returns of 1848–67, and records the sums at which tithe was commuted.

[71] For church courts and their records, see *Pilgrim Trust Survey* i, 15; Elton, *England 1200–1640*, 102 sqq.; Purvis, *Introduction*, 64 sqq.; Owen, *Records of the Established Church*, 36 sqq.; B. L. Woodcock, *Mediaeval Ecclesiastical Courts in the Diocese of Canterbury* (1952); I. J. Churchill, *Canterbury Administration* (1933); E. R. Brinkworth, *The Archdeacons' Court* (1942); Brinkworth, 'Archdeacons' Court Records', 93–9, and 97n., for references to archdeacons' court records in print. For an example of court of audience records, see M. Bowker, *An Episcopal Court Book for the Diocese of Lincoln, 1514–1520*, Lincoln Record Soc. lxi (1967).

the case.[72] Before the Reformation only a few such records exist, but they are more common from the mid-sixteenth century and, particularly, from the seventeenth century. Professor Elton warns scholars about the physical difficulties of using this type of material, while yet stressing its importance. The court records have in them much about relations between the clergy and the laity (including, as noted, tithe disputes), and the moral and spiritual life of parson and people. Cases cover immorality, blasphemy, drunkenness, neglect of duty by parish officers, non-payment of church rates, misbehaviour on the Sabbath, relics of popery, irregularities in the sacraments and the church services, clerical dress, plurality, unlicensed preaching, dissent, wills, church fabric, and so on.[73]

The records of the Court of Arches (formerly at the Bodleian Library but now at Lambeth Palace) are less useful, because they exist only from 1660, and also because as a court of appeal, the cases came from places over a large area. If search is made, however, they may yield information on rectories, vicarages, manners and morals, tithe disputes, and so on, for the parish being investigated.[74] The comparable court for York was the Chancery court.[75]

At Lambeth, too, are the records of the Faculty Office (from 1534) in which may be traced among other things

[72] Detailed extracts from both cause papers and act books will be found in Purvis, *Tudor Parish Documents.*

[73] Cf. Stubbs quoted by Jenkins, *Ecclesiastical Records*, 72. For examples from a consistory court, see A. J. Willis, 'Church and Laymen in the Eighteenth Century: A Study of some Archives of the Ecclesiastical Courts, *Amateur Historian* iv (1958–60).

[74] M. D. Slatter, 'The Records of the Court of Arches', *Jnl Ecclesiastical History* iv (1953); M. D. Slatter, 'The Study of the Records of the Court of Arches', *Jnl Soc. Archivists* i (1955–9); M. D. Slatter, *List of the Records of the (Canterbury Province) Court of Arches deposited in the Bodleian in 1941* (typescript, 1951) (since 1954 at Lambeth).

[75] See Jenkins, *Ecclesiastical Records*, 69; Owen, *Records of the Established Church*, 50–1, for this and other ecclesiastical courts.

dispensations for plurality and non-residence.[76] Capitular (dean and chapter) records, too, may sometimes be useful.[77]

The records of the parish itself if well preserved will, for the post-Reformation period, provide a great deal of minute evidence.[78] Vestry minutes, parish registers, constables' and churchwardens' accounts, and even overseers' accounts can be invaluable. They have been described and commented on in other chapters of this volume,[79] but because they are therefore briefly dismissed here the local historian of church affairs must not underrate them. Often they will provide richer detail – especially about the quality and nature of the religious life of a parish – and more easily culled than many of the other sources described above. Of them perhaps churchwardens' accounts are most useful for local church history, in particular with reference to the maintenance, repair, and reconstruction of church buildings, altars, fonts, pulpits, and organs, the use of prayer books and vestments, and details of church plate and church sittings.[80] Those for the periods of religious strife and upheaval in Tudor and Stuart times can be made to yield a great deal of significance. The minutes of the vestry deal with much secular business but also with church affairs, and are particularly useful for an indication of relationships with incumbents over, for example, services. Parish registers, described elsewhere,[81] may contain random

[76] Owen, *Records of the Established Church*, 51–2; D. S. Chambers, *Faculty Office Registers, 1534–1549: A Calendar* (1966).

[77] Jenkins, *Ecclesiastical Records*, 53–4; Owen, *Records of the Established Church*, 53 sqq.; *Pilgrim Trust Survey* i, 18–22; S. Bond, 'Chapter Act Books', *History* liv (1969).

[78] For a detailed study, see Tate, *Parish Chest*.

[79] See pp. 52–6, 77–9, 99–101.

[80] The best account is still J. C. Cox, *Churchwardens' Accounts* (1913). See also J. Blain. *A List of Churchwardens' Accounts* (1933); C. Drew, *Early Parochial Administration in England: The Origins of the Office of Churchwarden* (1954). For an example, see E. Hobhouse (ed.), *Church-wardens' Accounts of Croscombe, Pilton, Yatton, 1349 to 1560*, Somerset Record Soc. iv (1890).

[81] See pp. 52–6.

information apart from the lists of baptisms, marriages, and burials. They may reveal the otherwise untraced names of incumbents. For the nineteenth century, registers of services (service books) are invaluable for tracing the liturgical development of the parish.[82]

For recent times, parish and diocesan magazines, directories, and, especially, diocesan handbooks can provide a fund of detailed information. The local historian may find the fullest information in the diocesan handbooks or calendars, which may report the value of benefices, size of Sunday and day schools, improvements to church fabric, and the amount of seating accommodation available. Deserving mention, too, is the *Official Year-Book of the Church of England* (later the *Church of England Year Book*) (from 1884). Le Neve's *Fasti Ecclesiae Anglicanae* is also useful for information on clergy from the Reformation onwards. *Crockford's Clerical Directory*, first begun in weekly parts in 1855, is a mine of information for the clergy and their benefices for the past century or so. Biographies of each individual cleric are there, and for each parish are named the patron, present incumbent, curates, income gross and net (now net only), and the seating accommodation of the church.[83] Sometimes the diaries or journals of the incumbents have survived to provide details of the religious and general life of the parish.[84]

For the eighteenth century, the records of the Commissioners for Building Fifty New Churches, deposited at Lambeth Palace, may be of use, though they concern only London and Westminster.[85] Information on new church buildings in the nineteenth and early twentieth centuries, of

[82] R. Dunning, 'Nineteenth-Century Parochial Sources', *Studies in Church History* xi (1975).

[83] Similar is another periodical directory: the *Clergy List* (from 1843), publ. Kelly's Directories. For Le Neve, see p. 28.

[84] Dunning, 'Parochial Sources', 306–8.

[85] Owen, 'Canterbury Episcopal Archives', 147; H. M. Colvin, 'Fifty New Churches', *Architectural Review* cvii (1950).

which there were many, may be culled from the *Builder* (from 1834), the *Ecclesiologist* (1841–68), the records of the Church Building Society (founded 1818),[86] and diocesan registries.[87]

The records of the present Church Commissioners for England (established 1948) embrace also those of its predecessors, the Governors of Queen Anne's Bounty, the Church Building Commissioners, and the Ecclesiastical Commissioners for England.[88]

The Church Building Commissioners (1818–50) were most active between 1818 and the early 1830s, and their records include files for all the 1,077 new cures with which they were concerned, and surveyors' report books. Few of the original plans of the churches, however, survive.[89] The reports of the Commissioners form a series of parliamentary papers published between 1821 and 1856.[90]

[86] Now the Incorporated Church Building Society, 24 Great Peter Street, London sw1. Its files and annual reports give information on the churches it has helped since 1840. Files to 1860 are in the Lambeth Palace Library. Those from 1860 to 1880 will be deposited there. The records of later date and all minute books are with the society. For its records, see also H. M. Port, *Six Hundred New Churches* (1961).

[87] Hoskins, *Local History*, 62.

[88] At 1 Millbank, London sw1. The following is based on C. E. Welch, 'The Records of the Church Commissioners', *Jnl Soc. Archivists* i (1955–9); Owen, 'Canterbury Episcopal Archives', 146; E. J. Robinson, 'The Records of the Church Commissioners', *ibid.* iii (1965–9); E. J. Robinson, 'The Records of the Church Commissioners', *Local Historian* ix (1970–1). There is an N.R.A. report: *Lambeth Palace Library, Records of the Church Commissioners.* See also *The Central Records of the Church of England*, 15 sqq., 52 sqq.; G. F. A. Best, *Temporal Pillars: Queen Anne's Bounty, The Ecclesiastical Commissioners and the Church of England* (1964).

[89] Some of the records of the Church Building Commission are listed in Port, *New Churches*, which is a study of its activities; an appendix lists the churches concerned, with details.

[90] For references, see W. R. Powell, *Local History from Blue Books: Select List of the Sessional Papers of the House of Commons* (1962), q.v., also, for other parliamentary papers on new churches and parishes.

The records of Queen Anne's Bounty (1704–1948),[91] established to augment the income of poor benefices, consist chiefly of minute books (1704–*c.*1760); files containing reports of commissions enquiring into the state of livings and correspondence concerning grants; and files of legal correspondence concerned with the provision of grants. Plans and estimates for building parsonages exist from 1803. The work of the governors is summarized in parliamentary papers.[92]

The Ecclesiastical Commissioners were concerned mainly with the lands of bishops, deans and chapters, and other ecclesiastical corporations from the mid-nineteenth century until 1948. Surveys of these estates include particulars of the benefices of the parishes in which the lands were situated, and of the condition of their parish churches. They include maps of the glebe. Often these benefices were assisted by the Commissioners.

The reorganization of parishes by amalgamation or by subdivision, with which the Ecclesiastical Commissioners were concerned, can be traced in special Acts or Orders in Council printed in the *London Gazette*.[93]

Some parliamentary papers have already been mentioned. Others of importance include a return of benefices of 1818, the reports of a royal commission in 1835 and 1836, and the reports of the Ecclesiastical Commissioners from 1846.[94] These provide much information on incumbents, values of benefices, patrons, churches and chapels, and so on. The valuable 1851 religious census is described in detail in the next section.[95]

[91] See also above, p. 259.

[92] The first is *Livings Augmented by Queen Anne's Bounty, 1705–1815* (1814–15) xii. For others, including accounts, see the indexes to the parliamentary papers.

[93] Pugh, *Parish History*, 81.

[94] For these and others, see Powell, *Blue Books*.

[95] See p. 273.

PROTESTANT NONCONFORMITY

This section covers sources for the study of local puritan groups in the sixteenth and seventeenth centuries from which grew some of the nonconformist churches of the eighteenth century, and sources for the local history of official nonconformity after the Toleration Act of 1689, including groups formed later, such as the Methodists and more recently established sects.[96] Some of the sources described in this section are common to Protestant and Roman Catholic nonconformity and are, therefore, not dealt with again in any detail in the section on Roman Catholicism which follows this.

As with most topics it is difficult to carry out a local investigation without a background knowledge of the subject, and a local historian unfamiliar with this area of study should read some general works before starting.[97] He should

[96] General works on the topic include: W. R. Powell, 'The Sources for the History of Protestant Nonconformist Churches in England', *B.I.H.R.* xxv (1952); W. R. Powell *et al.*, 'Protestant Nonconformist Records', *Archives* v (1961); *Archives of Religious and Ecclesiastical Bodies and Organizations other than the Church of England*, British Record Assoc., Reports from Committees, no. 3 (1936); J. Smith, 'Nonconformist Records – A Neglected Opportunity', *Jnl Soc. Archivists* iii (1967); J. Smith, 'The Local Records of Nonconformity', *Local Historian* viii (1968–9). Wesley F. Swift, *How to Write a Local History of Methodism* (revised and added to by T. Shaw, 1964 edn), contains much information applicable to nonconformity generally. C. E. Welch, 'Archives and Manuscripts in Nonconformist Libraries', *Archives* vi (1964), has a useful list of libraries and depositories with an indication of the sort of collections they possess. C. Cross, 'Popular Piety and the Records of the Unestablished Churches, 1460–1660', *Studies in Church History* xi (1975), embraces earlier dissent.

[97] E.g., *Census of 1851: Religious Worship, England and Wales, Report and Tables* (1852–3) lxxix has a review of the teaching of various sects. See also D. Horton Davies, *The English Free Churches* (1952). More specific works include: A. C. Underwood, *A History of the English Baptists* (1947); R. W. Dale, *History of English Congregationalism* (1907); A. Peel, *These Hundred Years: A History of the Congregational Union, 1831–1931* (1931); R. T. Jones,

at least be aware that into the eighteenth century the division between sects was not as distinct as it later became, and congregations often changed allegiance with a change of minister; for some early congregations it is never quite clear to what sect they belonged. For this reason the careers of individual ministers may be of great importance.[98]

The first step is to search certain printed works.[99] G. Lyon Turner's *Original Records of Early Nonconformity*[100] provides references to early dissent culled from the state papers, domestic (to the Toleration Act of 1689), the returns of conventicles of 1665 and 1669, and the so-called Compton Census of 1676.[101] Alexander Gordon's *Freedom after Ejection* (1917) prints returns to enquiries of 1690–2 into the state of

Congregationalism in England, 1662–1962 (1962); W. C. Braithwaite, *The Beginnings of Quakerism* (1955); W. C. Braithwaite, *The Second Period of Quakerism* (1961); R. M. Jones, *The Later Period of Quakerism* (1921); W. J. Townsend, H. B. Workman, G. Eayrs, *A New History of Methodism* (1909); R. E. Davies, *Methodism* (1962); C. J. Davey, *The Methodist Story* (1955); L. F. Church, *The Early Methodist People* (1948); L. F. Church, *More About the Early Methodist People* (1949). For works on individual Methodist groups, see bibliography in Swift, *Local History of Methodism*, 19.

Early Nonconformity, 1566–1800 (a catalogue of books in Dr Williams's Library, published in 12 vols., by G. K. Hall & Co., 1968), contains references to many works bearing on the local history of dissent. For the resources of Dr Williams's Library, Gordon Square, London WC1, see 'Dr Williams's Library', *Local Historian* ix (1970–1), and *Rep. Historical Manuscripts Commission* ii (1872), 365–8. The John Rylands University Library of Manchester has the Hobill Collection of Methodist literature of which a typescript catalogue is available.

[98] C. E. Surman's bibliographical and biographical index housed in Dr Williams's Library contains reference to some 30,000 Independent and Congregational ministers.

[99] Listed in Powell, 'History', 215. This paragraph draws extensively on this excellent article.

[100] 3 vols., 1911. Vol. iii is a general introduction; vol. ii contains indexes; vol. i provides tabulated references, etc., Turner's original notes are in Dr Williams's Library.

[101] Taken only from the Lambeth Palace returns. For others, and further information on this return, see pp. 57–8.

Presbyterian and Congregational dissent, made by counties. Names of ministers are indexed with biographical information, and the indexed references to places sometimes give notes on local dissent. Two works by A. G. Matthews, *Calamy Revised* (1934), and *Walker Revised* (1948), provide information on, respectively, the ejected puritan clergy, 1660 to 1662, and the Anglicans who suffered during the years 1642 to 1660. G. E. Evans's *Vestiges of Protestant Dissent* (1897) gives dates of foundation, with names and dates of ministers, of all 'Unitarian, Liberal Christian and Presbyterian Churches', including Unitarian General Baptist churches still in existence in 1897.

From the nineteenth century local directories, especially Kelly's, give information on the more important dissenting congregations, and local newspapers should also be searched. Official year books, produced by the churches, are discussed below. Early maps, especially of towns, often mark the position of nonconformist chapels indicating their denomination.

Manuscript collections of general use include the Joseph Hunter manuscripts at the British Library, compiled in the first half of the nineteenth century. Of these, Additional MS. 24484, the 'Britannica Puritanica', comprises outlines of Presbyterian and Independent congregations after 1662, arranged topographically. Additional MS. 24485 consists of biographies of dissenting ministers compiled from diaries. At Dr Williams's Library are the John Evans manuscript, containing a survey of the state of Baptist, Congregational, and Presbyterian congregations in England and Wales (by counties) during the years 1715 to 1718;[102] the Josiah Thompson manuscript, which provides lists of English and Welsh

---

[102] It includes emendations and additions to 1729. There is some information on Quakers. A digest of this unofficial census is printed in 'The Baptist Interest under George I', *Transactions of the Baptist Historical Soc.* ii (1910–11), 95–109. A photographic copy in Dr Williams's Library is available on loan.

dissenting congregations in *c.* 1773 and of certain petitioning ministers in 1772[103] and gives details of the histories of certain congregations (mostly Baptist) drawn up in 1773;[104] and the Walter Wilson manuscripts, consisting of notes, compiled in the 1830s, on dissenting ministers and congregations in different parts of the country.[105]

The records of the Established Church will often contain information on local dissent. The episcopal returns of the 1660s and the census of 1676 have already been mentioned. More generally, visitation returns from the sixteenth century onwards very frequently report, often in great detail, on Protestant and Roman Catholic nonconformist congregations or on numbers of nonconformists or nonconformist families in each parish. These and other church records are important sources.[106]

Official government and local government records may also prove fruitful of search. The presentments of Protestant and Roman Catholic recusants are recorded in the quarter-sessions rolls from 1559,[107] as are the presentments (under the so-called Clarendon Code) of persons holding conventicles.[108] References in the state papers, domestic, at the

[103] 'Thompson's List of Conventicles' and 'Josiah Thompson's Survey of Nonconformity, 1773', *Transactions of the Congregational Historical Soc.* iv (1909–10), 49 sqq., v (1911–12), 205, 261, 372. A contemporary duplicate copy of the Thompson MS. is in the Museum Library of Bunyan Meeting, Bedford.

[104] See 'Josiah Thompson's Notes of 1799', *Transactions of the Baptist Historical Soc.*, NS, iii (1926–7), various pages, which prints details for places in Beds., Berks., Cambs., and Devon from this MS.

[105] There is a topographical index in Dr Williams's Library, and also a *Guide to the Manuscripts.*

[106] For an example in print, see *Archbishop Herring's Visitation Returns, 1743*, Yorks. Archaeological Soc., lxxi, lxxii, lxxv, lxxvii, lxix (1928–31).

[107] See also below, pp. 287–8, where the recusant rolls are described. These are as much a source for Protestant as for Roman Catholic dissent.

[108] For comments on these, see Powell, 'History', 214. Presentments were also made at the church courts.

Public Record Office may be traced through Lyon Turner's book, cited above, as well as through the *Calendar*. Included are the records of registration of licences under the Declaration of Indulgence of 1672.[109] The Privy Council registers contain much information on puritanism. [110]

The Toleration Act of 1689 required the registration of Protestant dissenters' meeting houses[111] with quarter sessions, the bishops, or archdeacons,[112] and an Act of 1812 required that the meeting houses should be certified with all three registering authorities. The quarter-sessions (usually in the order books), episcopal, and archidiaconal records may, therefore, contain petitions for and registers of these certificates or licences,[113] until an Act of 1852 brought the system to an end and inaugurated another which resulted in a series of records which will be discussed below. Sometimes the original certificates have survived in the records of the dissenting chapel or sect.

An Act of 1736 required the registration of nonconformist trust deeds and these are enrolled on the close rolls at the Public Record Office (Class C.54).[114] These, and the original deeds (found in local record offices as well as with the chapels concerned), provide (at least until 1890) a great deal of information on local congregations, their buildings and

---

[109] Original licences on printed forms were held by the congregations and are now to be found in local depositories: E. Welch, 'The Registration of Meeting Houses', *Jnl Soc. Archivists* iii (1966), 116.

[110] P.R.O. Class P.C.2 (indexed); some are calendared as *Acts of the Privy Council*.

[111] Only Unitarians and Roman Catholics did not benefit from the Act. From 1791 some of the provisions of the Act were extended to Roman Catholic congregations, and in 1813 to Unitarians, providing they registered their chapels.

[112] For details, see Welch, 'Registration of Meeting Houses'.

[113] *Ibid.* 118; Powell, 'History', 214; *Pilgrim Trust Survey* i, 15–16.

[114] For indexes, see *P.R.O. Guide* i, 18.

land, doctrinal beliefs, and administrative organization.[115]

Also at the Public Record Office are the invaluable records of the religious census of 1851.[116] These returns, sent in by almost all places of worship (including Anglican and Roman Catholic as well as Protestant dissenting congregations), should give totals of attendances at the various services on 30 March 1851, and the average attendances for the previous year. They also contain information on buildings and endowments, sometimes with informative remarks by ministers. As well as the original records there is a most useful digest published as a parliamentary paper.[117]

The Public Record Office now houses (Classes R.G.4, and R.G.6) a collection of some 9,000 nonconformist registers of births, baptisms, marriages, deaths, and burials (mostly for the period 1775 to 1837) which before 1961 were at the General Register Office, Somerset House, where they were deposited under Acts of 1840 and 1858. A parliamentary paper of 1838 lists about 7,000 registers of some 3,600 congregations and contains a great deal of useful material, including names of ministers.[118] The Registrar General in

[115] For details of these records, see E. Welch, 'Nonconformist Trust Deeds', *Jnl Soc. Archivists* iii (1968). A list is in *Thirty-Second Rep. Deputy Keeper of Public Records* ii, appendix ii (1871).

[116] P.R.O., Class H.O.129. The *Congregational Year Book* for 1855 prints a list of all Independent churches taken from this census. See also R. W. Ambler, 'The 1851 Census of Religious Worship', *Local Historian* xi (1975); D. M. Thompson, 'The Religious Census of 1851', in R. Lawton (ed.), *The Census and Social Structure* (1978). C. D. Field, 'The 1851 Religious Census: A Select Bibliography', *Proceedings of the Wesley Historical Soc.* xli (1978), is a valuable list, topographically arranged. For an example in print, see R. W. Ambler, *The Lincolnshire Returns of Public Worship, 1851*, Lincs. Record Soc. lxxii (1979).

[117] *Census of 1851: Religious Worship, England and Wales, Report and Tables* (1852–3) lxxxix.

[118] *Rep. R. Commission on Registers or Records of Births or Baptisms, Deaths or Burials, and Marriages, other than Parish Registers* (1837–8) xxviii; supplemented by another report: *Rep. on Non-Parochial Registers and Records* (1857–8) xxiii.

1859 published a list of these records then held by him.[119] Some of the registers deposited contained supplementary documents, such as minute books and ministers' diaries.[120] Not all congregations, however, deposited their registers.[121] Moreover, since 1837, with the introduction of civil registration of births, deaths, and marriages,[122] and the spread of the use of public cemeteries, the keeping of registers has become less common. It should be noted that the parish registers of the Established Church often contain entries of nonconformists since an Act of 1695 required notice of all births to be given to the parish priest, and an Act of 1753 restricted marriages (except of Quakers and Jews) to parish churches, though this was often ignored by Roman Catholics.

St Catherine's House holds a large collection of other records of use to the local historian deriving from changes in the licensing system.[123] An Act of 1852 transferred registration from the former authorities, noted above, to the Registrar General. At first registration was compulsory, and although in 1855 it became permissive, it had certain legal and financial advantages so that many congregations continued to register themselves. The cumulative Worship Register, still in progress, is arranged by registration districts in

[119] *Lists of Non-Parochial Registers and Records in the Custody of the Registrar General* (1859) (not a parliamentary paper; and unfortunately not often found in public libraries); but *General Register Office, List of Non-Parochial Registers, Main Series, and Society of Friends Series*, List and Index Soc. xlii (1969), incorporates the 1859 H.M.S.O. publication.

[120] E. Welch, 'Nonconformist Registers', *Jnl Soc. Archivists* ii (1964), q.v. for a full discussion of these records. See also, R. W. Ambler, 'Non-Parochial Registers and the Local Historian', *Local Historian* x (1972–3).

[121] Smith, 'Nonconformist Records', 283. For the whereabouts of others the *National Index of Parish Registers*, ii (1973), will be useful. For details, see above, p. 56 n. 36.

[122] Records at St Catherine's House, Kingsway, London WC2.

[123] For a description of these records, formerly at Somerset House, see R. B. Rose, 'Some National Sources for Protestant Nonconformist and Roman Catholic History', *B.I.H.R.* xxxi (1958), on which the following is based.

indexed manuscript volumes which may be consulted at St Catherine's House[124] They are extremely useful in tracing the existence and dates of establishment of dissenting congregations and their denomination. It must be noted, however, that since there is no financial or legal advantage in de-registration care must be taken before assuming the continued existence of a place of worship.

The Act of 1852 also resulted in the accumulation of retrospective material, for it required the submission by the former licensing authorities of returns of all Protestant nonconformist places of worship registered from 1689 to 1852, and of Roman Catholic chapels registered from 1791 to 1852. These returns comprise Public Record Office Class R.G. 31, and provide such evidence as the name, description, and location of each meeting house, its religious denomination, the names and personal details of the person certifying, and the date of registration.[125] Over 54,000 registrations are recorded, but they are incomplete and are more extensive for some areas than others. It should be noted, however, that they may include details of registration of which the originals no longer exist locally.

From 1837 registered meeting houses could also be registered at the General Register Office for marriages, and original certificates and the register are kept by the Registrar

---

[124] Some have appeared in print: those for 1856 and 1876 (both at St Catherine's House); *Returns of Churches, Chapels and Buildings Registered for Religious Worship* (1882) 1 (an extremely useful list). The *Official List of Places Registered for the Solemnization of Marriage* includes for 1902–15 (annually) all registered places of worship; from 1915 publication has been at intervals of several years with intermediary annual lists of addenda. The *Official List* does not provide the date of registration of those meeting houses which have closed.

[125] For a statistical analysis of the returns, see *Returns relating to Dissenters' Places of Worship* (1852–3) lxxviii. See also J. Nichol, 'Nonconformist Places of Worship Licensed under the Toleration Act', *Transactions of the Congregational Historical Soc.* vi (1913–15), 199–208.

General.[126] Duplicate registers were kept by the chapel and are often now deposited in local record offices or with the denomination's archives. Before 1902 the Registrar General issued frequent lists of licences registering for marriages; from then these have been published together with the lists of registration for worship.[127]

Certain other nineteenth-century surveys and investigations may be of use to the local historian. A parliamentary paper of 1836 gives accounts of dissenting meeting houses and Roman Catholic chapels registered up to that year provided by clerks of the peace, some of whom also give unrequested information on existing chapels and their history.[128] A census organized by the *Nonconformist* in 1865 for London, and another by the same periodical in 1872 for towns with over 20,000 inhabitants, give details of Anglican and Roman Catholic as well as Protestant nonconformist places of worship.[129] A private census for the early 1880s gives similar details, with figures of attendance at worship at various services for some 125 towns in England, Wales, and Scotland.[130]

[126] Welch, 'Registration of Meeting Houses', 118–19, 120.

[127] See p. 275 n. 124.

[128] *Return of Dissenting Meeting Houses and Roman Catholic Chapels in England and Wales* (1836) xl. A similar investigation in 1829 resulted in a parliamentary paper covering only Lancashire (*Churches, Chapels, and Chapels of Ease of the Church of England, and Places of Worship not of the Church of England, in Lancashire* (1830) xix (II)). Copies of returns for other counties may, however, be with the records of the clerks of the peace: e.g. [F. W. Steer], *Descriptive Report on the Quarter Sessions, Other Official and Ecclesiastical Records of West and East Sussex* (1954), 66; F. G. Emmison, *Guide to the Essex Record Office* (1946–8), 78.

[129] Published in the *Nonconformist*, 15 Nov. 1865 (Supplement); and in *ibid.* 23 Oct. 1872 (Supplement), and subsequent issues.

[130] A. Mearns, *The Statistics of Attendance at Public Worship as published in England, Wales and Scotland by the Local Press, Oct. 1881–May 1882* (1882). See also A. Mearns, *Religious Statistics of London, 1879* (1879); and, for Birmingham, *Birmingham News* for 1892. For others, see R. C. K. Ensor,

The printed and manuscript records and publications of individual sects and congregations form, of course, another important field for the local researcher. Although the important unit of Protestant nonconformist history is the individual congregation, some sects have or have had national or regional associations which have produced their own records and publications, and some have central depositories for their records.

From 1959 the Presbyterian Church of England had a national depository for completed records of individual local congregations. When the Presbyterians joined with the Congregational Church in England and Wales in 1972 to form the United Reformed Church the new church took over custody of the Presbyterian records.[131] These records include minutes of the national and district synods (from the 1830s), of sessions and committees, membership rolls, and baptismal registers. Some records belonged to congregations in existence before 1836 when they came together to form the later Presbyterian Church. Many Presbyterian records, however, were destroyed by enemy action in 1945.[132]

The Baptists possess no central record office. Minutes of the New Connexion of General Baptists for the period 1799 to 1890 are held at the offices of the Baptist Union of Great Britain and Ireland,[133] which also has some church trust deeds. Other trust deeds are kept locally, as are minute books

---

England, 1870–1914 (1949 edn), 308–9. A survey of religious attendance in a Cheshire town in 1968 is in W. B. Stephens (ed.), *History of Congleton* (1970), 204–5.

[131] At the United Reformed Church, 86 Tavistock Place, London WC1.

[132] J. T. Darling, 'Presbyterian Church of England Records', *Archives* v (1961); L. W. Kelly, 'Some Sources of English Presbyterian Church History', *Jnl Presbyterian Historical Soc. of England* ix (1948–51); J. C. Lancaster, D. M. Owen, and M. C. Poulter (eds.), *Archives, 1956–60*, Library Assoc., Occasional Publication, no. 1 (n.d.), 471.

[133] Baptist Church House, 4 Southampton Row, London WC1.

and other records of individual churches and regional associations, although some are at Dr Williams's Library.[134]

Congregational Church records,[135] where still extant, are usually held by individual churches or are deposited in local record offices. Such records may include church minute books, finance committee minutes, trustees meetings minutes, Sunday school minutes and registers, records of pew rents, charities, gifts to the poor, and so on. Records of closed churches may be with county association officers, and in cases where the former Congregational Union of England and Wales acted as a trustee, the deeds are now held by the United Reformed Church. In many cases deeds were held by Congregational county associations. Some of these remain operative and still hold their printed and manuscript records as well. Where the county association has closed, the deeds and records are normally held by the appropriate provincial office of the United Reformed Church at addresses listed in its year book. The Congregational Library[136] has some local church records, particularly of some old London congregations. Records of closed churches of the United Reformed Church are normally placed in local record offices.

Local Unitarian records, comprising usually deeds, minute books, letters, licences, and financial accounts are normally kept by individual congregations. There are, however, collections at Dr Williams's Library and other places.[137]

[134] A. H. J. Baines, 'Baptist Church Records', *Archives* v (1961). *Transactions of the Baptist Historical Soc.* i (1908–9), 123–4, has a list of sources.

[135] H. G. Tibbutt, 'Sources for Congregational Church History', *Transactions of the Congregational Historical Soc.* xix (1960–4) (which lists Congregational records held in public custody); H. G. Tibbutt, 'Congregational Church Records', *Archives* v (1961); A. Green, 'The Archives of Congregationalism', *Amateur Historian* iii (1956–8).

[136] Memorial Hall, Fleet Lane, London EC4. There is a two-volume catalogue of the manuscripts.

[137] See *Archives of Religious Bodies*, 10. Dr Williams's Library houses the minutes of the Presbyterian Board (from *c.* 1690), which became Unitarian and is unconnected with the later Presbyterian Church of England.

The minute books of the Countess of Huntingdon's Connexion (from 1823) may be traced through the Office of the Connexion,[138] and other records are at Cheshunt College, Cambridge.[139]

The Methodist Archives and Research Collection[140] includes many letters and other manuscripts relating to John Wesley and other early leaders, completed minute and account books for district synods and for some individual (particularly defunct) churches and circuits (though most of these are still held locally), and various private collections.[141] The Methodist Church Property Division[142] (formerly the Department of Chapel Affairs) has transcripts of trust records of all existing and closed Methodist chapels, annual reports of the department from 1855, and the circuit chapel schedules from which the reports were compiled. The head chapel of each circuit or its manse often has among other records trust deeds of the chapels in the circuit, minute books of closed chapels, completed minute and account books for quarterly circuit meetings, and circuit trust schedule books. These last summarize annual assets, liabilities, income, and expenditure in connection with all chapels in the circuit.[143]

[138] 66 Station Road, Croydon, CRO 2RB.

[139] E. Welch, 'The Early Methodists and their Records', *Jnl Soc. Archivists* iv (1971), 210.

[140] At the John Rylands University Library of Manchester, Oxford Road, Manchester, M13 9PP. See description of the Collection by F. Taylor, *Bulletin of the John Rylands Library* lx (1978).

[141] Smith, 'Nonconformist Records', 285, q.v. for further information.

[142] Central Buildings, Oldham Street, Manchester, M1 1JQ.

[143] The composition of circuits changed. Circuit plans, found in many places, are, therefore, useful documents. Some large collections of these are listed in *Archives* v (1961), 9; Swift, *Local History of Methodism*, 7. The Society of Cirplanologists was founded in 1955 to record the location of these plans, and it has published a *Register of Methodist Circuit Plans, 1777–1860*, and four supplements, indicating where they are. A journal, *Cirplan*, is published. There is a large collection of circuit plans at John Rylands Library.

Individual chapels may also have their own account and minute books, Sunday and day school records, and so on. It should be noted, too, that the Annual Conference of the Church now favours the deposit of records held by circuits with local record offices, so that there may often be found deeds, trust documents, marriage and worship certificates, other legal documents and the like.[144]

The Methodist Archives and Research Collection also includes the published *Minutes of Conference* (Conference being the central body of the church (from 1932)), and the printed central minutes of the Wesleyan Methodists (1744–1932), the Methodist New Connexion (1797–1907), the Primitive Methodists (1814–1932), the Wesleyan Methodist Association (1836–57), the United Methodist Free Church (1857–1907), the United Methodist Church (1907–32), and the Wesleyan Reform Union (from 1914).[145] In addition the Collection has the manuscript journals from which the minutes have been extracted, the district minutes (going back to 1800) of the various Methodist denominations, and the minutes of the various connexional committees.

The best organized nonconformist records are those of the Society of Friends.[146] The Society's library[147] will indicate where are the minutes for Monthly Meetings (meetings of all

[144] Some material is held at Methodist theological colleges: Swift, *Local History of Methodism*, 7.

[145] Powell, 'History', 224, q.v. for Bible Christians' minutes (1818–1907). The Wesleyan Reform Union, however, remains outside the Methodist Church and its manuscript records are located elsewhere (details from Church House, 123 Queen Street, Sheffield, s1 2du). Similarly outside are the Independent Methodists, who have their archives at Wigan.

[146] E. H. Milligan, 'Society of Friends Records', *Archives* v (1961); R. S. Mortimer, 'The Archives of the Society of Friends (Quakers)', *Amateur Historian* iii (1956–8). Re-location of records has taken place since these were written.

[147] Friends House, Euston Road, London nw1 2bj. See also the feature 'Reports on Archives' in the *Journal of the Friends' Historical Soc.*

congregations in a certain area), Quarterly Meetings (groups of Monthly Meetings), and Yearly Meetings (the central body for Great Britain). For the local historian the most significant are the Monthly Meeting minutes, many of which date from the late 1660s, and which provide information about meetings, meeting houses, membership, and finance. Also of interest are minutes of Preparative Meetings of local congregations in advance of Monthly Meetings.[148] There are at Friends House and with Quarterly Meeting records digested copies of the registers of births, marriages, and deaths now in the Public Record Office. The library at Friends House can supply a list of depositories (banks, local record offices, meeting houses) containing other Quaker records and their content. Mainly these consist of minute and account books, removal certificate books, records of early persecution, correspondence, and records of disownments (expulsions from the Society). A roll of Quakers affirming on admittance as attorneys is to be found in the Public Record Office (Class E.3).

The National Register of Archives[149] has some reports on records of individual nonconformist chapels and sects.[150] Leads to the records of other smaller nonconformist sects are footnoted below.[151]

[148] For examples, see B. S. Snell (ed.), *The Monthly Meeting Book of the Society of Friends for the Upperside Division of Buckinghamshire, 1669–90*, Bucks. Archaeological Soc., Records Branch i (1937); S. C. Morland (ed.), *The Somersetshire Quarterly Meeting of the Society of Friends, 1668–1669*, Somerset Record Soc. lxxv (1978); J. and R. S. Mortimer (eds.), *Minute Book of the Leeds Preparative Meeting of the Society of Friends, 1692–1712*, Yorks. Archaeological Soc.; Record Ser. cxxxix (1980).

[149] Quality House, Quality Court, Chancery Lane, London WC2.

[150] W. R. Powell, 'Protestant Nonconformist Records and the Local Historian', *Archives* v (1961), 5.

[151] For the Salvation Army, the Moravian Church, The Swedenborgians, the English and Welsh Calvinistic Methodists, the Presbyterian Church of Wales, and Strict Baptists, see *Archives of Religious Bodies*; Welch, 'Early Methodists'; and Powell, 'History'. For Welsh nonconformity generally, see E. D. Jones, 'Nonconformist Records in Wales', *Archives*

For some of the larger sects there are often bibliographies[152] and important record publications, while some contemporary works concerning them have become primary sources. N. Penney's *The First Publishers of Truth* (1907), for example, is an early eighteenth-century collection of Quaker records topographically arranged.[153] Penney also edited the *Journal of George Fox* (1911), another primary source for early Quaker history. Joseph Besse's *A Collection of the Sufferings of the People called Quakers* (1753) covers the persecutions from the Commonwealth to the Revolution and is based on local reports preserved now at Friends House. For early Methodism, the letters and journals of the Wesleys are important for the local historian.[154]

Denominational handbooks, directories, and year books frequently contain useful evidence, including lists of chapels, details of foundation dates (sometimes, however, unreliable), individual ministers, and architectural descriptions of chapels. Such periodicals include, for example, the *Baptist*

v (1961). Some records of the Calvinistic Methodists are at the National Library of Wales, Aberystwyth. The footnotes to the nonconformist sections of the volumes of the *Victoria History of the Counties of England* will also give leads. Those interested in British branch records of the Church of Jesus Christ of Latter-day Saints (Mormons) should contact the L.D.S. section of the Genealogical Department Library, Genealogical Society of Utah, 50 East North Temple, Salt Lake City, Utah.

[152] E.g., W. T. Whitley, *A Baptist Bibliography, 1526–1837* (2 vols., 1916, 1922); E. C. Starr, *A Baptist Bibliography* (25 vols., 1952–76); Underwood, *English Baptists*, bibliography; A. Lloyd, *Quaker Social History, 1660–1738* (1950) (has a good introduction to early Quaker records); Joseph Smith, *A Descriptive Catalogue of Friends' Books* (2 vols., 1867, and supplement, 1893). See also above p. 268 nn. 96–7.

[153] See also N. Penney, *Extracts from State Papers Relating to Friends, 1654–72* (1913), indexed.

[154] N. Curnock (ed.), *John Wesley's Journal* (8 vols., 1909–16) (a pamphlet of corrigenda is published by the Epworth Press); J. Telford (ed.), *John Wesley's Letters* (8 vols., 1931); T. Jackson (ed.), *Charles Wesley's Journal* (2 vols., 1849).

Handbook (annually since 1861),[155] *The Congregational Year Book* (from 1846),[156] the *Unitarian Almanack* (*c.* 1850–64), the *Unitarian Pocket Almanack* (*c.* 1860–90), and the *Essex Hall Year Book and Unitarian Almanack* (later *Essex Hall Year Book*; *Unitarian Year Book*; *Year Book of the General Assembly of Unitarian and Free Christian Churches*) (from 1890). The *Handbook of the United Methodist Free Churches* (various edns, 1836–99), gives lists of circuits. A *Methodist Who's Who* was published between 1910 and 1915.

Other individual publications provide similar information at certain points in time. W. Myles's *Chronological History of the People called Methodists* (4th edn, 1813) has lists of chapels, topographically arranged, giving dates of erection; T. Jackson's *Lives of Early Methodist Preachers* (6 vols., 1865–66 edn) is also useful for Methodism. So, too, is the series which first appeared as *Returns of Accommodation provided in Wesleyan Methodist Chapels* (1875), with later editions in 1882, 1892, 1902, 1912, and 1932. This statistical information was continued in returns for 1940, 1960, and 1970. Lists of Particular Baptist chapels in 1689 and 1763 exist.[157]

A Wesleyan publication, *Hall's Circuits and Ministers, 1765–1912*,[158] and Smith, Swallow, and Treffry, *The Story of*

---

[155] Till 1891 issued by the Particular Baptists; after that by the Baptist Union. Some regional Baptist associations also issued year books. Copies of all these are at the Baptist Union of Great Britain and Ireland, Baptist Church House, 4 Southampton Row, London WC1.

[156] From the 1899 volume onwards this has full statistics of churches. The volume for 1855 contains a list of all Independent churches in England and Wales.

[157] Respectively in *Rippon's Annual Register* iv (1803) and J. Ivemey, *History of the Baptists* (1830), iv, 13–21. For a similar list, see A. S. Langley, 'Baptist Ministers in England about 1750 A.D.', *Transactions of the Baptist Historical Soc.* vi (1918–19), 138–62. See also *ibid.* i (1908–9), 123–4.

[158] There is a supplement for 1919–23. For corrigenda and additions, see 'Hall's Circuits and Ministers, 1765–1912', *Proceedings of the Wesley Historical Soc.* xvii (1929–30), 96–8. For other similar lists, see Swift, *Local History of Methodism*, 11.

the United Methodist Church,[159] give lists of circuits and their ministers. William Hill's *Alphabetical Arrangement of all the Wesleyan Methodist Preachers* (1819, and thence at roughly five-yearly intervals) indicates where individual ministers served and provides a cumulative list of deceased ministers. There is a similar publication for the United Methodist Church.[160] Typescript lists of Primitive Methodist circuits and ministers compiled by William Leavy are at the John Rylands University Library of Manchester, which also has a similar typescript list (compiled by E. A. Rose) for the United Methodist Church.

Historical societies for some denominations publish not only articles but also record material, and the local historian should search their volumes. The *Transactions of the Baptist Historial Society* (now the *Baptist Quarterly*) (from 1908), the *Proceedings of the Wesley Historical Society* (from 1898), and the *Publications of the Welsh Baptist Historical Society* (from 1904) print much original material. The *Journal of the Presbyterian Historical Society* (from 1914) embraces the history not only of the modern Presbyterian Church of England but presbyterianism in earlier times and also contains information on early congregational and unitarian congregations. This journal and the *Transactions of the Congregational Historical Society* (from 1901) were merged in 1973 to form the *Journal of the United Reformed Church History Society*. Other such publications include the *Journal of the Friends' Historical Society* (from 1902), and *The Transactions of the Unitarian Historical Society* (from 1917).

Nonconformist periodicals, magazines, newspapers, and the like are too numerous to list here, but some may well be worth consulting.[161] The *Evangelical Magazine* (1793–1869)

---

[159] H. Smith, J. E. Swallow, W. Treffry (eds.) [1932].

[160] O. A. Beckerlegge, *United Methodist Ministers and their Circuits, 1797–1932* (1968).

[161] For Methodist publications of this kind, going back to the eighteenth century, see Swift, *Local History of Methodism*, 9–10; F. H. Cumbers, *The*

contains a great deal of local material.[162]

Some of these publications contain histories of individual chapels and congregations,[163] and there are, of course, many such histories locally published as pamphlets and booklets. Some of these are of a high standard. Many, however, are of dubious value, being largely exercises in hagiology; they may nevertheless contain information not available elsewhere.[164]

Some printed reports of unions and regional associations also exist. Regional Particular Baptist associations printed annual circular letters from about 1760 and these throw light on the histories of individual chapels.[165] The annual reports

Book Room (1956), appendix ii; *Bulletin of the John Rylands University Library* lx (1968), 271–2. Unitarian publications include the *Monthly Repository* (from 1806); the *Unitarian Herald* (1861–89); *Christian Life* (1876–1929). The Quaker publications the *Friend* (monthly, 1843–91, then weekly), the *British Friend* (monthly, 1843–1913), and the *Friends' Quarterly Examiner* (1867–1946; from 1947 the *Friends' Quarterly*) may be of use. The Evangelical Library, 78A Chiltern Street, London, WIM 2HB, has a good collection of periodicals.

[162] There is an index for 1793–1822 in the volume for 1822.

[163] E.g., the *London Christian Instructor* (later the *Congregational Magazine*) (1818–45) has a series of histories of Independent and Baptist chapels for counties alphabetically down to Devon; from 1826 it lists Congregational ministers and churches. Local chapel histories in Wesleyan magazines have been listed and indexed in *Proceedings of the Wesley Historical Soc.* i (1898) and vi (1908), and the publications of the various nonconformist historical societies often list new histories of individual congregations.

[164] Many are to be found in local libraries. Dr Williams's Library has a very large collection, and is especially strong in Unitarian histories. The Baptist Church House (4 Southampton Row, London WC1), the Congregational Library (Memorial Hall, 2 Fleet Lane, London EC4), the United Reformed Church History Society's library (formerly that of the Presbyterian Historical Society) (86 Tavistock Place, London WC1) (especially useful for London, Lancashire, Durham, and Northumberland), the Wesley Historical Society Library (Southlands College, Wimbledon Parkside, London SW19 5NN), the John Rylands University Library of Manchester, all contain many such histories.

[165] Copies in B.L. at 4135 aa 100.

of the General Union of Baptist Churches begin in 1832,[166] and particulars of local Quaker meetings may be found in the *Book of Meetings of the Society of Friends* (annually from 1801). The *Proceedings of Yearly Meetings of the Society of Friends* were first published in 1857. The *Reports of the Wesleyan Chapel Committee* (from 1855) are useful to the local historian down to 1939, particularly for chapel buildings.[167]

ROMAN CATHOLIC NONCONFORMITY

Many of the general sources described in detail in the last section (protestant nonconformity) apply also to the history of Roman Catholic nonconformity.[168] In particular may be mentioned the state papers, domestic,[169] the Compton Census, visitation returns,[170] quarter-sessions rolls, the religious

[166] Full set at Baptist Church House. The Congregational Union printed a report in the 1890s (and perhaps other years) for most of Somerset which includes lists of trust deeds relating to each chapel and brief histories of congregations: I am indebted to Dr R. W. Dunning for this information.

[167] Not in B.L. Full set at the Methodist Church Property Division, Central Buildings, Oldham Street, Manchester M1 1JQ; set from 1899 in Leeds City Library. At the Manchester office there is a card index providing a summary of particulars of chapels still in existence, and a ledger recording details and dates of sale of chapels.

[168] The best general account of Roman Catholic local sources is M. Greenslade, 'Sources for Post Reformation Staffordshire Catholic History', *Staffordshire Catholic History* i (1961), which is drawn on in the following account.

[169] See, especially, returns of recusants, e.g., for 1577–8. N.b. P. Ryan, 'Diocesan Returns of Recusants for England and Wales, 1577', Catholic Record Soc. xxii (1921). See also W. M. Wingfield, 'Religious Statistics Concerning Recusants of the Stuart Period', *Theology* xli (1940). For recusancy generally, see A. Davidson, 'Sources for Recusant History', *Local Historian* ix (1970–1).

[170] See, e.g., R. Trappes-Lomax (ed.), 'Archbishop Blackburn's Visitation Returns of the Diocese of York', Catholic Record Soc. xxxii (1932); W. Sharp and L. E. Whatmore, 'Archdeacon Nicholas Harpsfield's Visitation Returns, 1557, together with Visitations of 1556 and 1558', *ibid.*

census of 1851[171] and other (private) censuses, the Worship Register and other records at the Office of Population Censuses, St Catherine's House, parliamentary papers, directories, and local newspapers. Reference should, therefore, be made to what has already been said about these.

Early quarter-sessions records contain not only details of the presentation of recusants, more often Roman Catholics than protestant dissenters, but also the registration of Roman Catholic estates and wills under Acts of 1715 and 1717,[172] the registration of Roman Catholic chapels and schools under an Act of 1791,[173] and record of oaths of allegiance taken by papists in the eighteenth and nineteenth centuries.

At the Public Record Office the recusant rolls (Classes E.376, E.377)[174] are annual returns (1592–1691)[175] mainly by counties, of fines for recusancy and of lands distrained in connection with the fines.[176] It should be noted that the lists do not provide names of all recusants but only of those whose property was forfeit or on whom fines had been

xlv, xlvi (1950, 1951); J. S. Purvis, *Tudor Parish Documents of the Diocese of York* (1948), 80–1.

[171] See p. 273. For county totals for 1836, see p. 276 n. 128.

[172] Cf. R. S. France (ed.), 'The Registers of Estates of Lancashire Papists, 1717–88', *Transactions of the Soc. of Lancs. and Ches.*, xcviii, cviii (1945, 1960). See also B.L. Add. MSS. 30211, 15629.

[173] See above, p. 275. Roman Catholic chapels could be registered only at quarter sessions and not at the Anglican courts like other dissenting chapels.

[174] J. A. Williams, 'Recusant Rolls', *History* l (1965) (for detailed assistance in interpreting the rolls); J. A. Williams, 'Some Sidelights on Recusancy Finance under Charles II', *Dublin Review* (Autumn, 1953); H. Bowler, 'Some Notes on the Recusant Rolls of the Exchequer', *Recusant History* iv (1957–8) (and 'Corrigenda and Addenda' to this in *ibid.*).

[175] Unbroken only from 1673 for Charles II's reign.

[176] In print are: M. M. C. Calthrop (ed.), *Recusant Roll, no. 1, 1592–3*; H. Bowler (ed.), *Recusant Roll, no. 2 (1593–1594)* (an abstract in English); H. Bowler (ed.), *Recusant Rolls nos. 3 (1594–1595) and 4 (1595–1596)* (an abstract in English). These are published in the *Catholic Record Soc.* xviii (1916); lviii (1965); lxi (1970).

imposed, with their place of origin. Nor do the rolls indicate whether recusants were Roman Catholics or Protestants. Moreover, care should be taken not to draw too facile conclusions from the rolls (or from the quarter-sessions records cited above), for the evidence may reflect rather the incidence of persecution (which varied from place to place and time to time) rather than necessarily the strength of Catholicism. Moreover well-known recusants' names some-times do not appear.

Returns of papists are also to be found in Anglican diocesan records,[177] and receipts given to the payers of fines for recusancy may be found in Catholic family papers.[178] A diocesan return of recusants for 1577 in the state papers, domestic, and a list of 1588 of papists and recusants listed under knights and their wives or widows, and then under counties (in the British Library), have appeared in print.[179] So, too, has a British Library list[180] of recusants convicted in Charles II's reign, apparently based on the recusant rolls, covering Bedfordshire, Buckinghamshire, Berkshire, Hunt-ingdonshire, Dorset, Essex, Hertfordshire, the East and West Ridings of Yorkshire, London and Middlesex, Surrey, Devon, Norfolk, Newcastle-upon-Tyne, Somerset, Suffolk, Staffordshire, Hampshire, Sussex, Wiltshire, and Kent. It would seem, however, that many of these recusants were puritans.[181] The catalogues of the manuscripts in the British Library will reveal other documents listing recusants in various parts of the country.[182]

As well as the ordinary state papers, domestic at the Public

[177] See *Pilgrim Trust Survey* i, 16.

[178] Williams, 'Recusant Rolls', 195, q.v. for examples.

[179] See Catholic Record Soc. xxii (1921).

[180] B. L., Add. MS. 20739, printed (with doubtful accuracy) in J. Gillow and J. S. Hansom (eds.), 'List of Convicted Recusants in the Reign of King Charles II', Catholic Record Soc. vi (1909).

[181] See J. A. Williams, *Catholic Recusancy in Wiltshire, 1660–1791* (1968), pp. xiii, 266–7.

[182] E.g., Harley MS. 280; Egerton MS. 921; Add. MS. 35617.

Record Office (and, of course, their *Calendar*), the papers of the Committee for Compounding with Delinquents (Class S.P.23),[183] the Committee for the Advancement of Money (Class S.P.19),[184] and the Committee for the Sequestration of Delinquents' Estates (Class S.P.20)[185] contain much on Roman Catholic families and their assets since the committees were concerned with the property of delinquents, papists, and recusants. The state papers, Venetian (also at the Public Record Office, and with published *Calendar*), may also contain local information on the state of English Roman Catholics in the sixteenth and the early seventeenth centuries.

Also at the Public Record Office, the Privy Council registers (Class P.C.2) (printed for 1540 to 1631 as *Acts of the Privy Council*) contain information on recusants. The Privy Council papers (Class P.C.1) contain, amongst other things, returns of Roman Catholics who took oaths. Lay subsidy rolls (in Class E.179) sometimes mark recusants as liable to a poll tax. Returns made under an Act of 1715, by clerks of the peace, of names and estates of Roman Catholics (arranged for England and Wales by counties) are to be found in the forfeited estate papers (Class F.E.C.1).[186] Similar returns are in the Exchequer records known as returns of

---

[183] These are calendared as distinct volumes in the *State Papers, Domestic*, series. These volumes give a key to the names and indicate the references for the relevant records. For this period, see also G. Anstruther, *The Seminary Priests: A Dictionary of the Secular Clergy of England and Wales 1558–1850* (topographical index), (4 vols. published, covering 1558–1800 (1969–77); one vol. in preparation); C. Talbot (ed.), *Recusant Records*, Catholic Record Soc. liii (1961).

[184] Also calendared.

[185] These are not calendared. For use of Exchequer records for sequestration for recusancy, see *Staffordshire Catholic History* xviii (1978) (T. S. Smith).

[186] See E. Eastcourt and J. O. Payne, *English Catholic Nonjurors of 1715* (1885); J. O. Payne, *Records of the English Catholics of 1715* (1900), introduction. Both these works include examples of the records. See also P.R.O., *The Records of the Forfeited Estates Commissioners* (1968).

papists estates (Class E.174). The attorneys' oath rolls are lists of Roman Catholics taking oaths required for admission as attorneys, for 1790 to 1836 (Class C.P.10), and for 1831 to 1837 (Class E.3).[187] In the records of the petty bag office (Class C.205) there are certificates of various kinds concerned with recusancy: as, for example, certificates of delinquents' and recusants' estates sequestrated during the Commonwealth, and certificates of the time of Anne and George I of popish recusants and of persons concealed.[188]

The House of Lords Record Office contains certain important sources for the local history of Roman Catholicism in the Main Papers. Of these, the papists' returns of 1680 provide a general list of indicted papists extracted from lists presented to the Commons. Returns of 1705–6 by deputy lieutenants give names of Roman Catholics, with occupations and family relationships, topographically arranged.[189] There are also diocesan returns for 1706 (some also found in diocesan record offices, as at Salisbury). Returns of 1767 provide details of the age, but not the name, of each individual Roman Catholic, arranged by dioceses and covering the whole country, but unfortunately not calendared.[190] Some diocesan record offices may, like Salisbury, contain the original letters from incumbents from which the 1767 returns were compiled, with useful additional information. Returns of 1781 give totals only, parish by parish (but not complete).

The protestation returns of Charles I's reign, described

---

[187] See also Class C.P.37.

[188] See p. 134 n. 49 for index.

[189] Calendared in Historical Manuscripts Commission, *Manuscripts of the House of Lords*, NS, vi (1912), 417–23. A photograph of part of one is in M. Bond, *Records of Parliament* (1964), which contains (p. 27) a brief description of these records. Those for Staffordshire are in print, ed. M. W. Greenslade, in *Staffordshire Catholic History* xiii (1973), with introduction.

[190] The Catholic Record Society is soon to publish these as *House of Lords Return of Papists for 1767*, ed. E. S. Worrall. Cf. *Staffordshire Catholic History* xvii (1977).

elsewhere,[191] may indicate the existence of Roman Catholics in many parishes just before the outbreak of the Civil War. These also are in the House of Lords Record Office. Under an Act of 1625 Catholics were liable to pay double subsidy, so that subsequent subsidy rolls contain entries relating to them.[192] Roman Catholic wills are worth perusing for relationships, bequests, links with religious orders, foreign colleges, and so on.[193] An Act of 1657 'for convicting, discovering and regressing of popish recusants' gave rise to many lists of papists, now often in local record offices (as at Wiltshire and Somerset).[194]

The arrangement of the records in England of the Roman Catholic Church itself reflects its organizational history.[195] In the years following the Reformation little is available since, except for the Marian interlude, the administration of English Roman Catholics was directed from abroad. The Old Chapter or Old Brotherhood of the English Secular Clergy, a body with doubtful jurisdiction in England between 1631 and 1685, has records largely unused, but described as 'of more than ordinary value'.[196] A list of priests (1722–83), taken from these records, has been published.[197] The original

---

[191] See p. 66.

[192] See pp. 59–60.

[193] A selection of calendars of such wills is printed in Payne, *English Catholics*.

[194] See *Historical Collections for Staffordshire*, 4th ser., ii, 71–99. Cf. H. Bowler (ed.), *London Sessions Records, 1605–1685*, Catholic Record Soc., xxxiv (1934), pp. xlvi, 115–51.

[195] See *Archives of Religious Bodies*, 4–5, for a brief article on these records; J. H. Pollen, *Sources for the History of Roman Catholics in England, Ireland, and Scotland, 1533–1795*, S.P.C.K., Helps for Students of History, no. 39 (1921).

[196] Pollen, *History of Roman Catholics*, 39. See also *Archives of Religious Bodies*, 4n.

[197] R. Stansfield (ed.), 'Obituaries of Secular Priests, 1722–1783', Catholic Record Soc. xii (1913). See also R. Stansfield (ed.), 'Particulars of Priests in England, 1692', *ibid.* ix (1911).

records are at the Archbishop's House, Westminster, London sw1, but cannot be produced except by the permission of the president of the Brotherhood, and such permission is intended to be exceptional. Some of the archives, however, have been microfilmed for the use of students.[198]

From 1598 to 1621 the English Roman Catholics had an archpriest, and from then to 1655, and from 1685 to 1688, a vicar apostolic. Between 1688 and 1840 four vicariates were formed, each with a vicar apostolic; these vicariates were divided into eight in 1840, and replaced in 1850 by thirteen dioceses with the see of Westminster as metropolitan. The records controlled by the archbishop of Westminster now form a central collection. They include correspondence and 'memorials' to the papacy roughly for the period 1600 to 1688 relating to the whole of England and Wales. From 1688 to 1850 the Westminster archives cover only the London district, which included Middlesex, Surrey, Kent, Essex, Bedfordshire, Hertfordshire, Hampshire, Sussex, and the Channel Isles.[199] Documents relating to the sixteenth, seventeenth, and eighteenth centuries are likely to be of most use to the local historian.[200]

The records of the other vicariates,[201] from the late seven-

---

[198] I am indebted to Miss Elisabeth Poyser for some of this information. There are sets at the B.L. and the Catholic Record Society, 114 Mount Street, London w1y 6ah. A catalogue of the Old Brotherhood microfilms is published by the Catholic Record Soc. as: *The Old Brotherhood of the English Secular Clergy: Catalogue of Part of the Archives* (1968).

[199] Beds. and Bucks. to 1840 only.

[200] Greenslade, 'Post Reformation Staffordshire Catholic History', 6–7; P. Hughes, 'The "Westminster Archives"', *Dublin Review* cci (1934). The latter gives details of the arrangement of the archives at the time he wrote; the description is now somewhat out of date, but no other has been published.

[201] For a map showing the areas of the vicariates, see B. Hemphill, *Early Vicars Apostolic in England, 1785–1750* (1954), 17. A description of the areas is in W. Maziere Brady, *Annals of the Catholic Hierarchy* (1877). The areas may also be deduced from the annual directories in and after 1837 (see

teenth to the mid-nineteenth century, exist locally. For the
northern vicariate the chief depository is Usher College,
Durham, and there are also records at the Bishop's House,
Leeds, and with the Bishop of Hexham at Newcastle-
upon-Tyne. The records of the midland vicariate are at
the Archbishop's House, Birmingham.[202] The records of
the western vicariate are at the Bishop's House, Clifton,
Bristol; they date mainly from the 1770s, many earlier
records having been destroyed in riots of 1780. With the
establishment in 1850 of a Roman Catholic episcopal organization in this country each see keeps its own records.[203]

Roman Catholic registers of baptisms, burials, and marriages are common from the later eighteenth century, and
some exist for earlier periods.[204] Registers to 1858 are to be
found at the Public Record Office (Class R.G.4), and sometimes still in church hands. Many have been published by the
Catholic Record Society and local historical societies,[205]
while some originals are still to be found in individual
parishes. The registers often contain also other records
pertaining to the parish concerned.

The records of the English province of the Society of
Jesus[206] will often be of use to local historians. They are
mainly deposited at Stonyhurst College, Lancashire, and in

below), when missions were listed in their areas by counties, instead of
under counties alphabetically.

[202] Catalogue of the records at Birmingham have been published by the
N.R.A.

[203] For the Birmingham diocesan records, see the N.R.A. report cited
above, and *Newsletter for Students of Recusant History* vi (1964), 14.

[204] See pp. 56 n. 36, 273–4. For examples in print, see J. A. Williams,
Post Reformation Catholicism in Bath, ii, *Registers, 1780–1825, Catholic
Record Soc.*, lxvi (1976).

[205] See *Publications* (Catholic Record Soc., n.d.), a catalogue obtainable
from the Hon. Secretary; and *National Index of Parish Registers* (Soc. of
Genealogists, iii (1974); details above, p. 56 n. 36), for whereabouts of
some registers.

[206] The province included Wales, and (from 1815) Scotland.

London.[207] Those at Stonyhurst have been summarized by the Historical Manuscripts Commission,[208] and include most of the early papers from 1580 through the seventeenth century, and some later material. The later records, mainly from *c.* 1700, are in London.[209] From 1623 England and Wales were divided into areas of operation called 'colleges', each with subsidiary districts called 'residences', and the Jesuit records likely to be most useful to local historians are in the archives arranged by colleges and residences and consisting largely of financial accounts and reports and letters of individuals. The College of St Ignatius has records, chiefly financial, for London, Berkshire, Kent, and Hertfordshire from 1750; the College of the Holy Apostles covers Suffolk, Norfolk, Cambridgeshire, and Essex, with most papers relating to Norwich and Bury St Edmunds. The College of Blessed (later St) Aloysius embraced Lancashire, Cheshire, Staffordshire, and Westmorland, and has a very large collection of records from the seventeenth century onwards. The Old College of St Francis Xavier[210]

[207] At the Church of the Immaculate Conception, Farm St, London w1.

[208] *Hist. MSS. Commission, Reps.* i, 143–8; ii, 334–41. Other Stonyhurst MSS. of use to local historians are in *ibid.* xiii, 176–99.

[209] The following account is largely based on F. O. Edwards, 'The Archives of the English Province of the Society of Jesus', *Jnl Soc. Archivists* iii (1966), q.v. for a fuller description. See also H. Foley, *Records of the English Province of the Society of Jesus* (7 vols., 1877–83) (topographical indexes).

For the records of the monastic orders, see Pollen, *History of Roman Catholics*, 40–1; and *Downside Review*, v, vi (1886, 1887), and Catholic Record Soc., xii, xiv, xxxiii (1913, 1914, 1933) (for Benedictines); R. Palmer, *Life of Cardinal Howard* (1867) and Catholic Record Soc., xiv, xxv (1914, 1924) (for Dominicans). The Benedictine archives are at Downside and Ampleforth, and a MS. account of them exists at each abbey. For Franciscan records, see Fr Thaddeus, *The Franciscans in England, 1600–1850* (1898), and Catholic Soc. xxiv (1923). Rather more Franciscan material than is reflected in Thaddeus is preserved at The Friary, Forest Gate, London e7.

[210] Not the present institution of the same name.

included Wales[211] and parts of the Westcountry; its records date from 1743.[212] The records of the Residence of St John the Evangelist cover Co. Durham, Cumberland, and Northumberland (1717–1858). The College of St Hugh (formerly the Residence of St Dominic) covered Lincolnshire, the Residence (later College) of St Michael covered Yorkshire (the records pertain particularly to Richmond, Pontefract, Wakefield, Skipton, Huddersfield, Selby, and Leeds), and the Residence of St Mary, Oxfordshire, Buckinghamshire, Bedfordshire, and Nottinghamshire. The records of the Residence of St Thomas of Canterbury (1613–1839) cover Sussex, Wiltshire, Hampshire, and Dorset. The Residence of St George embraced Worcestershire and Warwickshire (from 1635). In addition to these topographically arranged records, a few collections are under the names of individuals.[213] One list of nineteenth-century Jesuits is a parliamentary paper of 1830, which is topographically arranged.[214]

For Roman Catholic history in any particular district the family papers of local Catholic families may well yield further information, and these should be searched out. They may be traced particularly through the volumes of the Catholic Record Society and the reports of the Historical Manuscripts Commission.

Other useful sources for Roman Catholic history are the *Laity's Directory* (1756–1839), which by 1773 included obituaries and in the nineteenth century lists of chapels and clergy,[215] the *Catholic Magazine*, published in the mid-nineteenth century, and the *Catholic Directory*, which dates

[211] North Wales only to 1666–7.

[212] For the Westcountry, see also the records of the Residence of Blessed (later St) Stanislaus, and the Residence of St Thomas of Canterbury (below).

[213] For these and some other records, see Edwards, 'Archives of the Society of Jesus', 112 sqq.

[214] *Return of Jesuits* (1830) xxx.

[215] For an account of this publication, see H. Thurston, 'An Old Established Periodical', in the *Month* (Feb. 1882). Obituaries from the

from 1838. There are also some regional directories, as, for example, the *Birmingham Archdiocesan Directory* (from 1882).

Finally the many volumes published by the Catholic Record Society (from 1905), already referred to in many footnotes, should be searched by local historians, for they may contain important evidence. *Recusant History* (formerly *Biographical Studies*) (from 1951) is also now issued by the Catholic Record Society as its historical journal and this, together with the *Newsletter for Students of Recusant History* (from 1959) may yield local information or details of records and record publications for the post-Reformation period.[216] In addition there are now numerous local Catholic history societies, some of which have publications which should be searched.

directory are printed in Catholic Record Soc. xii (1913). For the earliest known date of the *Laity's Directory* (1756) I am indebted to Dr J. Kitching, who points out that the date (1793) given in the *Catholic Directory* (1875–1949), is incorrect.

[216] See also, J. Gillow, *A Literary and Biographical History, or Bibliographical Dictionary of the English Catholics from 1834 to the Present* (5 vols., 1885–1902); J. Kirk, *Biographies of the English Catholics in the Eighteenth Century* (1909); and bibliography in G. A. Beck (ed.), *The English Catholics, 1850–1950* (1950).

CHAPTER 9

Houses, housing and health

This chapter is concerned not only with the study of the physical characteristics, ownership, and occupation of individual houses, but also with the investigation of housing generally in local communities, including housing density, typology of houses for different social groups, and aspects of the provision and financing of housing particularly in modern times. Some attention is also given to sources for the study of some aspects of health, especially in the nineteenth century when the housing and health of the multiplying population were often considered to go hand in hand.

BUILDINGS IN GENERAL

A great deal of research has been undertaken on notable buildings in most localities. Castles, moated sites of castles and homesteads, abbeys, stately homes, town walls, churches and cathedrals, and so on, are likely to have been examined by experts. It is not intended to deal with buildings of this kind here. Attention may, however, be drawn to the guides issued by H.M.S.O.,[1] and to a number of other works.[2] Other key works deal both with well-known buildings and with others less well known, but which are all of

---

[1] Listed in *Ancient Monuments and Historic Buildings* (Sectional List, no. 27, periodically revised). See also J. Harris, *A Country House Index* (1971).

[2] See, e.g., B. H. St J. O'Neil, *Castles: An Introduction to the Castles of England and Wales* (1973); D. Penn, *Norman Castles in Britain* (1973 edn) (deals with over 800 castles with references to the known information, 1066–1215); J. Forde-Johnstone, *Castles and Fortifications of Britain and Ireland* (1977) (a concise survey of the structures); F. V. Emery, 'Moated

architectural or historical interest. Mention must be made of Sir Nikolaus Pevsner's county volumes constituting the *Buildings of England* series. The investigator should know, too, of the topographically arranged 'Provisional List of Buildings of Architectural or Historic Interest for Consideration in connection with the Provisions of Section 30 of the Town and Country Planning Act, 1947'. This typescript was compiled for the Ministry of Town and Country Planning and copies of relevant sections are often available through local government authorities or may be found in local libraries and record offices. It gives brief descriptions with dates, and although it cannot be regarded as wholly reliable, it may provide a useful starting point.

The general volumes of the *Victoria History of the Counties of England* contain articles on the historic architecture of counties, and in the topographical volumes of this series, especially the more recent of them, there are very full descriptions of buildings, including domestic houses. The Royal Commission on Ancient and Historical Monuments and Constructions (England) has published detailed reports and inventories of historic buildings in different places.[3] At the Commission's offices (Fortress House, 23 Savile Row,

Settlements in England', *Geography* xlvi (1962); F. A. Aberg (ed.), *Medieval Moated Sites*, Council for British Archaeology, Research Report no. 7 (1978); J. le Patourel, 'Medieval Moated Sites Research Group', *Local Historian* xi (1974) (q.v. for the group's publications); (and also for moated sites: W. G. Hoskins, *Fieldwork in Local History* (1967), 54–5; *Field Archaeology* (Ordnance Survey, 1963), 122 sqq.); E. Gilyard-Beer, *Abbeys: An Introduction to the Religious Houses of England and Wales* (1972); D. Knowles and J. K. St Joseph, *Monastic Sites from the Air* (1952); H. L. Turner, *Town Defences in England and Wales, 900–1500* (1970) (topographically arranged). Also useful is H. M. Colvin, *Biographical Dictionary of English Architects* (1954). For churches, see pp. 250–1.

[3] Listed in *Ancient Monuments and Historic Buildings*. The Commission will provide reference cards for specified areas giving for each site a map reference, description, and bibliography.

London, WIX IAB) are supplementary collections of photographs and card indexes. The British Library and other repositories house the well-known Buckler watercolours and sketches, and other topographical drawings.[4] Now part of the Royal Commission on Historical Monuments (and at the same address) is the National Monuments Record (formerly the National Buildings Record). This possesses a very large topographically arranged collection of photographs and measured drawings of buildings, many of which have now been demolished. These records are open to consultation and copies can be purchased.[5] Also of possible use are the well illustrated annual reports of the Society for the Protection of Ancient Buildings (from 1878). For London, the volumes of the *Survey of London* (in progress) provide an extremely detailed architectural coverage.[6]

Some towns have modern surveys of historic domestic architecture.[7] There remains, however, much scope for initial survey and research into local houses, particularly of the humbler kind, for it is only comparatively recently that local historians have turned their energies to the systematic study of lesser houses, and of aspects of housing in general. Even in 1966 it could be said that in the study of urban history 'housing itself is oddly neglected',[8] yet there are

---

[4] W. G. Hoskins, *Local History in England* (1959), 34, 138; R. B. Pugh, *How to Write a Parish History* (1954), 34–5. See also M. W. Barley, *A Guide to British Topographical Collections* (1974) (collections of drawings, prints, and photographs listed by counties); J. Wall (comp.), *Directory of British Photographic Collections* (1977).

[5] N. H. Cooper, 'The National Monuments Record', *Jnl Soc. Archivists* iii (1967).

[6] For London, see also I. Darlington, 'The Register of Metropolitan Buildings and its Records', *Jnl Soc. Archivists* i (1955).

[7] See, e.g., M. W. Barley (ed.), *The Plans and Topography of Medieval Towns in England and Wales*, Council for British Archaeology, Research Report no. 14 (1976), 4.

[8] H. J. Dyos (ed.), *The Study of Urban History* (1968), 37.

plenty of sources, both documentary[9] and physical, and many topics worthy of attention.

HOUSES: OWNERSHIP AND ARCHITECTURE

The tracing of the history of a single dwelling house may in itself be something of an antiquarian pursuit,[10] but, set in the background of the general history of a locality, it may, for example, throw significant light on the domestic background of a particular family (either one of importance or one that typifies an occupational or social group), and the house itself may act as an example of a particular local building type.

The extension of such study to other houses in a town, village, or region may be considered more worthy of the local historian's efforts, for firmer general conclusions may then be drawn about such matters as the nature of the housing of various social groups and the life style that is suggested by the size, structure, and amenities of the buildings concerned, and sounder evidence be provided for comparison of the characteristics of one area with another. For pre-modern times, details of, for example, periods of significant alteration, extension, or decline of the local housing stock may give a clue to demographic and economic change and developments in the social and occupational structure of communities. Moreover, the study of the typology of domestic dwellings and of the regional variations and distribution patterns of different kinds of houses is developing into

[9] Useful are Historical Manuscripts Commission, *Architectural History and the Fine and Applied Arts: Sources in the National Register of Archives* (periodically produced, from 1969); J. H. Harvey, 'Architectural Archives', *Archives* ii (1953–6); H. M. Colvin, 'Architectural History and its Records', *ibid.* (published also in a revised version as *A Guide to the Sources of English Architectural History* (1967)).

[10] For details of such activity and much technical information on legal aspects of property ownership and tenantship in greater detail than can be given here, see J. H. Harvey, *Sources for the History of Houses* (1974), which is further drawn on below.

a distinct branch of local and general history. Those who come fresh to the subject would do well to read some good examples of secondary work in the field.[11]

The sources for tracing the ownership and occupation of houses are essentially those used for doing the same for landed property, and what is said here will be of value not only to those interested in houses, but especially to investigators of the history of local landownership and agricultural history generally, as well as to those interested in local topography. The documents of various kinds known collectively as deeds of title are centrally important from medieval times to the present day. The legal practices for conveyancing and leasing property which developed during the Middle Ages and in some cases lasted into modern times, are extremely difficult to interpret without special knowledge and experience, since they are not always what they appear or purport to be. Evidence includes the conveyancing documents known as feoffments, the bargain and sale, the lease and release, final concords (embracing feet of fines), and the common recovery. Investigators would be wise to consult such guides as are available before embarking on research based on deeds.[12]

There are many collections of deeds in record offices, and some are still in private hands, including those of solicitors, trustees of charities, and institutions such as hospitals, colleges, and schools. Since the Law of Property Act of 1925 limited the need to prove title to fifty years, large numbers of

---

[11] Useful, *inter alia*, are L. F. Salzman, *Building in England* (1967 impr.); T. D. Atkinson, *Local Style in English Architecture* (1948); M. W. Barley, *The English Farm House and Cottage* (1961); W. A. Pantin, 'Mediaeval English Town House Plans', *Medieval Archaeology*, vi–vii (1962–3); M. E. Wood, *The English Medieval House* (1965); J. T. Smith, P. A. Faulkner, and A. Emery, *Studies in Medieval Domestic Architecture* (1975); J. A. Wright, *Brick Building in England from the Middle Ages to 1550* (1972); and below, pp. 308–10.

[12] See references on p. 304 nn. 22–4, and in A. W. B. Simpson, *An Introduction to the History of the Land Law* (1964), chapters 6 and 8.

older deeds once privately held have been deposited in record offices. In towns where borough councils, important gilds, or churches owned much property, or where large urban landowners opened up areas for house-building, extensive collections of deeds and ancillary records, often catalogued, will probably exist and are likely to be found in the local record depository.

Extensive collections of deeds are to be found, too, in the Public Record Office in various classes, but generally categorized as 'Ancient Deeds' and 'Modern Deeds'.[13] By no means all deeds, of course, refer to or give details of buildings.[14] Where they do, however, they will provide evidence of ownership and occupation, though usually little on the actual building itself. Those for the modern period, particularly from the eighteenth century, are more likely than earlier deeds to contain full physical details of buildings.

Collections of deeds have far wider uses than the tracing of ownership of land and houses and the provision of much topographical information. Some refer to the use of buildings as various forms of workshop, giving clues to early economic history.[15] Deeds may form the basis for the investigation of urban building development, providing details of the landowners, builders, mortgagees, and house occupiers involved, and the mechanics of finance and building promotion, including dates of conveyancing of land and sale of houses, prices of land and property, amounts of

[13] See *P.R.O. Guide* i, 14, 57, 73, 82–3, 91, 111, 171; P.R.O., *Catalogue of Ancient Deeds* (1890–1906); and *Exchequer Augmentation Office, Calendar of Ancient Deeds, Series B, Pts I–III*, List and Index Soc., xcv, ci, cxiii (1973, 1974, 1975); *Exchequer Augmentation Office, Calendar and Index, Ancient Deeds, Series BB*, List and Index Soc. cxxxvii (1977); *Exchequer, Treasury and Receipt, Calendar of Ancient Deeds, Series A*, List and Index Soc., cli, clii (1978).

[14] See G. R. Elton, *England, 1200–1640* (1969), 138 sqq.

[15] D. Portman, *Exeter Houses, 1400–1700* (1966), 3–9; Hoskins, *Local History* (1972 edn), 105; Harvey, 'Architectural Archives', 19.

mortgages, and so on.[16] As well as the deeds themselves, copies or calendars may be found entered in cartularies,[17] and in borough, estate, and ecclesiastical records. There will also be registers of deeds which, though less informative than the original documents, are nevertheless useful for ease of reference, and for the provision of quantities of comparable evidence. They are of course especially valuable when the originals no longer exist.

Some collections of deeds have been printed in full or calendared form by local record societies,[18] and many of the so-called feet of fines preserved at the Public Record Office are published in this way.[19]

Legislation of Henry VIII's reign stipulated that deeds of bargain and sale should be enrolled in a court, and where these records of enrolment are available they are worth searching.[20] The registration of title will eventually become universal under an Act of 1925, but there is presently no right of search of the registers deriving from this Act. For Middlesex and the three ridings of Yorkshire, however, registers of abstracts of deeds were started in the eighteenth century and are available for inspection. The registers include extracts from wills bequeathing real estate. In most boroughs there has been from medieval times a prescriptive right of bequeathing landed property by will and this, too, has sometimes resulted in a system of civic record with deeds enrolled in

---

[16] C. W. Chalklin, *The Provincial Towns of Georgian England: A Study of the Building Process, 1740–1820* (1974), 348–9.

[17] See pp. 254–5, and D. Walker, 'The Organisation of Material in Medieval Cartularies', in D. A. Bullough and R. L. Storey (eds.), *The Study of Medieval Records* (1971).

[18] A good example is R. B. Pugh (ed.), *Calendar of Antrobus Deeds before 1625*, Wilts. Archaeological and Natural History Soc., Records Branch iii (1947).

[19] See p. 173.

[20] See p. 173 and n 43.

registers.[21] In the Middle Ages provision for the official recording of deeds existed by enrolment in the charter and close rolls.[22]

The tenure of many smaller houses, held by copyhold, as well as information on repairs and alterations to such property, can sometimes be traced down to modern times in manorial court rolls and books, rentals and surveys, though a good number of such tenures were converted to freehold in the nineteenth century.[23] Tenancy agreements, known as leases but not strictly speaking deeds, may also be important for the history of small houses, for they give sometimes quite detailed descriptions of buildings. These may be distinct documents or may form part of other records such as estate registers or accounts.[24] Estate documents may also include registers of leases, of sales of land, or of agreements to convey property. Many boroughs kept registers of leases of property owned by them.

Enrolment of bequeathed property has already been mentioned. Wills[25] in general may provide evidence not only of house ownership but brief details of the property concerned, such as the number of rooms and their use, the existence of attached workshops, brewhouses, bakehouses, barns and

---

[21] Harvey, 'Architectural Archives', 17; C. A. Archer and R. K. Wilkinson, 'The Yorkshire Registries of Deeds as Sources on Housing Markets', *Urban History Yearbook* (1977); F. Sheppard and V. Belcher, 'Deeds Registries of Yorkshire and Middlesex', *Jnl Soc. Archivists* vi (1980); G. H. Martin, 'The Registration of Deeds of Title in the Medieval Borough', in D. A. Bullough and R. L. Storey (eds.), *Medieval Records*.

[22] See S. J. Bailey, 'Thirteenth-Century Conveyancing from the Charter Rolls', *Cambridge Law Journal* xix (1961).

[23] A. A. Dibben, *Title Deeds: 13th–19th Centuries* (1968), 23–6; Chalklin, *Provincial Towns*, 349; Harvey, 'Ancient Archives', 20–4; and see pp. 51, 74–5, 169–70.

[24] See P. Roebuck, 'Leases and Tenancy Agreements', *Local Historian* x (1972–3).

[25] See pp. 63–5.

stables, and so on.[26] Connected with wills are probate inventories, the nature and whereabouts of which are described elsewhere;[27] these are useful for house history in the early modern period. They do not set out to describe the houses of the deceased, but since they often (though not invariably) list the dead person's effects room by room, indicating the function or name of each room,[28] and sometimes its physical relationship to other parts of the house, a good idea of the size and internal layout of a dwelling and its outbuildings may be obtained. It should, however, be borne in mind that rooms are not always distinguished and empty rooms are probably ignored. For many smaller houses deeds may well be lacking, and then probate inventories can provide the main source of information. Used in quantity, such inventories can throw a good deal of light on the types of dwellings in a locality inhabited by those classes – yeomen, craftsmen, farmers, and merchants – so often represented in these documents. Evidence of the nature and contents of the dwellings inhabited by a substantial cross-section of a community, and developments in house structure in a region, can be derived from them.[29] If inventories can be augmented by other evidence, perhaps by identification of one or more of the described houses still standing, a greatly enhanced impression is provided of the housing of the various social groups.

---

[26] For some examples in print, see E. Melling (ed.), *Some Kentish Houses* (1965), 6 sqq.

[27] See pp. 63–5.

[28] Useful here is M. W. Barley, 'A Glossary of Names for Rooms in Houses of the Sixteenth and Seventeenth Century', in I. Ll. Foster and L. Alcock (eds.), *Culture and Environment* (1963). For some examples, see Melling, *Kentish Houses*, 16 sqq.

[29] For reconstructive work based on inventories, see W. G. Hoskins, *Essays in Leicestershire History* (1950), 123 sqq.; W. G. Hoskins, *The Midland Peasant* (1965), 283 sqq.; F. W. Steer, *Farm and Cottage Inventories of Mid-Essex* (1969 edn). See also pp. 62–3.

More restricted in time, the seventeenth-century hearth-tax records can be of importance for housing studies. They do not describe houses, but list householders and the number of fireplaces their dwellings possessed. Since not every room would have a hearth, nor every similarly sized house the same number of hearths, the assessments are not precise enough to indicate exact house size. They are best used in the context of housing history to provide an approximation of the numbers and local distribution of larger and smaller dwellings. To be valid for this purpose, however, assessments and returns which include exempt as well as assessed householders must be used.[30] If hearth-tax evidence can be linked to other information its value is naturally increased. Where, for example, probate inventories for householders identified from the tax assessment are available, they may give an indication of the nature of, for instance, a one-hearth house in that locality. And it must be borne in mind that regional variations certainly existed in this respect, and also in the social status attributed to the inhabitants of similarly sized houses in different parts of the country. In rural Shropshire, for example, a one-hearth house was by no means identifiable with the poverty or near poverty usually indicated by such dwellings in some other places.[31]

For the eighteenth century the numbers of houses in different communities can be deduced from such records as the window-tax returns[32] and the increasing number of rate books (poor-law and other), especially those listing the exempt as well as the payers. Contemporary local histories sometimes actually state the number of houses in a given place, and numbers may also be deduced from the many local

[30] For details of these records, see pp. 60–1; and also, D. Foster, 'The Hearth Tax and Settlement Studies', *Local Historian* xi (1974–6).

[31] Ex inf. the late Alec Gaydon.

[32] These were, however, said to be defective, and houses with fewer than so many windows were in any case exempt: W. R. Ward, *The Administration of the Window and Assessed Taxes, 1696–1798* (1963).

population censuses.[33] The published decennial censuses from 1801 indicate the numbers of occupied and unoccupied houses, and as time goes on provide much more detailed information on local housing.[34] The census enumerators' books for 1841, 1851, 1861, and 1871, like some local directories,[35] may be used to relate housing to the types of occupant.

The parsonage house in early modern times is often well documented, and thus, since it was very often 'indistinguishable from that occupied by a typical husbandman at the same time in the same district',[36] can be used to throw light on the likely nature of housing of a significant section of the local community as well as to provide firmer evidence on the housing of the clergy. The prime source here is the glebe terrier, which exists in quantities for the sixteenth, seventeenth, and eighteenth centuries.[37] Episcopal faculty books and papers, sequestration papers, and the records of Queen Anne's Bounty[38] may also contain details and plans of parsonages and other ecclesiastical houses and of alterations to them.

From the seventeenth century, and more particularly the eighteenth, there are likely to be for many areas estate records[39] among church or family muniments or the archives of institutions owning land. Apart from deeds, already dealt with, these may include surveys, maps and plans, financial accounts, and craftsmen's bills, which may provide insight

[33] See p. 70.

[34] See *Guide to the Census Reports: Great Britain, 1801–1966* (Office of Population Censuses and Surveys, 1977), 100 sqq.; M. Bowley, 'Housing Statistics', in M. Kendall (ed.), *The Sources and Nature of the Statistics of the United Kingdom* i (1952).

[35] See pp. 67, 68–9.

[36] Hoskins, *Local History* (1972 edn), 156. Cf. Melling, *Kentish Houses*, 55.

[37] See pp. 177–8.

[38] See pp. 261, 267.

[39] See p. 200.

into the distribution and nature of various buildings – including houses, cottages, and farms – and details of their construction, alteration, and repair. Sometimes, for example, there are estimates for new farm houses or estate workers' cottages with plans. Manorial and estate surveys sometimes describe houses and other buildings on the estate.[40] Tithe, enclosure, Ordnance Survey, and other large-scale maps,[41] together with directories and rate books, will indicate the existence of particular houses at certain times, and perhaps give some idea of their size, as well as being the primary source of information on the expansion of built-up areas in towns.

In some places houses dating in part or in whole from early modern or even medieval times may still exist, and these provide physical evidence of types of constructions, building materials, layout, and size of dwellings more common in the past, and of phases in the growth of settlements and their character. Such survivals are particularly welcome where documentary evidence is sparse, or where houses for which written evidence exists can be identified. The dating of houses from these periods, and the identification of the original layout and of later alterations, require, however, both technical knowledge and experience.

Considerable local variations and, especially in rural areas, the continuance over long periods of particular building styles, complicate the study of traditional house types. Those who wish to make use of physical evidence would be advised to read widely in secondary sources,[42] paying particular attention to research into the vernacular architecture of their

---

[40] Hoskins, *Local History* (1972 edn), 159. The existence of large numbers of 'parliamentary surveys' for the seventeenth century should be noted: see p. 175.

[41] See pp. 30–5, 180–1, 193.

[42] A very useful initial guide is J. T. Smith and E. M. Yates, *On the Dating of English Houses from External Evidence* (1969), reprinted from *Field Studies* ii (1968). A journal, *Vernacular Architecture*, has been published from 1970. See also R. A. Machin, 'The Study of Traditional Buildings', in A.

district. Although the study of such building has blossomed only in the last two decades or so, there is already a significant corpus of valuable literature. For some areas relevant research may have been carried out, even if findings are tentative, and these should of course be studied.[43] Eric Mercer's *English Vernacular Houses* (1975)[44] publishes a large number of drawings, photographs, and written accounts of small rural dwellings in many counties and is well worth studying.

Many of the published sources already cited for the history of agriculture may provide information on rural housing, particularly that of the agricultural labourer. Among these are the *General Views*, the *Annals of Agriculture*, and the various parliamentary papers dealing with the employment of women and children in agriculture, agricultural customs, agricultural wages, periods of depression, and so on.[45]

Evidence which may be used for dating houses includes apart from actual date stones and dates on fireplaces, glass, drainpipes, and the like – types of building materials, techniques of timber framing and roof construction, and styles of mouldings and window tracery.[46] For the analysis of building evidence, a system that may be adopted by investigators and those wishing to record existing buildings has been

Rogers (ed.), *Group Projects in Local History* (1977); J. and J. Penoyre, *Houses in the Landscape: A Regional Study of Vernacular Building Styles in England and Wales* (1978).

[43] See J. A. Sheppard, 'Vernacular Buildings in England and Wales: A Survey of Recent Work', *Transactions of the Institute of British Geographers* xl (1966); R. de Z. Hall, *A Bibliography of Vernacular Architecture* (1972); D. H. J. Michelmore, *Current Bibliography of Vernacular Architecture*, i, *1970–76* (1979). Also useful are Barley, *English Farmhouse and Cottage*; works listed in Hoskins, *Local History* (1972 edn), 252–3; S. Davies, 'The Documentary Sources of Vernacular Architecture', *Local Historian* xii (1976–7).

[44] Published by the Royal Commission on Historical Monuments (1975).

[45] See pp. 183–6, 197–8.

[46] Harvey, 'Architectural Archives', 26–9.

devised by R. W. Brunskill,[47] and the Council for British Archaeology provides a guide on the recording and evaluation of the historical development of houses.[48]

For the typology of the domestic buildings of the last two centuries there is no analytical system comparable with Brunskill's for the vernacular architecture of earlier periods. Nevertheless, wide regional variations continued to exist in the eighteenth and nineteenth centuries and there is much scope for their study. Many more of these houses than the earlier ones still stand and are available for scrutiny, and a much greater variety of sources provides descriptions of local housing. Newspaper advertisements and sale and auctioneers' catalogues may exist for individual properties. Guide books often comment on the original character of the housing in various suburbs.[49] Directories, rate books, and census enumerators' books and electoral registers[50] are among the sources which can be used to find out who occupied particular houses. Indeed for the eighteenth and nineteenth centuries there is an almost embarrassing amount

[47] R. W. Brunskill, 'A Systematic Procedure for Recording English Vernacular Architecture', *Transactions of the Ancient Monuments Soc.* xiii (1965–6) (and separately published, abridged, 1975); a simplified version is in R. W. Brunskill, *Illustrated Handbook of Vernacular Architecture* (1970). See also P. Eden, *Small Houses in England, 1520–1820: Towards a Classification* (1969); J. T. Smith, 'Medieval Roofs: A Classification', *Archaeological Journal*, cxv (1958); R. A. Cordingley, 'British Historical Roof-Types and their Members: A Classification', *Transactions of the Ancient Monuments Soc.* ix (1961) (and separately published); W. A. Parkin, 'Medieval English House Plans', *Medieval Archaeology* vi–vii (1962–3).

[48] *Note on the Investigation of Small Domestic Buildings*, Council for British Archaeology, Research Report no. 3 (1964), reprinted from *Archaeologia Cambrensis* civ (1955). See, too, additional comment on this in Hoskins, *Local History* (1972 edn), 142–4.

[49] For the use of covenants in influencing the character of housing, see C. W. Chalklin, 'Urban Housing Estates in the Eighteenth Century', *Urban Studies* v (1968), 78 sqq.

[50] See, e.g., R. L. Gant, 'Electoral Registers as a Guide to Village Structures', *Local Historian* xi (1974–5).

of secondary and primary material from which to search for evidence of the extensive house-building that went with the great expansion of population, especially in urban areas. Pictures and photographs may exist of houses and other buildings which have now disappeared, and attention has been drawn above to collections of these.[51] They can, of course, be very useful.

Apart from the study of individual dwellings and of types of houses built in various places for the several social classes,[52] and the housing characteristics pertaining to different periods variously in towns, villages, and suburbs, local historians may wish to investigate other aspects of housing history. Worthy of enquiry are the agencies which promoted new housing, the local housing market and the financing of house-building (in particular the role of landlords, speculators, and others), and the contributions of such building to changes in the local topography. The social implications of housing development also open up a very large field for exploration, particularly of those problems, such as public health, arising from the concentration of housing on a large scale.

HOUSING AND HOUSING DEVELOPMENT

There exists, of course, a vast contemporary literature on the nature and problems of the housing and social conditions of the poorer classes, particularly in the towns and especially for London, to which specific guidance cannot be given here. The bibliographies and footnotes to the growing number of modern secondary works on these topics will soon provide the searcher with a quickly multiplying set of references.[53]

[51] See pp. 30, 229.

[52] See, e.g., bibliography in D. Rubinstein, *Victorian Houses* (1974), 273 sqq.

[53] See, e.g., A. Sutcliffe, 'Working-Class Housing in Nineteenth-Century Britain: A Review of Recent Research', *Bulletin of the Soc. for the*

He will also have to become familiar with the history of general and local Acts of Parliament,[54] and of local by-laws affecting housing, public health, and so on, for the matters discussed here cannot be understood or properly researched without this background.[55]

Many nineteenth-century periodicals contain articles and reports on housing and living conditions in different localities.[56] Certain journals are particularly rewarding in the search for details of local housing schemes and reforming activities as well as for descriptions of housing conditions in various towns. Most important is the *Builder* (from 1842), the pages of which no researcher in this field can ignore, and which is particularly rich in material for the years 1844 to 1883 when George Godwin was editor. Also useful for articles on local housing are the *Architect* (from 1869; from 1926 *Architect and Building News*), *Building News* (1854–69), and the *Lancet* (from 1825). The Statistical Society of London (later the Royal Statistical Society) took a particular interest in housing conditions in the 1830s and again in the last two decades of the century, showing special interest in the relationship between population growth and housing problems. Its *Journal* (from 1838) and the transactions of local statistical societies (sometimes reproduced in the London society's volumes) should therefore be searched. So, too, should the *Transactions* (later *Journal*) of the Sanitary Institute of

Study of Labour History xxiv (1972); and the bibliographies in: J. N. Tarn, *Five Per Cent Philanthropy. An Account of Housing in Urban Areas between 1840 and 1914* (1973), 197 sqq.; S. D. Chapman (ed.), *The History of Working Class Housing* (1971); H. J. Dyos, 'The Slums of Victorian London', *Victorian Studies* xi (1968); H. J. Dyos, 'The Speculative Builders and Developers of Victorian London', *ibid.*

[54] See pp. 21–2.

[55] See, e.g., Tarn, *Five Per Cent Philanthropy*, 7 sqq., 73 sqq.

[56] For the contents of the volumes of the *Nineteenth Century*, a journal containing such articles, see *Wellesley Index to Victorian Periodicals, 1824–1900* ii (1972).

Great Britain (from 1879), and the *Transactions of the National Association for the Promotion of Social Science* (1857–86), particularly for papers concerned with the living conditions of the poorer classes, and information on local housing reforms. The N.A.P.S.S., for example, published a survey in its 1881 transactions of housing in all towns where the Artisans' Dwellings Act applied (that is, towns with a population of 20,000 or more).

Since improvements in the housing and living conditions of the poorer inhabitants were often effected in part by the activity of local groups of individuals, the publications of such reforming groups, local newspaper articles,[57] and the biographies of local worthies, including particularly newspaper obituaries, can be of value.

The business of urban housing was undertaken variously by speculative builders and their financial backers, philanthropic bodies, self-help organizations, estate owners and landlords, industrial employers, and town councils. The extent and nature of their activities, as well as the types of housing they provided, form a rich and still largely untilled field for local investigation. The value of estate records for the activities of landlords in developing large-scale housing has been demonstrated by C. W. Chalklin, H. J. Dyos,[58] and others.

The records of building firms and individual craftsmen have not often survived, but may sometimes be traced through the lists of business records compiled by the National Register of Archives and local record offices and libraries. Builders may have worked on their own account in the speculative house-building trade (for much construction in the nineteenth century was of a speculative kind) or under contract to others in housing development and repair, and

---

[57] See A. S. Wohl, *The Eternal Slum: Housing and Social Policy in Victorian London* (1977), 348–9.

[58] Chalklin, 'Urban Housing Estates'; Chalklin, *Provincial Towns*; Dyos (ed.), *Study of Urban History*.

their accounts, contracts, correspondence, and other records, if in existence, are likely to vary greatly in the nature of their content. Bank records may sometimes provide evidence of credit given to craftsmen, builders, and others engaged in house-building.[59] The offices of solicitors and estate agents, though not easily accessible, may also have material.

The importance of fire insurance records for the study of speculative building and urban estate development has been demonstrated by M. W. Beresford,[60] and these records are described in detail elsewhere.[61] They are also valuable for the dates of erection and alteration, the typology of the buildings and their uses, and the kinds of materials used, as well as giving some rough idea of the value of the insured property.

Records of litigation[62] concerning land promoters, builders, and others involved in housing developments may also provide information. Such cases can, for example, be found in the order books (1710–1877) and enrolment books (1710–1859) of the Court of Chancery (P.R.O., Classes B.1, B.5).[63] Commissions of bankruptcy were published in the *London Gazette*. Exchequer bills and answers (P.R.O., Class E.112), arranged by counties, Chancery proceedings, and Chancery Masters' exhibits[64] will sometimes be found to

[59] Cf. Chalklin, *Provincial Towns*, 347. For London the monthly returns of the district surveyors from 1845 provide an enormous amount of information on builders and building: Dyos, 'Speculative Builders', 654–5. See also pp. 135–6.

[60] 'Building History from Fire Insurance Records', *Urban History Yearbook* (1976), which provides practical advice on searching the bulky records of the societies.

[61] See pp. 136–7.

[62] The following draws in part on the excellent 'Notes on Sources' in Chalklin, *Provincial Towns*, 342 sqq., as well as on F. H. W. Sheppard, 'Sources and Methods used for the Survey of London', in Dyos (ed.), *Study of Urban History*, 135–7. See also *P.R.O. Guide* i, 166–7.

[63] P.R.O., Class B.8, provides indexes to some of the enrolment books. The order books have indexes of names.

[64] See p. 134. For other Chancery classes, possibly useful, see Sheppard, 'Sources and Methods', 135.

concern disputes about the financial aspects of housing development and house construction. The Chancery Masters' exhibits include financial accounts, deeds, and correspondence. The other legal series consist of statements by plaintiffs and defendants. In using such material, however, it must be kept in mind that individual cases may not always be typical.

Among the House of Lords records are petitions, judges' reports, and draft Bills concerning estate Acts sought by landowners for urban land development, and also the committee books relating to the Bills. These records 'throw light on several aspects of the supply of building land, particularly the estimated gross rent per acre on the conversion of land to building use, or the price of building land'.[65]

From the later eighteenth century, building societies and freehold land societies[66] emerged as important agencies for the development of housing in many places particularly in the northern industrial towns.[67] Some of these societies were purely local, and their records, if they exist, will be of particular importance for their own areas, while other societies had wider interests. Their promotion of housing development is best studied through their annual reports and their rule books, though often such domestic records are not available. However, annual reports are sometimes reported in local newspapers, where advertisements, notices, and news reports relating to the societies may also be found. Some direct information on building societies may be obtained from the evidence recorded in certain parliamentary papers.[68]

[65] Chalklin, *Provincial Towns*, 346.

[66] For the distinction between these similar sorts of organization, see H. J. Dyos, *Victorian Suburb* (1973 edn), 114 sqq.

[67] E. J. Cleary, *The Building Society Movement* (1965), (q.v. for a very good bibliography); S. J. Price, *Building Societies, Their Origin and History* (1958).

[68] See below. For other useful sources, see P. H. J. H. Gosden, *The Friendly Societies in England 1815–1875* (1961), bibliography.

The *Builder* and the *Freehold Land Times and Building News* (1854; 1855–6 *Land and Building News*; 1857–1926 *Building News*) report on the formation and activities of societies, especially in the Midlands and the London area,[69] and the development of the estates promoted by the societies may be followed in Ordnance Survey and other maps and rate books.

Rate books, particularly in conjunction with building society records, with physical evidence, and with other written sources (such as directories and census enumerators' books), can also be used to indicate the extent of owner-occupation of housing at various times, the social composition of the membership of building societies, the degree of house letting and the use of the societies for speculative investment, and the actual quality of the housing involved.[70]

In addition to self-help organizations, philanthropic societies and trusts[71] promoted new housing and renovated existing houses for the working classes in the nineteenth and twentieth centuries. They flourished particularly in London, though they also existed in some provincial towns. Their activities, and those of housing companies, including co-operative housing companies, were facilitated by limited liability legislation from 1856 and may sometimes be traced in the volumes of the *Builder*.[72] Where they exist, the records of such organizations will of course be invaluable, but few appear to have survived.[73]

[69] M. Gaskell, 'Self-Help and House Building in the Nineteenth Century', *Local Historian* x (1972–3).

[70] See, e.g., M. J. Daunton, 'House Ownership from Rate Books', *Urban History Yearbook* (1976); R. S. Holmes, 'Ownership and Migration from a Study of Rate Books', *Area* v (1973).

[71] See D. Owen, *English Philanthropy, 1660–1960* (1964).

[72] See also the *Labourers' Friend* (1834–84), and J. Bowie, *Healthy Homes* (1854).

[73] But see T. R. Slater, 'The Cirencester Improved Dwellings Company, 1880–1914', *Business Archives* xl (1974); A. M. Green, 'Victorian Model Dwellings: Worcester, 1854–1876', *ibid.* xliii (1977).

The increasing interest of local authorities in urban development and other social matters makes it certain that local government records will contain much of value to the investigator of housing, especially in the larger towns.[74] The annual reports of town and county councils and other local government authorities, including, particularly, improvement and street commissioners,[75] and the minutes and reports of their committees (especially those of building committees), are obvious sources both for the regulation of house-building generally and for local government housing in particular. Where by-laws required the submission of plans and information on proposed building developments to local government officials, such records may still be available. In more recent times the records of planning and building departments should be searched. The annual reports of local medical officers of health will include information on slum clearance and rehousing. And for more recent planned developments, items in the *Journal of Town Planning* (from 1914), and the *Town Planning Review* (from 1910) may be of value.[76] The large number of parliamentary papers which deal with housing and public health are detailed in the next section.

The Public Record Office (Class H.L.G.2) holds files relating to mortgages, sales, and other transactions concerning corporation land covering the years 1831 to 1906. For the period from about 1909 the Public Record Office holds a large number of records which concern the involvement of central government and local authorities in the enforcement of housing and health legislation, town planning, and the

---

[74] For details of house-building collected from local authorities for some 80 towns, see S. B. Saul, 'House Building in England, 1890–1914', *Ec.H.R.*, 2nd ser., xv (1962).

[75] See Chapter 3 above.

[76] Useful here is W. Ashworth, *The Genesis of Modern British Town Planning* (1954); *Report of the Departmental Committee on Garden Cities and Satellite Towns* (Ministry of Health, 1935).

sale, transfer, or purchase of lands for various purposes including housing, and related financial transactions.[77]

PUBLIC HEALTH

It will have been clear that many of the sources for the history of working-class housing in modern times, detailed above, are also, directly or indirectly, relevant to the study of public health. These will not be referred to again in this section, and the reader should look back to previous pages. For both modern and earlier times the would-be investigator would do well to look first at the most recent edition of Charles Creighton's *History of Epidemics in Britain*, which contains not only references to many places, but also clues to source material. The editors have moreover provided a most useful bibliography.[78]

From the nineteenth century there is plenty of material for the specific study of public health and allied topics. For earlier centuries, material is more difficult to find, but there are some sources which may be mentioned. Borough council minutes from the sixteenth century will often contain information on such matters as water supply, sanitary regulations, street cleaning, and action taken in epidemics. The *Calendars of State Papers, Domestic,* for the early modern period, as well as the *Acts of the Privy Council* and the unpublished Privy Council registers, contain many references to 'plague' and government orders to prevent its spread or alleviate its results. For large towns there are often for this period miscellaneous records concerning epidemics.[79] More usually

---

[77] See *P.R.O. Guide* iii, 85 sqq. For official published material for very recent times, see also S. M. Farthing, 'Housing in Great Britain', in W. F. Maunder (ed.), *Reviews of United Kingdom Statistical Sources* iii (1974). See also below, pp. 321–5.

[78] Ed. D. E. C. Eversley, E. A. Underwood, and L. Ovendall (1965).

[79] E.g., W. E. A. Axon, 'Documents relating to the Plague in Manchester in 1605', *Chetham Miscellany* iii, Chetham Soc., NS, lxxiii (1915).

available sources are the burial registers, which lend themselves to serious statistical work over a long period of time,
perhaps from 1538 onwards. These may illustrate the ages at
which adults died, and sometimes the causes of death. They
can also show the effects of epidemics and the extent of infant
mortality.[80] From the sixteenth century, too, church wardens' accounts and more particularly the local records of the
poor law (especially, down to 1834, the overseers' accounts)
will show expenditure on sick paupers and indicate the
incidence of epidemics and the existence of parochial 'sick
houses'. From 1834 poor-law union records, especially the
reports of boards of guardians and records concerning
poor-law hospitals, will be useful.[81]

The records of local boards of health, urban and rural
sanitary authorities,[82] will of course be important.[83] Large-
scale local health maps, which the General Board of Health
encouraged local boards to produce, are particularly valuable: they show details of building densities, water supply,
sewerage, and so on.[84] Local directories may include details
of hospitals, medical missions and infirmaries, and local
newspapers sometimes contain reports of such institutions.
Since some of these were endowed charities, details of them
may be found in the reports of the Charity Commissioners.[85]

[80] See pp. 52–6 for parish registers. Cf. *The Plague Reconsidered*, Local
Population Studies (1977); C. Charlton, 'Historical Demography', in
Rogers (ed.), *Group Projects*, 103–6, and works cited there.

[81] See pp. 107–8.

[82] Records of Commissioners of Sewers go back into the sixteenth
century, but they were largely concerned with land drainage rather than
with the disposal of sewage: see A. E. B. Owen, 'Records of Commissioners of Sewers', *History* lii (1967); I. Darlington, *The London Commissioners
of Sewers and their Records* (1970).

[83] See *Return of Urban and Rural Sanitary Authorities* (1875) lxiv; *Returns of
Counties, County Boroughs, Urban Sanitary Districts, Rural Sanitary Districts
and Unions* (1888) lxxxvi; (1893–4) lxxvii.

[84] J. B. Harley, *Maps for the Local Historian* (1972), 18: E. W. Gilbert,
'Pioneer Maps of Health and Disease', *Geographical Jnl* cxxiv (1958).

[85] See pp. 111–12.

Occasionally, local philanthropic or reforming groups have left evidence of their investigations of public health, sanitation, and housing; for example, the Manchester and Salford Sanitary Association. For the larger towns there are usually published descriptions in the form of books and articles. Sometimes the records of dispensaries and hospitals exist in local record offices.[86]

For some places in the seventeenth century, and more generally in the eighteenth and nineteenth centuries, there are bills of mortality which collate the information in parish registers in towns, providing information on baptisms and burials and on the ages of those who died. They should be used with caution and not be regarded as particularly reliable sources.[87]

Central to the investigation of public health are the 'local reports to the General Board of Health' for some 300 places, published between 1848 and 1857.[88] These reports by government inspectors vary in length according, usually, to the size of the place concerned (some are of several hundred pages) and cover all aspects of the locality's sanitary conditions, often with statistics, correspondence, evidence of witnesses, maps and plans, and may include details of such matters as local Acts, mortality figures, information on water supply, drainage, slaughter house regulations, and the nature of tenements. They end with the inspector's final recommendations. The reports were not parliamentary papers, and there is no complete collection, but the most comprehensive are at the British Library and at the library of the Department of Health and Social Services. Many local reference libraries will, however, possess copies of the reports

[86] But see *Jnl Soc. of Archivists* v (1974–7), 181–3, 554–5.

[87] J. K. Edwards, 'Norwich Bills of Mortality, 1707–1830', *Yorks. Bulletin of Economic and Social Research* xxi (1969), 112–13; M. W. Flinn, *British Population Growth, 1700–1850* (1970), 15.

[88] H. J. Smith, 'Local Reports to the General Board of Health', *History* lvi (1971).

relating to their own localities, and some were printed in part or in full in local newspapers. Apart from these preliminary reports, which are the most important, there may be reports of further enquiries, usually on specific topics such as grave-yards.

The Public Record Office (Class M.H.13) holds the cor-respondence between the General Board of Health and Local Government Act Office, and local authorities, over the provision and administration of public health, sanitary, and other services under the various Acts covering these mat-ters.[89] The poor law union papers (Class M.H.12), 1834–1900, consist of the correspondence of the central government poor-law authorities with poor-law unions and other local authorities, and embrace public health administra-tion as well as poor-law matters.[90] Also relevant are the Local Government Board's correspondence files, 1868–1922 (Class M.H.48).[91] From the time local authorities established medi-cal officers of health, the annual reports of these officials were usually published with the council minutes. Other records of local authorities in the nineteenth and twentieth centuries which are concerned with health matters are too numerous to detail here.[92]

There are so many parliamentary papers which are concerned with or contain information on housing, living conditions, and public health, particularly from the 1840s, that it would be quite impossible to list them all here,[93] and the indexes to the parliamentary papers should be carefully searched. Mention may, however, be made of some impor-

---

[89] *P.R.O. Guide* ii, 172. Alphabetically arranged by urban and rural districts.

[90] See p. 109.

[91] For other P.R.O. classes concerned with twentieth-century health matters, see *P.R.O. Guide*, ii, iii.

[92] See above (housing section).

[93] See the official indexes, or the *Select List* of P. and G. Ford (see p. 17 n. 142), and also papers cited above pp. 109–10, 119–21, 216.

tant papers. The investigator should be reminded that such reports and the evidence they print cannot be regarded as indisputable truth since in many cases material has been carefully constructed and tailored to suit particular political and other interests.

The *Report of the Select Committee on the Health of Towns* of 1840[94] provides evidence on a number of places. Edwin Chadwick's *Report on the Sanitary Condition of the Labouring Population of Great Britain* is well known and contains a great deal of comprehensive information on aspects of public health, mortality, and housing,[95] and was accompanied by two volumes of local reports on various towns and counties.[96] The two reports of the Royal Commission for Inquiry on the Sanitary State of Large Towns and Populous Districts are very full of local information. The first[97] contains, for example, details for 50 towns of drainage, street cleansing, and water supply, and for a number of places of mortality and housing. Evidence from, among others, house builders is to be found in the volume. The second report[98] has special reports on working-class housing, mortality, sanitation, and like matters for 23 towns. The General Board of Health's *Papers Relating to the Sanitary State of the People of England*, published in 1858, has a section on rates of mortality from certain diseases in different districts.[99] A generation later the reports of the Royal Sanitary Commission[100] contain a great deal of evidence on dwellings, sewerage, epidemics, and so on. There is in the third volume (1874) an abstract

[94] (1840) xi, indexed.

[95] House of Lords sessional papers: (1842) xxvi. Also republished in an abridged form with an introduction by M. W. Flinn (1965).

[96] *Local Reports, England and Wales* (1842) H.L. xxvii; *Local Reports, Scotland* (1842) H.L. xxviii. There was also a supplementary report on burials in towns: H.C. (1842) xii.

[97] (1844) vii.

[98] (1845) xviii.

[99] (1857–8) xxiii.

[100] (1868–9) xxxii; (1871) xxxv; (1874) xxxi.

of answers to a questionnaire covering many boroughs and other local government areas on matters of housing, mortality, public health, sewerage, water supply, and hospital accommodation. The report of the General Board of Health on cholera epidemics in 1848 and 1849 contains reports on individual places; these throw light on housing and general sanitary conditions.[101]

The report of the Royal Commission on Water Supply of 1868–9 has useful evidence and excellent maps,[102] and for the late 1870s a report embracing all urban sanitary districts indicates details of sources of supply and the quantities of water used.[103] A report on sewerage schemes published in 1876 gives details for a number of towns,[104] and the reports of the Royal Commission on Sewerage Disposal in the early years of this century have much local information.[105]

The reports of the Royal Commission on Labour of the 1890s include information on aspects of health, workmen's dwellings, and rents. The reports are arranged by type of industrial employment, but much local information is embedded in them, while a series of reports on agricultural labourers contains information on selected districts in Bedfordshire, Hampshire, Huntingdonshire, Leicestershire, Nottinghamshire, Sussex, Wales, Scotland, and Ireland.[106] The *Report of the Inter-Departmental Committee on Physical Deterioration* of 1904 has some local information on health standards.[107] Specifically concerned with lower-class housing are the reports of the Royal Commission on the Housing

---

[101] (1850) xxi. There are other reports in the parliamentary papers on cholera and other epidemics in London and elsewhere: see P. and G. Ford's *Select List* (see p. 17).

[102] (1868–9) xxxiii.

[103] (1878–9) lxi.

[104] (1876) xxxviii.

[105] (1901) xxxiv (I–II); (1902) xlix; (1903) xxxi; (1904) xxxvii, xxxviii.

[106] (1892) xxxiv, xxxv, xxxvi (I–V); (1893–4) xxxii, xxxix; (1894) xxv; and (for agricultural labourers) (1893–4) xxxv, xxxvi, xxxvii (I–II).

[107] (1904) xxxii.

of the Working Classes of 1884–5 (which cover many places, urban and rural, and include information on the activities of building societies)[108] and select committee reports of 1902 and 1906.[109] The report of a Board of Trade enquiry into working-class rents and housing, and retail prices, published in 1908, contains information on many industrial towns.[110] The first report of the Royal Commission on Friendly and Benefit Building Societies has some details of individual societies in various parts of the country, while the fourth report contains accounts by Commissioners on the general position in various regions.[111]

In addition to these particular reports, information on the number of houses in different localities, their sizes, and the density of occupation, can be found in the volumes of the decennial censuses. From 1840 the annual reports of the Registrar General of Births, Deaths, and Marriages, offer statistical information to the local historian on the numbers of deaths in registration districts, and on ages at death, causes of death, and infant mortality. Similarly, the annual reports of the Poor Law Board give evidence on such matters as expenditure in different areas on medical relief and on poor law dispensaries, and include reports of workhouse medical officers. The annual reports of the succeeding Local Government Board from the early 1870s have information on health in various places, supplemented by the annual reports of the Medical Officer of the Privy Council and Local Government Board, which contain some local information. Prior to that,

---

[108] (1884–5) xxx, xxxi (Scotland). *Reps. from the Select Committee on Artizans' and Labourers' Dwellings Improvement* (1881) vii, (1882) vii, are almost exclusively concerned with London (with some information on Liverpool).

[109] *Rep. Joint Select Committee of the House of Lords and the House of Commons on the Housing of the Working Classes* (1902) v; *Rep. Select Committee on the Housing of the Working Classes Amendment Bill* (1906) ix.

[110] (1908) cvii.

[111] (1871) xxv; (1874) xxiii.

from 1859 to 1871, the annual reports of the Medical Officer of the Privy Council were published separately as parliamentary papers. The Board's reports themselves contain reports from local medical officers of health.

Apart from those parliamentary papers directly concerned with housing, health, and related matters, many others will contain incidental information on working-class housing, health, and living conditions. Among them are the various reports on the handloom weavers, reports on the employment of women and children in industry and agriculture, Boundary Commission reports, and reports on aspects of poor relief.

Index

Index

Index

Monasticon Anglicanum (Dugdale), 254
monopoly, patents of, 128–9
Moravian Church, 281n
Mormons, see Church of Jesus Christ of Latter-day Saints
municipal boroughs, see boroughs
Musgrave's Obituary, 27
music, 3
muster rolls and books, 58–9, 171–2
Myles, W., 283

National Association for the Promotion of Social Science, 224, 245, 313
National Association for the Promotion of Technical and Secondary Education, 245
National Buildings Record, 299
National Christian Education Council, 208n
National Farm Survey, 200
National Library of Wales, 281–2n
National Maritime Museum, 151
National Monuments Record, 299; see also Royal Commissions, Ancient and Historical Monuments and Constructions
National Railway Museum, York, 160n
National Register of Archives, 40, 76, 85, 281, 313
National Society for Promoting Religious Education, 208
National Society for Promoting the Education of the Poor, 208–10
navigation companies, 157n
Neild, James, 107
Neve, John le, 28, 265
Newcastle Commission, 213
newspapers, 22, 24–5, 30n, 84, 88n, 92, 94, 95, 125, 133, 136, 153, 154, 156, 160, 181, 186, 201n, 237, 241, 270, 287, 301, 313, 315, 319; nonconformist, 276, 284; see also periodicals
Nonconformist, 276
nonconformist registers, 8, 53, 273–6
nonconformist trust deeds, 272, 277, 278
nonconformity: Protestant, 10, 53, 57, 92, 260, 268–88; Roman Catholic, see Roman Catholic nonconformity; Welsh, 281n; see also conventicles; meeting houses; nonconformist registers; nonconformist trust deeds; puritanism; recusants; and under the names of denominations
Norden, John, 31
Notes and Queries, 25

obituaries, see biography and biographies; Musgrave's Obituary
occupational structure, 2, 54, 67, 69, 89, 165; see also social structure
Office of Population Censuses and Surveys, see St Catherine's House
Ogilby, John, 32
Old Chapter (Old Brotherhood) of the English Secular Clergy, 291–2
Old College of St Francis Xavier, 294–5
oral evidence, 41–5
'oral history', 41
order books, Chancery, 314
Orders in Council, 23, 267
ordination records, 261
Ordnance Survey, 16, 30n, 32–4, 49, 93–4, 159, 165, 182, 193n, 308, 315
overseers of the highway, see parish and parish records, highway surveyors
overseers of the poor, see parish and parish records, overseers of the poor
Owen, Robert, correspondence, 139

paintings, 299
palaeobotany, see botany
palaeography, 6
pamphlets, 54, 139n, 156; see also broadsheets
papal registers, calendar of, 257
papists: estates of, 289–90; see also recusants; Roman Catholic nonconformity
Pare, William, collection of press cuttings, 139
parish and parish records, 3, 38, 52–7, 72, 77–80, 159, 222, 232, 248–67 passim; 'books of record', 77; boundaries, 56n; charities, 113, 207; church, 38, 248–67 passim; churchwardens, 77, 78–9, 100, 115, 260, 264, 319; constables, 78–9, 264; councils, 77, 79–80; glebe, 177–9; highway surveyors (overseers, supervisors), 78–9, 154, 158; histories, 248; magazines, 209, 246, 265; marriage banns registers, 9; memoranda, 77; overseers of the poor, 78–9, 100–3, 105, 319; parsonage, 307 (see also glebe terriers); poor relief, 99–107, 319; rate books, 8, 62, 306, 310; registers, 8, 52–7, 66, 78, 101, 129, 214, 264–5, 274, 319, 320 (aggregative analysis of, 53–4); service books, 265; summaries (abstracts) of crops, etc., 195–7; vestries, 76, 78–9, 101, 103, 154, 264; see also Chapter 8 passim; schools

Index